For the Sake of Humanity

For the Sake *of* Humanity

Essays in Honour of Clemens N. Nathan

Edited by

Alan Stephens • Raphael Walden

Martinus Nijhoff Publishers
Leiden · Boston

ISBN 90-04-14125-1

First Edition 2006

Koninklijke Brill incorporates the imprints Brill Academic Publishers, Martinus Nijhoff Publishers and VSP.

www.brill.nl

Designed and digitally typeset by BooKraft@googlemail.com

Clemens Nathan's portrait © 2006 *Paul Whitehill, London*

Printed and bound in The Netherlands

Printed on acid-free paper

Clemens Neumann Nathan

CONTENTS

PREFACE

INVITING a group of highly qualified professionals and scholars to contribute to a collection of essays in honour of Clemens Nathan seemed to us an entirely appropriate manner in which to celebrate his remarkable position in public life. The response to our invitation was rapid and positive, and the essays contained in this book evidence not just an extraordinary breadth of interest, but also academic rigour, social concern and a commitment to historical truth, along with an adventurous and innovative spirit. All these qualities are to be found among the contributors, and in Clemens himself!

Elsewhere in this volume, Edmund de Rothschild has sketched some of Clemens Nathan's activities and achievements, and a little of his personal history; we have also included a brief *curriculum vitae*, to put on record some factual information.

However, it is our belief that the essays themselves say everything else that needs to be said about a man who, over a period of several decades, has stimulated and facilitated discussion, research and study on a striking array of topics. Clemens has built up a circle of friends, admirers and associates which allows him access to the best of thinking. He has exploited this access in a creative and constructive way; he has done this, in the words of our chosen title, *For the Sake of Humanity*.

We feel sure that these essays, written in honour of Clemens Nathan, will be read and re-read for many years to come, and can think of no more fitting tribute to a man of his nature and his calibre.

—*The Editors*

FOREWORD

I REGARD it as a great privilege to be given the opportunity of writing this foreword to a collection of essays in honour of a man of international stature.

Clemens Nathan is admired for his courage and respected for his tireless communal activities; he has led and has extended the boundaries of leadership in public office. The wide range of distinguished individuals who are associated with this *Festschrift* is a clear indication of the position he occupies in many minds as one of the outstanding Jewish leaders of our age.

His activities are breathtaking in their scope, but there is a common thread running through everything he has undertaken – the concept of voluntary service. The desire to put back into society the fruits of one's work and experience is a mark of voluntary service at its highest, and at its best.

Our paths have crossed frequently in the support of several important causes and in the work of great organisations. I shall make brief mention of some highlights.

THE ANGLO-JEWISH ASSOCIATION (AJA)

This is one of the two 'privileged bodies' in the Jewish community. It has always boasted a distinguished membership. The president succeeds by the use of influence rather than by the exercise of authority. Clemens Nathan was an outstanding president, highly regarded by Anglo-Jewry where he exercised his influence for the good. He extended that influence at the international level in his role within the Consultative Council of Jewish Organisations.

The CCJO is made up of the Anglo-Jewish Association and the Alliance israélite universelle, based in Paris. The organisation enjoys non-governmental status and has consultative status at the Economic and Social Council of the United Nations. He is chairman of the CCJO and has exercised tremendous influence in that capacity.

As a representative of the AJA, he has played a key role in the Conference on Jewish Material Claims against Germany and in the Memorial Foundation for Jewish Culture. He has worked tirelessly in order to obtain restitution for individuals from Nazi Germany and from Austria, and there are many people whose lives are the better for his efforts.

HUMAN RIGHTS AND INTER-FAITH COOPERATION

Born as he was in the first year of Hitlerite Germany (1933), Clemens Nathan realises only too well that the Jewish community, and indeed humanity as a whole, can enjoy stability only when there is a firm and perpetual commitment to Human Rights. The rôle of interfaith dialogue and religious cooperation is essential in this area. He has been at the forefront of those working to promote Christian–Jewish understanding for several decades. More recently he has devoted himself to the process of cooperation between all the Abrahamic faiths – Judaism, Christianity and Islam. These activities are well known both in the University of Cambridge and the University of Sussex.

Despite his many public interests, he did not neglect his business interests and has played a leading role in the textile industry, being seized of the importance of technology in this field. He is a founder member of Shenkar College in Israel, which is bringing much influence to bear upon the textile industry of the future.

These essays in honour of Clemens Nathan constitute an acknowledgement of the fact that he is amongst the outstanding Englishmen of today and one of the great Jews of our generation. I salute his contribution to progress and to humanity.

—*Edmund L. de Rothschild* CBE VMH TD

CURRICULUM VITAE

Clemens Neumann Nathan

HUMAN RIGHTS & INTERNATIONAL WORK

- Joint Chairman, Consultative Council of Jewish Organisations (CCJO), one of the oldest non-governmental organisations, founded by René Cassin, who received the Nobel Prize for human rights. Clemens Nathan worked with René Cassin when the latter was president of the Alliance israélite universelle and carried on his tradition of working for human rights for all.
- Active at the UN, mainly in Geneva and New York, the Council of Europe, and UNESCO, as Chairman of the CCJO.
- Board Member, Conference on Jewish Material Claims (dealing with problems associated with restitution and indemnification by Germany and Austria for gross violations of human rights perpetrated by the Nazi regimes). Chairman, Nominations Committee.
- Vice-President, Anglo-Jewish Association (President, 1983–89)
- Board Member, Memorial Foundation for Jewish Culture, New York
- Board Member, Three Faiths Forum
- Director, Sephardi Centre, London
- Board Member, Centre for Jewish–Christian Relations, Cambridge (One of the founders; chairman till 2003)
- Vice-President, Centre for German–Jewish Studies, Sussex University

DECORATIONS

- Knight and Order of Merit of the Italian Republic (1966)
- Medal from the State of Israel for contribution to its Economic Council (1973)
- The Officers Cross of Austria (1995)

PROFESSIONAL

- Chartered Textile Technologist and Fellow of the Textile Institute (Council member and past Vice-President)
- Medallist of the Textile Institute for outstanding work for the textile industry and the Institute
- Honorary Fellow, Shenkar College, Israel
- Fellow of the Royal Anthropological Society
- Fellow of the Royal Society of Arts
- Honorary Fellowship, Centre for Jewish–Christian Relations, Cambridge
- Past visiting Fellow of the School of Slavonic and East European Studies
- Freeman of the City of London
- Member of the Glovers Company
- On the board of various international trade organisations and companies, and educational institutions

PUBLICATIONS

- Various reports for governments and professional bodies on international trade and textiles
- Co-Founder of the Economist Intelligence Unit, Textile Outlook International

EDUCATIONAL

- Lectures at countless professional and human rights meetings, and at universities and colleges of further education in the UK and overseas. Developed scholarship funds for students from all over the world to study at British universities.

DAVID ABRAHAMSON

The Transition from Hospitals to Community Care

SUCCESS AS FAILURE

Large isolated hospitals 'rising unmistakable and daunting out of the countryside'[1] were for a hundred years the dominant response to mental illnesses. Their replacement by more varied and accessible alternatives has been welcomed by almost all those directly concerned and well-designed studies have demonstrated significant advantages for the new services.[2] Yet, as a leading authority has recently pointed out: 'ask any gathering of people who are not members of the psychiatric profession what they think of care in the community and most, if not all of them, will reply that it has failed.'[3] There is apprehension amongst patients and carers as well as professionals that this pessimism, which is boosted by much of the media, will be self-fulfilling by lowering expectations and increasing stigma and demoralisation. The author was privileged to work with a large number of patients in a hospital where

1 Powell, E. (1961) 'The Water Tower Speech'. Report of the Annual Conference of the National Association for Mental Health, pp. 4–10. The then Secretary of State announced in vigorous terms the policy of closing the large hospitals ('brooded over by the gigantic water-tower and chimney combined').

2 Leff, J. & N. Trieman (2000) Long-stay patients discharged from psychiatric hospitals: social and clinical outcomes after five years in the community. The TAPS Project: 46. *British Journal of Psychiatry*, 176:217–223. Priebe, S. et al. (2002) Do long-term hospitalised patients benefit from discharge into the community? *Social Psychiatry and Psychiatric Epidemiology*, 37:387–392. International comparisons suggest that success depends crucially on the socio-cultural context and the resources available.

3 Leff, J. (2001) Why is care in the community perceived as a failure? *The British Journal of Psychiatry*, 179:381–383.

many had spent twenty years or longer (up to an astonishing sixty years) to help them prepare for discharge and play a part in their subsequent lives. Despite all the difficulties involved, this was predominantly a gratifying experience and sometimes profoundly so. Most striking was their preservation of individual personalities and the potential for better qualities of life after such long periods of illness and institutionalisation. New generations of similar patients are a major proportion of care in the community service users and often come from groups marginalised for additional reasons, including poverty and ethnicity. Their interests are likely to be sacrificed to more intrusive demands, as in the hospital era, if care in the community is undermined rather than supported and strengthened.

REFORM UNDERMINED

How readily reforming ideals can be undermined was demonstrated by the large hospitals themselves. Mid nineteenth century legislation that mandated a network of public asylums in England and Wales reflected the efforts of a remarkable group of Victorian philanthropists and parliamentarians, whose optimism about improving the lives of the many mentally ill then in workhouses, prisons, private 'mad-houses' and on the streets was inspired by the moral treatment movement. The provenance of the term 'moral' in this context is confused, but it referred to psychological and social methods practiced in the earlier part of the century in a number of charitable asylums, most famously the Retreat, the Quaker foundation at York.[4] It was established that even severely disturbed patients were sensitive to the attitudes and behaviour of others, and could be influenced by personal interactions in a pleasant, active milieu where the shared humanity of patients and staff was constantly emphasised. This lesson has had to be re-learned repeatedly and still may be paid only lip service.

Moral treatment depended on the asylum being small and homely enough to facilitate interactions amongst patients and staff modelled on an extended family. But as the number of public asylums in England and Wales increased dramatically between 1827 and 1930, the average size grew tenfold: from around one hundred to over a thousand beds in each, often accompanied by deterioration in their milieus that horrified even enthusiasts. The Middlesex

4 Tuke, S. (1813) *Description of the Retreat*. Reprinted 1996, London: Process Press.

County Asylum at Colney Hatch, later Friern Barnet Hospital, opened in 1851 with 1250 beds and despite being described as a 'colossal mistake' grew to 2700.[5] Considerable variation in milieus remained and much depended on the local administration, the medical superintendent, and the funds available whether or not elements of moral treatment were maintained.[6] Overall, the lowest ebb was reached in the early twentieth century,[7] and despite subsequent improvements, bleak, sparsely staffed long-stay wards with 50–60 and even 100 patients locked into spaces appropriate for less than half the number, sharing clothing and toilet articles and bathed in groups, did not disappear until the 1960s: surely an antidote to the nostalgia that sometimes underlies disparagement of community care.

Causes of the huge growth in the number and size of asylums, which was replicated astonishingly widely in Europe, North America and Colonial Africa and India, have been more fully researched since the end of the asylum era than at the time. Revisionist opinion rejects Foucault's once fashionable thesis of a 'great confinement' of the poor, criminals, and the 'mad' sweeping over Europe (although the recent huge increase in prison populations is an uncomfortable echo). An initial influx of patients from prisons, workhouses and elsewhere, the longer term effects of an increasingly market based economy, and population changes including urbanisation, are emphasised instead. A family's inability to contain a mentally ill relative was often the immediate factor leading to admission: families remained under-appreciated and under-supported carers throughout the asylum era, as they were before it and have continued to be since.[8] The evidence, though incomplete, is against the widely assumed general increase in mental illnesses, but the criteria for admission widened. A significant proportion of asylum beds were filled by victims of a twentieth century epidemic of the terribly named, terrible disease 'General Paralysis of the Insane' (GPI): a late manifestation of syphilitic

5 Hunter, R. & McAlpine, (1974) *Psychiatry for the Poor*. Dawsons of Pall Mall.

6 Guyatt, M. A Semblance of Home: Mental Asylum Interiors 1880–1914. In: McKellar, S. & Sparke, P. Eds. (2004) *Interior Design and Identity*. Manchester University Press. A fascinating description of continuing attempts to provide homely environments in asylums. Furniture was purchased from high street retailers and interiors decorated and redecorated according to current fashions.

7 Lomax, M. (1921) *The Experiences of an Asylum Doctor*. London: Allen and Unwin. One of the accepted practices at that time was 'Behind the table' – patients confined all day between a table and the wall.

8 Melling, J. & Forsyth, B. (1999) *Insanity, Institutions and Society*. London and New York: Routledge.

infections that has been mercifully eliminated by penicillin. Long-term care for epilepsy, which now rarely requires residential treatment, was concentrated in asylums, whilst more prestigious and better staffed hospitals dealt only with acute cases.[9] There was also a marked increase in bed use because of a variety of alcohol related disorders – the consumption of spirits in England rose 57% between 1801 and 1901.

Reaction to these pressures was moulded by an increasingly pessimistic intellectual climate, in which the theory of degeneration, introduced by the psychiatrist B. A. Morel in 1857, and crude concepts of 'survival of the fittest' associated with Social Darwinism were important influences.[10] Fear and denigration of an 'underclass' that included the mentally ill and the destitute became widespread: and most asylum residents were both (many were admitted half-starved). This context is not without contemporary resonance and underlines how profoundly mental health services are influenced by aspects outside their control. New clinical concepts also tended to promote a sense of hopelessness. Several recognized syndromes were brought together with supposed progressive deterioration by Emil Kraepelin to constitute a disease entity termed dementia praecox[11] – early dementia in contrast with that associated with old age. This was shortly replaced by the concept of schizophrenia (more accurately the group of schizophrenias) introduced by Eugen Bleuler in 1911:[12] but the connotation of a downhill trajectory remained. His son, Manfred, summed-up the effects: 'the assumption of a continuous regressive process in schizophrenia . . . in its own secretive, insidious way, promotes hopelessness and resignation amongst doctors, nurses, families, and among the patients themselves.' He described his father's reactions after annual visits to former patients in an isolated rural hospital. Happy that they always greeted him warmly, he was depressed that 'most of them did seem to have deteriorated' and would ask 'is there really nothing that can stop this

9 Hunter & McAlpine, op. cit. An astonishing eighty grand mal fits occurred at Colney Hatch asylum during daylight hours (they were not counted at night); where five doctors looked after 2250 beds, in contrast to twelve for 75 beds at the elite National Hospital for Nervous Diseases.

10 Lewis, A. (1967) *Inquiries in Psychiatry*. London: Routledge and Kegan Paul.

11 Kraepelin, E. (1896) *Dementia Praecox and Paraphrenia*. Transl. R. M. Barclay (1919): Edinburgh: Livingstone.

12 Bleuler, E. (1911) *Dementia Praecox or the Group of Schizophrenias*. Transl. J. Zinkin (1950): New York: International Universities Press.

disease?' Manfred subsequently established that in fact improved patients had been discharged and overlooked.[13]

As the progression of established illnesses was considered inevitable, attention was concentrated on acute admission facilities, separated from the 'chronic' or 'back' wards 'where the layman who asks "if nothing can be done to help these wretched patients" will be told that nothing can be done: they are incurable.'[14] Many teaching hospitals went further and excluded long-term patients altogether – 'failures' of the time-limited treatment they offered were shipped off to hospitals with a fraction of their staff and resources. Generations of trainee psychiatrists were deprived of irreplaceable experience of complex conditions which exemplified the interaction of biological, psychological and social factors; and might be appointed mental hospital consultants after scarcely setting foot in a long-stay ward, as was the author in 1971. Nonetheless, there were significant improvements in the large hospitals from 1950 onwards, including the unlocking of most ward doors; mixed wards and staff instead of the traditional rigid gender separation – which had strikingly beneficial effects; and the development of specialist wards for old age disorders such as Alzheimer's Disease.

GROUNDS FOR OPTIMISM

The ground-breaking study that undermined the earlier pessimism was, happily, that of Manfred Bleuler who like his father became superintendent of the Bergholzi Hospital in Zurich. His personal assessments of more than two hundred patients with schizophrenic disorders for an average of twenty-two years demonstrated almost the opposite of progressive deterioration. A variety of intermittent and continuous courses were classified into seven main patterns, none of which showed overall worsening over time. Deterioration was largely confined to the first five years, followed by plateaus, and improvements were possible even after decades. Although temporary relapses could also occur at any point they were rarer later.[15] The essential features of these findings have been confirmed by many subsequent longitudinal studies in a number of countries – a summary of North American studies included over

13 Bleuler, M. (1972) *The Schizophrenic Disorders: Long-term Patient and Family Studies*. Transl. S. M. Clemens (1978). New Haven and London: Yale University Press, p. 413.

14 Bickford, J. A. R. (1955) The forgotten patient. *The Lancet,* II: 917–919.

15 Bleuler, M. op. cit.

1500 patients by 1988 – and by international comparisons.[16] Furthermore, a range of neuroimaging, psychological and developmental studies indicate that schizophrenic disorders fundamentally reflect neurodevelopmental rather than neurodegenerative processes.[17]

MORE THAN MEETS THE EYE

Emotional deterioration was another fundamental aspect of the founding descriptions of both dementia praecox and schizophrenia: 'Even in the less severe forms of the illness, indifference seems to be the external sign of their state; and indifference to everything – to friends and relations, to vocation or enjoyment, to duties or rights, to good fortune or to bad. What happens to others is of course of no concern at all to them.' But a number of anecdotes within the above account by Eugen Bleuler subvert the main thesis: 'Often patients can very well sympathise with another's situation or condition . . . A hebephrenic (schizophrenic), whose very speech was confusion, held the cigar-holder to the mouth of another patient suffering from muscular atrophy . . . with a patience and indefatigability of which no normal person would ever be capable. It sometimes happens that such schizophrenic Samaritans succeed in feeding an abstentious patient who could not be fed by anyone else.'[18] He had earlier successfully trained patients to act as nurses during a typhoid epidemic, and a century previously the remarkable Tilly Williams, a patient in Bethlem, had submitted detailed plans for a replacement hospital with sickrooms attached to each ward, because 'patients have a sympathetic compassion for their sick companions which no infirmary keeper can feel'.[19]

Some of the long-stay wards for which the author became responsible in

16 McGlashen, T. H. (1988) A selective review of recent North American long-term follow up studies of schizophrenia. *Schizophrenia Bulletin,* 14:515-542; Lin, K. M., Klirnman, A. M. (1988) Psychopathology and clinical course of schizophrenia: an international perspective. *Schizophrenia Bulletin,* 14:555–567; Harrison, G. et al (2001) Recovery from psychotic illness: a 15- and 25- year international follow-up study. *British Journal of Psychiatry,* 178:506–517.

17 Lewis, A. & Levitt, P. (2002) Schizophrenia as a disorder of neurodevelopment. *Annual Review of Neuroscience,* 25:409–432. Complex genetic influences and adverse events in the pre- and perinatal periods are thought subtely to impair certain brain developmental processes, and lead to later vulnerability to a range of stresses.

18 Bleuler, M. op. cit.

19 Jay, M. (2003) *The Air Loom Gang.* London: Bantam Press, p. 220.

1971 contained silent, withdrawn figures that seemed close to the original stereotypes. But it became clear there was more to them than met the eye – most movingly after his mother's death, when an apparently mute patient whispered 'Sorry about your mother'. This should not have been a surprise – 'Even patients in the agitated ward would feel a kind of obligation to be calm and make less noise if there had been a tragic event in the lives of one of the doctors' families.'[20]

Evidence from the previous century – had it been considered – would also have cautioned against taking 'indifference' at face value. Moral treatment depended on the opposite assumption, and indeed, the term was used of attitudes toward patients rather than their attitudes to others: 'That disregard to the feelings of insane patients ... this callous indifference proceeded, and is still manifested, in many cases at least, from the preposterous assumption that lunatics had no feelings, that they did not feel as other men.'[21] A number of asylum superintendents encouraged friendly personal relationships amongst patients, and commended them as confidants and even counsellors. Most remarkably, in one asylum female patients took charge of children from a local orphanage.[22] The Belgian psychiatrist Crommelinck was struck by the warmth of feeling of patients toward staff on visits to several asylums in Britain.[23]

Nonetheless, the idea of emotional indifference was revived when the terms positive and negative to categorise the symptoms of schizophrenia 'burst into the horizon as a recurrent comet' in Britain and the USA, followed by many publications.[24] Negative symptoms included 'blunted' and 'flat' affect and these striking metaphors remain prominent in modern diag-

---

20 Perlman, C. (1912) quoted in Shorter, E. (1997) *A History of Psychiatry*. New York: John Wiley & Sons, p. 39.

21 Scull, A. ed. (1991) *The Asylum as Utopia: WAF Brown and the Mid-nineteenth Century Consolidation of Psychiatry*. London and New York: Tavistock/Routledge, p. 159.

22 Scull, A. (1993) *The Most Solitary of Afflictions: Madness and Society in Britain, 1700–1900*. New Haven and London: Yale University Press.

23 Smith, L. D. (1999) *'Cure, Comfort and Safe Custody': Public Lunatic Asylums in Early Nineteenth-Century England*. 1999 London: Leicester University Press, p. 152. 'This attachment, which manifests itself sometimes by the most extraordinary proofs, is met with in the lunatic who has become incurable, as he who has become convalescent: one knows not whether to say it is stronger with the one than the other.'

24 Zubin, J. (1985) Negative Symptoms: Are they indigenous to schizophrenia. *Schizophrenia Bulletin*, 11(3) 461–490; Crow, T. J. (1985) The two-syndrome concept: origins and current status. *Schizophrenia Bulletin*, 11(3) 471–483)

nostic systems and textbooks.[25] But investigations of patients' speech, facial expressions, gestures and subjective responses to emotional scenarios support the anecdotal evidence that this appearance reflects impairments in expressing emotions, and attuning to those expressed by others, rather than in feeling.[26]

CLOSING THE HOSPITALS

The term 'institutional neurosis' was introduced in 1959[27] to describe a syndrome characterised by loss of individuality, apathy and submissiveness, due mainly to regimentation, inactivity, and domination by staff in enclosed, dehumanising environments. It was claimed to be established in all schizophrenic patients after two years in mental hospitals, and to occur in other large institutions including prisons, detention camps, orphanages and sanatoria. The concept excited widespread interest in the 1960s' climate of hostility to institutions of all kinds, although similar ideas had been current a century previously.[28] Valuable though it proved in many respects, its presentation glossed over the diversity of hospital inmates. Striking photographs of lines of stooped, expressionless long-stay patients became iconic, and reinforced earlier stereotypes: although the text also referred to 'the active cheerful patient who enjoys the facilities available'.[29] Oversimplification fitted the agendas of otherwise opposed interests. For 'anti-psychiatrists' it confirmed that psychiatric institutions of all kinds were intrinsically noxious and that long-term mental illnesses would no longer exist once they were abolished,[30] whilst for an influential group of neo-Kraepelinian psychiatrists it appeared to vindicate a progressive disease model: indeed the term dementia praecox

25 *Diagnostic and Statistical Manual of Mental Disorders* (DSM). Washington D.C.: The American Psychiatric Association; Gelder, M. G. et al. New Oxford Textbook of Psychiatry. Oxford University Press.

26 Silver, N., Shlomo, N. (2002) Anhedonia and schizophrenia: how much is in the eye of the beholder. *Comprehensive Psychiatry*, 43(1):65–68.

27 Barton, R. (1959) *Institutional Neurosis.* Bristol: John Wright & Sons.

28 J. T. Arlidge (1859) *On the State of Lunacy and the Legal Provision for the Insane.* London: John Churchill. 'In all cases admitting of recovery, or of material amelioration, a gigantic asylum is a gigantic evil, and figuratively speaking, a manufactory of chronic insanity.'

29 Barton, op. cit.

30 Sedgwick, P. (1982) Psycho Politics. London: Pluto Press.

was temporarily re-introduced.[31] Studies demonstrated that many features of the syndrome could be reversed within hospitals by measures strikingly similar to moral treatment, but it was also the case that severe disabilities might precede admission and be much more resistant.[32]

The confusingly similar term 'institutionalism' was coined in the 1970s to describe 'the gradual adoption of an attitude of indifference to leaving' the longer a patient had been in hospital. This was based on a statistical correlation between length of stay and negative attitudes to discharge, without reference to initial differences in the expectations of cohorts admitted decades apart or the accumulation of events such as the loss of family and homes.[33] It also overlooked patients' fears of losing contacts with one another and with staff, which in contrast to moral treatment's extended family model were given little attention at that time. One of the few studies carried out on long-stay wards reported social networks that, though often small as had been described for similar patients outside hospital, varied considerably and included some large networks.[34] An observational study in the patients' canteen at Friern Hospital suggested that for patients with the most restricted conversational skills and expression of emotion, the exchange of goods and services creates bonds similar to those that more usually result from shared confidences. Exchanges of tea, cigarettes and small change appeared to indicate friendship, toleration, sympathy, caring and the desire for contact.[35]

The concept of institutionalism made it easier to discharge long-stay patients without assessing their own attitudes, which were assumed to be uniformly formed by the process. But when investigated they often appeared to be realistic. The most common reason for wanting to stay was the absence of a family home to which to return. Only a minority had even a vague notion

31 Johnstone, E. C. Crow, T. J. Fwm, C. D. Stevens, M. Kreel L. and Husband, J. (1978) The dementia of dementia praecox..*Acta Psychiatrica Scandinavica*. 57:305–324.

32 Wing, J. K. & Brown, G. W. (1970) *Institutionalism and schizophrenia*: A comparative study of three mental hospitals 1960–1968. Cambridge University Press. Abrahamson, D. & Brenner, D. (1978) *A study of the 'old long-stay patients' in Goodmayes Hospital.* Final report of work carried out during tenure of a Department of Health and Social Security grant.

33 Wing & Brown op. cit. p. 86.

34 Defined formally as a specific set of linkages among a defined set of persons, social networks are maps of interactions within groups in which individuals can be represented by points and their connections by lines. They can be examined in relatively simple ways and by sophisticated mathematical analysis.

35 Dunn, M. et al. (1990) The TAPS Project. 4: An observational study of the social life of long-stay patients. *British Journal of Psychiatry*, 157:842–848.

of any alternative accommodation, and relevant information was shown favourably to influence attitudes to leaving. The second most common reason, inability to cope outside hospital, was offered predominantly by the more disabled patients, many of whom had no knowledge of any source of income outside hospital except employment, or of any available support. Some of those who reported liking hospital were amongst the least disabled: they had carved out active and independent lives in hospital and were puzzled at being asked why they stayed on in what they had come to regard as their home and even their place of employment.

Some quotations may bring to life the flavour of responses:

'I'm the only patient on this job, I've been doing it all the time I've been here, it gives me a sense of importance.'

'I'd like to go but employment would be a problem, I can't get a room until I've got some money.'

'I would miss the whole environment, the routine.'

'I don't want to go anywhere else, I might end up in a private posh place where they do things like playing bridge.'

'I stay with my mother every weekend: I wouldn't have enough to live on at home. I haven't got a watch or a lighter or any of the necessities.'

'I think there is more protection here than outside but I've never really been out, and I'm a bit scared to go.'

'I'd like my own flat but I'm overwhelmed by the thought of preparations; more confidence, knowing both sides to living.'

'You might be ready for something better.'

'I would gain a place of my own; a new life. I am not saying it would work but it might.'

'Learning how to cope with myself better.'

'What I would gain would be experience in looking after myself and perhaps looking after others.'[36]

From the 1970s onwards, these and similar patients were given the opportunity to move out gradually via preparation houses on the hospital campus, which provided domestic and social skills training and information about living in the community. They mainly moved on in compatible – yet often quite diverse – groups of four to six to houses in the locality, where they were

36 Abrahamson, D. et al. 'Do long-stay psychiatric patients want to leave hospital?' *Health Trends* (1978) 14:95–97 and (1989) 21:16–21.

supported by visiting nurses and social workers. Hoped for benefits appeared to be achieved: 'more support from others living here'; 'all muck in together'; 'understand each other'; ' 'If someone is not well we do their chores – if I am ill, the others will look after me'; and 'more myself'; 'more freedom'; 'We are all very individual.'[37] Attachments amongst a group of residents could override the tensions that develop in any small group living together, and it was again clear that even distant seeming relationships might be important. However, few fresh links outside were formed and some residents missed the range of contacts they had in hospital; although in other respects they were glad to be living outside.[38] Some of the increasing number of 'revolving door' patients, so called because of repeated short admissions, and the less numerous 'new long-stay', found small groups living difficult but became isolated on their own.

The range of choice was widened by a housing association development in 1984 of a core and cluster group of eighteen bed-sitters and flats, with communal dining and sitting rooms and a small number of part-time staff. A study during the transition from hospital and the first year of operation showed that social networks were considerably expanded and enhanced, although the general public remained sparsely represented.[39] Experience over twenty years has underlined the impression of an enduring small community and the importance of the mutual support available. The same is true of several later purpose built complexes of flats with communal facilities and 24-hour staffing, and as in the original scheme, the combination of space and privacy benefits both volatile residents and those whose main handicap is social withdrawal.[40]

37 Keays, M. (1986) *Group Homes – the heart of community care today?* Dissertation for Certificate of Qualified Social Worker.

38 Goldie, N. (1988). 'I hated it there but I miss the people': a study of what happened to a group of ex-long-stay patients from Claybury Hospital. Research paper 1, Health and Social Services Research Unit, Department of Social Sciences, South Bank Polytechnic, London.

39 Abrahamson, D. & Ezekiel, E. (1984). *The Social Networks of Patients Moving from Hospital into the Community*. Conference: Social networks in Hospital and in the Community. London: The King's Fund Centre.

40 Abrahamson, D. (1993) Housing and de-institutionalisation. In: *Dimensions of Mental Health Community Care*. Weller, M. P. I. Muijen, M. (Eds.) London: W. B. Saunders Company Ltd pp. 208–232.

CINDERELLAS NO MORE

Long-stay patients were transformed from Cinderellas to much sought after belles of the ball in the later 1980s, as the potential value of hospital land rose. Substantial funds – so-called dowries – were attached to each long-stay ward resident for their alternative care and were eagerly snapped up by the local authorities concerned. Although this proved to be a remarkably fruitful development overall, difference from the large hospitals tended to become a simplistic yardstick for the new services, and 'it's institutional' a catchphrase that restricted the range of alternatives. Most fundamentally, social networks implications were glossed over on the assumption that discharged patients would necessarily be engulfed in a putative, warmly welcoming entity termed 'The Community': an assumption that would have been unrealistic for any demographically similar group irrespective of disabilities. Possibilities were further narrowed by overemphasis on dispersal in small houses for two or three people that 'disappeared within the Community', reflecting fear of the 'ghettoes' of poor quality accommodation that had developed in the USA.[41] But dispersal may imply that social relationships within the stigmatised group are less valuable and prestigious than those outside it. Some discharged patients were discouraged from visiting their former hospitals or spending time with ex-patient friends elsewhere. When other contacts and friendships did not materialise as expected, 'Community Care' was officially transmogrified into 'Care in the Community', meaning care outside the traditional hospitals irrespective of the extent of community in its most important social network sense.[42]

Not surprisingly, social isolation and loneliness are major problems for new generations of patients 'in the community'. The current literature indicates that even by the time of their first admission, schizophrenic patients have in general smaller social networks than a range of comparison groups including patients with other psychiatric disorders, although there is considerable variation and some overlap. Friends feature less as constituents and there is a higher proportion of family members, who may themselves feel

41 Heginbotham, C. (1985) *Good Practices in Housing for People with Long-term Mental Illnesses.* London Good Practice in Mental Health; Torrey, E. F. (1997) *Out of the Shadows: Confronting America's Mental Illness Crisis.* New York: John Wiley & Sons, Inc.

42 Acheson, E. D. (1985). From the Chief Medical Officer – 'That over used word Community!' *Health Trends*, 17, 3; Scherer, J. (1972) Contemporary Community: Sociological Illusion or Reality? London: Tavistock Publications.

isolated, and of service providers. These characteristics tend to become more marked over time, due to unemployment and poverty as well as the direct effects of illnesses. Loneliness is a source of much hidden distress amongst long-term patients and there is evidence that it may be a factor in the association between psychiatric and physical illnesses.[43]

SECOND CLASS AGAIN?

There has been a longstanding tendency for mental health services, paradoxically, to allocate time to patients in inverse relationship to their difficulties in expressing themselves: schizophrenic patients with limited or disordered speech being habitually afforded the least time. Similarly, the more difficulty in expressing emotion, the more likely it is to be defined merely as blunted or flat affect rather than engaged with and explored. The loss this involves emerged clearly from two combined group and individual out-patient clinics for long-term patients, which have been operating for the past twenty years in one of the most socially deprived and ethnically mixed boroughs in London.[44] The unexpectedly lively discussions in the weekly groups include day-to-day issues, work and leisure, illness and medication, and bereavements and other losses. Mutual tolerance and empathy are striking and vocal members do not exclude the more withdrawn, who appear to enjoy the good humoured banter that is often a feature. Banter can shift rapidly to tactful attention to personal distress, and the predominantly optimistic atmosphere may give way to expression of the pain and even despair felt at times by long-term patients. The development of social links between attenders later stimulated the setting up of a weekly club, which has continued to be a focal point for many patients. Three-quarters of club members interviewed, most of whom had used it for two years or more, said they had made new friends there, and half that it helped them keep contact with old friends.

43 Lynch, J. J. (2000) A Cry Unheard: Medical Consequences of Loneliness. Baltimore: Bancroft Press.

44 Abrahamson, D. & Fellow-Smith, E. (1991) A combined group and individual out-patient clinic. Psychiatric Bulletin: *The Journal of Trends in Psychiatric Practice*, 15:486–487. Group out-patent clinics (Ward, D. J., 1975. *Journal of the Irish Medical Association,* 68:486–489) and the attractively named 'Coffee and ... psychotherapy' – Masnik, R., et al. (1971) *American Journal of Psychiatry*, 128, 164–167 – were influences; the immediate trigger was a complaint at a conventional out-patients that the waiting time was too short for the discussion between patients that was the best part!

Mixing and talking to fellow patients and staff was the most popular aspect, although there are members who attend regularly but rarely speak.[45] Club outings and holidays have ranged widely at home and abroad. The author has gained a great deal from being part of the club, where patients and staff become persons for each other.

Other rehabilitation services have had similar experience of long-term patients' potential, yet second-class status and time-limited treatment are creeping back. Early intervention services are high on the current centralised policy agenda, with the same assumptions as in the past. Hopefully, they may be more successful now, but there is already evidence that a significant proportion of their patients go on to need continuing care; and the same is likely for patients brought into the system by proposed new mental health legislation. Neglect of chronic conditions in general is reflected in media and political concentration on acute interventions as the main index of NHS performance. There is already pressure on community mental health teams to discharge 'the backlog of chronic cases'[46] in order to cope with growing emphasis on throughput, and community services will repeat the hospital pattern if long-term patients are given lower priority. A persistent, hopeful approach, with a range of therapies and social interventions as well as of medication, tailored to the individual, is clearly fully justified by the current state of knowledge. That it better meets the needs of patients and their carers is underlined by the recovery movement, which has become a key development internationally. Affinities with the moral treatment movement have been pointed out;[47] with in addition a more contemporary, strong emphasis on patients' own experiences and initiatives.

The meaning of the term would be clearer as 'in recovery': 'most definitions involve some component of acceptance of illness, having a sense of hope about the future, and finding a renewed sense of self', and the factors believed to facilitate it 'appear to have more to do with the person struggling with the illness than with the illness itself . . . hope, courage, and a sense of belong-

---

45 Godin, M. G. (1999) *An investigation into the extent and value of peer support amongst mental health service users*. Integrating Study: Bsc (Hons) South Bank University.

46 Singh, S. P. (2000) Running an effective community mental health team. *Advances in Psychiatric Treatment,* 6(6) 414–422 and DA & SPS 2001, 6(7)160. The journal title is intriguing!

47 Roberts, G. & Wolfson, P. (2004) The rediscovery of recovery: open to all. *Advances in Psychiatric Treatment*, 10:37–48.

ing'.[48] Its ethos is eloquently expressed by the mother of two patients: 'we must keep alive the hope that recovery is possible. There is reason to hope! Half to three fourths of all those with schizophrenia recover. This does not mean that they are cured . . . although this has happened in some instances. It means that over time, in an often long, difficult process, individuals come to terms with their illness. They learn how to accept it and then how to move beyond it, to believe in every cell of their being that they are not "schizophrenic", defined solely by an illness. They are individuals . . . with strengths as well as limitations, with the capacities to love and be loved, to work and to find joy and meaning in their lives despite an illness.'[49]

CHALLENGES

Terminology is contentious in this area and the plural 'mental illnesses' has been used to at least emphasise the wide variety of conditions involved. The hospital era illustrates the perils of attempting to impose a monolithic service on this diversity, and the even greater diversity of the individuals concerned. The public's disappointment with 'Care in the Community' may reflect expectation of a similarly high degree of visibility to the 'unmistakable' hospitals, and more dispersed services may be overlooked. These now include a range of multidisciplinary teams that provide a range of medication, social and psychological treatments; support teams that target social isolation and the pervasive occupation and employment needs, and supported accommodation of varying kinds. Unfortunately, some of the less successful components are the most visible, especially acute admission wards where the emphasis on crisis management and rapid throughput has been demoralising for patients and staff. Lessons about the principles and practices of therapeutic environments that had been learned in the moral treatment era and relearned subsequently are having to be learned yet again.[50] The prominence of secure units is also a cause for concern and is likely to be further promoted by a reactionary new mental health act, although there is no evidence of

---

48 Davidson, L. (2003) *Living Outside Mental Illness: Qualitative Studies of Recovery in Schizophrenia*. New York and London: New York University Press, pp. 14, 43.

49 Thornton, L.L. *Finding hope in schizophrenia: Healing and hope for everyone in the family*. Newsletter: NAMI-SCC National Alliance for the Mentally Ill (www.namiscc.org).

50 Muijen, M. (2002) Acute wards: problems and solutions. *Psychiatric Bulletin*, 26:342–343.

an increase in serious violence by patients since care in the community was introduced.[51]

Furthermore 'institutionalisation' in the large hospitals was promoted by a culture of overcontrol of staff as well as patients, and there is a risk that dedication, initiative and creativity in community services will be stifled as regulatory bodies proliferate:[52] 'There are more targets and procedures, which add to the stress and so people go off sick. This used to be a nice place to work in. There's been no laughter in this office for a long time' – a comment from within a team which like many struggles to provide the healing elements of personal interaction and concern.[53]

The public has a responsibility to support the best of care in the community, rather than undermine a humane reform, especially at a time when a previously optimistic climate has again swung to pessimism and fear. More informed attitudes to mental illnesses are overdue if the huge burden of stigma and discrimination is to be reduced.[54] Opportunities to enable patients and patient groups fully to join in and contribute to the network of communities that now make up 'The Community' need to be grasped by individuals and organisations; rather than being paid lip service as in the past.[55] The nameless and numberless patients, and the staff, who preserved humanity and altruism on forsaken long-stay wards, will be best remembered in this way.

---

51 An unprecedented alliance of many mental health and other organisations opposes the proposals (www.mind.org.uk); Walsh, E. et al. (2002) 'Violence and schizophrenia: examining the evidence'. *British Journal of Psychiatry*, 180:490–495.

52 Goldberg, D. (2002) The benefits and costs of continuous inspections: At what point does patient care suffer. *Psychiatric Bulletin*, 26:361–362.

53 *Changing Light Bulbs? Research into the Role of Mental-health Support-workers in East Suffolk* (2002) London: MACA.

54 Crisp, A. Ed. (2001) Every Family in the Land: Understanding Prejudice and Discrimination against People with Mental Illness. London: Sir Robert Mond Memorial Trust. Available online at www.stigma.org.

55 MIND, MACA (now 'Together'), SANE, and Rethink are among national organisations with such aims and are easily accessible, including via the Internet. They welcome interest and support.

ANNE BAYEFSKY

The Role of the United Nations in Countering Terrorism

THE DEFINITION OF TERRORISM

The key obstacle to the ability of the United Nations to play a constructive role in countering terrorism is the absence of an internationally agreed definition. Without defining terrorism UN states operate with impunity in parallel universes.

In July 2004, the Security Council held an open debate about the work of the Counter Terrorism Committee (CTC) – a Committee created in the wake of the events of September 9, 2001 and composed of all Security Council members. The Syrian representative told the Council "Syria reiterate(s) its deep commitment to the fight against terrorism and ... pledges its continued cooperation with the relevant organs of the United Nations working to eradicate that scourge."[1] Syria, however, is on the U.S. State Department list of state sponsors of terrorism and plays host to Hamas (the Islamic Resistance Movement), The Popular Front for the Liberation of Palestinian (PFLP), and The Popular Front for the Liberation of Palestine – General Command (PFLP–GC), all designated by the State Department as foreign terrorist organizations.[2]

Lecture delivered at the Conference on the Global Impact of Terrorism, the Israel International Policy Institute for Counter-Terrorism, Interdisciplinary Center (IDC), Herzliya, Israel, 12 September 2004.

1 Milad Atieh, Press Release SC/8152, 19 July 2004, p. 7, www. . ////2004/8152.doc .htm.

2 U.S. Department of State, Patterns of Global Terrorism, April 29, 2004, www.state .gov/////2003/31644.htm; Fact Sheet, Foreign Terrorist Organizations, 12 August 2004,

Similarly, the most recent Syrian report submitted to the CTC in July 2003[3] explains that various laws[4] codify "the procedures and measures adopted and in force in the Syrian Arab Republic aimed at the suppression ... and prevention of terrorist crimes, and ... the denial of safe haven, refuge, assistance or any form of help in the territory of ... Syria."[5] But a closer look at these laws, such as the Arab Convention on Judicial Cooperation, indicates that primary legal authority rests with Sharia or public policy in that country, and any moves to the contrary are unenforceable.[6]

The Arab Terrorism Convention and the Terrorism Convention of the Organization of the Islamic Conference (OIC) are both repeatedly invoked before the CTC, and define terrorism to exclude "armed struggle for liberation and self-determination."[7] This claim – which purports to exclude blowing up Israelis from the reach of international law and organizations – is central to interpreting every statement that Arab and Islamic states make in any UN fora purporting to combat terrorism.

The result is the pollution of UN action in the counter-terrorism context

---

www.state.gov/////2004/35167.htm; The Leading Palestinian Terrorist Organizations (August 2004), Intelligence and Terrorism Information Center at the Center for Special Studies (CSS), http:// .intelligence.org.il///8_04/.htm.

3 S/2003/725, 18 July 2003, http://ods-dds-ny.un.org////03/437/01//0343701 ?OpenElement; first report, S/2001/1204, 14 December 2001; second report, S/2002/1046, 19 September 2002.

4 The 1983 Convention on Judicial Cooperation between States of the Arab League (the "Riyadh Convention") and the Model Treaty on Extradition adopted by the Eighth United Nations Congress on the Prevention of Crime and the Treatment of Offenders (1990).

5 S/2003/725, 18 July 2003, para. 1.10

6 The Riyadh Convention permits a Recipient State (the signatory) to refuse to recognise the judgment of the courts of an Originating State where the judgment is contrary to Islamic law or the Constitution or public order of the Recipient State.

7 The Arab Convention for the Suppression of Terrorism, adopted by the Council of Arab Ministers of the Interior and the Council of Arab Ministers of Justice, Cairo, 22 April 1998, "Article 2(a). All cases of struggle by whatever means, including armed struggle, against foreign occupation and aggression for liberation and self-determination, in accordance with the principles of international law, shall not be regarded as an offence. This provision shall not apply to any act prejudicing the territorial integrity of any Arab State." Convention of the Organisation of the Islamic Conference On Combating International Terrorism, "Article 2(a). Peoples' struggle including armed struggle against foreign occupation, aggression, colonialism, and hegemony, aimed at liberation and self-determination in accordance with the principles of international law shall not be considered a terrorist crime," adopted at Ouagadougou, Burkina Faso, on 1 July 1999.

on every level from the adoption and implementation of resolutions, to the drafting of new conventions, to the application of the rules of self-defense.

GENERIC RESOLUTIONS

An example of UN inversion of principles in the terrorism context is the now annual resolution of the General Assembly and UN Commission on Human Rights called "human rights and terrorism."[8] At the last General Assembly the resolution was introduced by Algeria and sponsored by countries with poor human rights records such as China, Cuba, Saudi Arabia and Sudan.[9] The human rights and terrorism resolutions incorporate by reference the Arab and OIC Terrorism Conventions or similar pronouncements, like the 2003 "commitment" of the heads of state and government of the roughly 120 members of the Non-Aligned Movement[10] "to fight terrorism." This commitment includes the following:

> The Heads of State or Government ... reaffirmed the Movement's principled position under international law on the legitimacy of the struggle of peoples under colonial or alien domination and foreign occupation for national liberation and self-determination, which does not constitute terrorism.[11]

In the result, the resolution on human rights and terrorism is adopted by the

---

8 General Assembly Resolution A/RES/58/174, Human rights and terrorism, adopted 22 December 2003, 120 votes to 42, with 18 abstentions. Commission Resolution, 2004/44. Human rights and terrorism, adopted 19 April 2004, 31 votes to 14, with 8 abstentions.

9 At the 2004 Commission the sponsors were: Algeria, Bangladesh, China, Colombia, Congo, Côte d'Ivoire, Cuba, Ecuador, Egypt, Eritrea, Ethiopia, Gabon, India, Indonesia, Kenya, Madagascar, Mali, Mauritania, Nicaragua, Nigeria, Oman, Pakistan, Philippines, Qatar, the Russian Federation, Saudi Arabia, Senegal, Sri Lanka, the Sudan, Swaziland, Togo, Tunisia, Turkey, Uganda, Viet Nam and Zimbabwe.

At the 2003 General Assembly the sponsors were: Azerbaijan, Belarus, Bhutan, Cameroon, China, Colombia, Cuba, the Democratic Republic of the Congo, Ecuador, Egypt, El Salvador, Eritrea, Ethiopia, Georgia, India, Indonesia, Kazakhstan, Kenya, Kyrgyzstan, Madagascar, Mauritania, Nepal, Nigeria, Pakistan, Peru, the Philippines, Qatar, the Russian Federation, Saudi Arabia, Senegal, Sri Lanka, the Sudan, Swaziland, Tajikistan, Togo, Tunisia, Turkey, the United Republic of Tanzania, Venezuela, Viet Nam and Zimbabwe.

10 The Non-Aligned Movement is described on its website as a Movement representing the interests and priorities of developing countries. For list of member states see: http://.nam.gov.za//.htm.

11 A/57/759-S/2003/332, 18 March, 2003, see paragraphs 106, 108, 115.

Commission and the General Assembly only over the objection of virtually all Western democratic states.[12]

A COMPREHENSIVE TERRORISM CONVENTION

The definitional impasse has now stymied further codification. For many years, a working group of the Sixth Committee of the General Assembly has been attempting to conclude a Comprehensive Convention on International Terrorism. Even in the immediate aftermath of 9/11 it failed to adopt the Convention, and the deadlock continues to this day. The reason is very clear. On the one hand, stands the formal proposal of the Organization of the Islamic Conference. It seeks to add a paragraph stating "The activities of the parties during an armed conflict, including situations of foreign occupation . . . are not governed by this Convention."[13] Or, as the Syrian delegate described the standoff, "it emphasized the need for a clear definition distinguishing terrorism from the legitimate struggle of peoples against foreign occupation and alien domination."[14] And on the other hand stands the opposition of the Coordinator representing everyone else.[15] No state has any intention of moving forward by operating without consensus.

The absence of an internationally agreed-upon definition of terrorism is not an academic problem. It disables the UN from fair and non-selective criticism of terrorist acts.

---

12 Voting against at the 2003 General Assembly were: Albania, Australia, Austria, Belgium, Bosnia and Herzegovina, Bulgaria, Canada, Croatia, Czech Republic, Denmark, Estonia, Federated States of Micronesia, Finland, France, Germany, Greece, Hungary, Iceland, Ireland, Italy, Latvia, Liechtenstein, Lithuania, Luxembourg, Malta, Marshall Islands, Monaco, Netherlands, Norway, Palau, Poland, Portugal, Republic of Korea, Romania, Serbia and Montenegro, Slovakia, Slovenia, Sweden, Switzerland, The former Yugoslav Republic of Macedonia, United Kingdom, United States.

At the 2004 Commission on Human Rights voting against were: Australia, Austria, Croatia, France, Germany, Hungary, Ireland, Italy, Japan, Netherlands, Republic of Korea, Sweden, United Kingdom of Great Britain and Northern Ireland, United States of America.

13 A/57/37, Annex IV, Report of the Ad Hoc Committee established by General Assembly Resolution 51/210 of 17 December 1996; see also A/C.6/58/WG.2/CRP.2, Annex II, 8 October 2003.

14 A/C.6/58/WG.2/CRP.2, Annex III, paragraph 1, 8 October 2003.

15 A/57/37, Annex IV, Report of the Ad Hoc Committee established by General Assembly Resolution 51/210 of 17 December 1996; see A/C.6/58/WG.2/CRP.2, Annex II, 8 October 2003.

SPECIFIC RESOLUTIONS OF CONDEMNATION

Contrast UN action in response to terrorist incidents in Indonesia or Russia with terrorism in Israel.

In the case of the October 2003 hostage-taking crisis in Moscow, the Security Council adopted a resolution condemning the terrorist attack within twenty-four hours.[16] In the case of the bombing in Bali, also in October 2003, the Security Council adopted a resolution within forty-eight hours.[17] But it took the Council two weeks of intensive negotiation to adopt the resolution concerning the attacks in Kenya directed at Israelis.[18] Those attacks involved a suicide bombing at a hotel operated by, and catering to, Israelis, and a missile attack on an Israeli civilian airplane. The struggle behind the scenes occurred over references to Israel and Israeli victims. The original draft circulated by the United States, for example, read: "Condemns in the strongest terms the terrorist bomb attack against Kenyan and Israeli civilians." The final version omits the reference to "Israeli civilians" and reads, "Condemns in the strongest terms the terrorist bomb attack at the Paradise Hotel in Kikambala, Kenya, and the attempted missile attack on Arkia Israeli Airlines Flight 582."[19] In addition, while the Security Council resolutions on the Bali and Russian attacks urged cooperation with the Indonesian and Russian authorities in their efforts to bring the perpetrators to justice, the reference to cooperation with "Israeli authorities" was left out of the Kenya resolution.

On 31 August 2004 the Security Council refused to adopt a Presidential Statement condemning the terrorist attack on two civilian buses in Beersheva. The only response was a press statement – which has no status or distribution as a UN document – informing the public that Council members (not the Council itself) "strongly condemned these bombings that resulted in the loss of innocent lives. They also condemned all other acts of terrorism ... [and] denounced the escalation of violence in the Middle East and called

16 S/RES/1440 (2002), adopted 24 October 2002 concerning events of 23 October 2002.

17 S/RES/1438 (2002), adopted 14 October 2002 concerning events of 12 October 2002.

18 S/RES/1450 (2002), adopted 13 December 2002 concerning events of 28 November 2002.

19 S/RES/1450 (2002).

on all the parties for the continuation of the Middle East peace process."[20] Members of the Council like Algeria and Pakistan refused consensus for a strong unified Presidential statement on the grounds that it would be inappropriate to make selective condemnation of terrorist attacks; they insisted the Security Council has to treat all terrorist acts alike.

On the very next day, however, the Security Council issued a formal UN document in the form of a Presidential Statement in response to the hostage-taking and murder of Russian schoolchildren, parents and teachers. In stark contrast it read:

> The Security Council condemns in the strongest terms the heinous terrorist act involving the taking of hostages at a secondary school in the town of Beslan . . . as well as other terrorist attacks committed recently against innocent civilians in Moscow and on two Russian airliners, in which many lives were claimed and people injured . . . The Security Council expresses the deepest sympathy and condolences to the people and the Government of the Russian Federation and to the victims of the terrorist acts and their families. The Security Council urges all States, in accordance with their obligations under resolution 1373 (2001), to cooperate actively with the Russian authorities in their efforts to find and bring to justice the perpetrators, organizers and sponsors of these terrorist acts.[21]

THE IMPLEMENTATION MECHANISMS

The definitional problem has not been overcome by practical breakthroughs on the part of the UN's counter-terrorism apparatus.

a. The Counter-Terrorism Committee

The CTC has the job of reviewing reports of UN states on their implementation of Security Council resolution 1373.[22] By 30 June 2004 the Committee had received 515 reports. Every UN member had reported once, over half had reported three times, and some had produced four reports.[23] Still, sev-

20 Press Release SC/8177, 31 August 2004, www.un.org////2004/8177.doc.htm.

21 S/PRST/2004/31, 1 September 2004, http:// -dds-ny.un.org////04/475/84//04 47584.pdf?OpenElement.

22 S/RES/1373 (2001), 28 September 2001.

23 Press Release SC/8152, 19 July, 2004.

enty-one states (or about 40% of UN members) had overdue reports[24] and eighty reports are part of a backlog, reports submitted but not yet considered, by the CTC.[25] The Committee reads reports, asks questions of states about the content, and requires an additional report in response to each round of questions. Reports submitted from places like Sudan, Syria and Yemen[26] have not had a response by the Committee in a year. The work of the CTC is almost entirely behind closed doors. The questions posed to countries – which might exhibit some element of criticism – are confidential. The questions themselves must be approved by every member of the Security Council before being sent. The report of the Chair of the CTC to the Security Council in January 2004 pointed to another serious flaw: "... the main source of information for the CTC are the reports sent by member States answering ... the CTC's previous letters ..."[27] His recommendation – "to gather information from other sources ..."[28] – has yet to be followed up systematically.

Security Council Resolution 1373 requires that all States shall:

(a) Refrain from providing any form of support, active or passive, to entities or persons involved in terrorist acts, including ... eliminating the supply of weapons to terrorists;
(b) Take the necessary steps to prevent the commission of terrorist acts ...
(c) Deny safe haven to those who finance, plan, support, or commit terrorist acts, or provide safe havens;
(d) Prevent those who finance, plan, facilitate or commit terrorist acts from using their respective territories for those purposes against other States or their citizens ...[29]

But the CTC has never named a single terrorist organization, individual or state sponsor of terrorism. The CTC website has one sentence devoted to the

24 Press Release SC/8152, 19 July, 2004.

25 Counter-Terrorism Committee, http://www.un.org/Docs/sc/committees/1373/submitted_reports.html.

26 Sudan third report, S/2003/837, submitted 27 August 2003; Syria third report, S/2003/725, submitted 18 July 2003; Yemen third report, S/2003/1037, submitted 27 October 2003.

27 S/2004/70, 26 January, 2004, page 12, A.5.

28 S/2004/70, 26 January, 2004, page 12, A.5.

29 S/RES/1373 (2001), 28 September 2001, operative paragraph 2.

definition of terrorism. It refers interested parties to the ongoing discussion in the General Assembly's sixth committee over a comprehensive terrorism convention which "would include a definition of terrorism if adopted."[30]

In July 2004 the CTC was reorganized, and a new Counter-Terrorism Committee Executive Directorate was created. The CTC is now empowered to conduct country visits – "with the consent of the State concerned."[31] It is widely expected that the Committee will stay away from places like the Arab Middle East and focus on facilitating reporting and providing technical assistance to states which are willing, but unable, to comply with 1373. The CTC's Executive Directorate will recommend countries to visit, but all Security Council members will have to approve such recommendations.

A July 2004 letter from the Chairman of the CTC to the Security Council described "the Committee's main objectives ... [as] maintaining and strengthening the consensus within the international community on the importance of combating terrorism ..."[32] – a consensus which exists only so long as terrorism remains undefined.

b. The Sanctions Committee

A second Security Council resolution 1267, adopted 15 October, 1999, and directed at Al Qaeda and the Taliban, created what is called the Sanctions Committee.[33] This Committee gives rise to the only "UN terrorist list," but its reach is very circumscribed. A name can only be added to the list if all fifteen Security Council members agree. While not directly thwarted by the lack of a definition since the terrorist target has already been agreed, the sanctions committee has been beset by many difficulties:[34]

- the list does not cover all individuals or groups that are members of or associated with Al-Qaeda – only some three hundred individuals have been designated, despite the fact that some four thousand individuals have been

30 Counter-Terrorism Committee, "A Definition of Terrorism," http:// www.un.org/Docs/sc/committees/1373/definition.html.

31 S/RES/1535 (2004), 26 March 2004.

32 S/2004/541, 6 July 2004.

33 S/RES/1267 (1999), 15 October 1999.

34 This list is compiled from comments of various UN diplomats and secretariat officials, and in particular the article of Eric Rosand, "The Security Council's Efforts to Monitor the Implementation of Al-Qaeda/Taliban Sanctions," American Journal of International Law, vol. 98 no. 4, October 2004, pp. 760, 762.

arrested or detained in over one hundred countries on the basis of links to Al-Qaeda
- the identifiers on the list are unclear – with many commonplace or incomplete names
- states often fail to transmit the list to the national authorities responsible for monitoring borders or financial transactions
- diplomats report that some states fail to propose names of Islamic groups or individuals for fear of being seen as anti-Islamic
- more than one-third of UN states have failed to produce the required reports on compliance with resolution 1267
- most reports which are submitted fail to provide details of actions taken to implement the sanctions regime
- the travel ban and arms embargo have apparently produced few tangible results.

As American UN diplomat Eric Rosand concludes, after closely following the work of both the Sanctions Committee and the CTC, the Sanctions Committee has failed to reach any agreement on which States are not complying with their Chapter VII obligations, and has never submitted such a list of countries to the Council for a response – even if only to name the offending states publicly. Nor does the Council's most recent Al-Qaeda/Taliban sanctions resolution[35] contemplate such a move. In sum, neither the Sanctions Committee, nor the CTC, "are close to reaching agreement on the standards to measure States' performance, let alone on a list of the non-performers and whether to submit such a list to the Council" for action.[36]

THE GREEN LIGHT TO TERRORISM

These failures of neglect or omission are not the worst of the UN record on terrorism. UN moves go beyond complicity, and give a green light to terrorists who take aim at Israelis. For three years running the UN Commission on Human Rights has adopted a resolution which condones suicide bombing – that is when the target is Israel. The Commission adopted in April

35 S/RES/1526 (2004), 30 January 2004.

36 Eric Rosand, "The Security Council's Efforts to Monitor the Implementation of Al-Qaeda/Taliban Sanctions," American Journal of International Law, vol. 98 no. 4, October 2004, 745 at pp. 745, 762.

2004 another resolution,[37] sponsored by the Organization of the Islamic Conference, which through incorporation by reference speaks of "the legitimacy of the struggle [against] foreign occupation by all available means, including armed struggle" and the "right . . . to resist." The resolution passed by a substantial majority.[38]

Pronouncements of some of the judges of the UN's highest judicial body, the International Court of Justice, are similar. In its recent decision on Israel's security fence, Judge Abdul Koroma of Sierra Leone wrote: "It is understandable that a prolonged occupation would engender resistance."[39] Judge Nabil Elaraby of Egypt said, "Throughout the annals of history, occupation has always been met with armed resistance. Violence breeds violence." He "wholeheartedly subscribe[d] to the view" that there is "a right of resistance."[40] Judge

---

37 General Assembly Resolution A/RES/37/43, adopted 3 December 1982, says: "2. Reaffirms the legitimacy of the struggle of peoples for independence, territorial integrity, national unity and liberation from colonial and foreign domination and foreign occupation **by all available means, including armed struggle**" (bold added).

Commission on Human Rights resolution 2002/8, says: "Recalling particularly General Assembly resolution 37/43 of 3 December 1982 reaffirming the legitimacy of the struggle of peoples against foreign occupation." It was adopted 15 April 2002, 40 states for, 5 against, 7 abstentions.

Commission on Human Rights Resolution 2003/6 says: "Recalling particularly General Assembly resolution 37/43 of 3 December 1982 reaffirming the legitimacy of the struggle of peoples against foreign occupation and for self-determination." It was adopted 15 April 2003, 33 votes for, 5 against, 15 abstentions.

Commission on Human Rights Resolution 2004/10 says: "Recalling in particular General Assembly resolution 37/43 of 3 December 1982 reaffirming the legitimacy of the struggle of peoples for independence from foreign domination and foreign occupation and for self-determination, in conformity with international law." It was adopted 15 April 2004, 31 votes for, 7 against, 15 abstentions.

38 Thirty-one votes for, seven against, fifteen abstentions.

39 "9. . . . While it is understandable that a prolonged occupation would engender resistance, it is nonetheless incumbent on all parties to the conflict to respect international humanitarian law at all times." http:// www.icj-cij.org/icjwww/idocket/imwp/imwpframe.htm.

40 "3.1 . . . Throughout the annals of history, occupation has always been met with armed resistance. Violence breeds violence . . . The dilemma was pertinently captured by Professors Richard Falk and Burns Weston when they wrote, '. . . the illegality of the Israeli occupation regime itself set off an escalatory spiral of resistance and repression, and under these conditions all considerations of morality and reason establish a right of resistance inherent in the population. This right of resistance is an implicit legal corollary of the fundamental legal rights associated with the primacy of sovereign identity and assuring the humane protection of the inhabitants.' I wholeheartedly subscribe to the view expressed by Professors Falk and Weston . . ." http://www.icj-cij.org/icjwww/idocket/imwp/imwpframe.htm.

Hisashi Owada of Japan spoke of "the *so-called* terrorist attacks by Palestinian suicide bombers against the Israeli civilian population."[41]

NO SELF-DEFENSE AGAINST TERRORISM

There is a close nexus between active encouragement to terrorists who aim at Israelis and the effort to deny Israelis a rights of self-defense against terrorism.

In March of this year, the UN Human Rights Commission convened a special sitting on Israel's targeted killing of Sheik Ahmed Yassin.[42] The suffering of Yassin's victims, or the genocidal plight of millions of Sudanese, did not move the Commission to hold a special sitting. Instead, the UN's primary human rights body scheduled an extra three hours to denounce Israel over the death of one man – a man who personally instigated and authorized suicide bombing, ordered the firing of missiles at Israeli communities, and repeatedly exhorted his followers to armed struggle against Israelis and Jews "everywhere." Targeting and killing terrorists like Hamas' Ismail Abu Shanab, Yassin and Abdel-Aziz al-Rantissi,[43] even when there have been zero civilian

41 "31. Without going into the question of what is the causal relationship between the tragic acts of mutual violence resorted to by each of the parties and the question of whether the so-called terrorist attacks by Palestinian suicide bombers against the Israeli civilian population should be blamed as constituting a good enough ground for justifying the construction of the wall . . ." http://www.icj-cij.org/icjwww/idocket/imwp/imwpframe.htm.

42 "2004/102. Special sitting of the Commission on Human Rights during its sixtieth session: At its 17th meeting, on 23 March 2004, the Commission on Human Rights decided, by a recorded vote of 34 votes to 3, with 14 abstentions, to call for a special sitting of the Commission on an urgent basis to consider the situation in the Occupied Palestinian Territory resulting from the assassination of Sheikh Ahmed Yassin on the morning of 22 March 2004." E/2004/23, Report of the Commission on Human Rights.

43 The Hamas Charter includes:

- Israel will exist and will continue to exist until Islam will obliterate it, just as it obliterated others before it. (Preamble)
- The Day of Judgement will not come about until Moslems fight Jews and kill them. Then, the Jews will hide behind rocks and trees, and the rocks and the trees will cry out: "O Moslem, there is a Jew hiding behind me, come and kill him." (Article 7)

Abdel Aziz Rantissi: "We will kill Jews everywhere. There will be no security for any Jews, those who came from America, Russia or anywhere" (Abdel Aziz Rantissi, Chicago Tribune, July 23, 2002). "We have no choice but to kill the occupier, to kill him everywhere, every village and every city" (Rantissi, AP, March 11, 2002). Ismail Abu Shanab: "We are coming. We have accepted the challenge. We are coming to Tel Aviv. We are coming to every place in Palestine to purify it from the Jews" (New York Times, Oct. 28, 2000). See CAMERA, http://www.camera.org/index.asp?x_article=649&x_context=7.

casualties as was the case with Rantissi, have been criticized by UN officials – starting with the Secretary General – as illegal "extrajudicial executions".[44] On the contrary, the international law requirement of a proportionate response to a serious threat, posed by individuals who were part of the command and control structure of an armed gang, and whom Israel could not have arrested without much greater risk of casualties, was met.

Likewise, destroying homes which cover entrances to tunnels used for smuggling arms into Gaza was immediately criticized by the Secretary General as illegal.[45] However, the use of civilian property to support a military attack, by concealing weapons smuggling tunnels in civilian homes, is a war crime. The structures, having been used by terrorists in the midst of combat, constitute a legitimate military target.[46]

According to Israel Defense Forces sources, Yassin directly authorized suicide and bombing attacks, personally approving for example:

• The June 1, 2001, suicide bombing of a discotheque near Tel Aviv's Dolphinarium. Twenty-one young people were killed and 120 wounded when a Hamas bomber blew himself up while standing in a large group of teenagers waiting to enter the disco.

• The March 27, 2002, suicide bombing of the dining room of the Park Hotel in the coastal city of Netanya. Thirty people were killed and 140 injured, in the midst of their Passover holiday dinner (*seder*).

See Israel's statement to the UN Security Council by Ambassador Dan Gillerman, 23 March 2004, http:// www.aish.com/jewishissues/middleeast/Israels_statement_at_the_UN.asp.

44 SG/SM/9261, 17 April 2004, "The Secretary-General condemns Israel's assassination of Hamas leader Abdelaziz Rantissi. He reiterates that extrajudicial killings are violations of international law and calls on the Government of Israel to immediately end this practice."

SG/SM/9210, 22 March 2004, "The Secretary-General strongly condemns Israel's assassination of Hamas spiritual leader Sheikh Ahmed Yassin, which resulted in the deaths of eight others . . . He reiterates that extrajudicial killings are against international law and calls on the Government of Israel to immediately end this practice." Terje Roed-Larsen, S/PV.4824, 15 September 2003, "Both during and after the unilateral ceasefire Israel continued to carry out extrajudicial killings aimed at the leaders of Palestinian militant groups. The United Nations has repeatedly and strongly called on the Government of Israel to cease such attacks."

45 SG/SM/9307-PAL/1982, 14 May 2004, "The Secretary-General strongly condemns Israel's ongoing and widespread destruction of Palestinian homes in Rafah in the southern Gaza Strip. Reports cite the demolition of scores of buildings over the last two days, in addition to 130 residential buildings already destroyed this month. The Secretary-General has repeatedly called on the Government of Israel to address its security needs within the boundaries of international law. He urges Israel to uphold its obligations as an occupying power by immediately halting such actions, which are tantamount to collective punishment and a clear violation of international law." The Secretary General never mentions the tunnels used to smuggle arms beneath the homes destroyed.

46 Protocol Additional to the Geneva Conventions of 12 August 1949, and relating

DO SELECTIVE RULES FOR THE CONDUCT OF THE WAR ON TERRORISM MATTER?

At bottom, in the conduct of the war against terrorism the UN applies one rule for Israel and another for all other states. The vast majority of UN states and officials believe that this situation is either justified or at least tolerable. The ICJ case on the security fence, however, makes it even clearer, that the effects of such double-standards cannot be isolated.

The Court declared four new rules about the meaning of the right of self-defense in the face of terrorism today.

(1) There is no right of self-defense under the UN Charter when the terrorists are not state actors.[47]

---

to the Protection of Victims of International Armed Conflicts (Protocol 1), adopted 8 June 1977, entry into force 7 December 1979:

Article 51. Protection of the civilian population

7. **The presence or movements of the civilian population or individual civilians shall not be used to render certain points or areas immune from military operations, in particular in attempts to shield military objectives from attacks or to shield, favour or impede military operations.** The Parties to the conflict shall not direct the movement of the civilian population or individual civilians in order to attempt to shield military objectives from attacks or to shield military operations.

Article 52. General protection of civilian objects

1. Civilian objects shall not be the object of attack or of reprisals. Civilian objects are all objects which are not military objectives as defined in paragraph 2.

2. Attacks shall be limited strictly to military objectives. In so far as objects are concerned, **military objectives are limited to those objects which by their nature, location, purpose or use make an effective contribution to military action and whose total or partial destruction, capture or neutralization, in the circumstances ruling at the time, offers a definite military of advantage.**

Article 57. Precautions in attack

1. In the conduct of military operations, constant care shall be taken to spare the civilian population, civilians and civilian objects.

2. With respect to attacks, the following precautions shall be taken:

(a) Those who plan or decide upon an attack shall: . . .

(iii) Refrain from deciding to launch any attack which may be expected to cause incidental loss of civilian life, injury to civilians, damage to civilian objects, or a combination thereof, **which would be excessive in relation to the concrete and direct military advantage anticipated;**

(b) An attack shall be cancelled or suspended if it becomes apparent that the objective is not a military one or is subject to special protection or that the attack may be expected to cause incidental loss of civilian life, injury to civilians, damage to civilian objects, or a combination thereof, **which would be excessive in relation to the concrete and direct military advantage anticipated** . . .

47 The majority decision states: "139. Under the terms of Article 51 of the Charter of

(2) There is no right of self-defense against terrorists who operate from any territory whose status is not finalized, and who therefore attack across disputed borders.[48]

(3) Where military action is perpetrated by "irregulars," self-defense does not apply if the "scale and effects" of the terrorism are insufficient to amount to "an armed attack . . . had it been carried out by regular armed forces."[49] (The scale in this case is more than eight hundred Israeli civilians killed or the proportional equivalent of at least fourteen 9/11's.)

(4) Self-defense does not include nonviolent acts, or in the words of Judge Rosalyn Higgins: "I remain unconvinced that non-forcible measures (such as the building of a wall) fall within self-defense under Article 51 of the Charter."[50]

Each of these conclusions constitutes a direct assault on the ability of

---

the United Nations: 'Nothing in the present Charter shall impair the inherent right of individual or collective self-defence if an armed attack occurs against a Member of the United Nations, until the Security Council has taken measures necessary to maintain international peace and security.' Article 51 of the Charter thus recognizes the existence of an inherent right of self-defence in the case of armed attack by one State against another State. However, Israel does not claim that the attacks against it are imputable to a foreign State . . . Consequently, the Court concludes that Article 51 of the Charter has no relevance in this case."

48 The majority decision states: "139 . . . The Court also notes that Israel exercises control in the Occupied Palestinian Territory and that, as Israel itself states, the threat which it regards as justifying the construction of the wall originates within, and not outside, that territory. The situation is thus different from that contemplated by Security Council resolutions 1368 (2001) and 1373 (2001), and therefore Israel could not in any event invoke those resolutions in support of its claim to be exercising a right of self-defence." http://www.icj-cij.org/icjwww/idocket/imwp/imwpframe.htm.

49 "33 . . . in *Military and Paramilitary Activities in and against Nicaragua (Nicaragua* v. *United States of America)* (*Merits, Judgment, ICJ Reports* 1986, p. 14). It there held that military action by irregulars could constitute an armed attack if these were sent by or on behalf of the State and if the activity 'because of its scale and effects, would have been classified as an armed attack . . . had it been carried out by regular armed forces' (ibid., p. 103, para. 195). While accepting, as I must, that this is to be regarded as a statement of the law as it now stands, I maintain all the reservations as to this proposition that I have expressed elsewhere (R. Higgins, *Problems and Process: International Law and How We Use It*, pp. 250–251)." Per Judge Higgins. http://www.icj-cij.org/icjwww/idocket/imwp/imwpframe.htm.

50 "35. In the event, however, these reservations have not caused me to vote against subparagraph (3) (A) of the *dispositif*, for two reasons. First, I remain unconvinced that nonforcible measures (such as the building of a wall) fall within self-defence under Article 51 of the Charter as that provision is normally understood." http://www.icj-cij.org/icjwww/idocket/imwp/imwpframe.htm.

every UN member to fight international terrorism. The Court has gutted the potential of the UN Charter to confront violent non-state actors.

CONCLUSION

In conclusion, the United Nations has had a major negative influence on the ability to fight international terrorism. The sooner this battle cuts loose from the UN framework, the sooner the war will be won.

LOUIS BLOCH

L'universel et le particulier

LE 11 octobre 1870, alors que Paris était assiégé par les Prussiens, Gustave Flaubert écrivit à George Sand : « Ah ! comme je suis triste ! Je sens que le monde latin agonise. Tout ce qui fut nous s'en va ! » [1]

Le 11 septembre 2001 gageons que plus d'un Américain, voire d'un Européen aura repris à son compte la plainte de l'auteur normand : « Tout ce qui fut nous s'en va ! »

Cependant, en évoquant « le monde latin qui agonise », Flaubert ne songe ni à un folklore, ni à une race mais désigne une civilisation. Autrement dit, une échelle de valeurs. Or si l'attaque du World Trade Center aura déclenché la prise de conscience d'un renversement des valeurs, celui-ci lui est bien antérieur. Il date de la seconde guerre mondiale sinon de la première. C'est à la suite des actes abominables auxquels a conduit la barbarie nazie que l'Assemblée générale des Nations Unies a adopté et proclamé le 10 décembre 1948 la Déclaration Universelle des Droits de l'Homme.

Celle-ci rappelle dans son article premier que « Tous les êtres humains naissent libres et égaux en dignité et en droits... » Il ne sera pas fait de distinction fondée sur la race, le sexe, la religion, l'opinion politique ou autre etc... Toute personne « a droit à la vie, à la liberté et à la sûreté de sa personne ». Droit également à la justice, à l'éducation, à la propriété (art. 17), à la liberté de pensée, de conscience et de religion ce qui implique « la liberté de changer de religion ou de conviction ainsi que de manifester sa religion ou sa

1 Gustave Flaubert « Correspondance » (Gallimard – Paris).

conviction, seule ou en commun, tant en publique qu'en privé, par l'enseignement, les pratiques . . . » (art. 18). Il va de soi que cette énumération n'est pas exhaustive. Telle quelle, la « Déclaration », que son principal auteur, René Cassin, appela les « Tables de la Loi humaine », sans avoir valeur contraignante, remplissait son rôle de fournisseur de repères. Commentant l'arrêt Perruche, Ari Vatanen, député finlandais au Parlement européen, écrivait dans « Le Figaro » du 9 janvier 2002 « l'humanité a besoin de se reconnaître en des valeurs inébranlables ».

Or, il n'aura fallu qu'un demi-siècle après son adoption pour voir resurgir les démons qu'elle a voulu définitivement éliminer. Trois noms les évoquent et les résument : Phnom-Penh, Durban et, last but not least, Manhattan. Bien sûr, ce choix peut paraître arbitraire. Ni les Balkans, ni le Rwanda, entre autres, ne sont absents de ma mémoire. Mais si j'ai choisi le génocide des Khmers, le festival de haine antijuive qui s'est déroulé dans le cadre d'une conférence mondiale contre le racisme et l'attaque suicidaire et combien meurtrier du World Trade Center, c'est à cause du renversement des valeurs qu'ils exprimaient. Les « Khmers rouges » au Cambodge, les militants extrémistes arabes ou africains en Afrique du Sud, les membres du réseau « Al Quaida » à New-York et à Washington ont cru faire le bien. Les uns étaient mûs par un idéal nationaliste, d'autres par une idéologie politique ou religieuse : le choc des valeurs universelles avec celles qui sont propres à chaque individu ou groupe d'individus éclata ainsi au grand jour. Que s'ajoutent à ces considérations des éléments géopolitiques ou de domination économique n'y change rien. Le 20ème siècle aura requis la proclamation de la nature universelle de la personne humaine, le 21ème siècle devra s'atteler à la tâche de conjuguer les droits qui en découlent avec celui, tout aussi inhérent à la nature humaine, le droit à l'identité particulière.

Dans un colloque qui s'est tenu récemment sur « l'urgence d'un espace juridique et judiciaire mondial », le philosophe Alain Finkielkraut faisait remarquer que « la démocratie moderne est un mode tout à fait singulier d'articulation du particulier et de l'universel ». Alors que dans la démocratie antique on était citoyen en tant que membre d'une cité, « l'Athénien était citoyen d'Athènes », aujourd'hui, la démocratie étant fondée sur les Droits de l'Homme, « on exerce le pouvoir au nom de la nation, au nom du peuple mais aussi au nom de l'humanité. Nous disons spontanément que des actes qui peuvent être approuvés par une majorité mais qui sont contraires aux Droits de l'Homme ne sont pas démocratiques. Cela veut bien dire que l'humanité est présente ès qualité dans l'espace démocratique ». Selon Finkielkraut il y aurait danger à « déconnecter ou à découpler ce dispositif » pour renvoyer l'Humanité ailleurs, devant une cour pénale internationale ou ad hoc. Il pose le problème. J'ajoute que l'on peut entrevoir des solutions au niveau des traités internationaux. Mais ce n'est là qu'un exemple des difficultés qu'il y a à conjuguer l'universel et le particulier lorsqu'on veut s'engager dans la voie de sa réalisation concrète. « La justice sans la force est impuissante, la force sans la justice est tyrannique » constatait Pascal.[2] Cela reste actuel.

Il faudra donc que les droits inaliénables de l'individu énoncés dans la Déclaration Universelle prévalent sur les règles internes du groupe. Il faudra veiller à concilier les droits des minorités avec ceux de la majorité.

Et en aucun cas, dans les législations nationales ou supranationales, la mort ne pourra prendre le pas sur la vie.

☙

Trois ans et demi se sont écoulés depuis ce funeste 11 septembre 2001.

Malgré les actes de barbarie commis un peu partout, les prises d'otages, les assassinats – suicides, les incitations à la haine raciale et antisémite l'on sent que les principes énoncés plus haut commencent à s'incarner dans les mentalités et parfois dans les normes sociales.

Au Conseil de l'Europe, ce « laboratoire où se prépare et s'expérimente la coopération européenne » (Robert Schuman, discours du 10 décembre 1951) l'on était préoccupé en 2004 par le problème des migrations surtout concernant le courant « Sud–Nord ».

En fait, quel est le problème ? Un être humain quitte son pays, sa société avec ses valeurs, les coutumes, les rites qui les matérialisent pour vivre dans un autre pays où règnent d'autres valeurs, d'autres coutumes, d'autres rites. Dans la revue "L'Arche"[3] Benjamin Stora parle de son enfance à Constantine (Algérie) et de son installation en France, en 1962 : « . . . *nous avons été entraînés dans un processus, avec une forte envie de se fondre dans la masse. Nous sommes arrivés dans une France fermée, difficile, hostile. Notre mode de vie a été complètement bouleversé, socialement et humainement...* »

Aussi, avant tout dialogue, la société d'accueil devra respecter le nouveau venu dans sa différence. Et celui-ci, en retour, devra en faire de même à l'égard de sa nouvelle patrie. Notons au passage que les valeurs d'une société ne sont

2 Blaise Pascal – « Pensées » (Le Seuil – Paris).

3 « L'Arche », novembre – décembre 2003.

pas immuables. La France de Louis XVI n'était plus celle de Jeanne d'Arc ; l'idéal de celle du Siècle des Lumières ne correspondait pas à celui du Grand Siècle, le siècle de Louis XIV.

Autrement dit, ce qui permet le « vivre ensemble », ce sont les Droits de l'Homme. Ecoutons encore Benjamin Stora : « *paradoxalement, mai 68 a fait surgir la multiplicité des identités qui font la France. Enfin je pouvais dire : je suis Juif ! Je viens d'Algérie. Avec mai 68 . . . je pouvais assumer mes origines mais surtout je pouvais les assumer en les conjuguant avec les valeurs universelles.* » [4]

Cette identité particulière conjuguée avec les valeurs universelles résume très précisément les Droits de l'Homme.

Souvent les autorités du pays d'accueil demandent à l'immigré de « s'intégrer ». Aussi au regard des Droits de l'Homme quel sens donner au mot « intégration » ? Aucun car intégrer un être humain en respectant son identité particulière n'a pas de sens. L'étranger qui veut vivre dans un autre pays que le sien, s'il est respecté, respectera la nation qui l'accueille. Alors pourra commencer le dialogue qui permettra de lever les « blocages inconscients », souvent fruits de l'ignorance. Le Musulman citera le verset du Coran qui indique que si Dieu avait voulu créer toute l'humanité musulmane, il en avait le pouvoir mais il a préféré la diversité. [5] Ce qui corrige un tant soit peu l'idée que l'on a sur la volonté hégémonique de cette religion. Les Juifs, parfois perçus comme orgueilleux parce que membres du « Peuple élu » devront rappeler cette phrase du Talmud selon laquelle le Juste des Nations est l'égal du Grand-Prêtre d'Israël. [6] Les Protestants, les athées, les animistes africains etc… etc… Ainsi, dissipant les préjugés dus à la méconnaissance de l'autre, l'étranger et l'indigène auront jeté les bases du « Vivre ensemble ».

Edmond Jabès a dit : « Ne demande pas à un étranger d'où il vient mais où il va ». Cependant si vous croyez profondément aux Droits de l'Homme, si vous reconnaissez le droit à l'identité particulière tout en privilégiant les droits découlant de la nature universelle de l'Etre humain, alors vous pourrez lui demander d'où il vient. Et parce qu'il veut vivre avec vous il vous dira où il va.

4 cf note précédente.
5 Le Coran, sourate « Jonas », verset 99.
6 Sifra sur Aharé Mot, 13,13 et Maïmonide : Hilhot malakhim 8,11.

Le vingtième siècle aura vu éclore des déclarations et des textes de loi énonçant et garantissant les droits fondamentaux de tout être humain y compris, répétons le, le droit à l'identité particulière.[7] Le vingt et unième siècle devra, en vue de leur application harmoniser ces droits de nature universelle avec ceux, spécifiques, de chaque individu. Cependant cette tâche semble devoir concerner un autre domaine : celui des nations. A cet égard la comparaison de la Charte des Nations Unies avec le traité établissant une Constitution pour l'Europe se révèle particulièrement instructif.

D'abord la dénomination. Alors que la première se veut une « Charte » de « Nations » unies, la seconde n'hésite pas à se définir comme « Constitution » d'une « Union européenne ». Voyons maintenant les buts de l'une et de l'autre.

Pour les Nations Unies : « Développer entre les nations des relations amicales fondées sur le principe de l'égalité de droits des peuples et de leur droit à disposer d'eux mêmes . . . » (art. 1-2 de la Charte).

Pour l'Union Européenne : « Inspirée par la volonté des citoyens et des Etats d'Europe de bâtir leur avenir commun, la présente Constitution établit l'Union européenne, à laquelle les Etats membres attribuent des compétences pour atteindre leurs objectifs communs. L'Union coordonne les politiques des Etats membres visant à atteindre ces objectifs et exerce sur le mode communautaire les compétences qu'ils lui attribuent » (art. 1-1 de la Convention). Et encore : « La Constitution et le droit adopté par les institutions de l'Union, dans l'exercice des compétences qui sont attribuées à celle-ci, priment le droit des Etats membres » (art. 1-6 de la Convention).

Autrement dit, alors que la Charte des Nations Unies reflète un accord entre des nations indépendantes, le traité pour une Constitution européenne se veut supranational. Certains se sont penchés sur les mobiles qui ont animé les artisans de cette Constitution. Selon Georges Berthu,[8] député européen pendant dix ans, c'est la volonté de remédier à la désaffection des peuples vis à vis de l'Europe. D'où *« le processus de type étatique au niveau européen »*[9] que représente la Constitution. Et qui constitue une erreur, selon G. Berthu. « . . . *Si les citoyens se sentent effectivement étrangers aux procédures*

7 Convention européenne des Droits de l'Homme : art. 9 et 14 ; Déclaration universelle des D.H. : art. 18, 19, 20

8 Georges Berthu, « L'Europe sans les peuples » 2° édition, Editeur : F-X de Guibert – Paris 75016 – (2004).

9 idem.

de Bruxelles [. . .] c'est avant tout parce qu'ils reconnaissent mal la place de leur nation sur la scène européenne et que pour cette raison, ils ne parviennent pas à s'identifier ». [10]

Aussi peut-on se demander si la conjugaison de l'universel et du particulier, légitime quand il s'agit des êtres humains, garde sa légitimité quand on l'applique au niveau des institutions ou entités politiques.

Au regard de l'anxiété existentielle engendrée par le terrorisme, les conditions de vie dans nos sociétés actuelles, peut-être existe-t-il une nécessité de se hisser au niveau mondial ? Zygmunt Bauman, professeur émérite à l'université de Leeds le pense fortement : « *La grande question est de savoir si nous réussirons à soumettre le pouvoir – mondial, cette fois – à une politique conçue à sa mesure en rééquilibrant leurs puissances respectives, c'est à dire à des institutions politiques auxquelles nous ne faisons malheureusement que commencer à réfléchir...* » [11]

Dans l'incessant tourbillon des idées qui mijotent en ce début de siècle l'unité de l'humanité semble s'imposer chaque jour davantage et les organismes internationaux paraissent autant de marchepieds vers l'unité du monde.

N'oublions cependant pas cette perle de la sagesse africaine : « Tous les hommes ont une tête mais les têtes sont différentes. » [12]

---

10 Souligné par nous.

11 Z. Bauman, colloque de l'ECRI (European Commission against Racism and Intolerance) Strasbourg 18/03/04.

12 Proverbe akan Ghana in « Le droit d'être un homme » sous la direction de Jeanne Hersch – Edition : UNESCO/ Lattès – Paris.

SIDNEY BRICHTO

Religious Leaders Must Challenge Holy Scriptures

MY translating of the Old and New Testament was motivated by the desire to make the Bible accessible as literature to ordinary religious and secular readers. Out there was a large potential readership that was put off by the division into chapters and verses and the sanctity awarded to what most people believe are creations of the human spirit. Any book claiming divine authorship bars the reader from interacting with it. It is viewed as religious propaganda to be defended by believers, abused by humanists and ignored by the rest.

As I proceeded with my translation, I was struck by the number of times in both Testaments that I was required to dissociate myself from texts that called for wholesale murder of innocents or made wild accusations against a people that could incite genocide. Strangely, the same religious heroes guilty of these offences are also credited with sublime utterances and demands, which if followed could bring the world into the Messianic Age. Though my knowledge of the Koran is limited, I am confident that these comments also apply to the holy scriptures of Islam.

Let me in the first instance cite some examples of unacceptable immorality. In the Torah, a tale is told of the sinning of the Israelites at Baal-Peor. The blame for their idolatrous worship and licentious behaviour is laid at the door of the Midianite women. Moses selects 1000 men from each tribe to destroy Midian. They return victorious with booty and all the women and children as captives; they killed all the men. Moses vents his fury on them:

> Have you allowed all the women to live? Were they not the ones who led the Israelites to rebel against the LORD at Peor which in turn caused the plague in the LORD's people? Now, therefore, kill every male child. Also kill every woman who has slept with a man, but keep alive for yourselves every virgin.[1]

No religious, moral person could justify the words ascribed either to the great lawgiver or to the God who made him his spokesman on earth. Yet, it remains in the Torah, capable someday of being used as a precedent for brutality against a foreign enemy by religious literalists.

In the Gospel according to Matthew, Jesus is reported to have said to the Scribes and Pharisees,

> I am sending you prophets and wise men and scribes. You will kill and crucify some of them. Others you will scourge in your synagogues and will pursue to persecute from town to town, and so will fall upon you the punishment for all the innocent blood which has been shed on earth from the blood of the righteous Abel ...[2]

This curse on the Jews is attributed to Jesus. Because of their persecution of Christians, they will be punished for all the destruction of the innocent since the beginning of creation. This attack is consistent with making Jews into the Christ killers. As much as the Vatican repents of their part in the fomenting of anti-Semitism, such texts will continue to justify hatred of the Jews as a vile race.

Were one to suggest that these morally offensive passages were removed from the texts, there would be outrage in religious quarters. "How can you want us to change holy texts?" But that is the very point. Can such primitive calls for the destruction of the innocents or false accusations which led to such horrors be called holy?

There is another factor in the biblical narratives that entitles rational readers to question the need to respect them. If, as we are assured by the Jewish sages, the 'seal of the Lord is truth', are we to remain silent when we recognise that many of the texts have been written or distorted to promote the supremacy of a particular group?

Two further examples illustrate this point. In the Torah, in certain ge-

1 *Numbers* 31:15-18.
2 *Matthew* 23:34-35.

nealogical tables the progeny of Moses is ignored while that of Aaron his brother is fully recorded. A close reading of the texts would prove to the objective reader that they have been subverted retroactively to wrench power from Moses's descendants in favour of those of Aaron's. *Exodus*, *Numbers* and *Deuteronomy* are replete with stories and laws whose sole object is to give the the right of the priesthood only to the descendants of Aaron. Thus, when Korah, a Levite, and two heads of the tribe of Reuben, Jacob's first-born, question the authority of Aaron, they and all their households are swallowed up in an earthquake. The deception in this propaganda is that Moses is purported to have defended Aaron and to have caused this fierce divine punishment.

Yet, the narratives in *Judges* and *Samuel*, whose composition predates the Torah, proves that others did act as priests. Indeed, a wandering Levite pops up in the book of *Judges* who is employed by the entrepreneurial son of Delilah as a priest for his own local shrine. The shrine is looted and he is taken captive by the warriors of the tribe of Dan who are advancing to conquer the people of Laish in order to settle in their land. This priest who will serve in their idolatrous shrine is recorded to be Jonathan the son of Gershom the son of Moses![3] Can you believe it? The sages did not want to, so they superscribed the consonant 'n' between the 'm' and 's' of Moses so it could be read as Manasseh! And the Seer Samuel, who is not even a Levite is recorded as offering sacrifices on many occasions.

This same stricture of politically motivated falsehood applies to the Gospels. On another occasion I will seek to prove that the New Testament was a political as well as a theological treatise. For the purpose of this essay, I limit myself to one indisputable fact which is that for sectarian purposes the Gospels constantly question the intelligence and understanding of the apostles. This is no more apparent than in the treatment of St. Peter, the Rock of the Church: when Jesus asks the apostles their view on his status, Peter affirms that he is Christ, the Son of the living God. Jesus, according to the narrator, aware that such a belief would be a break with Jewish tradition, tells him that he could not have learnt this from any human faculty, but that God must have revealed this to him. A few verses later, after declaring Peter's

3 For a full treatment of this bizarre tale see *The Conquest in Canaan*, pp. 86-9, my translation of the books of *Joshua* and *Judges* in *The People's Bible*. Is this a factual history or the attempt to disqualify the descendants of Moses from the LORD's priesthood because his grandson was an idolator?

pre-eminence in the Church, Jesus describes his own fate – to be put to death and to rise up in three days. Peter, who as a Jew must have perceived Jesus as an earthly Messiah, "rebukes" him for this, whereupon Jesus declares, "Get from behind me Satan, you are an obstacle in my path because you think not as God thinks but as human beings do."[4]

The narrative needs to have Peter's inspired endorsement of Jesus as more than a human messiah but without denying that he could not accept the un-Jewish view of his being the sacrificial ransom for the sins of humanity. To achieve credibility in the Roman Empire, gentile Christianity required Jewish testimonies from the past – biblical prophesies – as well as from contemporaries – the apostles. The narrative, to its credit, does not conceal the reality that the Jewish Christians were waiting for the resurrected Christ i.e. Messiah to 'restore the sovereignty of Israel'.[5] Jesus as the Christ, the Son of God, the saviour of all mankind, was not the 'good news' of the Jewish apostles but it was that of St. Paul. Since the final composition of the New Testament took place after the dissolution of the Jewish Christian communities, it marked the victory of Paul's teaching over Peter's, who according to Paul's letters required Gentiles to convert to Judaism, which Paul did not.[6] Peter's acceptance of the negation of Jewish non-observance as recorded in *Acts*, because it is not first hand as are Paul's letters, must be discounted as a later gloss to vindicate Pauline Christianity.

The religious texts, therefore, which are the basis of Judaism and Christianity, as wonderful and morally elevating as they are, cannot all be relied upon as historically true, or for that matter as the inspired word of God. One could say that some scholars of Islam might also be embarrassed by a number of their own holy texts.

Had this essay been written by a humanist who decries the Bible as a fabric of lies to enslave human beings to superstition, it might be dismissed as an atheistic party piece, but it comes from one who loves the Bible, Old and New; who respects the Bible as the primary source of belief in the sanctity of every individual and the autonomy of the human conscience.

Until now, my respect for the sources of my faith compelled me to remain

4 *Matthew* 16:15-23.

5 *Acts of the Apostles* 1:6: 'Lord, has the time come for you to restore the kingdom of Israel?' *NJB*.

6 Evidence of this can be found in *Galatians* 2 and other letters attacking those *Hebraisers* who visited the Gentile communities to preach the gospel.

silent. I took comfort in that only the literalists accepted the divine origin of every biblical utterance and that these fringe movements could be ignored as they provided no danger to human freedom or safety. This is no longer the case. More religious leaders will begin to take my view when they realise how often they are being called upon to defend their religion against those crimes being committed in the name of their God, justified by their holy texts.

Almost all present conflicts are being fuelled by the belief of the combatants that they doing God's will – the belief that their true faith makes them superior to their enemies with the right to kill them. Wars are not being fought for personal freedom or for human rights. Struggles for national liberation are given a religious dimension where enemies are not only abused as infidels but are dehumanised as demons, dogs and pigs. Holy writ is used to glorify human sacrifice to achieve the destruction of the 'enemies of God'.

[October 9th 2004: I left my computer for a break from writing this to watch BBC News 24. The first thing I saw was the breaking news that a video had shown the beheading of the English hostage, Tim Bigley. The next day, *The Times*, in reporting his beheading, quoted what al-Zarqawi, the founder of *Tawhid wal Jihad* (Unity and Holy War) had said on the video showing the death of another hostage, the American, Jack Hensley, "Now you have people who love death, just as you love life; cutting the heads of the criminal infidels is implementing the orders of our Lord."]

The barbarisms in the name of God presently stem from the Islamic world, but this fact does not exonerate the potential dangers inherent in Christian or Jewish Scriptures. The Christian Crusaders of the Middle Ages on their path of destruction to conquer the Holy City from the Muslim infidels were crying out, "Kill a Jew and save your soul." A Jew massacred praying Muslims in Hebron; another assassinated Prime Minister Rabin for being prepared to surrender parts of Judea and Samaria, promised to Israel by God in the Torah.

It can be argued that these murderers from all faiths are simply fanatics or madmen, but there are too many of them now and are supported by governments. And the fact is that they find justification for their inhuman crimes in religious texts. When most of today's butchery in the name of God emanates from Islam, we still hesitate to question the morality of sections of the Koran because it could lead to accusations of Islamophobia. It could also call into question equally immoral judgements and commandments found in the Old and New Testaments. Giving undue respect to the sanctity of our texts now spells a greater danger to the credibility of the Abrahamic faiths than does our affirmation of the right of literalists to maintain their unreasoning faith.

Just as we in the democratic world have begun to realise that we can no longer give rights to those who would use them to destroy our civilisation, religious people can no longer tolerate the ascribed divinity to those texts that justify atrocious behaviour in the name of God.

The value and dignity of each and every human life is posited in *Genesis* in the affirmation that Adam was created in the divine image. This means the freedom and the autonomy of each person. The belief that all holy writ is the word of God hands over all power to its self-appointed priests, who can use those commands and images that incite hatred against those whom they perceive to be non-believers, i.e. those who do not share their faith in their own God. These texts, which spew out hatred against heretics, foreigners, and enemies of all sorts can no longer be reinterpreted or rationalised. Authorities of the Jewish, Christian and Islamic faiths need to acknowledge that parts of their sacred literature were never the word of God but motivated by political and aggressive ambitions.

What can be done about this? One cannot change the texts sanctified, if not by God, at least by time, faith and tradition. They were the reflections of periods in the birth of humanity that, regardless of their religious or moral credibility, we could no more alter than passages in the works of Homer or Shakespeare. But, what we could do, as we do with Shakespeare, is to provide footnotes immediately accessible at the bottom of each page, which would do more than explain the meaning; they would comment, when appropriate, on the change in moral perspectives since the time that the offensive texts were deemed to be acceptable codes of behaviour.

I have done this with my own translations. I do it with respect for the past and I often acknowledge that in some instances, for all our pretences of being superior, we have not improved all that much over our ancestors. For example, my footnote on the wholesale slaughter of the Midianites, excluding virgins:[7]

> The ruthlessness of Moses in this episode is chilling and cannot be justified. Vengeance against women who turned the Israelites away from God is at least subject to rationalisation but not that of innocent male children. This

7 *Moses, Man of God*, p. 109, *The People's Bible*, Sinclair-Stevenson.

story is a product of an age, which viewed other peoples as not entitled to the same justice and compassion as they would afford to members of their own community. Sadly, in many respects, contemporary ethnic wars reveal the same moral backwardness.

The Gospel according to John holds the Jews guilty for the killing of Christ by their response to Pontius Pilate:

At noon he said to the Jews, "Here is your king!"
– "Crucify him!"
– "Shall I crucify your king?"
– "We have no king but Caesar!"
So he delivered him to them to be crucified.[8]

My footnotes on this passage:

Pilate's question seems to compel the Jews to make this answer if they are to avoid being classed as rebels against Rome. It will soon become apparent that 'them' can only refer to the Roman soldiers.

But, of course, footnotes in an individual's translation will have no impact on changing perceptions of Holy Scriptures. They will require the authority of organised Churches. The Vatican would be in the best position to take on this challenge. Vatican 2 recognised the responsibility of Christian history and the false interpretation of the Gospels for the persecution of Jews leading to its climax – the Holocaust. They have sought to reverse the situation in several ways. Catholic scholars have acknowledged that certain passages which could incite anti-Semitism are not to be understood literally. The problem is that the praiseworthy attempt of the Vatican has not reached the grass roots of the Church. Only the insistence that all new authorized translations of the Bible provide page-by-page footnotes to dissociate themselves from the literal interpretation of certain passages would be proof of the Church's determination to undo the great wrong done to Jews, and through them to all humanity over centuries.

It would also give a wonderful lead to other Churches who have done little to mitigate the hatred that can be read in many passages of Holy Writ. The Jewish community could also be propelled into applying similar treatment

8 *John* 19:14-16. The footnotes appear on 74 of *The Apoclylpse, The People's Bible*

to odious texts in the Old Testament. Indeed, the Vatican might make this a condition for its own agreement to follow this radical initiative.

The response to this proposal may well be: “It cannot be done.” Why not? If the Church can cope with the fact that most of its believers, even their priests do not believe in the creation story, surely it can confess that its immoral and inhuman passages are not divine in origin. Indeed, while this is the right thing to do, religious leaders may find that in so doing they would also win back many to the fold without, at the same time, losing their core support.

We ministers of all religions ignore our responsibility for the evils perpetrated in God’s name unless we have the courage to challenge our colleagues and co-religionists who defame the name of God by using texts ascribed to him to justify their attacks on his creatures. In the end, if we do not live up to the standards of secular democratic values to which men like Clemens Nathan have devoted their lives, it will be the adherents of our faiths, and not secularists, who will be the ones limiting the faith of their founders in the human potential for moral growth.

JAN HERMAN BRINKS

Beyond Anne Frank
Dutch (pre-)Wartime Collaboration with Nazi Germany and its Aftermath

In 2000 the Dutch Government, together with the *Netherlands Bankers' Association* and the Amsterdam Stock Exchange, decided to put more than seven hundred million guilders at the disposal of Dutch survivors of the Holocaust who had been robbed of their possessions and, after the War, were often confronted with inadequate rehabilitation services. It is remarkable indeed that more than half a century after the Shoah this amount of money is to be handed over to the survivors or their descendants. However, this flow of money is not the result of belated pangs of conscience, nor are the 'machinations of a holocaust industry' to blame. Insiders have known for many years that these reparations were overdue. By its 'generosity' the Dutch Government is perhaps also trying to avoid a deplorable chapter of Dutch history getting too much international attention. For the great trust which the Netherlands has enjoyed for many years as a result of its reputed pro-Jewish attitude during the Second World War, and which is linked to the name of Anne Frank, rests on a myth.

The overwhelming evidence easily refutes the image of the Dutch resisting the Germans on a massive scale, and suffering because of the fate of their Jewish fellow countrymen. Contrary to popular belief, a far from harmless rapprochement between the Dutch and Nazi Germany had already taken place during the interwar period. At the root of this were both economic and ideological motives – a virulent anti-communism that had penetrated deeply into the Dutch elites. In 1917 the Bolsheviks had annulled all foreign debts. However, it was not the Dutch authorities or banks that had suffered but almost exclusively private individuals who had invested heavily in the empire of the Czar. One billion guilders was at stake, for those days an astronomical amount, and more than the total annual sum of Dutch expenditure.[1]

This anti-communism was not free from anti-Semitic undertones. The Minister of the Netherlands in Russia, Oudendijk, for example, argued in a report in 1918:

> I consider that the immediate suppression of Bolshevism is the greatest issue now before the world, not even excluding the [First World] War which is still raging, and unless as stated above Bolshevism is nipped in the bud immediately, it is bound to spread in one form or another over Europe and the whole world as it is organised and worked by Jews who have no nationality, and whose one object is to destroy the existing order of things for their own ends. The only manner in which this danger could be averted would be collective action on the part of all powers.[2]

The anger among the Dutch elites about financial losses and fear of the Bolsheviks may have contributed to the fact that the Dutch bourgeoisie was initially susceptible to Hitler's anti-Bolshevism, condoning his anti-Semitism for a long time.

After 1935, close Dutch–German collaboration was apparent with regard to the arrest of 'Marxist and Jewish elements'.[3] The immediate cause of this collaboration was the Dutch Government's fear of a stream of refugees from the German *Saar* that had advocated, on 13 January 1935, the *Anschluß* with

1 Cf. Zee, van der, Nanda, *Om erger te voorkomen: De voorbereiding en uitvoering van de vernietiging van het Nederlandse jodendom tijdens de Tweede Wereldoorlog* (To prevent worse: The preparation and execution of the destruction of Dutch Jewry during the Second World War), Amsterdam, 1997, p. 40.

2 'Withdrawal of Missions and Consuls: Subenclosure: Report of the Netherlands Minister relating to conditions in Petrograd', in: Publications of the Department of State, Papers relating to the Foreign Relations of the United States. 1918. Russia. (In three volumes); here vol. 1, United States Government Printing Office, Washington, D.C., 1931, p. 675–679; here. pp. 678 and 679.

3 In 1997, in a new *Bundesarchiv* in Berlin, Dutch historian Ger van Roon stumbled upon files with official notices about trips of Dutch officials to the Gestapo at the Prinz Albrechtstrasse and the *Kriminalpolizei* at the Alexanderplatz. Cf. Goudriaan, Huib, *Politietop al vroeg contact met Gestapo* (Senior Police Officers in early contact with Gestapo), *Trouw*, 18 December, 1997; also: Goudriaan, Huib, *Latere BVD-chef Einthoven op namenlijst Gestapo* (Future chief of BVD [National Security Service] Einthoven on Gestapo list of names), *Trouw*, 18 December 1997.

the German *Reich*. Many left-wing and Jewish Germans who had taken refuge there after Hitler came to power in 1933 now decided to flee.

On 16 January 1935, three days after the ballot in the *Saar*, the Attorney-General of Amsterdam, A. Baron van Harinxma thoe Slooten, argued, at the instigation of the Gestapo, in a confidential letter to the Minister of Justice, J. R. H. van Schaik: 'In my opinion the establishment of concentration camps where all undesirable communist elements could be sheltered who, in spite of the actions already taken by Your Excellency, will yet enter the Netherlands from the *Saar* and who are highly dangerous, not only with regard to internal peace but also because of less pleasant complications abroad, seems inescapably necessary.'[4] In March 1935 the Fortress Honswijk, south of Utrecht, was fitted up for this purpose.

Among the Dutch authorities, especially among senior police staff, there were not a few who offered their services to the Nazis during the inter-war years. They saw Hitler et al. as the most reliable defence against the 'Red Peril'. The Police Commissioner of Amsterdam, Broekhoff, for example, personally reported in 1935 to the Gestapo in Berlin that the Dutch Minister of Defence would co-operate in the common fight against '*kommunistische und marxistische Umtriebe*' (communist and Marxist machinations). Under the pen-name of 'David', Broekhoff took care of the exchange of information through which 250 German 'illegals' who had fled to the Netherlands immediately after the occupation in May 1940 were arrested by the *Sicherheitspolizei*.[5] Rotterdam's then Chief Commissioner of Police, Einthoven, also figured, together with seventeen other Dutch police officers considered to be '*deutschfreundlich*' (pro-German), in a Gestapo list of names.[6]

This pro-German atmosphere also affected the Dutch media. According to the Dutch historian Pieter Geyl, who worked as a journalist for the *Nieuwe Rotterdamse Courant*, this very influential newspaper sacked its Jewish foreign editor and acting editor-in-chief, Marcus van Blankenstein, as early as

4 Quoted in: Goudriaan, Huib, (Senior Police Officers . . .). The advice to house fugitives in concentration camps was less surprising than it may seem at first sight. In those days the Netherlands itself had two concentration camps: at Upper-Digul and Tanah Merah in New Guinea. Indonesian dissidents, among whom was the later prime minister, Hatta, were kept there for years, often without trial. Many of them died prematurely as a result of hardships.

5 Ibid.

6 Goudriaan, Huib, (Future chief of BVD . . .).

1936, because he took too critical and close a look at the developments in Germany.[7] In the opinion of the staff, whose interests were bound up with Rotterdam's port barons, it was better to avoid harming the interests of the state and the economy; that was why incurring Germany's displeasure had to be avoided.[8] As early as 1940, the Germans held the opinion that it was '*erstaunlich*' (amazing) how fast Holland's daily press had adapted to the new situation. In their judgement, 'the most severe censorship could not have had a better result'.[9] During the War, one of Holland's biggest newspapers, *De Telegraaf*, actively supported German anti-Semitism. On 17 May 1942, an editorial entitled 'For Consideration' appeared following the introduction of the yellow Star of David:

> For the German occupying forces, the Star of David is no joke but is in bitter earnest. This will separate the inhabitants of this country into two camps, friend and foe. Against the Jews and their dark forces are several million men – also Dutch – at the front. They fight against them and sacrifice everything for the sake of the future of their people . . . Those Dutch who cannot bring themselves to stop their friendly relations with Jews, or those who challenge the occupying forces by their provocative behaviour run the risk of being treated like Jews themselves with all resulting consequences for now and . . . in the future.[10]

During the marriage of the future Queen Princess Juliana, with the

7 Pieter Geyl explains that van Blankenstein was sacked because 'having a Jew as a foreign correspondent was considered dangerous in Rotterdam'. See Pieter Geyl, *Pennestrijd*, Groningen: Wolters, 1971, p. 340.

8 In 1935, the Germans had announced an advertising boycott. The German envoy in The Hague, the consul in Rotterdam, and the press officer of the Foreign Ministry informed the director of the newspaper that it had been especially the articles of van Blankenstein that had brought about this measure. Frank van Vree, *De Nederlandse Pers en Duitsland 1930–1939: Een studie over de vorming van de publieke opinie* (The Dutch press and Germany 1930–1939: A study of the formation of public opinion), Historische Uitgeverij Groningen: 1989, p. 131. The renowned Dutch journalist Menno ter Braak also became a victim of the *Zeitgeist*. On the eve of the Second World War, he was caught up in a remarkable accusation. Because of his critical comments about Hitler in a preface to Hermann Rauschning's *Hitler Speaks*, he was charged with 'slander of a friendly Head of State', as stated by Pieter Sjoerd Gerbrandy on 1 May 1940. Cf. Louis De Jong, *Het Koninkrijk der Nederlanden in de Tweede Wereldoorlog* (The Kingdom of the Netherlands in the Second World War), part 2, The Hague: Martinus Nijhoff, 1969, p. 153.

9 Groen, Koos, *Landverraad. De berechting van collaborateurs in Nederland* (High Treason: The trial of collaborators in the Netherlands), Weesp, 1984. pp. 202–3.

10 Ibid., p. 199–200.

German-born Bernhard zur Lippe-Biesterfeld in January 1937, it became clear how closely associated the Dutch elites were with Nazi Germany. Prince Bernhard, who, together with his brother had become a member of the *Reiter-SS*, was surrounded by friends who were active National Socialists. During a gala night which took place two days before the wedding in the Arts and Sciences Building in The Hague, the 'Horst Wessel Lied', the virtual hymn of the SA, was sung. Some of the invited guests, among whom was Queen Wilhelmina's uncle, Duke Adolf von Mecklenburg, who was standing next to the bride, paid their respects with the Nazi salute.[11]

The pro-German attitude of the Dutch authorities and elites was also confirmed by the German diplomat Wolfgang zu Putlitz, who, in 1938, after his return from London, where he had been for four years, was assigned to the post of Counsellor in The Hague.

In his autobiography, he mentions English politicians who were sympathetic to the Nazi cause, but, as shown by his observations, the situation in the Netherlands was particularly grave:

> In England I had never come across officials in leading agencies who expressed their sympathy for the new Germanism as enthusiastically as in the Netherlands ... The National Socialists of Mr Mussert [leader of the Dutch Nazis] had supporters in almost all ministries and even among the royal household ... There were Chiefs of Police who, summarily, at one signal from Butting [attaché at the German embassy] deported German emigrants at any time of day or night, and handed them over to the Gestapo ... I have never heard that the Dutch Government asked for a single document concerning such arbitrary acts, which were known to us by the dozen.

According to zu Putlitz the Dutch Government 'even willingly gave its approval when, later on, the Dutch people involved, who had shown a flagrant disregard for the law, were solemnly awarded the Order of the German Eagle, second or third class, which had been created by Hitler, at the suggestion of Butting or Schulze-Bernett [specialist in intelligence].'[12]

11 Kroon, John, '*Vijftig jaar huwelijksleven in een glazen huis*' (Fifty years of marriage in a glass house), *NRC-Handelsblad*, 3 January 1987; also: Laan, Geert-Jan; Robijns, Rien, '*Het geheim van Soestdijk: Prins Bernhard gaat in zaken*' (The secret of Soestdijk: Prince Bernhard goes into business), *Het Vrije Volk*, 17 December, 1977.

12 Putlitz zu, Wolfgang, *In Rok tussen de Bruinhemden: Herinneringen van een Duits*

Again after the Kristallnacht, 9–10 November 1938, it became obvious how apprehensive the Dutch authorities were of 'complications abroad'. Now, for the first time in the history of the Netherlands, the Government decided that the Dutch State would not take care of fugitives. Instead, Dutch Jews themselves had to care for several thousand Jewish fugitives from Germany. This was a radical break with the past, for during the First World War, one million Belgians who fled the acts of war in their own country found shelter in the Netherlands, which was a neutral country. At that time the Dutch Government took pity on them. But now, even if Dutch Jews wanted to help Jewish fugitives from Germany, they were often not permitted to do so.

On the eve of the Second World War, only seven thousand fugitives were allowed to enter the country. Most fugitives, among whom were complete families, were considered to be 'undesirable aliens' and were simply sent back to Germany at the frontier, or upon arrival at Schiphol airport from where they were about to leave for England or America.

On 15 November 1938, the Dutch prime minister Dr. H. Colijn explained this policy to Parliament:

> What I will say now comes from the bottom of my heart ... There is another reason why we cannot admit tens and tens of thousands to the Netherlands. I say this in the interest of our Dutch Jews themselves. These days not a single people is free from anti-Semitism; traces of this can also be found in our country, and if we were to admit here an unlimited stream of fugitives from abroad, the necessary consequence of this would be that the feeling in our own country with regard to the Jews would swing in an unfavourable way ...[13]
>
> The Government quite seriously has to bear in mind the consequences, all the consequences, including the consequence that were we to say at the moment: we will admit fifty thousand people and were it to turn out that [other countries] kept their doors locked, we would be at a loss what to do about those fifty thousand people, and this for ever. One should not

---

diplomaat (In Evening Dress among the Brownshirts: Memoirs of a German diplomat), The Hague, 1964, p. 210.

13 *Redevoering van Minister President Dr. Colijn op 15 november 1938 in de Tweede Kamer, 13e vergadering, 15 November 1938, Algemeene beraadslagingen over de Rijksbegroting voor het dienstjaar 1939, Handelingen der Staten-Generaal 1938-1939 – Tweede Kamer* (Address of Prime Minister Dr. Colijn on 15 November 1938 in the Second Chamber, 13th meeting, 15 November 1938, General deliberations on the national budget for the year 1939, Proceedings of the Second Chamber of the States-General 1938–1939), p. 262.

think that all this is a pleasant position for the Government . . . , but we also have as our vocation to serve the interests of our own people – not the interests in a lower sense, but also in a higher sense of the word – and we hope to be faithful to this.[14]

Aid from private persons like Gertrude Wijsmuller-Meijer, who helped hundreds of Jewish children escape from Germany during the War, was flatly condemned by the Dutch authorities. A press release from the Dutch Government exactly a week after the *Reichskristallnacht* ended with the words: 'The behaviour of Dutch people who transfer Jewish children by car or by train to the Netherlands has to be disapproved of. Such a disorderly arrival of fugitives naturally cannot be tolerated. Only an orderly flow is permissible and that to a very limited extent.'[15]

Initial plans to establish a camp for German fugitives in the Elspeterveld in the municipality of Ermelo, met with the objections of, from among others, Queen Wilhelmina, who considered the distance of twelve kilometres separating her country-residence Het Loo from the German asylum seekers to be insufficient. In 1939, after her authoritative utterance, the plan was abandoned and camp Westerbork near the German border was established, which gave shelter to 750 Jewish fugitives from Germany in May 1940.

However, the Dutch appeasement policy was of no use. On the night of 9–10 May 1940, German troops invaded the country. This was followed by the bombardment of the trade capital, Rotterdam, a five-year occupation, the murder of approximately three quarters of the Dutch Jews, the execution of numerous hostages, and an enormous trauma.

Among the ruling classes, however, quite a few quickly adapted to the circumstances. Immediately after the German occupation, Colijn, for example, who had headed four 'crisis governments' and was to become an icon for Dutch political Calvinism, published his book *On the Borderline of Two Worlds*, in which he criticised democracy and recommended acceptance of German domination: 'Europe and Germany; Germany and Europe: This will be a relationship to be reckoned with from now until any humanly foreseeable future. One must forget any preference one may have for one thing or

14 Ibid., p. 269.
15 Quoted in: Zee, van der, Nanda, 'To prevent worse', p. 37.

another: normally one's influence on the course of things is next to nothing, but in this particular case, it is literally nothing.'[16]

According to the well-known Dutch historian, Louis de Jong, the Netherlands also maintained its tradition of trade during the occupation. He says it possibly preserved this national feature *too* thoroughly. Dutch trade and industry probably lost touch with the goal of winning the war against the Germans, de Jong argues, because, until the end of 1943, the Dutch fulfilled 84.4 per cent of German orders – more even than the French, who achieved 70 per cent. According to de Jong, this punctilious discharge of business duties was certainly not absolutely necessary.[17]

It is a remarkable fact that for most Dutch collaborators, their collaboration remained without consequences after the War. Long before 1957, when former *Wehrmacht* general Hans Speidel became NATO's commander, the Dutch authorities were mostly of the opinion that the chapter of collaboration with the enemy was water under the bridge. Those who had served in the SS were sometimes shown remarkable mercy. The reasons for this state of affairs were expressed by the Dutch lawyer Professor W. Pompe, who explained in 1948 that 'taking part in the German battle at the western front has a more punishable character ... this was a fight against our immediate liberators, while the Russian armies only indirectly contributed to our liberation ... There is absolutely no mitigating circumstance for those who fought in the West, although fighting communism might have been a motive in the East.'[18]

As early as the end of 1944, Queen Wilhelmina's son-in-law, the husband of the future Queen Juliana, Prince Bernhard, held the opinion that a procedure for purging trade and industry was unnecessary. According to the Prince the economy would know who had behaved 'unpatriotically' and would be able to clean up its own ranks.[19] Of 32,232 cases of reported economic collaboration, 61 per cent were determinedly set aside. The Public Prosecutor

16 Colijn, H., *Saevis Tranquillus in Undis: Toelichting op het antirevolutionair Beginselprogram, Tweede druk, waarin opgenomen 'Op de grens van Twee Werelden'* (Elucidation of the anti-revolutionary manifesto, containing 'On the borderline of Two Worlds'), Amsterdam, 1940, p. 581–615, at p. 609.

17 Jong, de, Louis, 'The Kingdom of the Netherlands in the Second World War', part 7, (May 1943 – June 1944, first half), The Hague, 1976, pp. 120–30: at p. 130.

18 Groen, Koos, *Landverraad* (High Treason), p. 105.

19 Meihuizen, J. P., *Farce: De bestraffing van economische collaboratie 1944-1951* (Farce: The punishment of economic collaborators 1944–1951), Amsterdam, 1998, pp. 5, 6.

retained only 5,957 cases (18 per cent), of which only five hundred to seven hundred were brought before a special court of justice or a tribunal.[20]

Pressure was exerted up to government level to shield suspected industrialists from punishment. From beginning to end, economic and political interests deeply influenced the administration of justice. The Minister for Foreign Affairs, D. U. Stikker, for example, who was a member of the Central Council for purging trade and industry, staved off the imminent punishment of his friend M. H. Damme, who was Director of the *Werkspoor* company, which in those days was Holland's biggest machine manufacturer.[21] It was van Damme who had introduced Prince Bernhard into influential trade and commerce circles in 1936. Since then, he and the Prince had been close friends. Rotterdam's former Chief Commissioner of Police, Mr L. Einthoven, who had already collaborated with the Nazis before and during the War, was to become head of the Bureau of National Security, the *Bureau Nationale Veiligheid* which was the precursor of the secret service, the *Binnenlandse Veiligheidsdienst*. He also played an important role in purging procedures, which may explain why many collaborators got off scot-free.[22]

Immediately after the War, when the country was liberated, the relationship of the Dutch with the Germans reached an all-time low. Anti-German resentment and orgies of hate against real and alleged collaborators and their children (even child welfare refused to take care of them) rose from the ashes. This, by the way, did not prevent the Dutch economy from intensifying trade relations with Germany at the earliest opportunity.

Nevertheless, many Dutch now regarded themselves as the epitome of virtue and innocence, while every German was considered a villain. The Allies consciously tried to make use of this feeling. The American anthropologist Ruth Benedict was requested by the Office of War Information in Washington to write a memorandum about the Dutch. On the basis of this paper a pamphlet had to be composed by which American soldiers could acquire a basic knowledge of the Netherlands, to avoid friction with the population.

In her *Note on Dutch Behavior*, Benedict points out that 'Dutch self-

20 Ibid., pp. 38, 39.

21 Ibid., pp. 21, 22.

22 Brink, van den, Rinke, *Hitlers Orders: Nederlandse ambtenaren waren al fout vóór de oorlog* (Hitler's Orders: Dutch officials acted wrongly even before the War), Vrij Nederland, 10 January, 1998, p. 14–16; at p. 14.

confidence typically expresses itself, especially among the Calvinist majority, in [the] extreme conviction of having Right on its side.' With regard to 'Americans' ignorance of Dutch history and glory' she remarks:

> Except in what corresponds to our last years of high school, Dutch schools teach practically no history besides that of Holland. Most Dutchmen therefore will be shocked at American ignorance. They should be told that Americans have lived across an ocean in a figurative as well as in a literal sense . . . The sense of superiority which Dutch readers will get from this should be a valuable asset, for the Dutch, in contrast to many typical Germans, act with marked consideration and kindness when they feel themselves superior.[23]

This dialectic of moral superiority, however, was rather flimsy. Anne Frank, for example, was styled as a moral standard-bearer of the nation, and in the myth of resistance against the Germans she was illuminated in fairy lights. However, it is an unfortunate fact that this Jewish girl from Frankfurt am Main not only went into hiding in the Dutch capital but was also betrayed by the Dutch.

The fact that most Dutch Jews, in spite of a sympathy strike in February 1941, received only scant support from the non-Jewish population, and that many Jews were also betrayed by the Dutch, have been played down or hushed up.[24] When Simon Wiesenthal explained on Dutch television that the Dutch really could not have done more for the Jews than they actually did (for few Dutch houses had cellars in which to hide Jews), many people must have heaved a sigh of relief. However, it remains a fact that tens of thousands of non-Jewish Dutchmen were able to avoid forced labour in Germany by going underground in the Netherlands.

It is also difficult to maintain that the fate of the Jews that were deported was completely unknown to the Dutch population. Even a little girl like Anne Frank, who lived in hiding, had learned from her non-Jewish helper, Miep Gies, about their ultimate fate, and the child believed it. In a diary

---

23 Benedict, Ruth Fulton, *A Note on Dutch Behavior*. A complete edition of this text in: Ginkel, Rob van, *Notities over Nederlanders: Antropologische Reflecties* (Notes About Dutchmen: Anthropological reflections), Amsterdam/Meppel, 1997, p. 225–234. at pp. 226 and 232.

24 Probably one of the best accounts of the persecution of the Dutch Jews in Holland during the Second World War can be found in Jacob Presser, *The Destruction of the Dutch Jews*, New York, Dutton, 1969.

note of 9 October 1942 she writes: 'If even in Holland it is this bad, how will they live in the far and barbarian regions where they are being sent? We assume that most of them will be killed. The English radio speaks of gassing. Maybe that is after all the quickest method of dying.'[25]

After Queen Wilhelmina and the Cabinet fled the country, the Dutch civil service participated actively in the preparations for the elimination of Dutch Jews. Several permanent secretaries gave their fiat to the so-called 'declarations of Aryan origin'. It was Dutch policemen who arrested the Jews. And it was Dutch field security officers who guarded them in the Westerbork transit camp, from which they were deported to their death by Dutch railroad personnel.

Many Dutch policemen turned out to be loyal henchmen of the German occupiers. On 24 September 1942 the *Generalkommissar für das Sicherheitswesen* (Commissioner General of the Security Forces) in the Netherlands and *Höhere SS- und Polizeiführer* (Higher Chief of the SS and Police), Hans A. Rauter, informed his superior Heinrich Himmler in a secret letter with regard to the *Judenabschiebung*, i.e. the expulsion of the Jews, in the Netherlands: 'The new *Hundertschaften* of the Dutch police are doing an excellent job in the *Judenfrage*, and arrest the Jews by the hundreds day and night. In doing so the only risk that occurs is the fact that in places some policemen step out of line and enrich themselves out of Jewish property.' Himmler's commentary which was written at the top of this 'Interim report concerning the expulsion of the Jews' was a short and snappy 'very good'.[26]

The role of the Dutch railways is also a controversial one. In 1944, at the insistence of the Allies, a railway strike took place in the Netherlands. On 17 September, 1945, the first anniversary of this strike was commemorated. During a grand commemoration in The Hague, the Minister of Transport and Energy, Van Schaik, argued in front of the assembled railway personnel:

> I understand the struggle you have waged in your hearts when your trains carried off the stolen riches of the Netherlands, when our boys were moved across the border by your trains, or, even worse, to the concentration camps. You did your duty, knowing that in that stage of the war your refusal would

25 Frank, Anne, *Het Achterhuis: Dagboekbrieven 12 juni 1942–augustus 1944*, Amsterdam, Contact, 1947, p. 39; quoted in: Zee, van der, Nanda, 'To avoid worse', p. 127.

26 Facsimile reproduction of this letter in: Presser, J., *Ondergang. De vervolging en verdelging van het Nederlandse Jodendom (1940–1945)* (Destruction: The persecution and extermination of Dutch Jewry 1940–1945), part 1, The Hague, 1985, pp. 280 et seq.

have had consequences even far worse for the Dutch people than what has happened now. Your work served the welfare of the Dutch people but was to the advantage of the enemy at the same time.[27]

This 'advantage of the enemy' also implied that the Dutch Jews were deported with the help of the Dutch railways. However, according to the Government and the railways, an earlier strike which might have impeded the deportations was out of the question: 'Going out on strike', thus van Schaik, 'was a matter of balancing advantages and disadvantages, of choosing the lesser of two evils. For the time being the advantage of continuing to run was greater than the disadvantage; the evil attached to the continuation of the company was less than its suspension.'[28]

In other words, during the War, the economic interests could not be risked even when the 'lesser evil' implied that the Dutch Jews were sent to their deaths. However, on the orders of the Allies, this strike was quite possible. All the more so since a strike in September 1944 had only minimal consequences for the Dutch economy: 'The economy of the Netherlands', said Van Schaik, 'was *so* [emphasis in original] paralysed at the time, that your company was hardly necessary for its maintenance'.[29]

The words of Van Schaik, who did not mention the fate of the Jews at all, were not criticised in the Netherlands, though they may shed light on Adolf Eichmann's satisfaction; he allegedly argued that the transports in the Netherlands greased the wheels so perfectly that it was a treat to see.

Immediately after the War, there was no feeling of guilt among the Dutch authorities or most citizens towards the Dutch Jews. The surviving Jews were not taken care of by the authorities, but got help from the American Jewish Joint Distribution Committee. After the War the Dutch Government considered the surviving Dutch Jews to be 'Dutchmen like all Dutchmen'. For the authorities, Jewishness had no special meaning. This fallacy led to

27 *Rede van de minister van Verkeer en Energie, Ir. T.S.G.J.M. van Schaik tijdens de herdenkingsbijeenkomst van de spoorwegstaking op 17 September 1944 in het gebouw van de groenten- en vruchtenveiling in Den Haag op 17 September 1945. Plechtige Herdenking van de Spoorwegstaking op 17 September 1945* (Address of Minister of Transport and Energy, Ir. T.S.G.J.M. van Schaik during the commemoration of the railway strike on 17 September 1944 in the Vegetable and Fruit Auction Hall in The Hague on 17 September 1945. Solemn commemoration of the railway strike on 17 September 1945), Rotterdam, 1946, pp. 21–27; at p. 24.

28 Ibid.

29 Ibid., p. 25.

excesses: in two prison camps in Valkenburg and Sittard, 170 German Jews were detained amidst captured SS men and collaborators. Before the War, these German Jews had been granted asylum in the Netherlands; during the War they were deported to Bergen-Belsen, and after their liberation they finally arrived in the Netherlands where they were detained as 'Germans'.[30]

In the first twenty years after the War, the Dutch people had hardly any thought for the fate of their Jewish fellow-countrymen. The attention was entirely fixed on the resistance against the Germans and the occupation in general. This was the time in which the myth of the Netherlands as a 'country of resistance' developed; a myth that was willingly received abroad. There was more attention for the non-Jewish Dutch resistance fighters who had been detained in the concentration camps than for the Jews who had been killed there. In this respect there was little difference with the situation in the German Democratic Republic.[31] According to a rough classification by the Statistical Office in July 1945, forty per cent of the population of Holland's western provinces condemned the NSB (the Dutch Nazi party) for its treason and support of the enemy, eighteen per cent mentioned its support of dictatorship and terror, while seven per cent thought that its anti-religious character was the most reprehensible feature of the party. Only six per cent held the view that the racial theory, with its resulting anti-Semitism was the most repugnant aspect of the NSB. At the time it was already known that millions of European Jews, including one hundred thousand from Holland, had been killed.[32]

Many examples can be cited of the callous attitude which Jewish survivors encountered in the Netherlands until well into the sixties. To take one example: during the War, Dutch Jews were forced to surrender their money, stock-holdings, jewellery and works of art to the bank Lippmann Rosenthal & Co., for which they received a receipt. This Jewish property, however, was bartered away by the LIRO-bank against values that were much too low. After the War, some of these goods could not be reclaimed by their owners or their descendants, and as late as 1968/69 civil servants from the Amsterdam

30 Peeters, Frans, *Eenzaam, Berooid, ontheemd – en toch als iedereen* (Lonely, Destitute, Homeless – And yet like Everybody Else), *Het Parool*, 13 December 1997; cf.: Haveman, Ben, *Thuis na de Holocaust* (At home after the Holocaust), *De Volkskrant*, Vervolg, 20 December, 1997.

31 Cf. Brinks, J. H., Political Anti-Fascism in the German Democratic Republic, *Journal of Contemporary History*, vol. 32 no. 2, April 1997, pp. 207–217.

32 Groen, Koos, *Landverraad* (High Treason), pp. 49, 50.

branch office of the Ministry of Finance decided to sell off what was left of the booty among themselves, for symbolic amounts – valuables such as earrings, watches, gold fountain pens and silver cutlery. There was so much interest among the officials of the Ministry that they decided to draw lots,[33] but nobody ever had the idea of informing the Jewish community.

There are suspicions that many valuables that were stolen from the Dutch Jews and others remained in the Netherlands. This amounts to tens of thousands of houses, estates, works of art and stocks and shares belonging to war victims such as Jews, gypsies, homosexuals and Jehovah's Witnesses. Often these possessions fell into the hands of Dutch people who had had connections with the Nazis during the war, and of collaborators.

The restitution of art collections, including paintings, did not always proceed according to the regulations. After the War, paintings that were stolen from the Netherlands were stored at a collection of the *Stichting Nederlands Kunstbezit* (Council of Dutch Art Collections) which was responsible for tracing the owners or their descendants, and returning their property. However, this was only done in a few hundred cases. In 1997 this collection still contained 3,500 paintings. From the correspondence of the SNK, it appears that this organisation, immediately after the War, tried to change the laws involved in such a way that the works of art 'can be taken over by the State . . . in cases eligible for that purpose'.[34]

An example of this dubious policy is the case of the Jewish art-dealer Jacques Goudstikker, who, in 1940, in the course of his flight from Amsterdam to England, was killed in an accident. During the occupation Goudstikker's paintings were to a large extent 'purchased' by Göring, at bargain prices. After the War, the Dutch State recovered three hundred works of art from the Goudstikker collection, half of which were sold and half presented to Dutch museums. The heirs got nothing.

Under pressure from the Dutch authorities, Goudstikker's widow agreed

33 Houwink ten Cate, Johannes, *Niet historici, maar politici moeten Liro-zaak afwikkelen* (Not historians but politicians must settle the Liro-affair), *De Volkskrant*, 20 December 1997; also: *Joods eigendom onderhands geveild* (Jewish property auctioned privately), *NRC-Handelsblad*, 10 December 1997; *Nazi-buit bij ambtenaren* (Nazi loot and civil servants), *Algemeen Dagblad*, 10 December 1997.

34 Hollander, den, Pieter, *Staat aasde op roofkunst* (State had its eye on stolen art), *Algemeen Dagblad*, 12 December 1997; also: Heyting, Lien, *De kous is nog niet af: Verdwenen kunst, verdwenen eigenaren en talloze claims van regeringen en particulieren* (There's still no end to the matter: Disappeared art, disappeared owners and countless claims of governments and private persons), *NRC-Handelsblad, Cultureel supplement*, 28 November 1997.

in 1952 that her tax arrears should be cancelled in return for her giving up her husband's possessions. When, in 1997, this case became known in the United States, it gave rise to bad publicity for the Netherlands. Subsequently, the Dutch Ministry of Education and Cultural Affairs engaged the public relations agency Hill & Knowlton to make sure that the issue of looted art in the Netherlands would in future, according to a spokesman of the Ministry, 'be presented in the American media in an appropriate way'.[35]

Until recently Dutch historians were expected not to stain the myth that the Netherlands was a 'country of resistance' against the Germans. When, in an interview in 1993, Dutch historian Graa Boomsma compared the employment of military forces in the Dutch colony Indonesia after the Second World War with the conduct of the SS, this was enough as Boomsma noted, to have him accused of slander. Remarkable, indeed, considering the fact that there is circumstantial evidence that many men who had served in the German SS were sent for their 'rehabilitation' after the War to Indonesia, to maintain colonial order.[36]

After the judges had cleared Boomsma, the Public Prosecutor's office filed an appeal, which was quite unusual. In May 1994, even the international association of poets and writers, PEN, expressed its anxiety about the planned action against Boomsma in a letter to the Dutch Justice Minister Hirsch Ballin.[37] At the beginning of 1995, the suit was again dismissed, but this official action was a clear signal to Dutch historians as far as the assessment of the colonial past and the role of the Dutch in the Second World War is concerned.

---

35 Weidemann, Siggi, *'Ein schäbiger Vergleich'. Klage zurückgewiesen: Die Niederlande tricksen Beutekunst-Erben aus* ('A shabby exchange.' Case dismissed: The Netherlands outwits the heirs to looted art), *Süddeutsche Zeitung*, 16 March 1999.

36 Martin van Amerongen, "*Contrapunt: Reclassering anno 1949*" (Counterpoint: Rehabilitation in the year 1949), *De Groene Amsterdammer*, 15 September, 1993. See also Chris van Esterik, *Het litteken van een scheermes: SS'ers in Nederlands-Indië tijdens de politionële acties* (The razor scar: Members of the SS during police actions in the Netherlands East Indies), *NRC-Handelsblad*, 24 November 1984. In 1997, many former Dutch members of the SS put in an application for a pension from Germany, when it was made public that Germany had been paying war pensions to former members of the SS and war criminals all over the world. See, for example, *Keine Opferrente mehr für Adolf Hitler* (No longer a victim's pension for Adolf Hitler), *Süddeutsche Zeitung*, 28 February 1997.

37 *Brief aan minister Hirsch Ballin: PEN protesteert tegen vervolging auteur Boomsma* (Letter to minister Hirsch Ballin: PEN protests over proceedings against author Boomsma) *NRC-Handelsblad*, 24 May 1994; also: *Index on Censorship*, London: Writers and Scholars International, 3/94:179, 4–5/94:245, 2/95:181.

Such taboos belong to the past: the image of the Dutch resisting the Germans on a massive scale, and suffering because of the fate of their Jewish fellow countrymen is rapidly being refuted by overwhelming evidence to the contrary. However, much of this evidence is not really new and it looks as if the current, more differentiated view of the Netherlands and its relationship with Nazi Germany also serves contemporary Dutch–German interests.

The Dutch Government is anxious not to disturb relations with its neighbouring country, not least because of the economic dependency of the Netherlands upon unified Germany. Attempts are therefore being made to improve the image of Germany in the Netherlands and to establish a cordial relationship. These efforts, which are strongly supported by the royal family, are very vigorously pursued. At the beginning of 1995, Dutch newspapers even reported that the government of Social Democratic prime minister Wim Kok was trying to raise half a million guilders to finance a publicity campaign aimed at the development of a 'feeling' expressing 'togetherness-with-the-Germans'.[38] Many Dutch historians, journalists and politicians nowadays support this political line by drawing attention to Dutch complicity in Nazi crimes, while focusing at the same time on Germany's post-war democracy. Whether this will breed solidarity between neighbours in a 'Unified Europe' is doubtful. The Dutch Jews, however, may find that such a 'feeling' adds insult to injury.

38 *Ewoud Nysingh: Half miljoen gezocht voor 'wij-gevoel' Duitsland en Nederland* (Wanted: Half a million guilders for Dutch 'feeling' expressing 'togetherness with Germans'), *De Volkskrant*, January 26 1995.

MARTIN FORWARD

Replacing Replacement Theology

A Fresh Look at Relationships between the Abrahamic Faiths

CLEMENS NATHAN has a passion for the common good, to the point where he has taken up some remarkable causes. For example, few of us who are trustees of the Centre for the Study of Jewish Christian Relations, that innovative educational organization,[1] would have regarded the black churches as a primary focus of our activity. Yet Clemens, the first chair of trustees, discerns a latent anti-Semitism in much black theology, and constantly reminds us of our need to address that issue. So it seems appropriate that this essay should deal with what is a core problem between Jews and Christians that disturbs the common good, and suggest the beginnings of a remedy for it. The problem is replacement theology: in the context of Jewish–Christian relations, this is the Christian sense that it replaces Judaism as the religion required by God of humankind. More widely, it is the notion held by many religious people that their interpretation of religious reality replaces all others, within or outside their particular family of faith.[2] Hardly any people draw a line around such a narrow vision of religious truth and place themselves outside, amongst the 'unsaved'. This is one of the weaknesses of such a

---

Theology, narrowly defined, is rather a Christian enterprise, so some readers may prefer that I use a word like 'ideology'. But, within the Abrahamic faiths, transcendence is believed to be, at heart: one, personal God. Therefore I would defend the use of 'theology' as being the appropriate word to denote 'talk about God'.

1 For more information, see: http://www.cjcr.cam.ac.uk/

2 A very old yet intriguing and insightful work is by the pioneering Cambridge scholar of religions, Alan Bouquet: *Is Christianity the Final Religion?: A Candid Enquiry with Materials for an Opinion*, Macmillan, 1921.

world view, which is often about power and paranoia more than about truth. It seems best to admit straight away that this essay does not strive for a spurious objectivity, though it does attempt to be academically respectable and careful with the facts. To put it bluntly, 'replacement' theology is a menace and should be abandoned.

Clemens offers a good illustration of the problem of replacement theology for thoughtful Christians: his transparent humanity and goodness are so obviously derived from his Jewish faith that it seems absurd, even immoral, to suggest that the religion he holds is inferior or even valueless and should be replaced by another. So I offer him this essay as a token of affection and esteem.

Better sense can be made of this issue of replacement theology if we locate it in the wider context of the world's religions, with a special look at Islam's attitude towards it. So this essay will venture far and wide, in order to illustrate the problem. The author hopes that it may lead to further work in this area. Like many an academic, I am better at knocking down than at building up, though I will attempt to effect a modest refurbishment of the premises.

One important strand in contemporary interfaith relations is the desire to mend the world of the entail of the terrible consequences of bad attitudes towards the religious 'other'. The first Parliament of the World's Religions, held in Chicago in 1893, was perhaps the first example of this strand. Christian attitudes towards Jews have been described as 'the longest hatred',[3] yet members of these two religions have provided the most impressive recent scholarly example of the desire to mend fences and begin a more fruitful period in the history of these two religions.[4]

Not just scholars but church leaders have embarked on a more tolerant attitude towards the other. For example, on January 17, 2004, Pope John Paul II hosted a concert at the Vatican that aimed to bring together Christians, Jews and Muslims. Not only was he present, but also Israel's two chief rabbis and Muslim leaders. The Pittsburgh Symphony Orchestra played, whose members represented the USA's diverse religious population. One of the two pieces played, entitled *Abraham,* was new. (The other work was by Gustav Mahler, a Jewish convert to Roman Catholic Christianity, which may have been unwittingly tactless.) 'The Vatican says the musical evening was in-

3 The subtitle of Robert Wistrich's book *Antisemitism*, Pantheon, 1992

4 Many examples are given at: http://www.jcrelations.net/en/index.php.

tended to promote the commitment to peaceful co-existence among all the children of Abraham.'[5]

Few would doubt Pope John Paul II's commitment to good relations between Roman Catholics and people of other religions, particularly Jews. Yet he inherited a tradition that, in its mainstream, has marginalized the 'other', and sometimes even sought to exterminate it. As the popes grew more confident of their political power in the later Middle Ages, all the while aware of criticisms of and threats to their authority from a number of quarters, some made exclusive claims to the church's salvific role and to their own institution's central importance within it. For example Pope Eugene IV promulgated a papal bull in 1441 titled *Cantate Domino* during the Council of Florence. It includes the statement:

> It [the Church] firmly believes, professes, and proclaims that those not living within the Catholic Church, not only pagans, but also Jews and heretics and schismatics, cannot become participants in eternal life . . .

Here, the word 'pagans' seems to be a dismissive and imprecise catch-all for all those who do not fall within the other groups, yet are not members of the Catholic Church. The major group of people subsumed under this term at that time would have been Muslims. So this is an ambitious attempt to denounce as ungodly everyone not in communion with the Roman pontiff: not only people who held alternative visions of Christian faith and where its authority lay (especially followers of Jan Hus who had been declared a heretic and executed in 1415), but also members of other religions, to all intents and purposes at that time Jews and Muslims.

The following year the same pope issued an edict forbidding the building of synagogues, and preventing Jews from lending at interest, holding public office and testifying against Christians. Eugene IV was building upon a long history of Christian hatred of Jews. For example, in 600 Gregory I's policy of *religio illigitimo* protected Jews from violence but encouraged their conversion to Christianity and did not grant them equal status with Christians. During the crusading period, papal measures against Jews became more severe. In 1179, the Third Lateran Council prohibited Jews from having Christian servants and proclaimed that Christian testimony against Jews in lawsuits was to be accepted. The Fourth Lateran Council of 1215 went

5 http://news.bbc.co.uk/2/hi/entertainment/3406773.stm

further: Jews had to wear a distinguishing mark on clothing and live in segregated quarters; they could not exact interest on loans to Christians, nor could Christians do business with Jews who did not obey Church rules. Jews could not hold public office, and converts to Christianity had to stop Jewish observances. Furthermore, Jews were prohibited from hiring Christian women of child-bearing age as servants.

Clearly, Pope Benedict XVI and his successors have a long history of Catholic anti-Jewish policies to mull over and redeem. His great predecessor, John XXIII, pope from 1958 to 1963 and author of the reforms of the Second Vatican Council, began the process. Despite the shortcomings of the conciliar document *Nostra Aetate*,[6] finally proclaimed by Paul VI in October 1965, it began a genuinely new chapter in Jewish–Catholic relations, and has encouraged many Protestants also to examine their anti-Jewish rhetoric and history. Furthermore, it spoke warmly (if magisterially and condescendingly) of other revelations too, including those given to Hindus, Buddhist and Muslims. The document makes a great deal of 'the bond that spiritually ties the people of the New Covenant to Abraham's stock', by which it means the Jews. It is only a short step, which John Paul II took, to include Muslims within this West Asian family of faiths.

Indeed, it has become quite the thing to locate the spiritual ancestry of Jews, Christians and Muslims in the story of Abraham.[7] Whether this is as obvious as some scholars and practitioners of inter-religious dialogue imply is a moot point. If so, an unsentimental look at some of Abraham's actions would be welcome, such as his unquestioning willingness to sacrifice his son Isaac when he had at least tried to save Sodom from God's punishment (compare Genesis 18.16–33 with 22.1-19).[8]

Nowadays, considerable Catholic conservative reaction to Vatican II reforms calls into question the future of that church's commitment to a more generous attitude towards other religions. Much of that present debate centres on the issue of whether reform went too far, but some resisters to change

---

6 That document can be accessed at: http://www.jcrelations.net/en/index.php?id=1042

7 e.g. Kuschel, K-J., *Abraham: A Symbol of Hope for Jews, Christians and Muslims*, SCM, 1995; and, Feiler, B., Abraham: *A Journey to the Heart of Three Faiths*, Piatkus Books, 2002

8 An unsentimental and masterly assessment of part of Abraham's story, replete with insights for interfaith understanding, can be found in: Kessler, E., *Bound by the Bible: Jews, Christians and the Sacrifice of Isaac*, CUP, 2004

seem to suggest that all change is innovation and inauthentic.[9] Their hard line position expresses an attitude towards the importance of the immutability of tradition that is actually more central to the teaching of Eastern Orthodox Churches than of its proponents' own Roman Catholic faith. The fact that the Orthodox Churches have mostly been unable to review and repent their history of anti-Semitism shows one of the drawbacks of a fixed and unreflective attachment to a particular view of tradition: its inability to undo the bad as well as to affirm the good. In reality, all religious expressions change through time, even those that claim not to. A more scholarly and sensible attitude towards the past is to accept its importance, warts and all, and to rescue those bits that seem its appropriate expressions for the world in which we live. All religious people should be guided by the wisdom of the founder of Reconstructionist Judaism, Mordecai Kaplan, who observed that 'The past has a vote, but not a veto'.

Indeed, the attitude of the popes towards the Jews could be used to illustrate the point that religious tradition offers various paths, so believers must choose from among them which is best to follow in the contemporary world. The charitable attitudes of Pope John Paul II may not have much in common with some of his predecessors, whether remote like Eugene IV, or nearer in time like Pius XI (1939-1958).[10] Yet other pontiffs, not only John XXIII, also made benevolent choices. In 1236, Gregory IX condemned the excesses of the fifth crusade, specifically its violence against Jews. In 1429, Eugene IV's immediate predecessor, Martin V, re-enacted a bull protecting Jews. To be candid, these more tolerant attitudes and actions form a tributary stream flowing into a greater river of bigotry and even brutality. Yet most religions rarely express the fullest intentions of their deepest meanings. So it is very often only the foolish or fanatical who would claim that what a religion is mostly like, is what it really should be like. From time to time, minority religious traditions are recovered and transform families of faith into more authentic embodiments of what they should be.

Actually, the history of the late medieval papacy cannot be seen apart from its importance as a political as well as (perhaps more than) a moral and

---

9 e.g. A.S. Guimarães argues that ambiguity in the Council texts leads to a spirit of "tolerance toward the world and the false religions", in *In the Murky Waters of Vatican II*, Maeta, 1997, p.39.

10 It may be that Pius XII's anti-Semitism is overstated in Cornwell, J., *Hitler's Pope*, Penguin, 2000. A more accurate, yet devastating, judgment is found in: Cahill, T., *John XXIII*, Penguin, 2002. Cahill dubs Pius XII a 'moral pygmy' (p. 134).

spiritual institution. Yet the founder of Christianity, Jesus, seems to have had no interest in acquiring political power, and to have spurned messianic interpretations that emphasized its political possibilities. He rebuked his disciples James and John for requesting positions of authority rather than servanthood in the new age of God's kingly rule (Mark 10.35–45). Moreover, Jesus recognized that faith was a universal human quality, as likely to be found in a Syrophoenician woman (Mark 8.24–30) or a Roman soldier (Matthew 8.5–13) as in one of God's chosen people. It is hard not to think that the pretensions of some of the medieval popes to unrestrained political influence and totalitarian spiritual rule had moved them far away from the spirit of Jesus. In like manner, those present-day Roman Catholics who hanker after reconstructing that exclusive past seem to have lost the plot of the story of what the faith of Jesus and his followers should and could be.

If a strong stream of Roman Catholic teaching sees itself as replacing other versions of Christian faith, and other religions, then many Protestants have the same instinct that they hold a version of the Christian religion that should replace all other faith and faiths.[11] They may turn to the Bible rather than to the papacy or tradition to make this claim, but make it they often do. I suggest that, *mutatis mutandis*, reasons could be given to show that this Protestant version is just as ill-founded as the Roman Catholic one. It is time to move on to different ways of construing reality and the 'other's' relationship to it.

Christians might begin to realize how irritating and unpersuasive the claim to replacement (and its sister claim, finality) is if they, as outsiders, see it being made elsewhere. We can turn to the religion of Hinduism for an example. Despite the manifestations of Hindu intolerance in contemporary India, many people have a notion that Hinduism is basically inclusive and accepting, and that this is a good thing. It may well be better than some alternatives but, however well meant, it can be deeply insulting to others who resent being incorporated into Hindu views of reality.

Buddhism began in India as a rejection of some of Hinduism's major beliefs and practices. For example, for many (especially Theravada) Buddhists

11 Eastern Orthodox faith could contribute to a much more inclusive and accepting interpretation of the faith of others. See 'Why Am I an Eastern Orthodox Christian?' by Paulos Mar Gregorios, in Forward, M (ed.), *Ultimate Visions*, Oneworld, 1995, pp. 111-120. Sadly, however, maybe because of the traumas arising from the rule of many of their heartlands by Muslims or communists, the generosity of spirit revealed in this essay indicates a possibility of treasures as yet mostly unopened and unshared.

the gods exist but are powerless to help people, since they too are caught up on the wheel of becoming and re-becoming. The Buddha is the teacher of gods and men, because he helps both groups to wake up to reality. The awakened person (or god) is liberated from unnecessary attachments to transient things that get in the way of an astute diagnosis of the world's condition and its cure.

Buddhist teaching involves a sophisticated notion of the ephemeral self. Outsiders annex it instinctively to their own view of reality only at the cost of distorting and trivializing it. An outstanding example of this is the Hindu reading of Buddhism that interprets the Buddha as the ninth incarnation of Lord Vishnu. According to one Hindu belief, this incarnation was to preach non-violence and forbid animal sacrifice in religious ceremony. According to a second, it was to start a new religion to persuade demons to give up the worship of Lord Shiva. These interpretations could be said to intend to honour the Buddha, since the tenth incarnation of Vishnu will only be when the world is on the threshold of utter disaster. In fact, they completely distort his meaning as Buddhists see it. How paradoxical that someone who saw the impotence of the gods should be turned into one! One might also add: how ironic that a system, Buddhism, that aimed to replace the caste-system and brahminical domination of the Hinduism of its day, should find that its founder-figure has been absorbed into Hindu ways of life! Buddhism has mostly been expelled from India, the land of its birth, and found more congenial homes elsewhere; though it has made a modest comeback to its homeland in recent years.

If this problem between Buddhist and Hindus furnishes an empathetic Christian with a dispassionate insight into the problems of replacement theories, Islam provides a far more barbed example. For, just as many Christians claim that their religion replaces Judaism, so many Muslims maintain that Islam fulfils and replaces both Judaism and Christianity as God's preferred religion.

Muslim mythology (which a surprising number of Jewish and Christian scholars have swallowed uncritically) is that Islam was born in the full light of historical day, and that it is far easier to gain access to the historical Muhammad than to the historical Moses or the historical Jesus. In actual fact, it is not easy to ascertain what Muhammad did and what he did next, any more than it is with the other two religious leaders or many other figures from the past, sacred or secular.

Moreover, as the recent attachment by some Jews, Christians and Muslims to Abraham as an inclusive figure illustrates, the meaning we invest in 'historical' figures or read out of them is often only partially, if at all, related to what we can hope to know of their day to day lives on earth. Few scholars would see the biblical and rabbinical accounts of Abraham's life as furnishing accurate historical information. Even if we accept the broad outlines of Muhammad's life that past scholars took for granted – and within the last generation or so many have expressed considerable doubts about the historical accuracy of its sources[12] – how to interpret its meaning is quite another matter.

At first Muhammad probably thought that he stood in a line of prophets, each of whom brought revelation from God to a particular community, telling them of the certainty of judgment and the need to believe in one God and behave justly. The community to which he spoke was the Arabs. But gradually he came to see himself in a much more exalted light as the 'seal of the prophets' (Qur'an 33.40), the last and the greatest of God's messengers to humankind, the one with a universal mission.

To the historian (as opposed to many believers), it is unclear how far he saw that vision as replacing previous revelations.[13] Some quranic verses are generous about Jews and especially Christians, whereas others are strongly condemnatory of them. It would be possible to read this attitude towards sister West Asian faiths in different ways. Perhaps, whilst admiring much about them, Muhammad disliked some of their beliefs, such as the exalted status given by Christians to Jesus. Maybe a more compelling reason for his growing antipathy towards them was political: Jews and Christians were not impressed by his growing power, first within Medina, then over Mecca and much of the Arabian peninsular before his death in 632 CE. Since prophets are rarely systematic thinkers, it could be that Muhammad expressed different views at different times and in different contexts, and never gave much thought to the problem of making coherent sense of them.

12 Cook, M., *Muhammad*, OUP, 1984 provides a pleasingly admiring yet skeptical account of the Muslim construction of Muhammad's life. See also: Forward, M., *Muhammad: A Short Biography*, Oneworld, 1997, passim, but especially pp. 98-102.

13 The vast majority of Muslims believe the Qur'an to be the exact word of God. Outsiders do not and can therefore interpret the Islamic scripture as representing the mind of Muhammad. This need not be disrespectful. Most Christians believe, for example, that human beings wrote the Bible yet that it reveals the divine through its human words. This, they may argue, could also apply, *mutatis mutandis*, to the Qur'an.

Whatever the historian may judge to be the case, the fact is that the Qur'an and the Traditions of the prophet's life furnish an array of stories and sayings that allow a wide range of interpretations about the religious 'other', especially Jews and Christians. For example, one quranic verse has a generous attitude towards members of monotheistic faiths, allowing them a place in the delights of paradise,[14] whereas another seems to be strongly exclusive.[15] Muslims have a strong tradition of interpretive scholarship. Even those groups who are suspicious of interpretation as a human enterprise have, in effect, interpreted the tradition in order to create what they think of as God's point(s) of view. Muslims have debated much about the status of Jews and Christians (and other religions), but have reached no real consensus. The nearest to such was the development of the idea that members of monotheistic faiths should pay a poll tax (*jizya*) that would allow them to worship freely in Islamic territories (but not proselytize), and exempt them from certain duties, such as military service.

In traditional Islamic belief, faith and public life are strongly entwined. Muslims of this hue do not share the conviction that religion and politics should be separated, which some Christians, many North Americans and various others hold. This means that Muslims' attitude towards other religions in Muslim majority areas matters. If they see value in them, then other religions can co-exist and even flourish.

A good example of this was in the earlier years of the Muslim rule of the Iberian peninsular, when Jews and Christians worked alongside Muslims to create a remarkably tolerant and dynamic society. In later years, partly because of the threat to Muslims from North African groups and then from resurgent Christians, commitment to tolerance waned. An equal threat is when a pharaoh arises who knew not Joseph: the coming to power of someone who cannot see the point of co-existence. This happened, for example, in Mughal India, when the Emperor Aurungzeb (1658–1707) abandoned the tolerant policies of his predecessors. The problem with tolerant civilizations like Muslim Spain and India is that they are based, not on the premise that all must have equal access to human rights, but on the (from our contemporary

14 "Surely those who believe, and those who are Jews, and the Christians, and the Sabians, whoever believes in Allah and the Last day and does good, they shall have their reward from their Lord, and there is no fear for them, nor shall they grieve": Q2.62

15 "And whoever desires a religion other than Islam, it shall not be accepted from him, and in the hereafter he shall be one of the losers": Q3.85

perspective) condescending generosity of those in charge towards all others. What, then, when such liberality wanes?

It often wanes at times of political turmoil and trauma. From the eighteenth century until the middle years of the twentieth, Britain, France or the Netherlands ruled large tracts of the Muslim world. Since then, the USA has exercised considerable economic hegemony over the Muslim world. It has also supported rulers of Muslim lands who are despised and detested by many of their peoples. Since, with some justification, these countries are seen as Christian powers, it is hardly surprising that many Muslims have supported those of their co-religionists who have confronted rather than connived at foreign, 'Christian', influence in their homelands. Moreover, the modern state of Israel is also seen by many Muslims as a foreign, western power, dispossessing them of territory and even of 'honour'.

The 'religious' effect has been that many Muslims now emphasize strands from Islam's history which have portrayed Christians and Jews as dishonourable, manipulative, parasitical, and unable to distinguish true from false faith. Other more favourable interpretations have been shelved, and will probably return only when Muslims feel less vulnerable than now they do. In such a setting, it is easy to hear Islamic voices that condemn not just the politics of 'Christian' and 'Jewish' powers, but the religion. It has become commonplace to hear Muslims fulminate against the two religions, and to declare that Islam fulfils them.

Christians who hear such a diatribe, but who do not know whence it arises, might simply find themselves uncomfortable and even angry at having been declared religious dinosaurs, clinging on to a religion that is pushy and passé. It is to be hoped that they will see and perhaps even appreciate the irony that this is how many of their co-religionists have viewed Jews and Judaism.

Still, it is not enough to gain this insight. Considered reflection on why Muslims proclaim what they do might help point us to a route through replacement ideologies to more constructive ideologies. Most Muslims are poor, and many are refugees. Often religion is the only aspect of their life that gives them a sense of honour, status and empowerment. It is hardly surprising then that many underprivileged Muslims interpret Islam as the last and the best religion, which fulfils all others. It is equally predictable that many will emphasize the theocratic strand in Islam's past that assumes that it must govern and dominate where it exists. This is by no means the only way of interpreting Islam, whose jurists developed a range of ways in which Muslims who live under foreign rule could accommodate themselves to that condition.[16] Nevertheless, Muslims who feel oppressed and demoralized could conjure up visions of a romanticized past where they were the powerful, and yearn for its return, based upon the notion that, as the 'final' religion, they replace others.

Yet surely what is urgently necessary in the contemporary world is a sharing of power, not its transfer, whether by peaceful or warlike means, from others to one's own group. Replacement theologies tend to support views that disempower, marginalize, and dehumanize others. Not only Christians' treatment of Jews illustrates this sombre fact, but also Muslims' treatment of Baha'is, Ahmadiyyas and other post-Muhammad revelations that deny, implicitly or explicitly, that he was God's final messenger to humanity. One cannot exempt the third major monotheistic faith from this attitude. Indeed, it could be argued that the account of the entry of Jews into the promised land centuries ago under Joshua (in the eponymous biblical book) is an early example of replacement theology, with its concomitant acts of brutality and violence. Also, some settlers in present-day Israel seek for biblically-mandated borders and would exclude Palestinians from such a 'Greater Israel'.

Jews who hold an exclusive view of their religion tend to look backwards to scripture to find a mandate for their wish to replace others, whereas exponents of replacement theologies in Christianity and Islam are committed to the belief that later is better, at least until a certain revelatory moment, after which later is a great sin, perpetrated by those who have missed the right moment. In this manner have many Christians held Islam, thinking it to be a persistent and troublesome Christian heresy. So also, many Muslims regard Baha'is and other post-Islamic religions.

And this raises the intriguing notion that the best form of religion is not the latest model at all. Indeed, many people of faith value that which is long-lasting. They may include those who, in certain circumstances, assume that theirs is the last and pre-eminent religion, and who have not seen the incoherence of their vision of reality. Indeed, the recent emphasis upon Abraham as the common parent of West Asian monotheistic religions illustrates that important tendency in most religious people to value the longevity of reli-

16 e.g. Forward, M., *The Failure of Islamic Modernism?*, Peter Lang, 1999, pp. 8f.

gions. Such durability is a sign that their witness to how things really are has survived the test of time.

I am writing these words on 14 September 2004, which in the Muslim calendar is 29 Rajab 1425. When the Christian calendar was 1425[17] it was a time before the Protestant reformation and before the European expansion to the Americas and elsewhere. The English king was the young Henry VI, a pious and cultured yet ineffectual monarch (born in 1421 and king in 1422) who was to be deposed in 1461, then restored briefly in 1471 before being dethroned and murdered the following year. Nowadays, few of us would wish to return to restore the faith and practices of the medieval world, whatever the problems and shortcomings of our late modern one. It has proved tempting for some Christians, when faced with the uncritical avowal of Muslims that Islam is the final faith, to turn the argument upon its head and suggest that Islam could do with leaving the medieval world behind and undergoing a reformation. Admittedly, it can be satisfying to make such a claim to a Muslim who unthinkingly asserts his prejudice that Islam is the latest and best household of faith as an obvious fact. However, the wisdom of such a retort is questionable. For this response fulfils the same function that replacement theologies do – to denigrate and defame the other.

Is there any way to move beyond replacement theologies and the exclusive, even violent, attitudes they tend to instil in their devotees? It is often argued that they are so much a part of the religious traditions from which they spring that they must be accepted and even followed as the authorized or even 'true' version.

In this essay there is not the space for a detailed look at biblical and quranic evidence to challenge this false assertion (which I hope to do on another occasion). Nevertheless, to give just one example that would question it, the prophetic insistence upon justice that has shaped and guided Judaism, Christianity and Islam alike does not easily accommodate the unjust and immoral consequences of many replacement ideologies. For in practice, there is an ethical issue at stake. Replacement theologies are almost invariably wicked in their end results, and it is difficult to square this with a belief in a God of justice and mercy. The recent instinct among humane practitioners and even scholars of religions that the Golden Rule (some form of the affirmation that you must treat others as you would wish to be treated yourself)

17 Since Islam follows a lunar calendar and the Christian calendar is a solar one, this is not an exact match.

lies at the heart of all major religions,[18] also flies in the face of the ethics of replacement theologies. Let us therefore grant that replacement theologies are not the only way to read the religious traditions of the Abrahamic family of faiths, and that an emphasis upon justice and wider ethical issues should cause them to be discarded.

Another reason for disposing of replacement theologies is for the sake of the commandment not to bear false witness (Exodus 20.16; cf. Qur'an 4.135). Individuals may assume, on the basis of what they (falsely, be it noted) believe their own religion tells them, that the other is always duplicitous, or lacking or just plain false. Yet this is to impose a judgment upon them that may be denied by the quality of their religious lives, or the beliefs they hold that require them to act honestly and truthfully.

We have reached and raised a grammatical form of the centrally important yet slippery word 'truth'. It is natural that we should hold our religious path to be true. It is most unlikely that we would follow it if we believed it to be bogus and counterfeit. Even so, very many religious people puzzle over the issue of truth in a religiously diverse world. They ask, sincerely: how can many religions be true? As a response, many benevolent individuals assume or assert that all religions must be true paths for those who follow them. Yet this seems as simplistic and implausible a proposition as that which is held by those who identify truth entirely and selfishly with their own narrow, imperfect understanding of the meaning of life and death.

For example, an Aztec who practised human sacrifice seems far removed in religious insight and human empathy from someone who 'does justice, loves mercy and walks humbly with God' (Micah 6.8); which is not to deny that, in certain ways, Aztec spirituality transformed its followers for good. The complexity of issues surrounding truth causes many to place it on a back burner as far as good interfaith relations are concerned. This may be wise, up to a point, since such interaction thrives on trust, which is usually better established by tackling other issues first. Nevertheless, to avoid the question of truth altogether could seem to be deliberately avoiding the matter of valuing what the other believes and practices.

The problem with truth may not be with the concept itself but with the way it has been tackled. Most people think of it as static and essentialist, conveying an unchanging body of beliefs. Yet this essay has already queried

18 A useful summary of the 'universal rule' as expressed in several religions is found in Fisher, M. P., *Religion in the Twenty-first Century*, Routledge, 1999, p. 104.

the validity, let us say the truth, of such an approach, for it has argued that tradition changes and develops, and requires religious devotees to make life-enhancing choices from its pluriformity. Interestingly, according to John's gospel (3.21) Jesus talks about those who do or practise the truth, which gives to the meaning of truth dynamic and ethical qualities. Truth, in other words, is something we grow into as we attempt to live out its claims upon us. This notion of truth does not seem to cohere with its interpretation as a weapon to dispossess and replace others.

I have two final points. Christians have appropriated the Hebrew Bible for their own – very different from Jewish – interpretative needs; and Muslims have borrowed both Jewish and Christian biblical figures and made them look very Muslim in their meanings. This is not quite replacement theology, though it does mean that Jews, Christians and Muslims think that they know best how to interpret Abraham and many other common heroes and heroines of faith. How are we to deal with this problem?

Another dilemma is the political dimension of religion. This cannot be wished away. Indeed, claims to political authority are central to the self-identification of some strands of many religions, including Judaism, Christianity and Islam. Yet, as we have seen, such claims are often at the expense of issues of justice and peace. There is clearly the need for some careful and tough-minded reflection in this area, so as to affirm more inclusive and just visions of the social order, and to question some of the more grandiose claims to religious control over others.

I leave these for resolution on another occasion and likely by another person.

KENDRA H. GAINES

Writing into the Heart

THE young girl gazed at me from confused brown eyes now slowly welling with tears. Her frustration was palpable. Newly arrived as a freshman to the University of Arizona from Asia, she had been placed in an English 102 class where literature served as the focus, then sent to me for tutorial help. Her first assignment was to read a short story called "Araby" by the Irish writer James Joyce, and analyse the symbolism.

"But I cannot do this," she wailed helplessly. "I do not see any symbolism! There is a boy, he likes girl, girl does not like him, end of story."

I said, "Joyce was an Irish Catholic, and all his symbolism is Christian."

"Christian?" My student shook her head. "I know nothing of that religion."

And she didn't! She had grown up primarily in Burma where she learned something of both Buddhism and repressive politics, but nothing at all about any of the other great religions of the world. Glancing at the clock, I envisioned a succinct lecture on the foundational stories of Judeo-Christian tradition in the twenty minutes remaining of our tutoring session—and so I began.

Her eyes widened as I progressed through events in the Garden of Eden. "A snake?" she queried. "Apple? Just one bite and they must leave? Please"—she hesitated. "I mean no disrespect, but this is how great Christian religion begins?"

I was raised within the Anglican tradition and like most people, I had never addressed my tradition from an outsider's point of view. But as I explained the familiar stories to this young woman, I have to admit that they began to sound very peculiar indeed. In just a few eye-opening minutes, I saw my own religion as a total outsider might see it. But I persevered as my student took notes, and we were both gratified to see, two weeks later, that her remarkably capable English paper earned an "A".

This story remains in my memory for a number of reasons. First is, of course, the mental turn-around I had to perform to give my student the background she required to say something insightful about Joyce's story. As a veteran instructor of literature, I had always read his work as a fellow Christian, thoroughly familiar with the symbolic structure of his vision. But working with the story from the point of view of a young woman from Burma compelled me to see it with more objective, dispassionate eyes. She helped me—perhaps unknowingly—to comprehend the story on an entirely new level and from an entirely different perspective than I might ever have achieved on my own. In return, I helped her to grasp some of the key stories from the Christian faith and to analyse ways in which the symbolism from these stories had been put to creative use.

We learned from one another and we benefited from one another. Our different cultures, religions, and backgrounds did not matter in the least. In fact, in terms of our mutual benefit from our conversation, our differences became a positive asset in that they heightened our awareness of, and appreciation for, one another. The key to this kind of objective, analytical, open-minded approach lies in the context: the teaching of writing. Because we were focused on a specific and important goal—writing a paper—we were able to discuss easily topics that under other circumstances hold the potential for explosive encounters. The result was mutual understanding.

For this kind of interaction, and for numerous other equally uplifting reasons, I love to teach writing. I have done so now for over twenty years, working with both domestic American students and with international students from every possible continent. Every instructional encounter is unique, and without fail every such encounter yields insights into personalities that only the context of writing instruction could facilitate.

Writing is one of the most intimate and revealing acts of the human mind. In a person's writing, in some almost mystical way that I've never quite deciphered, true personality emerges from the verbiage. Even in the most formal of works, there beneath the words hovers the real person, usually without the writer's conscious permission. That random streak of rebellious humour that one tries to control—there it flashes, grinning madly. The pool of pessimism (or optimism) that one tries to restrain from a neutral, objective paper—somehow finds an unguarded crack and slips itself unnoticed into the text. This tendency of writing to declare the truth of a writer's nature frequently proves to be the source of so-called writer's block, or authorial anxiety. At some level, every writer cringes at the thought that something of oneself, something hitherto successfully hidden, might escape into the public limelight. Would it not be safer—one wonders—not to write at all?

It rather fascinates me that writers so rarely consider that what they reveal of themselves through writing might be actually superior in some way to their conscious deliberate utterances. Why might they not reveal that they are even better than they think they are? And perhaps more important, why not simply let out whatever wants to come out, grit your teeth, and let the world make of it what it will? Sometimes from such an act of bravado come new appreciation, awareness, and understanding, both from others and from oneself. It is a matter of having the courage to reveal yourself to perfect strangers as you write.

Lying—deliberately trying to be in writing what you are not—rarely works. At one time I tutored a young girl, a freshman, who eventually decided that she would like to transfer to a university in Colorado to be nearer to her boyfriend. She needed to write a personal statement to explain her reasons for the transfer. After several drafts, she finally produced a statement that we both agreed fairly represented her and was most likely to help her achieve her goal. I considered the matter successfully concluded. After the spring holiday, however, she returned, waving a paper and proclaiming, "Here's my final statement and it's *much* better!"

Somewhat puzzled, I read the statement, gazed at the eighteen-year old girl, and said, "I see. You're a man, somewhere in your forties, married but now divorced, educated in the eastern United States, and I think you're a lawyer. You also like to ski." Her eyes widened as I spoke, and I finally demanded, "*Who* wrote this?"

"Our neighbor," she gasped. "He's exactly what you said! My mother thought he could write a better statement than I could. But how did you know?"

How indeed. Personality finds the cracks and peeps through. I told her to mail her original statement immediately, no matter what her mother said! If I could discern the attempted deception, so could the committee at her chosen university. And of course, her transfer a few months later—under her own steam—was successful. If nothing else, this girl learned the value and necessity of writing with her own voice.

But one's own voice and personality still must often be subordinated to the greater task of considering and appealing to one's audience. This is often a difficult lesson to learn, especially when one's audience is potentially hostile to one's dearest opinions.

I well recall the young Hispanic man whose teacher for a literature class was an outspoken feminist. She had assigned the novel *The Awakening*, by Kate Chopin, in which the heroine perceives her life as too painfully crippled and ruled by men. Ultimately she swims far out into the ocean and drowns. For whatever reason, this young man detested Chopin's heroine with a virulence worthy of a real person. "She's stupid!" he growled one day. "She has everything—a great husband, kids, a big house. What more could she possibly want!?" He pounded his fist on my long-suffering desk.

"Isn't that the question the novel is asking?" I queried gently.

"I don't care. I hate her, and I'm going to write a paper saying so."

I reminded him that his instructor seemed practically to worship the heroine, and suggested that she might look ill at a blatantly hostile paper without adequate explanation for the hostility.

"I don't care," he shot back. "It's my right to say what I think."

"Yes, it is. But consider your audience. Think through why you feel so negatively. Then let's talk more. Let's explore what is troubling the heroine so deeply."

On deaf ears. He wrote a scathing paper, and over my objections, handed it in. The instructor assigned a grade of F to the paper but wrote, "This paper is anger without a cause."

Of course there was a cause; we just didn't know what it was. Neither, at least not consciously, did my student. But he was eager to rewrite, and after long conversations together, he decided to temper his hostile opinions with a slowly growing understanding of a hitherto foreign concept: that a woman might need a sense of self. He survived the course, and perhaps even gained some insight into women that otherwise he might never have grasped. I'll grant you that an improved grade might have been the primary incentive. But it seems to me more important to note that, through confrontation with his instructor, through heartfelt, passionate debates with me, and above all, through his own writing, he was able to achieve a perspective of which he'd never dreamt.

These last two tales focus primarily on personal insights that await students who are willing to benefit from their own writing. So many additional examples come to mind, but perhaps these two will serve to illustrate the utility of writing as a path to self-understanding. I will return, therefore, to my point of departure—namely, the mutual understanding that can arise, through writing instruction, between two people from distinct cultures and the astonishing benefits that accrue from such interaction.

One such benefit is ongoing friendship. My now dear friend, Parissa, had come to the United States from Iran, and had lived in the Midwest for some years before arriving at the University of Arizona and my tutoring desk. Her English was therefore fluent, and her love of literature and words well developed. I believed her to be thoroughly acclimated to U.S. culture, and indeed she was. That did not mean, however, that she had forgotten her Iranian roots. The occasional friction between those roots and her life of comparative freedom and individualism in the U.S. could and did create hot sparks, sometimes unexpectedly both to her and me.

Parissa arrived one day with her assignment in one hand and a newspaper in the other. Her assignment was to take a side on an issue of her choice and persuasively argue her position. The issue was supposed to be current, preferably gleaned from the day's newspaper. As luck would have it, the paper carried an article concerning the stricter enforcement in Iran of body-covering robes for Iranian women. I thought that perhaps, after so much elapsed time, Parissa would remain dispassionate about the ruling. My mistake. She was genuinely, passionately livid.

"How *dare* they? How dare the men claim that this is to secure the safety of women? Any idiot can see that what they're *really* saying is that men cannot control themselves! One glimpse of a female ankle and they become slavering beasts. And so *women* must pay the price! *Women* must cover their entire bodies away from sunlight and risk osteoporosis! How pathetic are these men, and how hypocritical. It's always the women that pay the price."

Living in an atmosphere of cultural tolerance, I had never considered the covering of Iranian women in quite this light. In Iran, of course, at this time, Parissa would never have been able to say such a thing. She was revelling in her freedom, now, to say what she honestly thought. But her anger prevented her at this stage from examining the issue in a more objective light, as, for example, a manifestation of a political power play. So, risking further ire, I played Devil's advocate, arguing that covering was a good thing for women, that they could more easily protect their modesty amid the turmoil of political change in Iran.

"But why should they have to?" she demanded. "Why can't *men* change?"

"Who is running the government?" I countered. "And who enforces the rules? How bound by U.S.-style rule of law are these people?"

Gradually, slowly, we began to formulate an argument founded on Iran's history, governmental intention, citizens' rights, and the role of women in modern Iranian society. Parissa's passion drove her essay and infused it with energy, but her rational intelligence considered her American audience, and formulated an objective argument calculated to speak to this specific audience. In the process, she came to better understand her own emotions—based on many stories of the Iranian social past that she had heard from her mother—and to enable me to grasp far more clearly the nature of the social upheaval playing out in Iran. Ultimately, her instructor read the final paper aloud in class, opening more eyes and widening ever more horizons.

If Parissa's project had an important impact on my thinking, Julie's project affected my life, and my husband's as well. Julie was her English name, but she came from central China. Her specific purpose for leaving China was to learn English well enough to help her father in his Los Angeles-based business. It was her duty to help her family, she told me. Julie had been placed in an English writing class structured especially for ESL (English as a Second Language) students, and her first assignment was to write about a personal experience that had affected her in some way. She chose to write about her first weeks as a teacher in an elementary school in her hometown.

As we worked together on this paper, I gradually became aware of the difference in attitudes and teaching styles that characterised her Chinese school, and those of American schools. Teachers I knew locally often complained that their students showed little respect for authority. In contrast, Julie's stories reflected the usual mischief-making of children, with resulting minor difficulties, but with an equal respect for authority. Julie radiated her deep affection for the children, but an affection tempered by the understanding that children need discipline and guidance to become responsible and contributing members of society. She was teaching them to think of others and to give back to their community. As we talked, I couldn't help but recall an overly-indulged sixteen-year-old American boy I'd worked with who had unequivocally announced to me one day, "My father *owes* me a car." The stark contrast between this boy's attitude and Julie's was almost painful.

Intrigued, I slowly ventured to ask Julie more personal questions about her family, and in response she brought photos. "There's my grandma," she told me proudly, pointing to a handsome elderly woman in one photo. "I love my grandma. She helps me learn about so many things." The family, I learned, survived through difficult years by growing and selling vegetables. As a young girl, Julie would rise before dawn, load her cart with the family's vegetables, and bicycle to market to sell them. When everything had been sold, she would return home in time to go to school. All the members of her family operated under the same rule: we will do everything we can to help one another. Julie was therefore highly motivated to write a superior paper for her English class because she would improve her English to help her father, and possibly she would earn an "A" which would help her grade point average and bring honour to the family.

She succeeded. She earned the "A", and her paper was chosen over hundreds of others to be included as the prize-winner in that year's freshman literary magazine. By then I had brought Julie home to meet my husband, and she in turn introduced us to her father when he came to visit her. I still remember her explanation of her father's English skills: "My father can say 'hello', 'OK', and 'bye-bye'. He has very efficient conversations!"

Over time, as my husband and I learned more about life in China and Julie's hometown, we made plans to fly to Beijing. Julie told us, with regret, "I cannot go with you. But you can take the train to my hometown and my family will meet you. You will be able to meet my grandma!" When we did join Julie's family at their home, meeting over a veritable feast prepared by Julie's mother, we were welcomed as if we were family, and—in true Chinese style—encouraged to eat until we could hold no more. A few years later we travelled to Los Angeles and rejoiced in Julie's wedding, happy to see this wonderful young woman working so successfully toward her own future and that of her extended family. By the time of her wedding, Julie's English had become fluent, and she had taken over all the correspondence necessary to her father's growing business. She had truly achieved her goal, to be helpful to her father through her mastery of English, and also through her growing business expertise. I doubt if she ever anticipated her role in opening our eyes, not to the China of tourists, but to the dynamics of this loving, mutually supportive Chinese family who open-heartedly included us within the circle.

As I have written this, hundreds of memories have surfaced of my writing students who have, perhaps unwittingly, shared so much of themselves with me. My job has been to guide and refine their writing skills; but my reward has been to learn from them in every possible way. Those who have come from around the world have taught me about their cultures, their family life, their struggles and determination to contribute something positive to the world. They have given me some of their language, shared vast quantities of superb regional food, opened my mind to geographic areas only dimly perceived from a one-dimensional map. They have taken the dry stuff of textbook history and given it human shape, with hopes, dreams, and eyes shining with real purpose. Collectively, they have given to me more than I could ever hope to repay.

And yet I have tried. Our home has been filled with young people from all over the globe—China and Iran, but also Mexico, Argentina, Burma, Nigeria, India, post-USSR Georgia. That is just the beginning of the list. When they leave, they write to us, in emails and real letters. They have learned their writing well, and I am proud of them. I like to think, wherever they are, that they carry with them—in addition to writing lessons—memories of hospitality and happy conversations, of genuine human sharing. I especially like to think, in what all too often seems like an increasingly politically hostile world, that they will remember and understand that when people come together and share their ideas in peaceful, measured terms, they can achieve a mutual understanding that transcends all politics. I like to think that the teaching and learning of writing has facilitated this mutual understanding.

From my perspective as a writing instructor, that is what my discipline *can* achieve, "for the sake of humanity." What is the root of hostilities, after all, if not a fear of the foreign, of what has often been called, the Other. And what more effective way to banish fear than to come face to face with this Other until it begins to lose its Otherness. Such an act of courage, however, simultaneously requires the facing of oneself, the same sort of confrontation that paralyses so many writers. "What will come out?" we ask ourselves. "Will we like ourselves? Will others like us?" And perhaps, "Will I still be able to feel superior?"

Such questions themselves create fears and reveal our own deep-seated insecurities. Perhaps, I sometimes think, as I read the news of endless global conflicts, it seems easier to fight than to come to terms with such questions. And yet, while fighting yields only pain, self-confrontation holds the promise of a new, more intimate understanding of ourselves. In turn, we can become more willing and able to see that the Other struggles with the same fears that have haunted us. In this way begins the true communication that leads to a mutual understanding. Such an understanding does not depend necessarily upon *agreement*—but on the gradual realisation that the Other, and ourselves, are much the same.

Writing can make all this possible. I well recall the wisdom of E. M. Forster's query: "How can I know what I think until I see what I say?" He was encapsulating a too-little recognised truth—that the act of writing can help us to understand what we are truly thinking and feeling. No doubt more scientific people than I could explain the process rationally; but I can certainly testify that the simple act of committing thoughts to paper can help us identify the kernel of our ideas. Amid the welter of conflicting thoughts that teem in our brains, there is usually one coherent, overriding concept that is often overwhelmed and lost. But it *can* emerge, to enlighten us about ourselves, if we give it an avenue through our writing. The writing need not, at least initially, be public, nor need it be particularly grammatical. It simply needs to be honest, for in that one adjective lies self-discovery—and that is the beginning of it all.

From private, personal writing then comes more public, assured writing, writing that reflects the hard-won truth of the writer. And from the entire process come a more open mind, clearer vision, and a willingness to acknowledge and accept *both* the similarities and differences that characterise human beings.

I offer, then, for the sake of humanity, my discipline of writing. I have seen for myself the magic that can arise from teacher and writer determined to create a communicative document, and I already know that the benefits from such an endeavour stretch far into the future—and into the human heart.

LUCIEN GUBBAY

Muslims and Jews – Then, Now and in the Future

RELATIONS between the world-wide communities of Jews and Muslims have never been so bad. Muslims outnumber Jews by almost one hundred to one and their present hostility to Jews is being felt everywhere. Even in Europe, mass immigration of Muslims to France has already made its Jews feel unsafe in their own country; and in London, Jews have learned to accept the necessity of tight security in their synagogues and at their public functions.

But it was not always so. Though the prospect of peaceful co-existence may now seem remote, the situation was very different before the start of the latest Palestinian uprising against Israeli occupation only five years ago. Positive contacts between Jews and Muslims at all levels were increasing; and on two occasions I personally witnessed a majority of Muslim students at colleges in the University of London successfully sidelining their own extremists in order to continue realistic debates with Jewish speakers. The future looked promising.

Can such conditions return or are we doomed to endure a descending spiral of recrimination and hatred? To answer that question, we must first learn what we can from the lessons of the past, then look more closely at the underlying causes of the present conflict and, *for the sake of humanity,* do our utmost to steer both communities towards better mutual understanding.

Jews and Muslims have lived side by side for the past fourteen hundred years, with the majority of the Jewish people subject to Islamic rule for most of that time. Even as late as the sixteenth century, there were still over twice the number of Jews in the Muslim Ottoman Empire as in the entire territory of Poland, Lithuania and the Ukraine in which most Ashkenazi Jews had by then sought refuge. Of course there were disasters, riots, persecutions and massacres, especially on the fringes of the Muslim world such as Morocco, Yemen and Iran. But those were violent times in which every section of society was subjected to very similar tribulations and when the poor of all nations suffered continuing hardship. No doubt Jews, being utterly defenceless, were especially vulnerable to the savagery of enraged mobs – but wherever possible they were protected by Islamic law or by the Muslim rulers. It is all too easy for us today to compile lists of massacres, forced conversions and gross humiliations from over fourteen hundred years of living together with Muslims; but harder to uncover the other side of the picture.

A balanced view of the Jewish condition under Islam is that, in return for accepting a subordinate position in society, Jews were granted security for their lives and property, freedom of worship and a large measure of self-government. The Jews of Islam fared reasonably well when times were good but did badly in periods of general hardship and decline. They participated in the flowering of the brilliant international civilisation created by the then almost world-wide conquests of the Arabs, and bound together by Islam and the Arabic language. Under the relatively tolerant sway of Islam, Judaism itself was enabled to develop and then to crystallise into very much the religion we know today.

Much is made today of the subordinate status of Jews and Christians under Muslim rule, especially as we have now become accustomed to a world dominated by European ideals – a world in which human expectation can be summarised in the words of the American Declaration of Independence: *We hold these truths to be self-evident, that all men are created equal* . . . But in none of the great civilisations of the past was there any notion of the fundamental equality of human beings. On the contrary, inequality was part of the natural order, woven into the very fabric of society – with the rulers and the ruled, the superior castes and the inferior castes, the men, the women and the slaves. The civilisation of Islam was no exception; and it is grossly unfair to judge past times in terms of the ideal standards of today – especially as these are still very far from being achieved. When the Arab empire was first established in the seventh century, it would have been inconceivable for the Jews – a distinct nation living in lands conquered by Islamic warriors – to have been assigned a status equal to that of the triumphant Muslims. What is remarkable though, and in striking contrast to Christendom, is that they were granted well-defined rights, guaranteed by law.

On the whole, I think the historian Salo Baron was right to conclude that, though second-class subjects of the countries in which they lived, Jews hardly ever lost their rights. Unlike the Jews of Christendom, they suffered few economic restrictions, were not expelled arbitrarily from their countries of residence and only very rarely were they forced to abandon their religion. Their disabilities and even their humiliations must have seemed a relatively small price to pay for their freedom to live full Jewish lives within their own communities; and there can be little doubt that, until the nineteenth century, their lot was a far happier one than that of most of their brethren under Christian rule.

Jews were always a small minority in the Muslim world and, as such, posed no threat. Jews may not have been liked and were often despised as unbelievers; but it was an almost casual contempt, very different from the visceral fear and loathing of Jews so prominent in Christian Europe. It is significant that when the new form of anti-Jewish hatred first reared its head in the Middle East as a result of the Arab–Jewish conflict in Palestine, anti-Jewish texts in Arabic did not exist and had to be specially translated from European languages.

In the past, the relationship between Muslims and Jews was governed by two factors. The first was the conquest by Islamic warriors of that part of the world in which most Jews then lived – and the subsequent reduction to subordinate status of all those who refused to embrace Islam. The second was the Prophet Muhammad's own attitude to Jews, as revealed in the Qur'an and the Hadiths (Traditions).

The Qur'an is a complex and multi-layered account of Muhammad's encounter with the Divine. Its meaning is often distorted by determined propagandists, who do not scruple to quote passages out of context and to ignore contradictory material. A careful study of the Prophet's attitude to Jews, as portrayed in the Qur'an, will give a very different picture to that given by casual browsers with an anti-Jewish agenda.

The Qur'an frequently refers to the Jews and the Christians, who had received earlier revelations from God but had corrupted them. Though some of its verses mention Jews and Christians in friendly terms, and are quoted in support of Islam's tolerant attitude to fellow monotheists, others display different sentiments. Monotheistic non-believers, though protected by Islam, were generally despised because of their wilful persistence in refusing to accept the words of God recorded in the Qur'an. However, unlike Jews in Christian Europe, they were neither hated nor demonised.

Muhammad, the Prophet of Islam, was forty years old when an angel commanded him to commence his mission as the 'Messenger of God' to the pagan Arabs. His revelations were badly received by his fellow townsmen in Mecca, who first sneered at his pretensions and then made his life intolerable. So, in the year 622, Muhammad and seventy followers fled from Mecca to Medina, some 250 miles to the north.

Medina was then occupied by three Jewish tribes and two pagan tribes who had once forced their way into the previously Jewish oasis: each tribe lived separately in its own fortified village. The dominant pagan majority at once accepted Muhammad as leader; and he concluded a treaty of mutual support with the Jews.

The pagans of Medina, who had long lived alongside Jews, accepted the abolition of their old gods by Muhammad without protest. They were thrilled by the presence in their midst of God's Messenger to the Arabs, with his revelations in their own language. There was a rapid tide of conversions to Islam; and Arab historians praise the Jews for preparing the ground for the favourable reception of the Prophet's message.

As a fellow monotheist, Muhammad must have looked to the Jews as his natural allies; and no doubt he hoped that they would accept him as their long-awaited Messiah. In fact some Jews did so at once and many others converted later. In what seems to have been a deliberate attempt to reconcile the Jews and gain their acceptance, the Messenger at first adopted Jewish-style forms of worship for his new religion. His followers were directed to face towards Jerusalem in prayer and to recite three daily prayer services and special Friday evening prayers. In the early days of Islam, Muhammad repeatedly compared himself to Moses and regarded himself as Moses' successor. According to the Qur'an, 'Before this book there was Moses' book . . . and this book confirms it in the Arabic language.'

Sadly for them, the Jews of Medina failed to reach an accommodation with the new religion. Not only did they refuse to accept Muhammad as their Messiah but they also subjected him to criticism and mockery. The Messenger was a proud man who could not tolerate ridicule; and so, only eighteen months after his arrival in Medina, his attitude to the Jews changed radically. He demonstrated his displeasure and his growing independence by changing direction and steering his followers away from Jewish practices. Muslims were ordered to turn towards Mecca in prayer and no longer towards Jerusalem, with five daily prayers services instead of the (Jewish) three. All traces of the Sabbath were eliminated and Friday was declared a day of public prayer on which work was allowed. In a change of emphasis, Muhammad began to lay greater stress on Abraham than on Moses: Abraham, he proclaimed, was the first Muslim.

The three Jewish tribes of Medina then came to be seen as a threat to the young Muslim community in its struggle with its pagan enemies in Mecca. One by one Muhammad accused them of treachery and of having broken their treaty with him. He declared that they had conspired against him with the pagans of Mecca and also with waverers within his own Muslim ranks. Muhammad eliminated the Jewish tribes by first expelling two of them from the oasis and then by massacring the third.

Here it must be stressed that Muhammad's actions appear to have been prompted by the politics of his struggle for power in Arabia, and not by hatred of Jews as such.

Indeed, the Messenger of God offered generous terms to the other Jews and Christians of Arabia to persuade them to submit quietly to the new order: 'Those . . . who hold fast to their own religion, whether Jews or Christians, will not be obliged to change it. They must pay the poll tax, one dinar for every adult . . . He who pays this tax to God and his Apostle has his security guaranteed . . .'

Following the death of their Prophet, and welded together by their new faith as well as by their poverty and their greed, the half-starved Bedouin nomads erupted out from Arabia with extraordinary vigour. The Byzantine Empire was stripped of most of its territory and the Persian Empire was totally destroyed during the first twenty years of warfare. By 732, only one hundred years after the death of Muhammad, the Arab Empire stretched from the Atlantic in the west to modern Pakistan in the east. At one stage, the vanguard reached a point in France, only two hundred and fifty miles from Dover, before falling back into Spain. Progress was slower after that, with Sardinia, Sicily and parts of Southern Italy only gradually added to the Islamic world. Though Spain was lost to the Christians several hundreds of years later, the Muslim world expanded again to include the Balkans, the northern part of Africa, the whole of northern India and much of south east Asia.

Once the first invasions started, belief in the one God who had chosen the Arabs and rewarded them with success after success became inspirational. God was clearly on their side in their bid to conquer the entire world for Islam. Another important factor in the overwhelming success of the Arabs was the generosity of their surrender terms. All could also join the ranks of the conquerors by simply declaring: 'There is no God but Allah, and Muhammad is his Messenger.'

It soon became known that Jews, Christians and Zoroastrians would not be harmed by the Muslims so long as they submitted to the new order by paying the poll tax – and as the poll tax often amounted to no more than the tax demanded of them by the former regimes, that was not too onerous. The result was that, in time, almost all the members of the defeated nations aspired to the name *Arab.*

The Muslim civilisation, in which the Jews played their part, was a civilisation before which we can stand in awe today. Its first phase peaked at a time when Europe was only just emerging from the barbarism of the Dark Ages. It was built on the cultures of Persia, India and China as well as those of ancient Greece and Rome – all enhanced by the Muslims. Though its language was Arabic, its poets, artists, historians, scientists, mathematicians and traders, all proud to be called *Arabs*, came from the conquered peoples; and it was they who created the first international Muslim Empire.

By the thirteenth century, much of the Muslim Empire had fallen into the hands of mercenary Turkish soldiers, who had usurped power from their former Arab masters. These alien rulers oppressed the local Muslim populations and caused widespread economic decline. As the conditions of the Muslim masses worsened, their jealousy and resentment of minorities grew. The position of the Jews deteriorated and remained low until the rise of the Ottoman Turks in the fifteenth century.

The expansion of the Ottoman Empire brought relief to the Jews, who became a trusted, prosperous and very useful Ottoman middle class. Especially favoured by the greatest of the Ottoman sultans, they then enjoyed over two centuries of privilege and well being – all at a time when their brethren in western and central Europe were experiencing the deepest misery. Unfortunately, good times do not last forever, and the Jews fared badly again during the long decline of the Ottoman Empire, when they gradually lost their privileges and descended into poverty and obscurity.

Islam, claiming to be God's last and perfect revelation to mankind, extended toleration to members of the older monotheistic faiths on condition that they submitted humbly to its rule. According to tradition, the Christian Patriarch of Jerusalem offered detailed terms of submission when he surrendered his city to Khalif 'Umar in 638. That treaty of surrender, called the *Dhimma*, was incorporated into holy law and became the basis for the treatment of all monotheists forced to submit to the rule of Islam. Its purpose was to guarantee the superiority of Islam for all time. In return for accepting a status in society inferior to that of Muslims, the *dhimmis* (protected people) were guaranteed their lives, their property and their freedom of religion. They were free from economic restriction and could follow almost any occupation they chose. Except in the Hejaz, they could live wherever they pleased; only very rarely were they forced into ghettos.

Dhimmis lived within their own communities, which enjoyed almost full autonomy in internal affairs. Each small community of Jews was ruled in accordance with Jewish law and administered by its own elected rabbis, judges and officials. Providing they paid their taxes and kept the peace, ordinary people were left virtually undisturbed by the Muslim state.

Respect for Islam and for Muslims was fundamental to the Dhimma, and submission to Islamic rule involved the acceptance of many restrictions, some of them deeply humiliating when strictly applied. Its principal manifestation was the poll tax. This, demanded on the authority of the Qur'an, was imposed everywhere without exception until European notions of equality began to prevail in the latter part of the nineteenth century. Here I quote directly from the Qur'an: 'Fight against those ... who do not practice the true religion, among those who have been given the Book, until they pay the *jizya* from their hand, they being humbled.'

In practice though, most Muslim rulers were more concerned with the efficiency of their tax-collecting system than with imposing petty humiliation on taxpayers: so the extreme demands of Islamic theology were often disregarded. Indeed, it made sense to keep dhimmis sweet when the success of the economy depended so much on their efforts.

Here we come across the typical Muslim contradiction in the attitude to minorities. The harsh rulings of the religious authorities, when applied rigorously resulted in the humiliation and oppression of those affected; but when tempered by the goodwill or the pragmatism of Muslim rulers, they were transformed into relatively minor disabilities. It depended very much on the prosperity and self-confidence of each particular Islamic society as to which view prevailed at any one time or place.

Mainstream Islam's attitude to the Jews was and, still to some extent, is governed by a contradictory two-pronged approach. On the one hand, Muslims shared the old pre-Islamic Arab friendship for their Jewish neighbours, who were praised for their loyalty, hospitality, generosity and usefulness. Even in modern times, Muslims unhesitatingly formed business partnerships with Jews and lived with them on terms approaching mutual trust and respect. The other parallel approach uses the same facts but interprets them in a negative way. Though worshipping the same God, Jews and Christians refuse to accept the authenticity of his revelation to Muhammad. Instead, they perversely falsified their sacred books and distorted God's message. Jews in particular are distrusted because the Jewish tribes of Medina, by rejecting the Prophet and refusing to support him in his war against Mecca, became his enemies. Present-day fundamentalist thinking goes much further in its portrayal of the Jews as eternal enemies of Islam, forever plotting its destruction.

The descendants of those Arab warriors who poured out of Arabia in the seventh century to overcome the mighty empires of Persia and Byzantium and conquer a vast swathe of territory in the name of Islam had no doubt about the purpose of their enterprise or of its future. Their belief in God was absolute. So too was their faith that the steady expansion of Islam and the rapid conversion to their faith of countless millions of people was a sure sign of God's approval. To them, Islam was God's final and perfect revelation to mankind, superseding the corrupted versions contained in Judaism and Christianity. The course of history, the working of God's purpose in the world, was clear. Islam would spread until its devotees ruled the entire world in the final age of mankind.

All went well for the first five hundred years after the death of the Prophet. Not only did Arab and Muslim arms triumph almost everywhere, but their victories were also rewarded with widespread prosperity and the establishment of an advanced civilisation without parallel at the time.

It was only later that things started to go wrong. Christian Europe began to exert pressure on the frontiers of Islam. And within the Muslim world, alien rulers from the steppes of Central Asia ruined the economy and oppressed the native peoples. Muslim self-confidence faltered as the result of those unaccustomed checks to the serene advance of Islam – and the result was turbulence and hardship.

What must have seemed the natural course of history was again resumed in the fifteenth century with the rise of the Ottoman Turks and the irresistible advance of their armies to the gates of Vienna – the capital of the Hapsburg Empire and the very heart of Christian Europe. That respite lasted for only two or three hundred years for, from the eighteenth century onwards, the decline of the Ottoman Empire was accompanied by an inexorable rise in the power of the Christian West that undermined Muslim confidence in the worth of its own society.

The first signs of the rapid technological advance of the previously backward countries of Western Europe came with Christopher Columbus's crossing of the Atlantic in 1492 and Vasco da Gama's rounding of the Cape of Good Hope to reach India a little later. Though not realised then, the supremacy of the land-bound realm of Islam was doomed just as soon as the ships of Western Europe encircled and outflanked it. There is no doubt that it was by vastly superior technology that Christian Europe first seized world markets for itself – and then went on to dominate the globe and to impose its own ideas upon it. Islam turned in on itself and became more intolerant in the process.

That sharp reversal of roles between East and West was followed, in the modern period, by the total collapse of the Muslim world and its domination by Europe and America. It reacted with a crisis of confidence – a crisis so deep-seated that it continues to this day as the driving force behind Islamic fundamentalism.

Scholars are now falling over themselves in attempts to answer the question of what went wrong with the Muslim world and why it failed so utterly to adapt to new conditions?

At a time when Europe was sunk in the barbarism of the Dark Ages, Islam had already established a brilliant international civilisation, a peak of human achievement. A highly innovative culture flourished in its cities, where its science, mathematics, arts and commerce led the world. Islamic lands were fertile: North Africa, the former granary of the Roman Empire, was thickly forested, Mesopotamia was extensively irrigated and present-day Iraq was a veritable Garden of Eden.

Contrast that with the position today. The once fertile lands of Islam have been transformed into arid wastelands, incapable of feeding its peoples. The economy of some of its nations is based entirely on a single non-renewable resource – oil – discovered, extracted and transformed into ephemeral wealth by foreigners. The development of science and technology, the spirit of inquiry and the quest for new ideas hardly exist. And a small but increasing number of its despairing, poverty-stricken masses have come at least partly to sympathise with a desperate fundamentalist ideology centred on martyrdom and death.

It is not difficult to trace the course of this decline. The first nomadic conquerors, who established the conditions under which Muslim civilisation flourished, carried the seeds of decay with them; and their mistakes were repeated by those who came after them – the usurping mercenary dynasties from Central Asia and the sultans of the mighty Ottoman Empire. The Arabs and their successors failed to move on from their initial policy of exploiting their vast territories solely to enrich themselves at the expense of the conquered masses. They failed to encourage farming and industry: they failed to foster the welfare of the people they governed.

To make matters worse, the Arab conquerors, and those who eventually took over the reins of their empires, were nomadic warriors and traders who despised agriculture and industry. They took no interest in the land: for them, it existed only as the source of the wealth that could be extracted from it. They did not settle on the land or farm it; and their insatiable greed caused them to tax the countryside almost to extinction. They ruined the rural economy and drove its people into the towns.

Forests were cut down. Grasslands, spoiled by over-grazing, could not renew themselves because of the shortage of rainfall. The fine irrigation systems inherited from pre-Islamic times either collapsed or were destroyed – and they were not rebuilt. Bedouin nomads repeatedly ravaged large areas of Syria and North Africa. Soil erosion followed inevitably in the dry and ecologically fragile environment of North Africa, Arabia and the Fertile Crescent – and the area was transformed from a leader in world food production to a series of saline steppes and deserts. As the scientist Jared Diamond so eloquently put it, the Muslims committed ecological suicide.

Another fatal flaw was the inability of the ruling class to maintain a frugal Muslim lifestyle when confronted with the wealth that poured so effortlessly into its coffers. Lack of self-discipline coupled with excessive luxury led to the moral, physical and intellectual degeneration of the élite; and that resulted in the neglect of firm government and to the fragmentation of their empires. This process was repeated again and again; and you have only to see the theoretically puritanical Wahabi rulers of Saudi Arabia at play in the casinos of London today to see how little has changed.

Of course the Islamic world did not exist in isolation; and by the sixteenth century Western Europe had embarked on the process of technological transformation that enabled it to eclipse Islam and dominate the globe. European society was founded on technology, and on the investment and reinvestment of capital to enable it to reproduce its resources indefinitely. In contrast, the economy of Islam could rely for advancement only on achieving an agricultural surplus – and that was just not possible in its ruined heartland. Islam failed to compete with the new Europe; and by the time the Ottoman Sultans realised how far behind they had fallen, it was already too late. A process that had taken Europe three hundred years to complete could not be instantly reproduced.

A common feature of industrialised economies is their need to expand to find new markets abroad – so, inevitably, Europe began to colonise the agrarian countries beyond its boundaries. Muslim society tried to counter this alien colonisation; but its modernising response proved superficial and ineffective.

Some Muslim leaders tried to bring their countries closer to Western models – but they all failed in a fundamental sense. Kemal Ataturk in Turkey and the last Shah of Iran imitated many aspects of Western society and sought to confine Islam to a personal religion, separate from government and public affairs. The Turkish army, as heir to the Ataturk revolution, still struggles hard to preserve the secular state: but in Iran, the Shah's westernising reforms were swept away in a ferocious fundamentalist backlash. The Egyptian and Algerian forms of nationalism have so far managed to keep fundamentalism at bay, but at heavy cost in human life. In Egypt, Muslim fundamentalists have regularly been executed since the time of President Nasser; and in Algeria the death toll remains horrific.

The world of Islam, having lost its position as a leader of human civilisation, was reduced to dependent status by the European powers. Muslims were then exposed to the contempt of European colonialists, who could see only their backwardness, inefficiency, fatalism and corruption – and the majority of their populations was simply left to rot. All of this had dire consequences for Muslim self-esteem and contributed to a collapse of confidence.

It is not hard to see why the Muslim world reacted to its own sharp decline with a crisis that was so deep-seated that its resolution still remains in doubt. But why did it fail so badly in competition with the West? Why did it ruin the basis of its agricultural economy, fail to rid itself of its tyrants and crippling taxation, fail to develop its own commercial skills into full-blown capitalism, fail to modernise its institutions and industrialise its production? Why did it neglect to emancipate its women? And in the all-important realm of ideas, what became of the tradition that once spawned world-leading scientists and mathematicians?

Most modern Muslim thinkers accept the fact of their society's malaise and look back with nostalgia to their ancient glory. They all agree that fundamental internal reform is needed to stop the rot but differ as to how this may be accomplished. Three distinct trains of thought have emerged in the race to identify causes and allot blame.

The first and simplest is the religious argument. Traditionalist thinkers attribute all present failures to God's punishment for neglecting Islam – and where have we heard that argument before? If people will only return to their faith and live in accordance with the holy Shari'a then, as surely as day follows night, world history will again be set on its proper course – culminating in universal acceptance of divine rule under Islam. It is interesting to note that, according to this thesis, the Christian West is not the prime culprit in Islam's present humiliation; for it has only acted as God's agent in this chastisement. The real fault lies with Muslims themselves, and with no one else.

The second argument is that of the fundamentalists, who go even further than other traditionalists by insisting on a literal return to the attitudes and laws of the earliest Islamic community. Their belief in the concept of *jihad* (holy war) is very important for, unlike mainstream Islam, fundamentalists interpret jihad as a permanent state of active warfare between Islam and its enemies; and those enemies include their own national rulers and all fellow Muslims who betray Islam by refusing to live under its ancient laws.

The third and most thought-provoking idea, only just emerging from the shadows, needs courage to articulate. This is that the faulty interpretation of the religion of Islam itself is directly responsible for engendering intellectual stagnation and national decay in its followers.

In today's political climate, most outsiders would hesitate to criticise the religion of Islam openly: some Muslims, however, are not so reticent. One of the most significant recent attempts at self-analysis was received with applause at the Islamic Summit Conference of October 2003, when the then prime minister of its host country, Malaysia, addressed the assembled delegates in an attempt to disprove the perception of Islam as a religion of backwardness and terror.

Former prime minister Mahatir is very well known for his outspoken hostility to Great Britain, Israel and the United States – so he could not possibly be accused of pandering to Western values or of betraying Islam when he proclaimed that Muslims themselves are responsible for their present state of decay.

After an exhortation to unite against their foes, he went on to say that there is nothing wrong with Islam itself – only with its interpreters. He described the glories of the past, when Muslims led the world in all fields of the knowledge of their times, and then put his finger on what he thinks is the root cause of their decline:

> But halfway through the building of the great Islamic civilisation came new interpreters of Islam who taught that acquisition of knowledge by Muslims meant only the study of Islamic theology. The study of science, medicine, etc. was discouraged. Intellectually the Muslims began to regress. With intellectual regression the great Muslim civilisation began to falter and wither. But for the emergence of the Ottoman warriors, Muslim civilisation would have disappeared with the fall of Granada in 1492. The early successes of the Ottomans were not accompanied by intellectual renaissance. Instead they became more and more preoccupied with minor issues such as whether tight trousers and peaked caps were Islamic, whether printing machines should be allowed or electricity used to light mosques. The Industrial Revolution was totally missed by the Muslims.

Prime Minister Mahatir's words, deploring the suppression of the spirit of empirical inquiry that is the mainspring of science and technology, might have resonated with some Jews in his wider audience – especially when, speaking of religion, he said: 'We are more concerned with the forms rather than the substance.'

That very same process occurred in Judaism, though rather later than in Islam; and small sections of the Jewish community today still vehemently turn their backs on secular learning of all kinds. In modern times, Jews as individuals contributed most to world culture only after they had loosened stifling religious constraints. Christian listeners too might have pondered the fact that that it was only after the peoples of Europe had freed their minds from the restrictive shackles of the Roman Catholic Church that they started on their own amazing transformation.

Mr Mahatir concluded his remarkable address with practical advice to his Muslim brethren on how best to overcome their many foes – and he sees enemies of Islam everywhere. After condemning futile wars and mindless violence against Israel and the West, which he said have got Muslims nowhere, he quoted the example of the Prophet in urging negotiation and compromise, even if on unpalatable terms.

Turning now to the traditionalist and fundamentalist approaches, it is understandable that a small minority of Muslims, when confronted with the problems of their own society with its immense disparity between rich and poor, should seek spiritual certainty in the myth of a return to an idealised past; but that is hardly realistic for so large a part of the human family. The contemporary perversion of old ideals into a lifestyle that suppresses freedom of thought, heaps restrictions on women and glorifies death cannot be an acceptable basis for human continuity.

The Europeans, who so humiliated the Muslim world in the nineteenth and twentieth centuries, introduced their own novel idea of the equality of all men and women and rejected the concept of dhimmis as subordinate subjects. Some Muslim rulers, from the reforming Ottoman sultans of the nineteenth century onwards, co-operated with the Europeans and attempted to adopt many of their attitudes. Thus Jews gradually lost their status as dhimmis and emerged from the obscurity into which they had descended into the full light of day. They saw themselves as people equal to all others in their legitimate aspirations and eager to join the new world then opening under European influence. Many of them prospered, some few exceedingly, under European tutelage.

Traditional Muslims, horrified to see the frustration of God's grand design as their world plunged into crisis, were outraged to see Jews, in league with Europeans, emerge from their subordinate place in society. Jews thus became a prime symbol of Muslim humiliation; and the establishment of the State of Israel, in which Jews ruled over Muslims on what they regarded as their own sacred territory, was the last straw.

In the old Islamic world, Jews were hardly worth hating: it was only when they occasionally forgot their assigned status in society and rose to prominent positions of wealth and power that they provoked hostile reaction. A far harsher approach to Jews has been substituted in this uncompromising fundamentalist ideology. All the negative attitudes in traditional Islamic sources are emphasised at the expense of the pragmatic and accepting practical approach adopted throughout the ages. Gone are the days of easy contempt and practical tolerance.

To quote the historian Ronald Nettler, the former casual contempt for Jews has been transformed by fundamentalists into a virulent hatred that is uniquely modern. This in turn has spawned an anti-Semitic literature in which Jews are demonised to an extent only previously seen in Christendom.

It is all too easy for fundamentalists to justify this new attitude to Jews by referring to Muslim history as portrayed in the Qur'an and the Hadiths – but suppressing the more tolerant passages. Though the Jews are the recipients of an earlier revelation from God, they falsified his words and killed his prophets. The Jews of Medina rejected Muhammad's hand of friendship and conspired with his enemies against the early community of Islam: they insidiously undermined its message by sowing doubt amongst its supporters. That same Jewish conspiracy continued after the Prophet's death; for, according to one Arab historian, it was a converted Jew with bizarre religious notions who created the first split in the unity of Islam by leading a revolt that ended in the murder of the third Khalif: such a split would have been inconceivable without the insidious and destructive influence of the Jews.

From this it is not too large a step to the sentiments expressed in the following quotation from the writings of Sayyid Qutb, a father of Islamic fundamentalism:

> The Jews have confronted Islam with enmity from the moment the Islamic state was established in Medina . . . This is a war which has not been extinguished . . . for close on fourteen centuries its blaze has raged in all the corners of the earth and continues to this moment . . .

Qutb went on to blame the Jews for the internal degeneration of the Muslim world:

> Just as, in the past, it was the Jews who had disrupted the early Islamic community . . . it was the Jews who had more recently undermined Islam by installing a generation of fifth-columnists in its midst, posing as true Muslims but in reality betraying the Muslim cause . . . The Jews have installed . . . a massive army of agents in the form of professors, philosophers, doctors, researchers . . . some even from the ranks of the Muslim religious

> authorities . . . intending to break the creed of the Muslims by weakening the Shari'a in many ways . . . with this and that they fulfil the ancient role of the Jews . . .

The execution of Sayyid Qutb by order of President Nasser of Egypt in 1966 did not stop the spread of his ideas, which continue to be widely quoted.

Any attempt to summarise the lessons to be learned from history and from the present situation must start with the proposition that, despite the subordinate status assigned to them in traditional Islamic society, Jews managed to live alongside Muslims in reasonable harmony for the greater part of 1400 years.

The summary would continue with the observation that as the Islamic world declined, lost its leading position and finally collapsed as the result of its failure to compete with the rapidly developing technological might of the West, the position of its Jews deteriorated.

It might conclude with the suggestion that the explosive Muslim backlash now being experienced against all things Western and Jewish is the prime symptom of a deep internal malaise that now affects the Islamic world – a world that has lost confidence in its own values and abilities. The fifteen million or so Muslim immigrants to Europe during the past fifty years, and the further millions who have emigrated to the United States of America – the supposed arch-enemy of Islam – is another telling symptom of that same despair.

The future remains inscrutable. One certainty is that it will not be easy for Muslims to come to terms with the Western world, let alone repair their old relationship with its Jews, until the sickness at the heart of Islam is remedied. Another is that a cure can be effected only by Muslims themselves and not imposed from the outside. There is always a chance that, just as a fever racking the body of a human being eventually subsides – if it does not first kill – fundamentalism will follow a similar course; but it must be admitted that there are few grounds for such optimism.

It is more likely that, just as happened in Europe, many generations must pass before real progress is made and Islam finds the way to renew itself in a more moderate and accommodating manner. Whilst maintaining the noblest elements of its own tradition, it will have to recognise and then build on the human advances made since the days of the Prophet. Islam will somehow have to find a way to enter into a wider world than that predicated by its more conservative theologians – a world imbued with the ideas of Jefferson and modern democracy, of Newton, Freud and Einstein; a world enriched by the work of Stevenson, Pasteur and Salk. It is to that world that it must eventually make its own unique and valuable contribution

Claims advanced by many European commentators that the Arab–Israeli conflict is the root cause of the clash between the Islam and the West are not credible. My own belief is that this dispute is little more than a convenient outlet for accumulated frustration and despair. Let us hope that, after the passing of the present ageing leaderships, a compromise of sorts will eventually be achieved in the Middle East that will enable the majority of Arabs and Israelis to rebuild their formerly more positive relationship; but it must be recognised that for some few Muslim fanatics, peace will never be achieved while Israel continues to exist. Despite some appalling episodes, Israelis seem better able to control their own extremists. More serious is the problem posed by the fact that several generations of schoolchildren have already been indoctrinated with a hatred of Jews and the West; and that is truly depressing. After all, it took Christian Europe over a thousand years to rid itself – and then only partly – of the disease of anti-Semitism: how long will it take the Islamic world to undo what is now being inculcated?

It would not be appropriate to end an essay in a volume published in honour of Clemens Nathan and entitled *For the Sake of Humanity* on so bleakly pessimistic a note. Though powerless to affect the resolution of a profound historical process, people of goodwill on both sides of the Muslim/Jewish divide will continue to strive to do what they can to mitigate its baleful effects. Individual Muslims and Jews will, one hopes, redouble their efforts to avoid the demonisation of their perceived foes and bring about better mutual understanding. The Muslim and Jewish communities in Britain also have an important role to play in working together for the common good.

The large Muslim community of this tolerant country of ours has a unique opportunity to point a way out of the present morass of negative thinking. It must first marginalise and then isolate its vocal minority of extremists; and the British media can help it by highlighting the efforts of courageous imams and other leaders rather than focussing only on the crazed views of fanatics. A start is already made in the setting up of a training college in England for future religious leaders who, hopefully, will attempt to achieve an acceptable synthesis between the best of Muslim and Western ways. And let us not forget that the increasing number of Muslims, educated here and now joining this country's professional and business élite, will soon be exerting their own influence on the thinking of their community.

My own ancestors acquired British nationality in the early years of the nineteenth century. Though motivated primarily by material factors in their own move out of the world of Islam, they were also conscious of the advantages of a European lifestyle. They made a determined effort to fit in with the ways of their host country; and adapted well without losing too much of their own Jewish heritage. It has proved a happy compromise; and so far as I am concerned, I can declare with sincerity that *je suis bien dans ma peau*.

Is there not an example here of how the longer established Anglo-Jewish community can help the newcomers? Some Jews have extended the hand of friendship and offer practical advice based on their own hard-learned experience of settling down and preserving the best of their own culture in alien surroundings. Communal, educational and other organisations are already working together; and, though this is very limited so far, it is at least a start. The Jews of Israel too, once they have overcome fears about their own safety, have their part to play in the softening of mutual hostility: more sensitive awareness of the suffering of others, in the interests of their common humanity, would help to ease tensions.

I conclude this essay in honour of Clemens Nathan with a quotation from the *Ethics of the Fathers*, an important part of the Jewish liturgy:

> Rabbi Tarphon said: The day is short; and the work is great; and the labourers are sluggish: and the reward is much; and the Master of the house is pressing.
>
> He also used to say: It is not your duty to complete the work; but neither are you free to desist from it . . .

GENERAL THE LORD GUTHRIE OF CRAIGIEBANK

Terrorism: How Dangerous is the Threat?

TERRORISM has been around since the dawn of history. It has not just been invented. In the twentieth century, terrorism was a familiar phenomenon. Many countries suffered: France, Northern Ireland, the UK, Spain, India, Pakistan, the Middle and Near East and Russia. The list could go on and on. Some countries were more fortunate than others and have had less of a terrorist problem. Until recently, the United States could be numbered amongst them.

Although terrorism has always been with us there is still no common agreement on how to define a terrorist. Politicians, the military and the United Nations cannot agree. There is well known saying, an unhelpful one but which has some truth in it, that one man's terrorist is another man's freedom fighter. Palestinians, who take their own lives when killing others, are described by some as heroes going on martyrdom operations and by others as evil suicide bombers. It was only a short time ago that many United States citizens advocated and funded the cause of the IRA who were killing British soldiers and civilians. I am not going to attempt to give you a definition but have some sympathy with the Judge who said he could not define pornography but knew what it was when he saw it. The paradox of terrorism and violence is that most of us both condemn it and condone it. Violence is widely abhorred, yet frequently employed.

Are we now, since 9/11 in New York, really living in a different world? Are the Russians really living in a different world because of Chechnyan terrorists? Is the world at war with terrorism? There is a serious divergence of opinion. Many do not accept the idea of a 'war'. They believe good policing, good intelligence, justice, human rights and good governance solve terrorism. Many fear that the United States is engaging in an endless war and became engaged without considering all the possible consequences. The Americans use the term war more freely than we do. They talk about 'a war on drugs', 'a war on poverty'; neither of which incidentally look like being won.

I don't think we should be surprised that attitudes are different. What happened in New York created an urgency and a reaction, which was not replicated elsewhere, where it was felt that in the recent past terrorism could be managed with democratic measures. Moreover, the rhetoric of the United States – 'Axis of Evil', 'crusade', 'smoke them out', 'kick butt' and the very term *war* itself – was less than helpful. Understandably, many governments in Europe and elsewhere were also anxious not to stir up or frighten their own Muslim populations, who needed to be calmed down rather than excited.

These differences do not help, but I do believe we need a new and more international approach. I speak as someone who spent a surprisingly large part of his forty-four years as an army officer on active anti-terrorist operations in different parts of the world – in Malaysia, Cyprus, East and West Africa, the South Pacific, the Yemen, Oman and Northern Ireland. Unlike some of today's terrorists, none of those I was operating against, though some were Islamic, wished to die for their cause like some Muslims do today. I was never confronted by a suicide bomber.

We may not be at *war*, but much of today's terrorism is, in some ways, *different* to what we knew about; and I suggest we should have faced up to this some time ago. The signs were there well before 9/11. But the Twin Towers brought brutally home to us what the problem was. Al Qaeda and Osama bin Laden were known about in the 1980s. They committed atrocities, but governments were very coy about doing anything about it: about spending money, about cooperating internationally with intelligence and defining threats, about even discussing the problem, and about having a common approach to terrorism. They hoped the problem would go away; at the very least it would be another government's problem, not theirs. How often did the USA or UK discuss Al Qaeda with Russia or vice-versa? How often did we share intelligence? I was very struck how when I retired my Russian opposite number told me that he felt we, the British, should wake up to the threat from Islamic terrorism, and that we had Islamic terrorists living in England plotting against Russia. Russia, I think, was more aware of the threats than we were; but when I asked General Krasnin, my opposite number, for evidence of terrorists living in the UK, none was produced.

Today several developments have made societies more vulnerable. Modern civilisation, with its high technology, has certainly made our lives more efficient, comfortable and easy, but many of our vital systems such as air, road and rail travel, information systems and energy are easy targets to attack and disrupt and lead to catastrophe. Sophisticated states, societies and businesses are easy to damage.

We also see technology helping the terrorist in other ways. Weapons of mass destruction can now be made that are small, light and cheap. They used to be expensive and unwieldy. A terrorist who highjacks a high-tech aircraft can also find himself flying a devastating weapon for little more than the price of an airline ticket, as the Twin Towers illustrated.

The information revolution has provided an inexpensive means of communication to ill-intentioned groups and individuals. Once, such communications were so expensive that only governments, the military, the police and multinational companies could afford them. Today terrorists in London, New York, Bali, Afghanistan and Moscow can cheaply hold a conference call. Plotting, searching for and exchanging information, and planning is easier for the terrorist than it ever was. Terrorists do not have to meet together before they carry out an operation.

Another difference with terrorism today, a new trend, is *what* motivates terrorists. In the mid twentieth century most terrorists tended to have relatively well defined political objectives, such as liberation from colonial rule, and the righting of perceived or real social and ethnic grievances and the release of political prisoners. Sometimes governments supported and controlled terrorists, often covertly supporting terrorism in other countries. Towards the end of the century, radical groups grew up on the fringes of several religions. Most numerous were the thousands of young Muslim men who went to fight against the Soviet occupation of Afghanistan. Many were recruited to organisations with an extreme view of the religious obligation of *jihad*. Terrorism has become more brutal and indiscriminate. This is reinforced, for some terrorists (though by no means all or even a majority), by promises of rewards in another world. At the touch of a button a young suicide bomber can be transported to eternal paradise.

Terrorist organisations have changed. For example, Al Qaeda's network of ten thousand people with loosely affiliated cells in some sixty countries give it a scale well beyond anything we have seen before. I stress loosely affiliated: slum dwellers in Cairo, second generation Pakistanis in the UK, Afghan *mujahedin*, Muslim fanatics in the US, Chechnyans, and Algerian and Moroccan immigrants in France have little in common – except a roughly similar ideology. They certainly do not have a chain of command as we know it. Terrorists can now operate both internationally and cross-border. Because terrorists are now loosely affiliated, less structured and less hierarchical, they are very much harder to penetrate.

We now have two new aspects of terrorism – the first technological, the second ideological – which have increased our difficulties in dealing with Terrorism.

Today we have terrorists who embrace globalisation. Because of 9/11 and the unprecedented scale of Al Qaeda and their affiliates, the current focus is on terrorism associated with Islamic extremists. But we should not forget that every large group of people has some members who deviate from the norm; and some of these are bent on destruction and creating catastrophe.

Some examples:

First, the worst case of terrorism in the USA before 9/11 was perpetrated by Timothy McVeigh in Oklahoma. He killed 168 people and injured 600. He was a purely home-grown anti-US-government fanatic. Second, the Japanese cult that applied sarin gas in the Tokyo subway system in 1995 – when thousands were hospitalised – had nothing to do with Islam, like Timothy McVeigh. I could give many more examples of non-Islamic terrorism. Islamic terrorism may be what currently preoccupies much of the world, but the threat can be multifaceted and we would be unwise to forget this. What about the anti-abortionists in the USA who have killed doctors who work in abortion clinics, or even the anti-animal-vivisection fanatics who kill those who carry out experiments on animals? They are terrorists.

Today a pathological individual can, by himself or with very little help, kill thousands. It is not inconceivable in the future that he could kill millions. In the past, when pathological killers murdered vast numbers – people like Hitler and Stalin – they could only do so with the apparatus of a state behind them.

Lethality has been increasing. The 9/11 attack cost thousands of lives. Beslan cost hundreds. These did not happen because of weapons of mass destruction. Much of the new terrorism is not like the seventies' terrorism of the IRA in the United Kingdom, ETA in Spain, or the Red Brigades in

Germany and Italy. The what you might call 'business as usual' attitude towards curbing terrorism is not enough. Although I do not think we should over-emphasise the threat, one must face the fact. The risk of a dirty 'radiological' bomb is increasing. In 1996 there were eight incidents of smuggling of radioactive materials suitable for such a device. In 2003 there were fifty-one. We know Al Qaeda wants to acquire radiological materials, but, as I said, we should not over-emphasise the risk. There are huge problems for those who wish to make such a device, and there are other ways to terrorise which are cheaper. We know they exist today because they have been used.

What should we be doing to tackle terrorism? Can we succeed? We should seriously ask ourselves whether we have the will. It may be impossible to eliminate all terrorist incidents, but if we can reduce their numbers, their frequency and their lethality, our societies will greatly benefit. I do not think we will ever be able to stop every terrorist, but we should be able to find an acceptable level. We must not view it all as too difficult and inevitable.

Many would disagree with me about even talking about an acceptable level. I was certainly very much criticised by the British prime minister, Margaret Thatcher, when, as chief of the defense staff, I told her we could not eliminate every terrorist in Northern Ireland but should be able to reach an acceptable level of violence. Can we develop a strategy?

First, Terrorism cannot be solved unilaterally. Multinational cooperation is essential. It is everybody's burden. Some countries, I think mistakenly, may wish to avoid the budgeting burden of military and civil measures or of providing assistance. Even more dangerous is the temptation to think that by appeasing terrorists, paying them off, you can avoid trouble for yourself. This is very unlikely to be a solution in the long term. Saudi Arabia has been accused of doing this – paying Al Qaeda not to attack them.

Secondly, there is inevitable tension between the need for security measures and the need to protect freedoms. Issues of national security can never justify abandoning the rule of law. But neither can the law be so interpreted as to frustrate legitimate measures designed to protect the public against terrorism. I think it is absolutely right to consider changing our laws because of recent developments and new threats. I recognise that this is an extremely difficult area to reach agreement over and, of course, our liberties are of the greatest importance to the nation, but so are the lives of innocent people. It seems to me that what the government proposed, and I speak as a crossbench peer who spends more time criticising the government over defence and security than supporting it, was thoroughly sensible. It recognised people's concerns. The nintey days proposed was not like internment in Northern Ireland, and those who suggested it were either ignorant or disingenuous. Every seven days the police would have to argue before a high court judge why they needed to detain a suspect. The burden of proof was on the police. Surely, high court judges are capable of ensuring procedures are fair. The government also added a sunset clause to alleviate fears of unnecessarily prolonging the legislation.

Terrorist organisations are now far more sophisticated and international than they were. Investigations are complicated and often involve searching for evidence in other countries. The trail could lead to Pakistan, Indonesia or the Philippines – and needs to be followed if outrages in our own or other countries are not to occur.

I think the government and police deserved our support over this. The hysterical and shrill protests of some, including certain law lords, was misplaced, and our country is now faced with greater risk than it need be. To say we are being propelled towards a police state seems to me to be complete nonsense.

Illegal measures such as torture very rarely assist in terrorist operations. Very occasionally they may in the short term, but hardly ever in the long term. Torture is almost bound to make matters far worse. It brutalises the torturers and rots the soul, adding to those who sympathise with the terrorist. Study the French army in Algeria. Torture should never be condoned or excused, and those who carry out torture must be pursued and severely punished.

Third, every effort must be made to suppress the financing of terrorist acts. This is a hugely important area. It involves governments, banks, financial institutions and regulators and is an international challenge. So far the international community has failed to achieve much success.

Fourth, the military certainly has an important part to play – a part only they can play. But civil measures are also very important: perhaps more so. The police, judges, drafters of constitutions, prison officers, *et al.* are crucial. This is what we call 'soft' power as opposed to 'hard' power. Having spent forty-four years in the army I am sure conflict is easier than conflict resolution which is almost always more expensive than the conflict itself and goes on for longer.

The aim I think must be to combine correctly what one calls hard power (military power) and soft power (civil measures), and that is a very difficult balance to arrive at.

Intelligence has to be more widely shared. This is not as easily done as it sounds. Sources have to be protected. It would be ridiculous to share intelligence with certain countries many of whose people may openly or secretly sympathise with the terrorists. But we do need to assess long-term threats together and share both strategic and tactical intelligence whenever we can. It is costly; huge sums of money have been spent on technical intelligence, particularly by the USA but, in my view, inadequate funds on human intelligence, on spies, agents and friends.

In the past, the US – particularly the administrations of President Carter and President Clinton – appears to me to have been rather squeamish about agents and human intelligence-gathering. They had been embarrassed by the criminal activities of some of their agents. But if you want to find out about nasty, evil people – terrorists – you probably need to send nasty people to penetrate them and mix with them. Agents and spies take many years to develop and at the time of 9/11 we had very few. We need to actually understand why the terrorist is a terrorist and why he follows a certain leader before we can develop a coherent approach.

To illustrate my point: Why is Osama bin Laden followed? Whether we like it or not he is a hero to many Muslims. Why is he such an attractive leader? I would suggest several reasons:

He is a fine looking man. This matters. He looks the part.

He speaks beautiful Arabic. He is articulate and advocates his beliefs well. He has a simple message he repeats again and again.

He understands Arab history. Most Arabs have an interest in history. I have rarely heard an Arab saying 'Oh that is history', dismissing the past as though it did not matter. You do hear history being dismissed in Europe and the USA as having little relevance to the future. Osama bin Laden plays on the Arab interest in history and has talked about the once all powerful and civilised Islamic world as being humiliated since the fall of the Ottoman Empire eighty years ago. Bin Laden has often spoken about this. Many Arabs do feel humiliated and their shame is crucial for us to understand.

Osama bin Laden is also unusual in that he has actually shared the same dangers as his followers. He has been on the mountains of Afghanistan and been bombed by US planes. He has taken the same risks, and he has given his wealth to the cause. He came from an immensely rich family, and he himself sponsored Al Qaeda. He is no longer immensely rich. All these things make him charismatic and an icon for tens of thousands of Muslims worldwide.

In Kano, a Muslim town in Nigeria, of one hundred boys born in the government hospital in one week, seventy-two were given the name Osama.

Bin Laden has a very simple message: remove from the region the despotic Arab rulers and their evil supporters, the US and her allies. Having such a simple message is important. It must be easy to understand if it is to be effective.

I find it alarming that in the Muslim world there are many people who still believe that Al Qaeda will prevail. They say, first, Al Qaeda is resolute and is totally committed to its cause. Is the USA? What do they really believe in? What are Americans passionate about and willing to die for? Many of them – and I am not talking about uneducated Arabs – are certain the US will abandon Iraq. They are convinced the US always does leave when the going gets tough. They quote Beirut, Somalia and, of course, Vietnam. They also say the US will abandon her allies. Certainly many Pakistanis feel that they will be abandoned. They say they were abandoned before by the US after the Soviet Union had left Afghanistan and they were no longer useful. The fact that the United States did not stand by the Kurds or the Marsh Arabs when they had been encouraged to revolt against Saddam Hussein and were brutally suppressed is well remembered. It is depressing that this is the perception of too many in the Muslim world. Whatever we think, it matters what they think.

I have digressed, but there is an old Army maxim 'know your enemy'. We need to study them. The indicators are there, and we need to recognise them and take appropriate actions.

We also need to develop a common approach towards proliferation. Weapons of mass destruction are not science fiction. They have been used. Although, as I have said, it is difficult, it is not inconceivable for a terrorist to make a nuclear weapon if he can get his hands on the necessary nuclear materials. These could be procured. They are not all in safe hands. Nuclear fissile material is certainly not impossible to find.

Today the suicide bomber is armed with explosives; tomorrow, if the opportunity arises, he or she could be armed with much more deadly nuclear, chemical or biological devices.

Next, what do we do about failed or failing states? Failed states are fertile breeding grounds for terrorists; it is in our interests to coordinate our efforts to help them. Helping is, of course, not only about funding and aid. It is much more. Every failed state is different. Some require firmness, some encouragement. But if the ultimate goal is good governance, dignity, and human rights, the more the international community can adopt a common approach the better. We need to identify states before they fail.

Lastly, religion and conflict are ancient partners that remain inextricably bound. Many wars and conflicts in human history were supported by at least one religious institution. But if religion sometimes supports war or conflict, it is most important to remember religion is also usually the basis of antiwar and peace movements. The trouble with the current situation is that while good, civilised men and women from different religions can have dialogue and understanding, they have no influence whatsoever with the extremists who come from the fringes of their own religion and are intent to destroy.

We, and moderate Muslims throughout the world, are up against extremists, a few of whom believe in death and regard the innocent people they kill as a passport to paradise. They represent a radically new danger. To me perhaps the greatest downside to the war in Iraq today is that many moderate Muslims became sympathetic to the extremists. I firmly believe that moderate Muslims, more than anybody else, are far better equipped to handle Muslim extremists in the long term than Christians or Jews. The war has made it harder for this to happen.

To me terrorism can never be excused or condoned. We are faced with a long and gruelling struggle against our enemies, many of whom have a passion for their cause and have no doubt they will prevail. Whether one was for or against the USA and British actions in Iraq, the support should now be unequivocal. Too many people in the world would like to see the United States humiliated further and fail. If this happens, terrorists around the world – not just Muslim terrorists – and their sympathisers will be energised, and the forces of tolerance and progress will be on the run.

The threat is very serious, but it is crucial that we keep a sense of balance. The terrorists are certainly not getting it all their own way. They have suffered serious reverses. In many areas they have been weakened and their operatives killed or captured. The security services have done well and thwarted numerous attacks. We owe them much in the UK. But we must not drop our guard. Terrorists only have to get lucky once. We need to hold our nerve and not falter. Do we really have the will to prevail?

ARTHUR HARVERD

World War II Compensation Schemes

INTRODUCTION

Clemens Nathan has devoted his life to the cause of human rights and the alleviation of oppression. Included in this field is his important contribution to the work of The Conference on Jewish Material Claims Against Germany. Clemens has served the Claims Conference for several decades.

A recent annual report of the Claims Conference defines its mission as to secure a small measure of justice for Jewish victims of Nazi persecution. This goal has been pursued through a combination of negotiations and legislation, disbursing funds to individuals and organisations, and seeking the return of Jewish-owned assets lost during the Holocaust.

The Claims Conference works towards the following goals:

- To gain indemnification for injuries inflicted upon individual Jewish victims of Nazi persecution and restitution for Jewish-owned properties confiscated or destroyed by the Nazis.
- To obtain funds for the relief, rehabilitation and resettlement of Jewish victims of Nazi persecution, and to aid the rebuilding of Jewish communities and institutions devastated by the Nazis.
- To administer individual compensation programmes for Nazi victims.
- To recover unclaimed Jewish property and allocate the proceeds from their sale to institutions that provide social services to elderly, needy Nazi victims and that engage in Holocaust research, education, and documentation.

The Claims Conference also addresses the needs of the aging population of survivors through grants to organisations around the world, primarily funded today by the sale of unclaimed Jewish property in the former East Germany and by the German Foundation, 'Remembrance, Responsibility and the Future'. Grants are also administered from the governments of the United States, Austria, France and Spain, and by funds from the Swiss Bank Settlement designated for such assistance to survivors.

As a longstanding and dear friend of Clemens, our association commencing at the age of seven in the same primary school class in Amersham, Bucks, during the War, I thought that it may be of interest to describe the work of two World War II compensation schemes with which I have been involved to provide an indication of the way in which these schemes operate. The two schemes are the UK Government Enemy Property Compensation Scheme and the International Commission for Holocaust Era Insurance Claims, which is based in the United States. These schemes are independent of the Claims Conference and are not administered by it, but there is a general unity of purpose in the endeavours undertaken. All of the many compensation schemes benefit from the pioneering work and direction of the Claims Conference.

UK GOVERNMENT ENEMY PROPERTY COMPENSATION SCHEME

At the commencement of World War II the UK Government introduced Trading with the Enemy legislation. The purpose was to take into British Government control assets located in the United Kingdom belonging to individuals and companies who were resident in the belligerent countries. The aim of this legislation was to ensure that enemy-owned assets in this country could not be utilised by enemy authorities to assist their war aims against the United Kingdom and its allies.

The seized assets were placed under the control of British Government Custodians of Enemy Property, there being separate Custodians for the various enemy countries such as Germany, Hungary, Romania and Bulgaria.

The belligerent countries fell into two categories. Those with which we were at war and countries occupied by the enemy which came under the control of enemy administration. These latter countries were called technical enemies. After the end of World War II monies seized by the British Government belonging to technical enemies were released to the original owners where found. The governments of belligerent enemies which subsequently fell behind the Iron Curtain took control of the monies returned by the British Government. The original owners could not then claim against their local governments for the return of their assets because it would have been dangerous for them to do so. Individuals in those countries were not permitted to possess bank accounts or other assets in foreign countries and severe punitive action could have been taken against them if the authorities were so informed.

After decades of debate as to whether and how the seized assets could be returned to their rightful owners the British Government decided in 1997 that individuals who lived in the belligerent countries but were themselves victims of Nazi persecution had suffered an injustice in not having their seized UK assets returned directly to them. Such individuals could not be considered as enemies. The Prime Minister invited Lord Archer of Sandwell, QC, to examine the matter and develop an appropriate compensation scheme. As Peter Archer, MP, Lord Archer had been solicitor general in the Wilson and Callaghan governments during the 1970s. Lord Archer devised a compensation scheme which was approved by Parliament. The scheme required that a panel of assessors be appointed to determine any claims that may be made under the scheme. A team of officials from the Department of Trade and Industry was formed to provide a secretariat to the panel. Their duties were to promote the existence of the scheme, to publish the names of those who had their assets seized under the Trading with the Enemy legislation, to liaise with claimants throughout the world, to prepare claims documentation for the panel, and send remittances to the successful claimants. In January 1999 Lord Archer was appointed chairman of the Panel of Assessors and shortly afterwards the scheme got underway.

Individual account cards going back sixty years or more, which detailed the assets which had been seized by the Custodians were found in the Public Records Office. Every single owner, or joint owners, of seized assets had their own account card which identified the assets that had been seized and their value at the date of confiscation. Where the seized assets had been subsequently returned after the war, the account cards duly recorded that fact.

Early in 1999 the existence of the compensation scheme was widely publicised through refugee organisations, British embassies overseas and other relevant entities. The names of the account card holders were published on a website and original owners and/or their descendants were invited to apply for compensation.

Questionnaires which had to be completed by the claimants were printed in several languages and were distributed to them.

Over 1,100 claims were received and a few late claims still continue to arrive from individuals who had not previously heard of the scheme. Where descendants or siblings of a deceased original owner apply for compensation, they are required to prove their family relationship to the original owner or owners with documentary evidence. Because of this the panel of assessors has often had to construct elaborate family trees from birth, marriage and death certificates and wills and other forms of inheritance documents written in many different languages.

Most claims were determined by the panel of assessors on a documents only basis, there being sufficient evidence in the documents to enable a decision to be made. From time to time oral hearings were needed in order to establish facts that could not otherwise be confirmed in the documents provided. There could, for example, be concerns when more than one family claimed for the same asset. Oral hearings were held in many countries, usually in the local British embassy or consulate.

A key issue that often had to be resolved was to establish who the rightful owner of the asset would have been if it had not been confiscated. For example, if there had been a divorce, a question could arise as to whether a proportion of the asset should be repaid to the divorced wife or her descendants.

Many of the account cards record that the asset had already been repaid to the original owner or his or her descendants, many years ago. It was occasionally argued that payment had been made to the wrong person or persons. Where this was found to be, the claimed payment was made to the rightful person or persons.

Compensation is paid only to victims of Nazi persecution, and claimants were required to demonstrate that the original owner and/or the claimant suffered such persecution. It is not sufficient to assert that the original owner was in favour of Britain and was sympathetic to its policies during the war, or assisted in hiding Jews, however noble and unbelievably brave that was. The original owner and/or the claimant had to show that these actions led to persecution. In this respect, several Christian families and organisations were successful in their claims because in hiding Jewish refugees they themselves suffered persecution.

Many claimants suffered persecution under Soviet regimes either during World War II or subsequently behind the Iron Curtain. The terms of reference of the compensation scheme did not include Soviet persecution and regrettably several claims were rejected for this reason. The Baltic States suffered badly under successive Nazi and Soviet regimes during the war. In one case an individual from one of these countries was persecuted by the Soviets and deported to Siberia. The claim failed as the original owner was not subject to persecution by the Nazis. His descendants took the case to the High Court for judicial review on the grounds that as a result of the Ribbentrop/Molotov Pact between the Soviets and the Nazis, the Soviets were carrying out Nazi persecution policies in the Baltic States by agreement. The Court held that there was a distinction between Nazi and Soviet persecution and the appeal failed.

There has been no financial limit on the total amount of compensation paid. The assets were valued at the time of confiscation and the values were recorded on the individual account cards. Where an award was made the value at the time of confiscation was multiplied by the UK Retail Price Index since that time, hence successful claimants receive the current value of the asset. The financial impact of the award of compensation on the recipients varies depending on their present financial circumstances. It is fair to say that the amounts paid, in particular, to individuals resident in former Iron Curtain countries can have a significant impact on their standard of living.

Over four hundred of the claims have been successful and over £20 million to date have been returned to the original owners or their descendants. This numbers is likely to increase reasonably substantially by the time that the scheme is terminated. The largest individual payout so far has been £2.7 million.

The Scheme incorporates a private appeals mechanism which enables a claimant who is dissatisfied with the panel's decision to appeal. A retired Court of Appeal judge, Sir Christopher Staughton, was appointed as the appeals adjudicator. He has heard over fifty appeals, but on only three occasions has he overturned the findings of the panel. In several appeals, however, the claimants produced new documentation which had not been seen initially by the panel. In these cases the claims were remitted to the panel for their further consideration and the new evidence sometimes led to a revised decision.

Inevitably, it was often a harrowing experience for members of the panel and the support secretariat to review the claims as they brought to life stories of the most extreme persecution and deprivation. At the same time, stories of bravery and resilience in the face of terrible odds inspired all those engaged in this task.

The original owners of the seized assets were mainly prosperous businessmen who traded internationally and knew how to arrange for funds to be transmitted to the UK. This was done to provide financial security for owners' families in the event of war. In some cases funds were transferred for specific purposes, such as to cover the expenses of a child sent to the UK for educational purposes, including his/her upkeep at school or university. In several cases it was not necessary to remit funds to Britain. The businessman may have sold goods to a UK customer and instead of requiring payment to be made directly to his business overseas, he would request that the debtor remit the amount owed to a British bank account. In this way a fund could be gradually built up to provide the desired financial security.

Some of the original owners travelled briefly to the UK before the war for the express purpose of depositing cash in a newly opened bank account in London. The owners or their descendants sometimes did not know, or could not recall, after the passage of time, the name of the bank where the funds were deposited. The panel and the secretariat would often seek the assistance of the banks' archivists in trying to ascertain whether funds were still held in their banks. The archivists gave great assistance in this respect and were willing to go to considerable lengths to help. The advice of leading historians was also obtained from time to time to assist with obtaining details of events in particular regions in Europe during the war.

In one case where the name of the bank could not be remembered, the documents provided with the claim included a copy of a diary which recorded some capital letters and a number which could have been some account identifying mark. A telephone call to one of the well known depository companies in London revealed the existence of a deposit box within a few minutes.

Another source of funds was legacies from UK estates for the benefit of residents in the belligerent countries which were retained in British bank accounts.

The information provided by the claimants constitute a rich source of important historical material about the life of individual Jewish families in Europe during the 1930s, their experiences during the war and what happened to the survivors subsequently. The claim files are being retained so that historians may have access to them.

INTERNATIONAL COMMISSION FOR HOLOCAUST ERA INSURANCE CLAIMS

The International Commission for Holocaust Era Insurance Claims (ICHEIC) is headquartered in Washington, D.C. The Commission is chaired by former secretary of state Lawrence Eagleburger.

ICHEIC's main function is to act as the conduit for the payment of proceeds of unclaimed life insurance policies taken out by Jews in Europe before World War II to the original policyholders, where still alive, or to their descendants. In the vast majority of cases the original policyholders perished in the Holocaust and the proceeds of the life cover had never been paid out.

Four large European insurance companies have participated in the ICHEIC compensation scheme. On receipt of a claim ICHEIC attempts to match the name of the policyholder with the records of the relevant insurance company. Where a match is found the policyholder (or his/her descendants) enter into negotiation with the relevant insurance company with a view to reaching agreement as to whether a policy was in existence and, if so, the amount of the policy proceeds that should now be paid out. If agreement is reached, the funds are paid to the claimant and that is the end of the matter.

Where agreement between the claimant and the insurance company is not reached, and this can be because the insurance company maintains that there is no relevant policy or offers an amount that is unacceptable to the claimant, the dissatisfied claimant can lodge an appeal with ICHEIC. ICHEIC established a tribunal of some sixteen arbitrators located in about eight countries to determine appeals from claimants. The insurance companies and the claimants make written submissions on the issues and the appointed arbitrator makes his decision on the facts and arguments submitted by the parties.

Two problems regularly arise. First, several of the East European insurance companies were, during the 1930s, subsidiaries of the insurance companies participating in the ICHEIC scheme but were nationalised by their local governments after the war and records of the policies are no longer available. Secondly, many claimants possess no documents relating to the policies and do not know the amounts insured, the premiums that were paid or the number of years that the policy was in existence. In cases where it seems plausible that an insurance policy was in existence, but no further details can be found, the arbitrator may award the claimant an amount from a special humanitarian fund set up for this purpose. Where the existence of a policy is established, but there is no record of the amount of insurance cover, average values are paid out.

OTHER COMPENSATION SCHEMES

There are several other compensation schemes, the most well known being payments in respect of dormant Swiss bank accounts. Others involve compensation to slave labourers and to nationals of particular countries, e.g., Holland, who suffered as a result of the occupation.

A compensation scheme for victims of Nazi persecution who had assets in Palestinian banks as they then were, may soon become operative in Israel. Many refugees from the belligerent countries found a haven in Palestine and deposited funds in Palestinian banks before or in the early stages of World War II. As Palestine was then a British mandate the UK authorities seized the assets in Palestine of those refugees in the same way that they did in the United Kingdom. Many years after the end of the war the British Government repaid to the State of Israel the monies that had been seized. During the last few years a Knesset committee has been supervising an exercise to identify those who may have valid claims. In January 2005 the Knesset Committee stated that the State of Israel and five Israeli banks should return more than $30 million in assets held since World War II in the accounts of Holocaust victims to the victims or their heirs. Up to nine thousand people may be eligible for payments.

It is a tragedy that it has taken nearly sixty years after the end of the war for compensation to be paid, when few of the original owners of the assets are still alive. Nevertheless, for those now engaged in some small way in this sacred exercise, it is of comfort that restitution is now being made.

The high level of practical activity in this field during the past decade is an eloquent tribute to those who have tirelessly and persistently campaigned for justice over many decades on behalf of those who suffered in the war. Clemens Nathan has played an important role in this exercise and it is pleasing that his efforts, and those of many others, have had a successful outcome.

PRINCE HASSAN OF JORDAN

Towards an Ethic of Human Solidarity

An individual has not started living until he can rise above the narrow confines of his individualistic concerns to the broader concerns of all humanity. (Martin Luther King, Jr)

REFLECTING some months ago on the tragedy that perhaps more than any other has marked the beginning of our twenty-first century and shaped our attitudes towards one another, I expressed the hope, shared by millions, that never again will we see something as tragic as the billowing smoke that enveloped the collapse of the Twin Towers and all who were in them on 11 September, 2001. That horrendous and surreal sight should be remembered as a symbol not just of a heartbreaking day, but also of a tragic schism in humanity. I also expressed the hope that the Twin Towers will be replaced, not only by the exquisite towers of light that were first conceived, a year later, to fill the horrible void where they used to stand, but also by a common perception of the twin concepts of civilisation and culture. That would mean that we had finally risen above the hostile energies revealed on that day, to a higher plane of insight into the steps to be taken to ensure our shared future.

I believe it was Gandhi who counselled, 'You should not lose faith in humanity. Humanity is an ocean: if a few drops become dirty, the ocean does not become dirty.'

And there are many encouraging signs. Recent years have witnessed a surge in peoples' movements globally, sometimes in support of or in conjunction with governments, sometimes in opposition to them, to improve the lot of the ordinary man. The demands for a fairer system of debt relief, the several 'velvet' revolutions, the emergence of citizens' movements and assemblies, and the growing focus on global poverty spring immediately to mind, whilst the global response to the tsunami disaster was incontrovertible evidence of the possibility of man's *humanity* to man. Simultaneously we have seen a mushrooming of bridge-building initiatives between peoples of all nationalities and faiths, many of them in response to 9/11, designed to educate, build trust and foster peaceful coexistence.

In my own small sphere, I am proud to be a member of the Parents' Circle, bringing together families who have lost their loved ones on both sides in the Middle East conflict, in a mutual support network; a founding member, together with John Marks, of Search for Common Ground, of the Partners in Humanity programme which aims to address mutual fear and suspicion between the West, especially the US, and the Muslim world based on perceived and real injustices, inequalities and stereotypes; a patron, founding member and member of numerous interfaith and humanitarian organisations, including the Independent Commission for International Humanitarian Issues, Rights and Humanity, the World Conference of Religions for Peace and the Club of Rome, to mention but a few.

Yet it would be abject foolishness to think that all is well with our world. Never before has man wielded so much power over his destiny, or indeed over the destiny of the very planet itself, yet modern man is at peace neither with himself, his brothers, nor with his environment. It is crucial that we now ensure that wisdom and foresight prevail over the rule of war, crisis management and (blind) technological advancement.

In my view the challenges faced by contemporary society can only be met by placing human welfare at the centre of national and international policy making. Or to quote Martin Luther King Jr: 'We must rapidly begin the shift from a "thing-oriented" society to a "person-oriented"' society. When machines and computers, profit motives and property rights are considered more important than people, the giant triplets of racism, materialism and militarism are incapable of being conquered.'

It is this issue which has shaped my own personal vision for the future, a vision which I have tried, over the past three decades or so to transform into a tangible reality. Action based on humanitarianism, hinged on an ethic of human solidarity; the creation of a culture of participation and a culture of peace; dialogue and its humanising aspect; knowledge, innovation and imagination: these should become our guiding principles.

Crucial to the above are the upholding of civil liberties, observance of the rule of law, by state and non-state actors alike, and protection of the human habitat, inclusive of water, energy and the human environment.

Sadly, in stark contrast to the above, leadership today in all too many parts of the world appears to operate within a matrix of fear and isolation, resulting in unilateral militarism and cultural disengagement. America's 9/11 and Spain's 11/3 have become symbols of an all-encompassing sense of global insecurity, leading at national level to often extreme anti-terrorist measures which risk both curtailing national freedoms and exacerbating the very problems they are supposed to solve (fundamentalisms and phobias), whilst at international level, as in the 'war on terror', prompting crisis/panic driven responses which, though multilateral in ideology, are unilateral in reality, and frequently inimical to sound international and humanitarian law.

The great issues of our time affect us all and can only be confronted multilaterally, through the combined action of governments, international and regional organisations, and, most important of all, the people immediately affected. However, global problems do not necessarily have global solutions. Every region and every culture has its own specificity. While some of today's most pressing problems and threats to world peace – the population explosion, the deteriorating environment, AIDS, poverty, terrorism, the proliferation of weapons of mass destruction, to mention a few – require the cooperation of governments as well as other organisations and individuals, their particular solution may call for differing treatment. Thus it is vital that we recognise that even global issues require flexibility in approach. But our future depends not only on finding technical solutions to the problems we face, but also on reaching a consensus about the ethical basis of our response.

The question confronting us today is whether we can move from a culture of war to a culture of peace.

Sadly, in some quarters it would appear that the lesson gleaned from 9/11 is that one must '... go on the offence and stay on the offence'.[1] Simultaneously, as Andrew J. Bacevich has pointed out, high-tech warfare and surgical strikes have enabled a belief in an acceptable 'coercive diplomacy' – war, by any other name – in sharp contradiction to the prevalent, and in my opinion wholly correct view following the two world wars that to those on the ground, armed conflict, however waged or named, is nothing but 'barbarism,

1 *The Normalization of War*, Andrew J. Bacevich, TomDispatch.com, 21.4.05 (President Bush quoted in).

brutality, ugliness and sheer waste ... an orgy of destruction that devoured guilty and innocent alike';[2] evidence of the failure of diplomacy.

Few if any in authority seem to question the wisdom of an open-ended global war on terror; rather, military might is the order of the day. Yet, I doubt the validity of such an approach. We need to examine carefully those situations on the ground that terrorists find useful to their causes and consider whether we are addressing them wholeheartedly and effectively, ignoring them, or in some cases even conniving at them.

In this context it was interesting to note the results of Robert A. Pape's research into the motivation behind suicide attacks. Analysing the results of his database of suicide bombings and attacks around the globe from 1980–2003, he states that while religion may be used as a tool in recruiting, there is far less of a connection between suicide terrorism and religious fundamentalism than most people think. Rather, 'what nearly all suicide terrorist attacks actually have in common is a specific secular and strategic goal: to compel modern democracies to withdraw military forces from territory that the terrorists consider to be their homeland.'[3]

The time is long overdue for the construction of a peace culture that employs pragmatic and effective methods to foresee and avoid crises and eliminate strife and offers people tangible proof of the viability of peace. Although agreements and treaties have long been recognised as essential instruments for regulating the conduct of states, far less attention has been given to a more comprehensive approach engaging individuals – the citizens of those same states. I am reminded here of the constitution of Unesco which states emphatically that 'since war first begins in the minds of men, it is in the minds of men that defences for peace should be built.' This entails a reconsideration of the meaning usually understood by the term 'security'. Security must not be restricted to its military definition; for social and economic security, culture and identity are also a prerequisite of stability. We cannot talk of violence, terrorism and security without talking of root causes. We ignore the importance of soft security at our peril.

In this context, we must become more sensitized to the consequences of the insidious weight of pessimism that is the result of exclusion and helplessness. All people have the right to a dignified life, free from terror and despair, and states must be encouraged to respect and enforce basic human rights if

2 Ibid.

3 Robert A. Pape, *Blowing up an Assumption*, NYT, 18 May, 2005.

their citizens are to avoid political, ideological or other forms of exploitation. Equally important is the development of a global initiative employing innovative combinations of policies, inclusive of economic, technological and cultural resources, to stimulate the evolution of a culture of participation amongst all elements of society and of a genuine civil society, to eradicate poverty and exclusion and to advance mechanisms for reconciliation.

Peace is not the mere absence of war. Peace is not a nothing which happens; rather it is a something which must be actively created. It derives from the teaching and taking of responsibilities; education for ethics, legislation for justice and post-war special processes. We have laws of war; is it not time to introduce a law of peace?

In this context I should like to emphasise the importance of working *for* something universal, rather than merely against the specifics of various phobias. Culture inclusive of human rights is security. The key is understanding and respect for human dignity. Neglected elements of society are easy prey for extremist organizations. Particularly at risk are the young, who presently make up the majority of the developing world's population. It is the recognition of this fact which gives us one possible starting point – the promotion of a global peace culture among young people. If the culture of peace can become the norm that permeates all aspects of their lives, it will represent a high-yield investment in our common future. Violence and terror are often born out of political and economic despair since extremism thrives when people believe they have no future. Peace is born of hope. Surely we can give our children the very thing that they symbolise to us: hope for the future.

And here I would like to mention the invaluable work of the Seeds of Peace[4] programme which brings teenagers from regions of conflict together to dispel myths and fears and learn peacemaking skills.

Turning for a moment to my region (the Greater Middle East), we are presently at a crossroads in our history. These times may be viewed by future generations as an era when the region finally began to move towards establishing the conditions for sustainable peace, sustainable development, justice and democracy for all alike. Or, they may see these as days presaged by yet more false dawns; days when we wasted opportunities and squandered our chances. Time is of the essence, as the authors of the latest UN-sponsored Arab Human Development Report made clear, expressing their hope for an

4 http://www.seedsofpeace.org.

'historic, peaceful redistribution of power within Arab societies',[5] and their fear that if the overwhelming desire for people's participation is not met, the next few years may be punctured by 'chaotic upheavals'.[6]

In order to ensure the smooth transition from non-participatory systems to democratic models, our part of the world, as I said in a recent Statement to the US Senate for Foreign Relations Committee, requires as many initiatives for reform and development as can be imagined, both from within and from the outside. For the reality is that these areas, variously described as the Middle East North Africa Region, the Greater Middle East, West Asia, or South Asia are in fact regions only in name. Their institutions function poorly, multilateralism barely exists. But to succeed, reform initiatives must be undertaken in partnership, not patronage, and all importantly, be culturally attuned and inclusive of civil society. This area, which for a number of years I have referred to as the 'Arc of Crisis', extending from the Maghreb in North Africa to the Arabian Sea, and from Sudan to the North of the Caspian Sea, is simultaneously the most populous, the poorest and the most volatile part of the world today. It is also home to the greatest energy reserves. And the equation is simple: instability pushes up the price of oil, the revenues from oil are spent on weapons, and petro-politics, rather than anthropolicies yet again become the guiding force. But a new thinking is emerging in the region, in its widest sense, perhaps indeed across the developing world, in which the traditional drive for strategic and economic dominance have no place, no more does 'preventive war'.

The scientific and technological revolution, as well as the economic globalisation process, have opened up huge opportunities, which were not available before. They have also opened people's eyes. What is needed for the development of global peace is imaginative leaps into non-traditional combinations of policies.

The schisms in the world today are so numerous, the inequities so stark that today, more than any other time in the past, an ethic of human solidarity and a new international humanitarian order are needed. A universal respect for human dignity that brooks no exceptions must be brought back into the consciousness of the international community.

There are inherently universal values that we all share, irrespective of our particular tradition. Whilst there may be different cultures, all have contrib-

5 UNDP Arab Human Development Report 2003.
6 Ibid.

uted to universalism. Our common humanity therefore must be our starting point as we learn to live with multiple perceptions of the truth.

Yet, despite what we may call the universality of universalism, there are still, alas, too many unacceptables remaining in our world: an unacceptable level of illiteracy; an unacceptable lack of women's empowerment; an unacceptable North–South divide, with the rich getting richer and the poor poorer; an unacceptable level of inequality; unacceptable demands on the environment due to, among other things, an unacceptable level of pollution exacerbated by an unacceptable lack of international agreement on policy. The list goes on.

Dealing with such unacceptables, therefore, is one of the main challenges. A Common Minimum Agenda to tackle these and associated problems is essential for the well-being of the people of our planet. It could include the following: recognising the sovereignty of the citizen, controlling population growth, economic growth with equity, restructuring institutions of governance, redefining the role of the State, social development emphasising common culture. The bulk of the agenda appears to be domestic, some of it is regional. Both are essential to take the citizens of our respective regions from the present state of unmitigated and pernicious poverty, degradation of human dignity, poor quality of life and most important, the severe problems of governance which they face. The citizens must therefore come together within their own countries, as well as regionally, to work towards better governance.

Simultaneously, it is time we developed effectively the Conference on Security and Cooperation for which I have been calling for many years, to promote and preserve peace and harmony between the communities and countries of the region and contribute to socio-economic, as well as political stability. Issues on the agenda would range from the promotion of a WMD-free zone, the taking of concrete steps to address both state and non-state terrorism, to the establishment of a Community of Water and Energy, and a socio-economic road map geared to human well-being and peace-making at the grass roots level. Issues such as resources, water and energy, the environment, refugees and arms control are by their very nature transnational and must therefore be addressed collectively. This includes not only the regional players, but the international community as well.

And there are some encouraging signs.

The European Union has not only recognised the linkages between development, poverty and conflict, and the role of development cooperation in conflict prevention, but has called for conflict prevention and peace-building to become a central part of development policy. And I am particularly encouraged by the development of a Global Marshall Plan Initiative by the Club of Rome, over which I have the honour to preside. The plan offers a viable method, complementing both the Millennium Development Goals and the EU Development Programmes, based on the core concepts of co-financing and the establishment of mutually agreed economic, social, cultural and ecological standards, for stimulating worldwide sustainable socio-economic development.

But I counsel again, if economic and political decisions are made without reference to human culture – and especially the transparent fostering of human dignity and self-worth for *all* human beings – then they cannot succeed in improving people's lives and they lose credibility.

Our actions, whether in developing or developed countries, impact upon us all, and our future depends not only on finding technical solutions but also on reaching a consensus about the ethical basis of our response – a universal code of conduct and an ethic of human solidarity.

Writing some fifteen years ago, Hans Kung emphasised that the world would not survive without a world ethic, that there would be 'no world peace without peace between the religions', and 'no peace without dialogue between the religions'.[7] Dialogue is an effective tool in building bridges of cooperation between representatives and people of different cultures and faiths by unmasking stereotypes and clarifying misconceptions. It not only reveals hitherto unsuspected areas of agreement, but encourages the holders of conflicting opinions to recognise that neither side has a monopoly on the truth; rather, the two share the truth between them and each has a vision which is incomplete without the other.

We have come a long way in the field of interfaith relations, though, sadly, at the present time, phobias of all kinds are again on the increase. Some thirty years ago, when I first embarked on seeking to 'Meet and to Greet',[8] interfaith relations were dominated by three fears: fear of the 'other'; fear of the folks back home; and, in my region, fear of peace – ironic, when it should only ever be fear of war. In continuing efforts to encourage dialogue, two

7 Hans Kung, *Global Responsibility: In Search of a New World Ethic*, SCM Press, 1990.

8 Kenneth Cragg, *To Meet and To Greet*, Epworth Press, London 1992.

years ago, in cooperation with Professor Ihsan Dogramaci, president of the Hacettepe University Foundation and president and chairman of the Board of Trustees of Bilkent University, we founded the Parliament of Cultures to promote understanding amongst different religions and cultures and to enhance dialogue between their thinkers and intellectuals, whilst, in Jordan, I had the honour of founding the Royal Institute for Inter-Faith Studies in 1994. Originally established as a centre for the study of Christian and Jewish traditions in the Arab world, it has since broadened its scope to include cultural or civilisational interaction world-wide, recognising that regionality can no longer afford isolation in the contemporary world.

Sadly, at the current time, I see a three-way Venn diagram of extremists (be they Muslim, Christian or Jewish extremists, American, Israeli, Arab, or any other kind), all of which fuel each other, leading to greater polarisation. What is required is corresponding circles of moderates to shore up the middle ground. I believe that the concept of centrism – *wasatiyya* – which was the headline topic at the recent Assembly of the Arab Thought Forum in Bahrain, is an important one not just in theoretical terms, but in terms of a practical application which can motivate and mobilise civil society.

The whipping up of phobias, the carrying out of terrorist action comes from the minority, but with vast potential support to draw on, if what I would like to call the 'coalition of the sane' – those of us who are part of the mainstream – remain in the shadow. We must be prepared now to step forward, yet it is crucial that we also become a 'coalition of the coherent' adopting policies informed by wisdom and experience.

And today I call on all faith leaders to exercise their responsibility towards the creation of world peace. This does not imply indifference to transcendental concerns, nor a need for any form of syncretism, but simply a recognition that hate-speech, incitement to violence, and even indifference to the plight of other human beings are unacceptable to any true adherent of our various religions. East and West, South and North need to rediscover the ecumenical way between fanaticism for truth and forgetfulness of truth.

All our religions, and secular humanism too, call for action, not inaction, in the face of oppression, tyranny, violence, and suffering. All our cultures treasure art, music, dance, the power of creativity and the values of justice, mercy, wisdom, courage and benevolence. We have these things in common. We cannot allow crimes of omission to escape through loopholes of international law and for international apathy to decimate our cultures until they are no longer capable of considering values because they are too busy considering how at all costs to avoid their bodily demise.

My concern for the future of humanity manifests itself in global caring and sharing; in building global participatory democracy; in shifting from imposition, force and violence to a culture of respect, dialogue and mutual understanding. Economic structures will fail if not built on democratic values and ideals, and on human rights. They should accommodate religious, linguistic and historical values. They should respect diversity in all its aspects and manifestations. Imported culture cannot be imposed with imported commodities. The challenge facing society is how to build peace and foster development in a rapidly changing world. To be sustainable, development must be founded on justice. Justice, in turn, depends on the framework of ethical references called democracy.

I participate; therefore I am. If I do not participate, I do not exist as a human being, let alone as a citizen. This is how democracy deteriorates into market research, oligarchy, plutocracy, bureaucracy and technocracy. Peace, development and democracy should be built up by education, not by force; they should not be regarded as a gift. Education is the key to liberty. If we wish to reduce the social disparities that are a source of conflict, if we wish to improve the quality of life, if we wish to guarantee food and education for all citizens, if we wish to provide employment and mitigate poverty, then we must stop paying the price of war and pay the price of peace.

Great achievements are almost invariably inspired by a great imagination that is informed by both heart and mind. This is true of all the explorations and innovations that have opened new horizons for humanity – whether in land, sea, space, the human psyche, the gene, the computer with all its accessories and so on. Building on knowledge and the inspiration of the greats of all cultures, it is imagination that leads the way. It is its intensity that consoles us, moves us, sustains our hopes and drives us on to change our world to a better place, especially at times of crisis. I do not think we are mere dreamers if we invoke imagination to combat evil – violence, aggression, man's inhumanity to man and man's cruelty to his environment. Nor if we summon imagination to forge a moral code of conduct based on universal values and, more to the point, attempt to uphold it at all times.

I have worked for over thirty years to help create a world in which dialogue, cooperation and peace are so commonplace that they excite no comment; but the world I seek still eludes me. Today I invite you to join in my quest. Together, let us pursue the vision of a world beyond discrimination, in which each and every individual has the right and the opportunity to develop without prejudice, intolerance or oppression of any kind. Let us hold sacrosanct Franklin D. Roosevelt's four freedoms – freedom from fear and from want, freedom of belief and of expression. Let us add our voices to the call for a human charter, allied to the ethic of transnational human cooperation, to foster the conviction that the proper focus of politics, economics and security is the individual human being. For however the collectivity may be expressed – as community or culture, civilisation, society or state – it is composed of individuals, each of unique value, with unique needs, abilities and aspirations.

The great poet of Islam Jalalu'l-din Rumi, in his poem 'The Burden of Existence', put it beautifully: 'I am like a jaded camel: the saddle of free will has sorely bruised my back.'[9]

Yet we have free will and it is my firm belief that we must accept with joy the bumps and bruises along the path and continue to strive for a better world for all people wherever they may be, for the sake of humanity.

---

9 Jalalu'l-din Rumi, *The Burden of Existence,* Mathnavi IV.

K. HANNAH HOLTSCHNEIDER

Jean Améry
Cultural Exile, Homelessness and Jewish Solidarity

BORN in 1912 as Hans Mayer (Jean Améry), an assimilated Austrian Jew, was, according to his own account, forced to 'inhabit' his Jewishness when confronted with the impact of the Nuremberg Laws after the annexation of Austria to the German *Reich* in 1938. Améry's home was the German cultural context, shaped by the intellectual environment of Vienna of the 1920s and 1930s. Fleeing Austria in 1938, Améry sought asylum in Antwerp and joined a political resistance movement. He was arrested and imprisoned first in Gurs, France, then in Breendonk, Belgium, where he was tortured. When it was discovered that he was Jewish, he was deported to Auschwitz from which a death march brought him to Bergen-Belsen. Liberated, Améry chose Belgium as his residence, making writing his profession. He committed suicide in 1978.

Améry first gained recognition in Germany when he began to write explicitly for a German audience in the mid-1960s. Having refused to travel to Germany and to write for German speakers since the end of the war, Améry followed the invitation of journalist and poet Helmut Heissenbüttel to write about his experiences of the Holocaust and to read the resulting essays to a German radio audience before publishing these as a book. From 1964 onwards, Améry wrote for an almost exclusively German (speaking) audience and undertook a number of lecturing tours through Germany and Austria.

Jean Améry, his pen name, is a direct translation of Hans Mayer, Jean being the French equivalent of Hans (short for Johannes) as well as a reference to his 'intellectual mentor' Jean-Paul Sartre, and Améry being a French-sounding anagram of Mayer. Améry is best known for his autobiographical writings which provide an important commentary on the post-war West German political scene, although he also published fiction, yet never gained much acclaim for this work.

This essay aims to explore, firstly, how Améry located himself in the context of German–Jewish relations, and how he interpreted his attachment to German culture and to Jews. Secondly, I am interested in the implications of this self-definition for discussions of contemporary Jewish identity and current Jewish–non-Jewish relations in Germany. Much has been written on Améry and his relationship to German culture and to Judaism, and his name appears in many discussions of the Holocaust and post-war German–Jewish relations. As Jean-Michel Chaumont observed, Améry's identity as Jew and German was based not only on the destruction of his self-understanding in Auschwitz, but equally on his desire to contribute to a 'reconciliation' between victimisers and victims of the Holocaust.[1] Given that this is the case, how can Améry's thought speak to current encounters between Jews and non-Jews in Germany and contribute to the formulation of Jewish identities in this changing context?

Améry explored the effect of the Holocaust on his life, interrogating his identity as 'German' and 'Jew', as neither and yet forced to be both, particularly in his autobiographical collection of essays entitled *At the Mind's Limits: Contemplations by a Survivor on Auschwitz and Its Realities*. German was the only language in which he felt 'at home', while at the same time he had been violently exiled from this cultural–linguistic context.

Améry expressed his Jewishness in negative terms, having encountered it as a personal reality only through his victimisation and brutalisation by other Germans, and being unable, before or after the Holocaust, to find a positive attachment to Judaism and Jewish culture. Améry felt trapped by his Jewishness which was forced on him by being a victim of the Holocaust. Yet, at the same time, he voluntarily adopted it as his self-definition and affirmed his Jewishness as an identification of solidarity with Jews all over the world and in particular with those in the State of Israel. Drawing on Existentialist philosophy to elaborate on his position, Améry seems to have fallen victim to one of Existentialism's key concepts, 'bad faith', i.e. 'coming

1 Chaumont, Jean-Michel, 'Geschichtliche Verantwortung und menschliche Würde bei Jean Améry', in *Über Jean Améry*, ed. Irene Heidelberger-Leonard, Beiträge zur neueren Literaturgeschichte 102, (Heidelberg: Universitätsverlag Winter, 1990), p. 32.

to construe himself as he is for others'.[2] Trapped in his 'German–Jewish' dilemma, Améry appeared locked into 'bad faith' regardless of his assertions that he chose these identifications voluntarily. He often lamented his feeling of being determined by the accidental fact of his birth and upbringing which, with its destruction by the Nazis, left him with a sense of longing without ever again being able to 'belong', i.e., having a home that is acknowledged by society as rightfully one's own and, when distant from this home, both in time (childhood) and geography, having the ability and right to 'long' for it. This contradiction in his own approach can hardly have escaped Améry's attention. His writings explore themes of 'loss' and 'alienation', his work reverberates with Existentialist terminology. Why, then, did Améry apparently fail to follow Existentialist advice to keep 'reinventing' himself, to shed 'old' attachments and to emancipate himself from the notion that birth, *Heimat* and society have the ultimate power to determine who he is? Or did he liberate himself? Was this 'trapped' existence one that aspired to the best Existentialist ways of living in the world and for others?

Reflecting on his first reading of the Nuremberg Laws, Améry claimed that these appeared to clarify a situation of which he had been dimly aware.[3] Améry's sense of a society which was his natural home, linguistically and intellectually, was irreparably destroyed. His writings suggest that, from 1938 onwards, all he had taken to be rightfully his own he saw as no longer valid.[4] Reflecting on this situation as a refugee in Belgium he writes:

> I was excluded from the fate of the German community and thus from its language. 'Enemy bomber' – fine; but for me these were the German bombers that were laying the cities of England in ruins, and not the flying fortresses of the Americans, which were attending to the same business in Germany. The meaning of every German word changed for us, and finally, whether we resisted or not, our mother tongue became just as inimical as the one they spoke around us.[5]

2 Cooper, David E., *Existentialism*, Introducing Philosophy 8 (Oxford et al.: Blackwell, 1999), p. 117.

3 Cf. Beckermann, Ruth, 'Unter der Bank gelesen: Jean Améry und Österreich', in *Jean Améry (Hans Maier)*, ed. Stephan Steiner (Frankfurt am Main: Stroemfeld, 1996), pp. 176ff.

4 Cf. Rosenfeld, Sidney, 'Gegen die Unmoral der Geschichte: Jean Amérys Kampf um die Identität', *Tribüne*, 93 (1985), p. 110.

5 Améry, Jean, *At the Mind's Limits: Contemplations by a Survivor on Auschwitz and Its Realities* (Bloomington: Indiana University Press, 1980), p. 53.

A language is validated by the community that owns it. But the reverse can also be asserted, that a language creates a community. According to Améry, who found his interpretation validated by Sartre, one who is excluded from such a community not only loses the rights of social belonging, but also the ability to interpret the world with the language of the community which excluded the individual.[6] And yet, in contrast to Améry, Sartre also argued for the power of the individual to transcend society's definitions by continually shaping and reshaping one's own identity. Améry's life and work rely on his access to German language and culture. He referred to Thomas Mann's saying 'Wherever I am is German culture' as follows,

> The German-Jewish Auschwitz prisoner could not have made such a bold assertion, even if by chance he had been a Thomas Mann. He could not claim German culture as his possession, because his claim found no sort of social justification. Among the émigrés a tiny minority was able to constitute itself as German culture, even if there was not exactly a Thomas Mann among them. In Auschwitz, however, the isolated individual had to relinquish all of German culture, including Dürer and Reger, Gryphius and Trakl, to even the lowest SS man.[7]

However, his work appears actively to subvert his exclusion from German as his mother tongue, essential for his identity formation and yet denied him by the German cultural community. By continuing to use German as his own language, he uses it in a sense against himself and against itself, i.e., against the wider community of German speakers who had expelled him and did not invite him back as one of their own. And in doing so he forced himself and his audience to confront the destruction of his identity.

Améry identifies *Heimat* as 'security', a context which can be taken for granted. He perceived the fact of being violently expelled from his home by representatives of the society he identified with and then having to live in a different cultural context as causing the irretrievable loss of his entire cultural system of reference. Non-Jewish Germans who voluntarily went into exile could claim that they were the 'real' representatives of German culture,

6 Cf. Altounian, Janine, 'Jean Améry legt Zeugnis ab über Hans Mayer, den seines Namens, seiner Sprache, seines In-der-Welt-Seins Beraubten', in *Jean Améry, der Schriftsteller*, ed. Irene Heidelberger-Leonard/Hans Höller, Stuttgarter Arbeiten zur Germanistik 385, Unterreihe Salzburger Beiträge 39 (Stuttgart: Heinz, 2000), p. 127.

7 Améry, *At the Mind's Limits*, p. 8.

since German society had not taken away their right to identify as German. Améry's violent and irreversible exclusion from German society, and hence from the interpretive context of the German language and culture, threw him into a sense of isolation (*Einsamkeit*) which, throughout his life, he was not able to replace with a renewed attachment to any community. Jews with a strong affiliation to Judaism as a religious and cultural community had a sense of belonging independent of the wider linguistic and social community of Germany and Austria with which they also shared a cultural heritage. When the Nazis violently severed the social ties of these Jews with Germany, such Jews were able to retain their individual, social and communal identities, since these were still validated by a community to which they already had belonged and felt attached before the rise of the Nazis.[8] Améry and other assimilated Jews in Germany had completely identified with German culture and society and felt that they could not resort to another communal identification which would keep alive their sense of belonging. Without any community on whose solidarity Améry could rely despite his expulsion from German society and culture, he felt completely disowned.

> We, however, had not lost our country, but had to realize that it had never been ours. For us, whatever was linked with this land and its people was an existential misunderstanding. What we believed to have been our first love was, as they said there, racial disgrace. What we thought had constituted our nature – was it ever anything else but mimicry?[9]

Améry had lost not only his identity, but also the means to express this loss in his own language. His mother tongue, German, and in particular the dialect of his native Styria, no longer felt his own, having become the language of the Nazis, who were legitimated both by German society and by the international community as the representatives of Germany. Améry's sense of the lack of public accountability for the Jews' exclusion from German society, or for their subsequent murder, and the persistence of publicly-expressed German antisemitism, contributed to his inability to reclaim country, culture and language fully as his own, while he was also not able or willing to substitute another for these.

Améry's interpretation of his Jewishness was influenced by Sartre's influential book *Réflexions sur la question juive*, which emphasises that non-Jewish

8 Cf. Beckermann, 'Unter der Bank gelesen', p. 176.

9 Améry, *At the Mind's Limits*, p. 50.

society determines the identity of Jews to the extent that Jews themselves try to conform to antisemitic stereotypes.[10] Améry did not receive a Jewish education and, although he was aware that his own family was regarded by others as Jewish, his own Jewishness became significant only with the application of the Nuremberg Laws to Austria in 1938. Believing that a positive identification with a culture and community cannot be acquired later in life, but is transmitted early in one's childhood, he connected only negative associations with his Jewishness, such as having been made Jewish by the same law that excluded him permanently from the community of Germans and therefore from ownership of German culture. Améry suggests that, from the time he first read the Nuremberg Laws, he felt like 'a dead man on leave',[11] characterising his identity as a Jew also as being 'not a non-Jew'. In this sense, his Jewishness was like an illness which had overtaken him, and from which he could not recover.[12] This 'illness' was brought on by the fact that society ceased to validate Améry's identity as German. Thus, his private perception of himself was validated by his acceptance of the notion of identity as a social category. In his view, only if one's identity is recognised by a social group is it viable.

> Society, concretized in the National Socialist German state, which the world recognized absolutely as the legitimate representative of the German people, had just made me formally and beyond any question a Jew, or rather it had given a new dimension to what I had already known earlier, but which at the time was of no great consequence to me, namely, that I was a Jew.[13]

Améry contends that the number tattooed on his arm tells more about his Jewishness than any religious text or tradition could. This tattoo stamped a forced identity onto him which he felt he had no mandate or power to define himself, but which he also could not relinquish.

10 Cf. Heidelberger-Leonard, Irene, 'Jean Amérys "Meisterliche Wanderjahre"', in *Überlebt und unterwegs: Jüdische Displaced Persons im Nachkriegsdeutschland*, ed. Fritz Bauer Institut, Jahrbuch 1997 zur Geschichte und Wirkung des Holocaust (Frankfurt am Main/New York: Campus Verlag, 1997), p. 298.

11 Améry, *At the Mind's Limits*, p. 86.

12 Cf. Altounian, 'Jean Améry legt Zeugnis ab über Hans Mayer . . .', p. 128.

13 Améry, *At the Mind's Limits*, p. 85.

> To be a Jew, that meant for me, from this moment on, to be a dead man on leave, someone to be murdered, who only by chance was not yet where he properly belonged; and so it has remained, in many variations, in various degrees of intensity, until today.[14]

Jean Améry insisted on being a 'catastrophe Jew', someone who draws on the murder of European Jews and the possibilities this stands for in terms of Jewish experience, and makes this the basis for his Jewishness. Identified as a Jew by the society which expelled him as well as by the international community, he decided to accept this identification and at the same time to rebel against it, struggling to find himself in the concepts that were forced on him.[15] Améry's writings express the tension between forced identification and chosen identity, as Jew and German, mainly in direct confrontation with West German society – his native Austria possibly being too close for him to endure this tension continually.

It is here that his 'Existentialist' stance is most poignantly expressed, as well as his moral voice, shaped by a philosophical position indebted to the Enlightenment notions of 'progress' and 'reason'. Choosing consciously what had been forced on him (Jewishness) and also what had been denied him (German language and culture), Améry adopted the position of a moral voice towards West German society, hoping for a resolution of this tension in a reconciliation with the society which had brutalised and expelled him. His *ressentiments*, directed chiefly at Germany and the nature of its social-political developments after the war, express his sense of frustration and anger at a society which apparently wanted to reach for the future without a consciousness of the past. *Ressentiment*, a French word, resembling the English 'resentment', is also used in German, and refers to a strong emotional opposition, often connected with notions of revenge and bitterness. Yet, while this is also the case with Améry, according to Chaumont, he moved beyond the impasse of such a situation and attempted to use his *ressentiments* to call for the need of confronting and ultimately overcoming the injury caused by Nazi Germany to Jews.[16]

True to Sartre's characterisation of patterns of Jewish identity in non-Jewish societies, and in an embodiment of Existentialist attempts to escape

14 Ibid. p. 86.

15 Cf. Rosenfeld, 'Gegen die Unmoral der Geschichte', p. 12.

16 Cf. Chaumont, 'Geschichtliche Verantwortung und menschliche Würde bei Jean Améry', p. 32.

foreign determination of the self, Améry's identification as a Jew was a rebellion against his imposed Jewishness with all the negative stereotypes this entailed. With this voluntary adoption of the Jewishness forced on him he intended to force the society of victimisers to realise their error and change their perception of him[17] – that he does so with texts written in German heightens the rebelliousness of his identification.

Améry's Jewishness also expressed his solidarity with all Jews who are threatened, in particular in the State of Israel, and, as commentators have suggested, by extension, his solidarity with all who are persecuted and whose human rights are violated.[18] Here Améry's stance is comparable to that of other Jews who have been deeply affected by the Holocaust such as Elie Wiesel, René Cassin and Gerhard Riegner.

Yet, rising antisemitism on the political Left in Germany and the 'normalisation' of German society, a society which did not respond to Améry's frequently expressed *ressentiments*, led to his sense of failure as a writer and political critic. Understanding his autobiographical writings as expressing not only his personal experience but also as documents of contemporary history, his final suicide attempt in 1978 appears thus also as a logical consequence of his writing. His suicide attempts (the first in Breendonk after he was tortured, in order not to give away his wife's address in hiding, the second in 1965) succeeded in 1978 when he took an overdose of tranquillisers in a hotel in Salzburg, Austria. He felt that his efforts to confront and reconcile had failed, and that therefore his identity was ever more defined by what Nazi Germany had imposed on him, rather than by his ability rebelliously to transcend this societal identification. To commit suicide remained an option of asserting himself in his freedom of choosing his own identity.

Whether he regained control in other than a personal sense is arguable, given that today his work and death are not widely remembered in Germany. His suicide, instead of signifying rebellion and liberation, could also be read as resignation. His warnings about the antisemitic politics of the German Left having gone unheard, his 'mission' failed, Améry saw himself as a redundant person. He had begun his career as a writer for a German context only in his fifties, and felt that he had come too late and accordingly had failed as a professional writer. Commentators have repeatedly noted that

17 Cf. ibid. p. 45.

18 Heidelberger-Leonard, 'Jean Amérys "Meisterliche Wanderjahre"', in *Überlebt und unterwegs*, p. 298.

many German intellectuals appeared to treat Améry as an 'institutionalised conscience', as a 'professional Jew' one could call on in times of distress, but whose message otherwise could go unnoticed.[19]

However, Améry's writings have impacted on the first generation of non-Jewish Germans born after the war who listened to this Jewish voice in its commentary on and criticism of political and social developments in West Germany. While novelists such as Alfred Andersch and Ingeborg Bachmann were inspired to works of their own by Améry's texts,[20] and literary critics and political scientists have regularly commented on Améry's works, and even increased their output of articles and books on him in the 1990s, his thought does not appear to have had a lasting influence beyond a specialist academic audience. Améry is no longer in fashion, his faith in Enlightenment ideals being overtaken by post-modern critiques of such values.[21]

Beyond Améry's moral message to German society vis-à-vis Jews, his writings could yet become a reference point for investigations of the impact of the Holocaust on Jews who were and are biographically attached to German (speaking) cultural contexts. Améry, caught between two impossibilities, and his resulting 'identity in crisis', can help us to understand the ways in which history, memory and identity are connected in language and culture. Notions of *Heimat* and belonging, central to Améry's writings, are regularly posed as issues in contemporary Germany, a society which is struggling to come to terms with the fact that it is an immigration country, and particularly for Jews. While his moral message about the need for a reconciliation between victimisers and victims of the Holocaust through a confrontation of Nazi definitions of insiders and outsiders still has currency, its attachment to the notions of 'reason' and 'progress' makes it a questionable basis for debates about German and Jewish identities today.

However, the tensions contained in Améry's self-understanding lend themselves to explorations which push the boundaries of his thought to an inclusion of post-modern notions of identity formation and ideas of belong-

---

19 Cf. Heidelberger-Leonard, Irene, 'Jean Améry's Selbstverständnis als Jude', in *Über Jean Améry*, p. 25; Brandenburg, Rainer, 'Zwischen Morosität und Moral: Jean Améry im Spiegel der Kritik', *Modern Austrian Literature*, 23:1 (1990), pp. 69-84.

20 Cf. for example Andersch's novel *Efraim* as response to Améry's essay on his Jewishness and Bachmann's story *Drei Wege zum See* as reflection on Améry's essay on torture (cf. Heidelberger-Leonard, 'Jean Améry's Selbstverständnis als Jude', p. 17).

21 Cf. Heidelberger-Leonard, Irene, '*Lefeu oder der Abbruch – summa der eigenen Existenz?*' in *Jean Améry, der Schriftsteller*, p. 8.

ing, which – in contrast to Améry's perception of post-modernism – do not need to lead to an abandonment of responsibility for the humaneness of society. Examining the dilemmas, conflicts and choices confronted by this individual of such extraordinary intellectual lucidity can assist current scholars of Jewish–non-Jewish relations to sharpen their categories of interpretation of the 'German-Jewish symbiosis' which, in post-war Germany, has also been described as a 'negative symbiosis'.[22] Améry's 'identity in conflict' could contribute to the ongoing debate about the possibilities of being German and Jewish in a post-Holocaust context.

22 Diner, Dan, 'Negative Symbiosis: Germans and Jews After Auschwitz', in *Reworking the Past: Hitler, the Holocaust, and the Historians' Debate*, ed. Peter Baldwin (Boston: Beacon Press, 1990), pp. 251–261.

EDWARD KESSLER

Israel and Jewish–Christian Relations

It is a great privilege to be invited to contribute to a Festschrift in honour of Clemens Nathan, who has devoted much of his adult life to improving understanding between religions and between people of religion. Although he was forced to flee Germany with his parents in 1936, Clemens has spent many years building bridges and fighting intolerance. His many friends in the Church of England, the Roman Catholic Church and the Muslim community helped him to look at religion and human rights as something everyone needs to know more about and to encourage better understanding of other people's traditions and cultures.

Hans Kung has aptly pointed out that peace between religions is the key to peace in the world. He has declared there can be no peace among the nations without peace among the religions. Yet, destruction is now to be found on such a massive scale that we are bound to ask whether people of different faiths are capable of working together to create a better world. Considering all the bloodshed which wars and disputes between religions have caused and still cause, I would like to acknowledge Clemens Nathan's dedication towards the development of a *chevruta* (partnership) with like-minded people for the sake of *tikkun olam*, the healing of the world.

Nowhere is the subject of peace and understanding, or perhaps more realistically, violence and misunderstanding, more evident than in the Middle East, and more discussed than in the tea rooms and coffee parlours of Jerusalem and Tel Aviv as well as Ramallah and Bethlehem.

The apparent constant instability in Palestinian controlled areas, combined with threats from some orthodox Jews in Israel against Ariel Sharon because of the proposed pull-out from Gaza, are reminders of what seems to be an intractable conflict between Israel and the Palestinians. A story is told about an Israeli and a Palestinian leader meeting with God and asking whether there will ever be peace in the Middle East in their lifetime. 'Of course there will be peace,' God told them. They looked relieved. 'However,' God continued, 'not in my time.' One hundred and twenty years after the beginning of modern Zionism, a peaceful solution seems some distance away.

How did we get from statesmanlike handshakes on the White House lawn to Palestinian children falling victim to Israeli gunfire and Israelis being butchered in the streets of Tel Aviv? What became of the hopes? Why did the dream of a lasting peace evaporate?

A series of failures on both sides contributed to the collapse of the peace process. On the Palestinian side, virtually nothing had been done to develop a mentality of peace. This is a significant failure of Palestinian leadership, notably by Yassar Arafat, who during his lifetime, as one Israeli politician remarked, never missed an opportunity to miss an opportunity. The language of hatred and violence continues unabated in the media, in educational programmes and in religious institutions. On the Christian side, Patriarch Sabah made some statements urging reconciliation, but no programme was established to inculcate a new attitude of peace.

On the Israeli side, there was a failure to understand the pent-up economic frustration of the Palestinians. There had been a lot of talk about progress – but to many Palestinians, especially in the refugee camps, such statements rang hollow. Israel was viewed as the sole culprit for their terrible sufferings, but the Palestinian leadership failed to make a concerted effort to divert international aid to benefit the people who needed it most.

For Jews, the centrality of the land of the Bible, as well as the survival of a third of world Jewry, is at stake. Christians, for their part, not only disagree as to the place of Israel in Christian theology, but many understandably feel particular concern for Arab Christians who live in Israel and in the future state of Palestine. Israel is controversial because it cannot be viewed simply as a geographical and political entity whose emergence is like the establishment of any new state. Political, social, cultural and religious concerns all affect its place in the Jewish–Christian relationship.

The land and state of Israel are intricately related to a number of subjects in that relationship. For example, it is impossible to examine the covenant of Israel with God if no account is taken of the place of land. In the Bible, possession of the land of Israel was an indispensable condition of self-fulfilment both for the individual and for the community. When dispossession and powerlessness arose as a result of the destruction of the Temple in 70 CE, the Jewish response consisted both of the hope of divine restoration and of the mystical idea that God was also exiled with His people. Both Jews and Christians agreed that the exile occurred partly as a result of divine punishment. Traditional Christian interpretation emphasised punishment for failing to believe in Christ, whereas Jewish interpretations explained it as a result of internal Jewish strife and argument. Nevertheless, the rabbis taught that God's Presence (*Shekhinah*) joined the exile and that there were positive consequences such as Jewish teaching being spread far and wide. The traditional Christian emphasis on divine punishment provided the basis for replacement theology – in other words, the belief that Christians replaced Jews as the people of God. This teaching became dominant through the centuries, contributing greatly to antisemitism. The Church Fathers consistently used the historical tragedies of the Jewish people as 'proof' that God had rejected them definitively because of their rejection of Jesus. As long as Jerusalem and the Temple lay in ruins, and Jews remained in exile, it appeared that Christians were correct in claiming that Judaism had lost its legitimacy.

These views have been undermined for many reasons, one of which is the emergence of the State of Israel, in which Jews are a sovereign majority and Judaism the established religion of the land. Christianity's minority status is emphasised by the diminishing number of Christians living in Israel alongside an increasing and significantly larger Muslim Arab population. Genuine contact between Arab Christians and Jews is overshadowed by the Israeli–Palestinian conflict. As a result, dialogue between Jews and Christians (and Muslims) is often transformed into dialogue between Jews and Palestinians or Jews and Arabs, with national identities emphasised far more than religious differences.

In recent times, a Palestinian theology of liberation developed out of replacement theology and the everyday experiences of Palestinian Christians living in Israel since 1948. It is not too extreme to state that the Palestinian Church has faced a major theological crisis since the establishment of Israel. A considerable part of this crisis has been due to a belief that the Bible has been used as a political Zionist text. Naim Ateek argues that 'before the creation of the state, the Old Testament was considered an essential part of Christian Scripture, pointing and witnessing to Jesus. Since the creation of the state, some Jewish and Christian interpreters have read the Old Testament largely as a Zionist text to such an extent that it has become almost repugnant to Palestinian Christians' (*Justice and Only Justice*, p.77). The continuing problems faced by the Palestinian people have added to the crisis. Palestinian Liberation theologians ask, with some justification, for their fellow Christians not to ignore the Palestinian people, their loss of homeland and struggle for liberation.

Yet the problem remains that some Palestinian liberation theologians are politically partisan, hostile to Jews and Judaism and naive about the possibilities of dialogue with increasingly militant Arab Islam. A wholly negative attitude towards Israel on the one hand and an embrace of a radical Palestinian Liberation theology on the other are unhelpful. In fact, they are as unhelpful as some more extreme forms of Christian Zionism which view any action by Israel as wholly positive. The truth lies somewhere between the two.

As far as Jewish hopes are concerned, the will to survive in the Diaspora generated Jewish messianic hopes of redemption, which occasionally led to a high level of anticipation and the extraordinary claims of self-appointed messiahs such as Bar Kokhba and Shabbetai Zvi. One of the common features of these times of messianic fervour was that the Promised Land became a symbol of redress for all the wrongs which Jews had suffered. Thus, modern Zionism is in part the fusion of messianic fervour and the longing for Zion. Jews took their destiny into their own hands and stopped waiting for a divine solution to their predicament. This was a dramatic break from the Diaspora strategy of survival, which advocated endurance of the status quo as part of the covenant with God. For many Jews, the Jewish state offered the best hope not only for survival in response to the breakdown in Europe in the late nineteenth and early twentieth centuries but also for fulfilment. This was the response of what became the major forces in the Zionist movement, the Zionism of Herzl, of Ben Gurion as well as Jabotinsky, of the left-wing Palmach and the right-wing Irgun. Indeed, Zionism has frequently been described as a form of secular messianism. For many Jews the establishment of a Jewish State offered the best hope not only for survival but also for their religious and cultural fulfilment.

Martin Buber explained the Jewish historical attachment to the Land of Israel in a letter to Mahatma Gandhi, written in response to Gandhi's

November 1938 declaration, which was critical of Zionist aspirations. Gandhi had recommended that Jews remain in Germany and pursue *satyagraha* ('holding onto truth' which was the basis for his non-violent resistance to British rule) even unto death. Buber forcefully rejected this argument and explained the connection between the Jewish people and the land as follows:

> You say, Mahatma Gandhi, that a sanction is 'sought in the Bible' to support the cry for a national home, which 'does not make much appeal to you.' No, this is not so. We do not open the Bible and seek sanction there. The opposite is true: the promises of return, of reestablishment, which have nourished the yearning hope of hundreds of generations, give those of today an elementary stimulus, recognised by few in its full meaning but effective also in the lives of many who do not believe in the message of the Bible. (*The Letters of Martin Buber*, ed., N. N. Glatzer and P. Mendes-Flohr (1991) NY: Schocken pp. 479–80)

Yet not all Jews supported a Jewish state, particularly before the Holocaust. Indeed, Zionism resulted in vociferous arguments within and between all Jewish groups, secular and religious, Reform and Orthodox. Today most ultra-Orthodox Jews reject the Jewish state arguing that Israel should be a divine and not a man-made creation.

From the Christian perspective, perhaps because land is not central to Christian theology, Christians have found it hard to grasp that the Jews feel tied to a particular territory. One eminent American theologian, Walter Brueggemann argues that the subject of land should move to the centre of Christian theology, and suggests that Christians cannot engage in serious dialogue with Jews unless they acknowledge land to be the central agenda. In his view, controversy over the State of Israel highlights the lack of a theology of place in contemporary Christianity (*The Land*, p. 23).

Roman Catholicism's attitude towards Zionism changed greatly in the course of the twentieth century. In 1904, Pope Pius X (1903–14) rejected Herzl's plea for support, unequivocally stating that 'the Jews have not recognised our Lord, therefore we cannot recognise the Jewish people.' However, Vatican II and the 1965 document *Nostra Aetate*, while not explicitly mentioning Israel, began the process which eventually led to the Vatican's recognition of the State of Israel in 1994. Increasing awareness among Roman Catholics of the place of Israel has become much more noticeable during the papacy of John Paul II. His acknowledgement of its significance to Jews can be seen as early as 1984 when in his Good Friday Apostolic Letter he wrote: 'the Jewish people who live in the State of Israel, and who preserve in that land such precious testimonies to their history and their faith, we must ask for the desired security and the due tranquility that is the prerogative of every nation and condition of life and of progress for every society.'

Ten years later the State of Israel and the Holy See exchanged ambassadors, and the process begun in 1965 reached another significant landmark with the Pontiff's pilgrimage to Israel in 2000, and the everlasting image of his visit to the Western Wall. Israeli prime minister Ehud Barak spoke for many when he welcomed the Pope stating that he has 'done more than anyone else to bring about the historic change in attitude of the Church towards the Jewish people ... and to dress the gaping wounds that festered over many bitter centuries'. Following Jewish tradition, the Pope placed a written prayer in a crevice of the Western Wall. The short typed prayer with an official seal read: 'God of our fathers, you chose Abraham and his descendants to bring your Name to the Nations. We are deeply saddened by the behavior of those who in the course of history have caused these children of yours to suffer, and asking Your forgiveness we wish to commit ourselves to genuine brotherhood with the people of the Covenant.'

Nevertheless, even though there have been great changes in Christian teaching on Judaism, a resurgence of anti-Israeli attitudes, particularly in Europe, has taken place in the last few years and the feeling remains that whilst the Church has for many years been grappling with issues related to Christian antisemitism, attitudes towards the Land and State of Israel continue, from the theological perspective, to be more difficult to tackle. Theological difficulties have made a Christian re-orientation to Israel problematic. Simply put, it has been easier for Christians to condemn antisemitism as a misunderstanding of Christian teaching than to come to terms with the re-establishment of the Jewish State. As a result, the subject of Israel has probably caused as much disagreement and division within the Church as any other topic in Jewish–Christian dialogue. Alice Eckhardt is one of a number of scholars who points out the contrast between Christian willingness to tackle antisemitism and the Shoah with Christian reticence on the subject of Israel. Rather controversially, Eckhardt argues that Christians are more likely to think about the Shoah than the State of Israel because the former accords with the traditional stereotype of Jews as a suffering and persecuted minority. Israel however challenges this assumption, transforming the victim into a victor ('The Jewish State in Christian–Jewish Relations', *European Judaism*, vol. 25, p. 4).

The Christian reluctance to accept the implications of the new State in the Jewish–Christian relationship only served to reinforce its centrality in discussion. The fact that Israel is the only state in which Jews form the majority also has important consequences for the Jewish–Christian relationship. For example, all the Christian holy places are now in Israel or in Israeli controlled territory, which means that the entire Christian world takes a close interest in the developments. This has led to strong reactions – both of a favourable and unfavourable nature – but the very existence of this spotlight shining so strongly on Israel, and especially on Jerusalem, gives particular importance to any attempt at mutual understanding between Christian and Jew, inside Israel. The recent controversies over the Nazareth mosque are a good example of this phenomenon. At the same time there is always the potential hope of a future meeting with the other great monotheistic faith, Islam.

However, there is danger in arguing that what was once an interpretation about the nature of the biblical word and promise is now in the situation of Israel concretised in a contemporary event. The challenge to Jewish–Christian dialogue as a result of an emphasis on fulfilment of biblical prophecy can be seen in the writings of some evangelical Christians as well as fundamentalist Jews.

What happened a hundred years ago to the Jews outside of Israel is considered by some as historically remote compared to biblical events, which are viewed as almost contemporary. The present becomes transformed into biblical language and geography, which leads to the danger of giving metaphysical meaning to geographical places. The fundamentalist Jew in Israel interprets the ownership of the Land of Israel in terms of a divine gift. This creates a great danger of bestowing divine importance to Israel and the vocation of the Jew becomes a dedication to the existence and the restoration of the cosmic state. Thus, the return to the Land is a fulfillment of the divine promise and reflects a return to the original fullness. However, the biblical promises do not define the same borders and by choosing the widest ones the fundamentalist abuses the idea of the promise, which is related to the Land.

There are also dangers when those who, in the name of dialogue, move from a position of commitment for the well being of Israel to one of almost

Israel can do no wrong. This is not conducive to dialogue for it is not an honest and sober conversation firmly related to present realities. For example, although Evangelical Christian Zionists strongly support Israel and especially the Settler Movement, their agenda is dominated by an eschatological timetable. Their hope, as they freely admit, is that the Jewish return to Zion will be followed by a second-coming and the acceptance of Jesus by the entire Jewish people.

David Flusser, the eminent Israeli scholar of first century Judaism, once told the following story, based on his encounter with a group of evangelical Christians visiting Israel:

> 'Why should we quarrel?' I asked. 'You believe in the coming of the Messiah – so do we. So let us both work for it and pray for it. Only, when he arrives, allow me to ask him one question first: Excuse me sir, but is this your first visit to Jerusalem?'

The majority of Jews feel that some Evangelical Christians who rejoice in the Jewish return to Zion are simply utilitarian, i.e., the Jews are pawns on the chessboard of history, being used to fulfil the final predetermined game-plan. Many Christians also express great concern about what they regard as the evangelicals' exploitation of biblical prophecy. The General Assembly of the Presbyterian Church in the United States criticised such interpretations and commented that 'the State of Israel is a geo-political entity and is not to be validated theologically'. The problem with this statement is that it completely removes the theological aspect of the Land of Israel from the agenda of Jewish–Christian relations. As has already been suggested, Israel cannot simply be viewed as a political entity but also needs to be viewed from a theological perspective. On the other hand the approach of dispensationalists such as Falwell is also problematic because of their reliance on the predictive nature of prophecy.

For Christians, the ongoing debate about Zionism mainly revolves around to what extent Zionism is an integral part of being Jewish, as the vast majority of Jews of believe. Many Christians share this position. However, for some Christian critics, joined by an even smaller number of Jews, Zionism is intrinsically incompatible with Judaism.

In conclusion I would suggest that in the aftermath of the Holocaust and after two millennia of Christian anti-Jewish teaching, Zionism has become a pre-eminent part of Jewish identity. Of course, there continue to be passionate arguments over its desired future course, and the debate about the place of Israel among Christians and Jews will continue in the future for God-knows how long. Unless we intend to fulfill the story I told towards the beginning of this article, we need to change our course. Listening to each other's views with generosity would be a good place to start.

ZVI C. KOREN

Color My World

A Personal Scientific Odyssey into the Art of Ancient Dyes

PROLOGUE

"An ordinary day," I mused. This was to be a normal day at the lab for my student and me. Today we were continuing our quest to decipher the makeup of certain ancient colorants adorning various woolen fibers from sheared and washed fleece, yarns, and weaves. Leah was attempting to extract the coloring substance from the minuscule purple-colored fibers in preparation for subsequent analytical chemical and intrumental tests. "Something is not going right here, Zvi," she exclaimed. I turned my eyes from the computer screen and asked her what was wrong. It seemed that the colorant on the fibers was so stubborn that it was not leaching into solution. Up to this moment, I and other assistants and students had worked on numerous fibers dyed with various shades of red, from scarlet (orange-red), to salmon, pink, bright red, crimson (bluish-red), brick-red, and red-purple. In the past, all of these reds yielded themselves to the attractive powers of the liquid potion – the solvent that strips the dye from the fibers, which is the prerequisite step in the overall scheme of dye analysis. However, today would be different.

My first reaction was that Leah did not follow all the requisite procedures that I had formulated for dissolving that pigment; perhaps she used the wrong solvent system, the temperature was not as high as it should be, or the time elapsed was not sufficient for the dye to dissolve. So, I gave her a typical "try it again" answer, and returned to my computer work. But something was still troubling me as to why that red dye was not being solubilized with the highly acidic alcohol concoction that we have been using. Leah was an excellent student and chances were good that she did everything right. I couldn't completely focus on my computer work, and so this time I had one eye on the computer screen and the other on her experimentation as she began to repeat the process. After the necessary time had elapsed for the possible dissolution of the dye, we both looked at the liquid inside the extraction vial and then looked at each other, puzzled. The liquid was colorless – no colorant was extracted from the fibers. Mystified at first as to why a reddish dye would not yield to the powers of the extracting solvent, I then trembled at the thought of what this could portend regarding the nature of that colorant. I had known from my and other scientists' experimental work that there is only one pigment of a red-purple (maroon or bordeaux) or violet hue that would not budge when treated with that solvent system. It was never discovered on any textile from ancient Israel and its discovery would be historic.

This time I had to perform the analysis by myself in order to witness first-hand the awe-inspiring result that I anticipated should inevitably materialize. With hands nearly shaking and with much trepidation, I placed a few fibers from that minuscule purple fragment excavated at the famous Judean Desert archaeological site at Masada into a vial. When tiny droplets of the special organic elixir that is specific for that dye were added to the fibers, nothing developed for the first few seconds. But soon thereafter the colorant finally began yielding itself to the powers of that liquid, with the noble red-purple colorant forced to produce a beautiful sky blue solution. As the dissolving process had finally begun, I shuddered with astonishment and I must have uttered a divine exclamation of some sort. I hastened the stripping of the dye from the fibers by raising the mixture to a high temperature. Though more tests were needed to be performed on this dye solution, I nevertheless already knew that in my hands was one of the most important biblical treasures that have been found – a royal and priestly color of historic proportion. One key to the puzzle of the trilogy of sacral colors was now deciphered.

A PERSONAL HISTORICAL ODYSSEY

When he entered my office about a decade ago, I thought a cherub had descended from the sky. That was the first time I had met this great humanitarian, an enthusiastic supporter of the fusion between science and art for the sake of humanity. Clemens was, is, and will always be the cheerleader that one needs, especially when hitting a seemingly dead end in one's investigations. Meeting him at the time was a much-needed catalyst to continue searching for newer and creative pathways in my scientific investigations of ancient colorants.

My first experience with ancient colorants, a field that is of special appeal to Clemens, began nearly fourteen years ago, exactly a year after hearing the call of Zionism beckoning me and my family to make *aliyah* (literally "going up") to Israel in the summer of 1990. I had left the dream positions of professor of chemistry and chairman of that department at the School of Engineering at the Cooper Union for the Advancement of Science and Art in the East Village of Manhattan in New York City, where I had begun my academic career in January 1977. That institution was founded in 1859 by the wealthy industrialist Peter Cooper, a son of New York City, whose mandate was to give free higher education to deserving students in engineering, art, and architecture. In 1860, Abraham Lincoln spoke there while electioneering for president and gave his famous "Right makes might" speech. Thomas Alva Edison studied there. To this day, Cooper Union is the only tuition-free private institution in the United States offering baccalaureate and master's degrees in these fields. My appointment to this position was thanks to the noted chemists, Professor John Bové and the late Professor Julius (Jack) Klerer, to whom I will be eternally grateful.

During my first year in Israel, I was able to sample the academic programs at five institutions, including Shenkar College of Engineering and Design, the institute with which I am now permanently associated. The variety of institutions would allow me to study the nature of academia in Israel and thus I would be better equipped to decide at the end of that year where I would like to direct my academic and research energies. But fate played its hand before I had a chance to venture into the long and elaborate decision-making process, and I was offered a proposition that I could not refuse.

During that first year, I had read that Professor Mary Virginia Orna, a Sister of the Order of Saint Ursula (OSU), of the College of New Rochelle in New York, had co-authored a textbook, *Chemistry and Artists' Colors*. This was a field I knew nothing about but that sparked my interest. Mary Virginia has become an international expert on inorganic pigments used in historic paintings and illuminated manuscripts as well as a leader in the field of chemical education.

She and I go a long way back. My first meeting with her was in 1976, a year before I received my PhD in physical chemistry from the City University of New York, where my doctoral research was performed at Brooklyn College, my *alma mater*, in the area of stable isotope separation by means of inverse vapor pressure effects. That first meeting was actually an interview for a position at her college, a most prominent all-women Catholic institution. I remember giving a seminar to the students and faculty on laser-induced chemical reactions, a very hot and exciting field in chemistry at the time. I believed that my talk and subsequent interviews went well, but alas, I didn't get the job, because, as Mary Virginia later explained, they were looking for someone with biochemical-related research. However, she and I remained collegial friends and every few years would run into each other. Our last meeting while I was still living in the States was at the national American Chemical Society annual conference in Boston in the spring of 1990, where I presented a paper on a consumer-oriented spectrophotometric investigation of sunscreen ointments.

The scene now skips ahead one year to my first year in Israel; I am teaching part-time in Shenkar. I read that her book was coming out and contacted her to inquire how I would be able to acquire a copy, as I was living in Israel. She wrote back that, as it turns out, she would be visiting Israel soon and would be glad to bring me a copy. She also stated that she would be visiting a certain institution here and it would be good if I could meet her there. She wasn't sure if I knew where the college was, but I could of course inquire as to its location. She told me the institution's name was Shenkar College and that it was located somewhere in the city of Ramat Gan. I then coyly responded that, yes, as a matter of fact I happened to know where it was, and I would meet her there with a surprise in store.

At our meeting, she was most surprised to find out that not only did I know where Shenkar was, I was already teaching here. The purpose of her trip was not completely clear to me at the time, but she told me that she was sent by a Dr. Sidney M. Edelstein to do a feasibility study – both academic and financial – to determine whether Shenkar could host a center dedicated to the analysis of Israeli antiquities. I learned later that Dr. Edelstein was chairman of the board of the Dexter Chemical Corporation in the Bronx, New York – a great philanthropist who supported many educational programs both here and in the States, and a great fan of science for the sake of archaeology. I also discovered later that he himself studied the colorants on textiles excavated in the early sixties by the dean of Israeli archaeologists,

Figure 1a (from left to right): *Dr. Sidney M. Edelstein and Mrs. Mildred Malka Edelstein (both of blessed memory), Professor David Samuel, and the author (1993).*

Figure 1b (from left to right): *Professor Amotz Weinberg, Professor Heini Zollinger of Switzerland (of blessed memory; an international expert on color chemistry and champion of the State of Israel), and the author (1995).*

Yigael Yadin, and published widely on the topic of textile chemistry. I didn't know much else about the subject she was pursuing and wished her success with her work and visit in Israel. At the time, I didn't realize the impact of her main mission here and continued with my academic business.

A few weeks after she returned to the States, I was approached by two prominent academicians at Shenkar who were eager to speak to me concerning a most pressing matter. One was the then president of Shenkar College, Professor David Samuel, third Viscount Samuel of Mount Carmel, a peerage he had inherited from Lord Herbert Samuel, his grandfather (fig. 1a). The other individual was the head of the Department of Textile Chemistry at the time, Professor Amotz Weinberg, who is the current president of the College (fig. 1b). They explained to me that Mary Virginia had submitted a glowing report to Dr. Edelstein. It concluded that Shenkar was the right

Figure 2. The author with the former president of the State of Israel, Chaim Herzog (of blessed memory), perusing the doctoral dissertation of President Herzog's father, Rabbi Dr. Isaac Halevy Herzog (of blessed memory), at the inauguration of the Edelstein Center in 1994. Rabbi Herzog, who was the chief rabbi of Ireland from 1921 and later the first Ashkenazi chief rabbi of the newly established State of Israel wrote his seminal thesis for the University of London in 1913 on Hebrew Porphyrology, the biblical Tekhelet and Argaman dyes, a field that is today one of the major scientific research areas of the Center. © Zvi C. Koren

institution in Israel to host a center for the analysis of Israeli antiquities as it possesses capable faculty and staff who would be able to perform investigations in these areas. Dr. Edelstein's motive can be termed "blue-and-white" after the colors of the Israeli flag; that is, his Zionistic ideals dictated that what is found here is investigated here. After discussing the matter with Dr. Edelstein, and with his approval, they now approached me and asked if I would like to head a center dedicated to the analyses of ancient artifacts. I asked what such a position would entail, and more importantly, what I would do in such a post. Their answer was simple and to the point: "We don't really know. Just do something." There had never been a position like it in Israel, so there was no precedent on which to tailor it. Everything would need to be built from the ground up.

I agreed to the challenging undertaking, but was still not sure what would be expected of me. The more global question, one I had been pondering ever since deciding to make *aliyah*, was how I would be able to contribute to the academic and research fields of this still nascent country Israel. While not completely fathoming the activities I would undertake as director of the Edelstein Center, I began to understand that herein lay the meaning of my Zionism. The position would allow me to put Israel on the international map in the new area of scientific investigations of ancient colorants, for the sake of humanity.

In my first year in this new position I carried out discussions with museum curators, archaeologists, artists, and scientists in order to learn of the scientific needs and results that each sector desires. In the following year, I understood what my course of action would be: to develop modern, state-of-the-art analytical instrumental methodologies that would reveal the technologies associated with one of the oldest crafts – the dyeing of textiles – and investigate the dyes and pigments associated with the color industry and artistry of antiquity.

Thus began the Edelstein Center for the Analysis of Ancient Textiles and Related Artifacts, whose permanent lab was officially inaugurated in 1994, shortly after the departure of Dr. Edelstein, of blessed memory, from this world (figs. 2, 3). My interaction with Mary Virginia continued, and she was honorably chosen as a Fulbright scholar for 1994–5 and spent the fall semester at the Edelstein Center here at Shenkar (fig. 4).

Since the inception of the permanent home of the center, we have been privileged to have made a number of hitherto unknown discoveries, some of which are described in this essay.

STUDY OF ANCIENT COLORANTS FOR HISTORY AND HUMANITY

The study of the coloring matters produced by the ancients opens a historical window to understanding the processes associated with one of the oldest chemical technologies – textile dyeing. Color analysis of a textile involves the identification of the colorants and of the processes utilized to produce that color or hue on the textile, as well as the identification of the fiber material, the substrate, which can also influence the final hue produced. The analytical investigations involve chemical detective work to help decipher the identities and sources of the dyestuffs used in antiquity. Research into the colorants used by ancient peoples involves a multidisciplinary approach that combines history, archaeology, religion, botany, entomology, marine zoology, and forensic microscale analytical and instrumental chemistry methods.

Knowledge of the natural dyes used in different regions in antiquity increases our understanding of local and international trade and commerce in ancient times. The identification of the dyestuffs used can indicate the movement of dyed goods and the transfer of dyeing methods from one geographical area into another. Such an examination of the textiles of past cultures uncovers the development and technological advancement of the 'scientific art' of textile dyeing through various archaeological periods. In addition, the study of ancient textiles enhances our understanding of the standard of living, textile art, fashion, and color preferences of ancient peoples.

Conservation treatments on degraded textiles require knowledge of the nature of the coloring substance so that the colorants will not be damaged during this process as different colorants can react differently to the cleaning solvents. If a textile artifact is to be partially or fully restored, then the philosophical ideal is for the restoration to be performed with the same fibrous materials and natural colorants that were used in the original fabric in order to maintain the historical and cultural integrity of the artifact. In addition, a technical reason for restoring with identical materials is to maintain the uniformity of the overall hue of the

Fig. 3. The Edelstein Center's scientific activities involve (above) *designing and performing chemical experiments on natural dyes and pigments, and* (below) *computerized chromatographic and spectrometric instrumental analyses of these colorants.* © Zvi C. Koren

fabric. Different colorants have different light fastness properties and the addition of a foreign colorant in the restoration process may, in time, yield a different shade in the restored part from that of the original. The varying fading rates of different colorants is also an important factor in determining the length of time that such an artifact should be displayed under the appropriate lighting conditions in a museum or exhibition gallery.

THE ADVENT OF DYEING

One of the oldest 'pictures' portraying colored garments is from Beni (or Bani) Hasan in eastern central Egypt (fig. 5). This is an important Middle Kingdom archaeological site dating from about 1900 BCE, and situated on the eastern bank of the Nile, about 150 miles south of Cairo. The site is known for its rock-cut tombs of important officials from the eleventh and twelfth dynasty (2125–1795 BCE). In the tomb of Khnumhotep II, a high-ranking Egyptian official, there is a wall painting that depicts Egyptian men with skirts of white linen, the typical haute couture for them at the time, whereas the Asiatics or Canaanites – Semites – are wearing colored striped skirts and colorful clothing as they enter Egypt at the time of the Patriarchs.

Were these colored garments worn by our forefathers? Did Joseph's amazing striped dream-coat resemble any of these clothes? We of course can never know for sure, but what is definite is that this painting is conclusive, though indirect, proof that the dyeing of fibers in vivid colors of blue and red existed at least about four thousand years ago.

THE COLORANT RULE

In antiquity, both inorganic and organic colorants were used for decorating various substrates. Mineral-based inorganic pigments were primarily used for adorning and painting such objects as walls, sarcophagi, clay vessels, and the surfaces of burial shrouds. Organic colorants, which originated from flora and fauna sources, were typically used in the dyeing of textiles. The vegetal sources for these dyes were certain roots, leaves, stems, and flowers of various plants, and the bark, branches, leaves, and berries of certain trees. There were two animal sources for the dyes: entomological and marine. Certain species of scale insects produced red dyes of crimson (bluish-red) or scarlet (orangey-red). From the sea, certain mollusks produced purple and violet pigments that were used for the dyeing of fibers to be used in royal and sacral vestments. The material that was best suited for the chemical uptake of these colorants was protein-structured wool, a practice that began probably about four millennia ago. Linen from flax was also sometimes dyed in less vibrant colors than in the case of wool, and that practice originated at least six millennia ago (see below). Dyed cottons, which have a cellulosic molecular structure similar to linen, appear from about the later Roman to Byzantine Periods, nearly two thousand years ago.

As a general rule, with only a few exceptions, we see an interesting empirical law practiced by the ancient colorist: "organic on organic, inorganic on inorganic". That is, inorganic pigments were in use on stone and clay, whereas organic dyes were utilized for natural organic fibers such as wool.

It is important to understand the difference between coloring by means of painting and by dyeing. Decorating a fabric by means of painting would not be used for everyday garments that need to be laundered on a regular basis, since the surface-applied pigment would simply wash out of the cloth after a few washes. However, for burial shrouds there was of course no desire to wash the surface-colored fabric, and thus that simple technique of color application was satisfactory. True dyeing, as opposed to painting, consists of a process whereby the dye has been dissolved in an aqueous solution, allowing the individual dye molecules to penetrate into the interior of the fibers and bond to them through physical and chemical attractions. This dyeing process rendered a relatively stable color production on the fibers and good wash-fastness.

METHODOLOGY OF A DYE DETECTIVE

There are several essential steps involved in the chemical identification of an organic dye or pigment present on a dyed textile (a dyeing) or on a pottery shard from a dyeing vessel or vat. Most analyses proceed according to the following scheme (Koren 1993a, 1994a, 1995a).

First, an appropriate chemical reagent is administered to a very small sample that has been removed from the dyeing in order to strip the dye off the fibers and dissolve the extracted colorant. After filtering this mixture, a colored solution is obtained (fig. 3, *top*).

The next stage is the identification step, and it usually involves running

Figure 4. Professor Mary Virginia Orna, Sister of the Order of Saint Ursula (OSU) and an international expert on inorganic pigments, with the author at the American Chemical Society awards ceremony honoring her with the Pimentel Award in Chemical Education. Anaheim, California, 1999. © Zvi C. Koren

Figure 5. Artist's reconstruction of fragments of a wall painting from Beni Hasan, Egypt, showing (top) *Semitic women and* (bottom) *men, dressed in variegated garments, 1900 BCE.*

Source: M. Soloweitschik 1926. *Die Welt der Bibel. Ein Bilderatlas zur Geschichte und Kultur des biblischen Zeitalters*. Jüdischer Verlag, Berlin; figure 179. These figures were reproduced from: C. R. Lepsius 1849-1859. *Denkmaeler aus Aegypten und Aethiopien*. Abtheilung ii, Band iv. Nicolaische Buchhandlung, Berlin, page 133.

the dye solution through an instrumental detection setup. The instrument can be a spectrometer, which radiates light typically in the ultraviolet, visible, or infrared regions of the electromagnetic spectrum. The intensity of light absorbed by the extracted dye solution at different wavelengths is electronically measured, and a graph – or spectrum – of the resulting absorptions is obtained. This profile can be characteristic of the major dye component present in a specific natural dyestuff source. This spectrum is compared with other spectra of known components and when a match is obtained, the dye source – vegetal or animal – can be ascertained.

Another analytical instrument that has been the major workhorse of dye analyses is known as a chromatograph, so-named for its ability to separate out various colorants (chroma = color). The main instrument for such analyses is known as a high-performance liquid chromatograph (HPLC), and is highly capable in separating out all the major components present in the natural dyestuff. This is a major advantage over spectrometric techniques alone (fig. 3, *bottom*).

In the HPLC instrument, a sample consisting of ten or so microliters of the extracted dye solution is injected into the instrument by means of a special accurately calibrated syringe. The liquid is then chased after and mixed with a series of solvents – called the eluents – that also flow through the system and whose composition can change with time. These solvents drag the sample into a separation column filled with a certain densely packed material, so that the sample and eluents need to be pushed through this column at pressures as high as 250 times normal atmospheric pressure. The sample is then both attracted to the material in the stationary phase as well as to the solvents in the mobile phase. This mutual competition can be unique for each component and thus produces the necessary separation. The time that it takes for each component to be retained in the separation column before being eluted out by the eluents can be unique and is used to characterize that component. This chromatographic property is known as the sample's retention time.

Additionally, each separated component passes through a spectrometer, known as a photo-diode array (PDA) detector, which measures the sample's ultraviolet and visible spectrum. This spectrometric information is combined with the other chromatographic property, and when all systems have been properly calibrated, the identity of the dye can be determined.

Figure 6. Aerial view of the remnants of the first century BCE *Herodian palace-fortress atop the imposing Masada cliff in the Judean Desert.*
Source: J. Aviram, G. Foerster and E. Netzer (eds.) *Masada IV. The Yigael Yadin Excavations 1963–1965. Final Reports*: Israel Exploration Society, Jerusalem. Reproduced with the kind permission of Dr. Richard Cleave.

MASADA EMOTIONS

One of the first textiles I examined was excavated at Masada, the fortress-palace erected by King Herod in the last quarter of the first century BCE atop an imposing cliff in the Judean Desert overlooking the Dead Sea (Yadin 1980) (fig. 6). The name of this site is derived from its Hebrew appellation – *Metzadah* being Hebrew for 'fortress'. That palatial fortress was also the setting for one of the worst tragedies befalling the struggling Jewish nation in the second half of the first century, about a century after the Herodian complex was built. Masada became the last stronghold of those Jews who were militarily opposed to the Roman rule in ancient Israel from 66 to 73 CE (Josephus 1995). When defeat became imminent, the nearly thousand men, women, and children living in this mountaintop fortress chose a tragic end rather than await their doomed fate at the hands of the Roman captors. The saga of Masada still resonates in the psyche of the modern State of Israel as it has become a symbol of the renaissance of the new Jewish Nation, nearly two millennia later; a kind of phoenix rising out of the ashes of the exiled Jewish people who have sworn that "Masada shall not fall again".

The tragic story of Masada is related by the Jewish-Roman historian Josephus Flavius (37–100 CE) who chronicled the history of the Jews. His previous name was Yosef ben Matityahu, of the priestly and royal Hasmonean dynasty, and he led the Galilee brigade, fighting the "Great Revolt" against the Roman occupation of Judea in the seventh decade of the first century. However, as he was vastly outnumbered by the Roman army, he surrendered to General (later Emperor) Titus Flavius Vespasian, whose son Titus finished the decimation of the Jewish revolt. After being taken to Rome he was granted Roman citizenship. He appended the name Flavius to his Romanized Hebrew name, Josephus, to honor his patron, the emperor Vespasian, founder of the Flavian dynasty. In these new Romanized surroundings, as history has noted, Josephus embarked on his new – and invaluable – role as historian of that period.

In chapter 9 of his epic *Wars of the Jews*, Josephus recounts the ghastly mass self-carnage that was performed by nearly one thousand men, women, and children desperately attempting to stave off the mighty Roman army. After three years of fighting, when the end is near, their leader Eleazar passionately appeals to the masses atop this palace-fortress. According to Josephus (*Wars of the Jews*, bk. 7, ch. 8:7), he ends his exhortation with these words:

> Let us die before we become slaves under our enemies, and let us go out of the world, together with our children and our wives, in a state of freedom ... Let us therefore make haste, and instead of affording them so much pleasure, as they hope for in getting us under their power, let us leave them an example which shall at once cause their astonishment at our death, and their admiration of our hardiness therein.

In the following chapter, Josephus relates the bone-chilling events that transpired immediately after Eleazar's speech (ch. 9:1):

Now as Eleazar was proceeding on in this exhortation, they all cut him off short, and made haste to do the work, as full of an unconquerable ardor of mind, and moved with a demoniacal fury. So they went their ways, as one still endeavoring to be before another, and as thinking that this eagerness would be a demonstration of their courage and good conduct, if they could avoid appearing in the last class: so great was the zeal they were in to slay their wives and children, and themselves also! Nor indeed, when they came to the work itself, did their courage fail them as one might imagine it would have done; but they then held fast the same resolution, without wavering, which they had upon the hearing of Eleazar's speech, while yet every one of them still retained the natural passion of love to themselves and their families, because the reasoning they went upon, appeared to them to be very just, even with regard to those that were dearest to them; for the husbands tenderly embraced their wives and took their children into their arms, and gave the longest parting kisses to them, with tears in their eyes. Yet at the same time did they complete what they had resolved on, as if they had been executed by the hands of strangers, and they had nothing else for their comfort but the necessity they were in of doing this execution, to avoid that prospect they had of the miseries they were to suffer from their enemies. Nor was there at length any one of these men found that scrupled to act their part in this terrible execution, but every one of them dispatched his dearest relations. Miserable men indeed they were! whose distress forced them to slay their own wives and children with their own hands, as the lightest of those evils that were before them. So they not being able to bear the grief they were under for what they had done, any longer, and esteeming it an injury to those they had slain, to live even the shortest space of time after them – they presently laid all they had in a heap, and set fire to it. They then chose ten men by lot out of them, to slay all the rest; every one of whom laid himself down by his wife and children on the ground, and threw his arms about them, and they offered their necks to the stroke of those who by lot executed that melancholy office; and when these ten had, without fear, slain them all, they made the same rule for casting lots for themselves, that he whose lot it was should first kill the other nine and after all, should kill himself. Accordingly, all those had courage sufficient to be no way behind one another, in doing or suffering; so, for a conclusion, the nine offered their necks to the executioner, and he who was last of all, took a view of all the other bodies, lest

> perchance some or other among so many that were slain should want his assistance to be quite dispatched; and when he perceived that they were all slain, he set fire to the palace, and with the great force of his hand ran his sword entirely through himself, and fell down dead near to his own relations. So these people died with this intention, that they would not have so much as one soul among them all alive to be subject to the Romans. Yet was there an ancient woman, and another who was of kin to Eleazar, and superior to most women in prudence and learning, with five children, who had concealed themselves in caverns under ground, and had carried water thither for their drink, and were hidden there when the rest were intent upon the slaughter of one another. These others were nine hundred and sixty in number, the women and children being withal included in that computation. This calamitous slaughter was made on the fifteenth day of the month Xanthicus [Nisan].

It was with this calamitous Masada background haunting me that I braced myself to study those very same textiles that were used by these Jewish rebels and their families. The first time I had the opportunity to marvel at and to actually touch those fabrics was so momentous and mind-boggling that it took me several days of resolve in order to be able to begin analyzing the weaves. These were the garments that clothed their bodies, the most personal of any material effects one can possess, and the household furnishings used in their homes. And so I began to analyze the worldly possessions of our brave and controversial ancestors who departed to an after-life of divine tranquility rather than be enslaved in earthly captivity.

MASADA REDS, PURPLES AND BLUES

There were many stunning examples of colorful and intricate weaves found at Masada. Looking at their majestic beauty, I couldn't help but notice that the color was of such high quality and so miraculously endured the ravages of time that many of these textiles did not look like they were dyed nearly two thousand years ago, but practically only yesterday! Three such examples are shown in figure 7 (Sheffer and Granger-Taylor 1994).

From the dye analyses that I and others have performed on numerous historic textile dyeings from ancient Israel (Koren 1993b, 1994b, 1995b, 1999, 2005a), including Masada dyeings (Koren 1994b; Koren, Sheffer, and

Figure 7. Beautifully dyed ancient woolen weaves excavated at Masada, first century CE, *by the late Yigael Yadin; these fabrics belonged to the Jewish zealots whose last stand against the Roman occupation of Judea finally resulted in their calamitous mass-suicide, as described by the Jewish–Roman historian Josephus. Prior to producing the various patterns in the following textiles, sheared and washed woolen fleece fibers were appropriately dyed, then spun into yarn, and finally woven to construct the design of the weave.*

Figure 7a (left): *Probably from a garment, perhaps a mantle; the salmon pink ground fibers were dyed with madder, and the purple of the notched weft band was produced by double-dyeing fleece fibers with the red-producing madder roots and with the blue indigo-producing leaves of probably the woad plant.*

Figure 7b (top right): *Perhaps from a tunic; ground fibers were dyed with madder red, and the weft band fibers with indigo blue.*

Figure 7c (bottom right): *Possibly a cushion cover; part of a repeated design of stylized flowers and leaves in a geometric framework using indigo blue and undyed fibers.*

Source: J. Aviram, G. Foerster and E. Netzer (eds.) *Masada IV. The Yigael Yadin Excavations 1963–1965. Final Reports*: Israel Exploration Society, Jerusalem. Reproduced with the kind permission of the Israel Exploration Society.

Figure 8. Madder plant roots held by the author near Avignon, France, exposing the location of the red dye in the inner part of the roots. Dyeing with this dyestuff is effected by pulverizing the roots, adding water, and heating to less than boiling to dissolve mostly the dye, and then introducing the wool that has been treated (mordanted) with a hot solution of the mineral alum.

© Zvi C. Koren

Granger-Taylor 1994), a picture of the botanical expertise of the ancient dyer becomes apparent. Results show that practically all of the red dyeings from about two millennia ago were produced by the use of the inner root parts of the plant known as dyer's madder, or botanically as *Rubia tinctorum* (literally "red dye") after the system devised by the botanist Linnaeus (fig. 8). During the Roman Period, this plant was grown in the Levant as well as in Europe, and a related species was also native to India and environs.

In order to perform dyeing with this vegetal colorant, the sheared and washed woolen fleece first had to undergo a pre-dyeing mordanting stage. In this step, the wool was immersed in a hot solution in which the mineral alum had been dissolved in water allowing the molecules of the aluminum compound to impregnate the interior wool fibers. This alum "bites" into the fibers and is thus considered a "mordant" (from the French *mordre*, to bite). After about an hour or so has elapsed, the mordanted wool – wet or dry – is introduced to a hot liquid mixture in which the colorants from the madder roots have been extracted. This dye extraction is accomplished by mixing the ground powdered madder roots with very hot water. As the colorants in solution come in contact with the textile, they bond better to the alum, which is already bonded to the fibers, than to the fibers themselves. Hence, the mordant alum acts as an intermediary and as a bridging agent between the fibers and the colorants and yields more vibrant and more stable colors than if the dye were to bond directly to the fibers. Such alum-mordanted

Figure 9. The author holding a lump of dark blue-violet indigo pigment. This was produced by fermenting the leaves of the woad plant in order to reduce and dissolve the forerunner to indigo blue, the yellow colorant from the leaves. Air was then bubbled into the solution, allowing the colorant molecules to couple via air-oxidation and form the insoluble indigo pigment. © Zvi C. Koren

dyeings yield various hues or shades of red including salmon-orange, red, and brick-red colorations. These shades are possible as there are various colorants in the madder roots; two of the principal colorants are the orange-red dye known as alizarin and a purple one known as purpurin, named for the dye's hue. Examples of the use of the madder roots to produce red dyeings can be seen in the in the grounds of the following Masada textiles: the salmon-pink of figure 7a and the red of figure 7b.

The dyeing with plant-extracted blue was effected by means of a fermentation process involving the steeping of certain plant leaves in warm water made alkaline by either stale urine, lime, plant ash, or the mineral natron (carbonate of soda), also known as *nitron* in Greek, *nitrum* in Latin, and as the biblical and Talmudic Hebrew *neter*. The process could now continue in one of two directions. If dyeing is to be performed at this stage, the fleece is added to the greenish yellow solution containing the dissolved and reduced colorant. After the textile is removed from the dye bath, the dye molecules in the fibers undergo air-oxidation to produce the blue insoluble pigment in and on the fibers. In the second possibility, if the dyeing is not to be immediately performed, then the dye solution is beaten and stirred in order to introduce as much air as possible so that the solid blue pigment will precipitate and settle to the bottom for later use (fig. 9). This type of dye is known as a vat dye, which requires it to be dissolved by reducing it to another state, followed by air-oxidation to form the solid pigment. This dye has been identified as indigotin (or indigo, for short) and it was the only source for the production of a blue dyeing in the ancient world.

In the Levant and Europe of the Roman period, the source available for the blue indigotin pigment was undoubtedly the leaves of the woad plant, *Isatis tinctoria* L., whereas *Indigofera tinctoria*, known as the "indigo" plant native to "India" and environs, as its name implies, was another source for the blue pigment in that far-flung part of the world.

Examples of the use of the blue dye indigotin were detected in the Masada weaves of figure 7: in the weft band of the red textile (fig. 7b) and in the floral patterned fabric (fig. 7c).

A most interesting use of indigotin blue is in producing purple bands, such as the example in figure 7a. In addition to reds and blues, purple hues were also the haute couture color of that period. The most noble of these was known as Tyrian purple, which was produced from the hypobranchial glandular extracts of various *Murex*-type sea snails (Koren 1995c, 2005b). The violets and purples produced from these mollusks were the most expensive, complex, sacral, and royal of all the dyes used in antiquity, and adorned the textiles of emperors, caesars, kings, military generals, Israelite high priests, and temples (see below). Various edicts were enacted to "persuade" the common folk that it would not be advisable for them to wear such real purple-dyed garments. All of these technical and legislative obstacles precluded the dyeing of *Murex*-purple by those who were on the lower rung of the socioeconomic scale. Nevertheless, the clever dyers found a means of circumventing these difficulties by developing a double-dyeing process to produce these popular hues, which I call the "poor people's purple." This "fake" purple was fabricated by dyeing with a red colorant, such as by using madder roots, followed by vat dyeing with blue indigotin, or in reverse order. The ancient color theorist realized that a combination of blue and red yielded purple colors whose desired hue could be fashioned by controlling the relative quantities of the red and blue components. Dye analyses on the above-mentioned purple notched band showed that it was produced by this double-dyeing process.

THE BENI HASAN BLUES

Let us return to that famous Egyptian burial site of Beni Hasan that was previously discussed. Officials at the Egyptian Antiquities division at the

British Museum in London gave me a small fragment from a linen cloth (EA 38007), perhaps from a burial shroud, found in a pot at one of these tombs. Traces of light blue stripes were noticeable on the edge of this fabric (fig. 10). The chromatographic analyses performed on this colorant clearly showed the unmistakable trademark of the blue indigotin dye. Thus, this nearly 4000-year-old blue-dyed linen sample is one of the oldest surviving blue dyeings, as are other contemporaneous examples that are on display at the British Museum.

THE BAR KOKHBA REBELS' TEXTILES

Many textile fragments belonging to the rebel leader Bar Kokhba and his followers and possibly their families were found in one of the caves in the Judean Desert (Yadin 1963). This site has been named "Cave of Letters", as various documents and correspondences written on scroll parchments were found and were attributed to these rebels.

It is important to understand the historical milieu of the analyzed textiles so that the impact of their discovery, examination, and interpretation is fully appreciated not just on the scientific level but also on the emotional and human scale. The accounts associated with the above-mentioned archaeological site of Masada and the Bar Kokhba rebellion are well known in Jewish history as they represent national tragedies during the Roman occupation of Judea.

The third and last wave of rebellion against the Romans in ancient Israel during the reign of Hadrian was waged from 132 to 135 CE by Bar Koziba, literally "son of Koziba" (Koziba probably being his native town). As history recounts, he was a charismatic leader and to some a messianic figure. In fact, historically he is known more by his famous *nomme de guerre*, Bar Kokhba (Son of a Star), which was coined by the Talmudist Rabbi Akiba, who believed that Bar Kokhba was the Messiah who would redeem the Jews from their Roman troubles. R. Akiba applied to him the verse in Numbers 24:17–18:

> There shall come a star [*kokhav*] out of Jacob, and a scepter shall rise out of Israel, and shall strike the corners of Moab, and destroy all the sons of Seth. And Edom shall be a possession, Seir also, his enemies, shall be a possession, and Israel shall do bravely.

Figure 10. Microscope pictures of a 1900 BCE *weave fragment from a linen shroud at Beni Hasan, Egypt. Figure 10a* (top) *shows two undyed warp yarns and traces of indigo blue dyed weft yarns; 10b* (bottom) *shows at higher magnification the beautiful indigo blue fibers at the ends of some weft yarns.* © Zvi C. Koren

The revolt met with initial success, and Bar Koziba maintained his independence for about three years until the disastrous siege of Beitar, at which Bar Koziba was killed. That tragic end to the war was more colossal than the expiation of any individual, as it also was a great tragedy to the Jewish nation as a whole, leading to the final exile of many Jews from their homeland. The catastrophic consequences of this military venture lead many Talmudic-period Rabbis to be utterly contemptuous of Bar Kokhba's actions, as we can see from the following legendary tale in the Talmud (Sanhedrin 93b):

> Bar Koziba reigned two and a half years, [and then] he said to the Rabbis, "I am the Messiah." They answered, "Of Messiah it is written that he can smell [a man] and judge [him, whether he is innocent or guilty]. Let us see whether you can smell and judge." When they saw that he was unable to judge by the scent, they slew him.

Additionally, so distraught were the Rabbis of the time with the tragic results of Bar Koziba's rebellion that they ridiculed his family name (pronounced "Kozeeva") by stating that it was derived from *kazav*, whose etymological root denotes a lie and a disappointment.

It is with this background in mind that I set out to perform dye analyses on the Bar Kokhba textiles, which were first analyzed by the landmark pioneering work of Dr. Sidney Edelstein, who founded the center which I now head, and the then vice president of his company, David Abrahams (Abrahams and Edelstein; 1963, 1964). An example of a beautiful Bar Kokhba weave is the scroll wrapper decorated in a variety of colors, where the madder roots described above were used for the red background (fig. 11). The various weft bands are blue from indigotin, and yellow and green from a combination of the blue and yellow colorants.

Various shades of purple fleece were also found at this site. An example is shown in figure 12. The early analyses, performed more than four decades ago, reported that this purple was produced from the double-dyeing of the blue indigotin dye and a red colorant extracted from certain insects (see below). However, when I analyzed such purple samples it was conclusively shown that, in addition to blue indigotin, the red colorant used was that from the madder roots, as seen in the Masada example of figure 7a described above (Koren 2005a).

The finding of a dyed fleece is demonstrative of the stages associated with textile manufacturing in antiquity: The technological order was for the sheared and washed fleece to be dyed first (this is known as "dyeing in the fleece") and then spun into yarn, which is used for weaving. As I was investigating these colored fleeces, I marveled at how the ancient passage in the Mishnah, a body of religious and secular laws compiled around the first two centuries of this era (a timeframe contemporaneous with these textiles),

(left) *Figure 11: A multicolored scroll wrapper from the Bar-Kokhba Cave of Letters, second century* CE.

© Zvi C. Koren; adapted from Y. Yadin, *The Finds from the Bar-Kokhba Period in the Cave of Letters (Judean Desert Studies)*: Israel Exploration Society, Jerusalem, 1963; plate 61.

(opposite) *Figure 12: Purple fleece of various shades found at the Cave of Letters, second century* CE. © Zvi C. Koren

was in complete harmony with these findings. The Talmudic exposition from tractate Shabbat (Mishnah 7:2; p. 73a) relates to the work-related activities that are forbidden on the Sabbath, the day of rest:

> The primary labors are forty less one: . . . shearing wool, bleaching it, carding it, dyeing it, spinning, stretching the yarns, the making of two meshes, weaving two threads, dividing two threads, tying, and untying, sewing two stitches, tearing in order to sew two stitches . . .

INSECT SOURCES FOR DYES: COCHINEAL AND KERMES

Entomological dye sources in the Levant for the production of red dyeings, alone or in combination with other dyestuffs, were the scale insects commonly known as cochineal and kermes. These were obviously more prestigious and expensive than botanical sources for biological and chemical reasons. Whereas dye plants can be grown practically in one's backyard, the biology of these unique insects required them to breed only on certain host plants located in specific geographical areas. Additionally, the chemistry of these insect dyes produces certain mordant-to-dye bonds in the fibers that result in more vibrant reds than those obtainable from plant dyestuffs.

In the ancient Middle East, the obvious cochineal to be imported into this area would have been the one that goes by the popular names of Ararat, Armenian, or Turkish cochineal, as well as by kirmiz, and entomologically as *Porphyrophora hamelii* Brandt. This cochineal breeds on the ground-level upper roots of certain grassy weeds. The dried, dark brown mature female insects are relatively flat, with lines or scales on their shell. The main colorant extracted from this cochineal is carminic acid, which produces crimson (bluish red) dyeings on alum-mordanted wool.

The other red-producing insect is known as oak kermes, *Kermes vermilio* Planchon, which breeds on the branches and leaves of certain oak trees at relatively high altitudes. The 'etymology of entomology' is quite interesting, as the Biblical name for kermes in 2 Chronicles has an equivalent name – *karmil*. The round, pea-shaped, dark brown mature female insects are collected together with their larvae for the dye production. Their dye content consists primarily of two components: orange-red flavokermesic acid and the red-purple kermesic acid. Modern kermes dyeings on alum-mordanted wool produce scarlet (orange-red) hues. This insect is the source of the Biblical *shani* dye, which provided flaming orange colors on the vestments of the High Priest and on the textile furnishings of the Tabernacle.

THE FRUGALLY RICH INSECT RED

The skills of the dyer and weaver in so many artistic weaves have been found in many textiles. However, the combination of the economics and beauty of the final product can be evidenced from a rare red fabric excavated at a late Byzantine site at 'Ein Boqeq in close proximity to the Dead Sea, the lowest point on Earth. This site probably served as a way-station along the famous spice route from the Nabatean capital of Petra (now in Jordan) to the Gaza port and on to further points of commerce.

I was given a small red yarn sample to analyze by Avigail Sheffer, a veteran researcher of the physical structure of ancient weaves, who was investigating the various textiles excavated at this site. I found that the red colorant was produced by using the roots of the madder plant. When Avigail then showed me analyses performed in the early 1970s on the same red fabric, I was perplexed. Researchers in Belgium had reported that the red dye was of insect origin. I was stunned. My scientific analyses clearly showed the presence of the two main colorants making up the madder plant, an orange colorant named alizarin, and a purple one called purpurin. There was no mistaking that result. But the Belgian researchers were top-notch scientists; their report was also iron-clad. I was befuddled.

I then asked for and received a very small weave sample containing warp and weft from the red fabric. Looking at this fabric, I still could not understand why the Belgians and I were getting radically different results. I then placed the minuscule fabric under a microscope, and I noticed immediately that not only did the fabric consist of bright, shining, crimson-colored red yarns, but also of some dull red yarns, considerably visually inferior to the brilliant color reflected from the crimson yarns (fig. 13). This must have been the reason for the discrepancy in the results obtained. Upon further inspection, I noticed that all the dull red yarns formed the warp of the red weave, while the weft yarns were of a dazzling crimson.

Chemical instrumental analyses then showed that the dull-red warp yarns were the ones dyed with the madder roots, whereas the vivid crimson weft yarns were in fact dyed with the dye produced by scale insects. Based on the chemical signature of the components found in this crimson colorant, and also based on the geographical and archaeological context of this textile, I surmised that this dye originated from the Ararat (or Armenian) cochineal insect that breeds on the ground-level upper roots of certain grassy weeds

Figure 13. Microscope picture of a fragment of the woolen red patch from 'Ein Boqeq, dating from the seventh century CE *late-Byzantine period. Visible are three light red warp yarns produced from madder red, and brilliant crimson weft yarns whose fibers were dyed with the exotic Ararat or Armenian cochineal scale insect.* © Zvi C. Koren

growing at the base of Mt. Ararat. This was the first direct evidence of the use of such an insect dye in a textile from ancient Israel.

Another amazing aspect of this red patch is the clever integration of these two differently colored yarns into the weave. This red fabric is a weft-faced tabby, so that the most visible element of the weave is the crimson weft, while the dull-red warp is largely concealed in the background. The ancient weaver was interested in producing a crimson look for the textile, so the relatively expensive cochineal-dyed yarns took the weft center stage in the production, while the inexpensive red madder-dyed yarns were backstage in the warp. With an eye to the aesthetics of the finished product, red-dyed warp yarns were nevertheless used – not undyed ones – just in case a warp here and there would peek through and become visible.

THE SACRAL INSECT SCARLET

The 2000-year old archaeological site known as 'Ein Raḥel (Spring of Rachel), a Nabatean fort in the 'Aravah valley, southwest of the Dead Sea, yielded a surprising and rare weave. A purple band was present in a few of the excavated textiles; however, this color was unlike any of the other purples I had investigated. The major dye component of this band was the purple kermesic acid dye, which can only be produced from the oak kermes insect. Thus, as in the case of the crimson 'Ein Boqeq cochineal-insect dyeing mentioned above, this too was the first time that a dyeing from ancient Israel containing another insect – kermes – was found.

However, the surprising find – or lack of it – was that the orange-red flavokermesic acid colorant, which is always found together with kermesic acid in modern kermes dyeings, was decidedly absent. The absence of this dye is most probably not due to the use of a specific kermes species that only consists of the purple dye constituent, but due to the degradation of the unstable orange-red colorant over the archaeological time frame.

The modern-day implication of ancient kermes dyeings is that "what-you-see-today" is not "what-you-had-yesterday". As the orange component has decomposed over two millennia, it is obvious the original hue of the band in the 'Ein Rahel textile was not purple, but possessed at least a tad of orange to it. This is an important fact in attempting to reconstruct the original color of this and other bands. Were we to find a kermes dyeing from Biblical times, though it would now appear purple, we would know that when originally dyed in antiquity, it would have been the Sacral Scarlet *Shani* dye.

THE SIX THOUSAND YEAR OLD WARRIOR'S BURIAL SHROUD: THE OLDEST DYEING YET FOUND

In 1993, numerous archaeologists embarked on a daring mission code-named "Operation Scroll" in the Judean Desert to find more remnants of Dead Sea type scrolls. Every known cave was searched, but instead of finding significant scrolls, they made a spectacular find of a different sort. Inside a cave located in the cliffs of the lower Wadi el-Makkukh, near Jericho, they discovered the intact burial site of an adult male, a full skeleton in a fetal position, probably a warrior or hunter of high rank, dating to the early fourth millennium BCE (late Chalcolithic Period). The find included several rare, exceptionally well-preserved funerary objects: a coiled basket, a wooden bowl, a pair of leather sandals, a flint knife, and a bow broken into two parts. The bow had been deliberately and ritually broken, testifying to the ancient mortuary rite of "killing" the bow as a way to symbolize the end of its use upon the death of its owner. The presence of these remains and artifacts at this archaeological site is the basis for naming it the "Cave of the Warrior".

These remarkable personal articles, and the skeleton, were found in the largest textile yet found from this era, an incredible two-by-seven meter linen-weave, which was folded in four. Additionally, two elaborate and beautifully woven linen textiles were found within the very large shroud that wrapped the body.

The linen textiles I examined showed various earth colors, from beige and brown to dark-brown (nearly 'black'). The large textile also had reddish spots, composed of the red pigment haematite (red ochre), an iron oxide, which were distributed randomly. This pigment was undoubtedly sprinkled onto the shroud enveloping the skeleton as part of the burial ritual. Red ochre, symbolizing life-blood, has been used in the funerary rites (painting of skull, bones and other parts of the deceased) of various ancient cultures (Brunello 1973).

The decorative bands forming the warp ends in each of the textiles contained dark, brown, and beige yarns. Dark yarns were also present as outer warp threads on both sides of the large textile, and on weft yarns from the decorative bands of the large and the smaller textiles. The sources of these colors were analyzed via microscopic, chemical, and chromatographic tests.

Though the nature of the blackish dark-brown organic colorant has not been completely identified yet, it is nevertheless clear that the Chalcolithic Warrior textile is the earliest example of yarn-dyeing yet discovered anywhere in the world (fig. 14). The colors on even later Neolithic textiles discovered so far were produced by surface coloration – painting or smearing – of part or all of the bulk textile, in contrast to the Warrior textile. In the Warrior weave, the dyeing of individual yarns was performed and then these were introduced during the weaving stage. In addition, the relative uniformity of the dark brown color along the length of the inner dark fibers that comprise the decorations in the Warrior textiles is remarkable, given that this textile is nearly six-thousand-years old!

THE BIBLICAL HERODIAN ARGAMAN

"An ordinary day," I mused; this was to be a normal day at the lab for my student and me. However, in my hands was one of the most important biblical treasures ever to be found – a royal and priestly color of historic proportion. One key to the puzzle of the trilogy of sacral colors was now deciphered. Those minuscule red-purple fibers, mentioned above in the prologue, established at last the true color of the biblical *argaman* dye used for kings, high priests, and in the textile furnishings of the Tabernacle.

Figure 14. Microscope picture of part of the decorative band trim of the linen burial shroud found in the Cave of the Warrior. The shroud is six-thousand years old (late Chalcolithic Period). Visible are weft yarns dyed brown-black prior to weaving. © Zvi C. Koren

The rare molluskan pigment known as royal purple has also been referred to as Tyrian purple, after one of the capitals of the sea-faring Phoenicians, the foremost traders and merchants of the ancient world, whom history has credited with perfecting the craft of purple dyeing. This pigment was produced in antiquity from the substances contained in the colorless fluids of the hypobranchial glands of certain sea mollusks commonly referred to as *Murex* snails. As described by Greek and Roman historians, such as Aristotle and Pliny, respectively, the dyeing of wool and silk with the solubilized reduced form of this pigment was undoubtedly one of the oldest and most complex of biochemical technologies in the ancient world. During certain eras, this precious dye was worth more than twenty times its weight in gold (Bridgeman 1987). This is no wonder, as experiments performed in my laboratory have shown that approximately ten thousand such snails were needed to dye just one royal cloak from head to toe! The scarcity of this animal dyestuff and the majestic beauty of murex-purple dyed textiles endeared it to kings, emperors, caesars, and ecclesiastics. History has recorded that this purple was the fashion of royalty in the empires of Assyria, Babylonia, Persia, Greece, and Rome. Military generals and nobility were also permitted to adorn at least part of their garments with this imperial dye.

The textile that Leah and I analyzed was excavated along with other textiles and artifacts in an expedition at Masada led by the late Yigael Yadin, the dean of Israeli archaeologists, between 1963 and 1965 (Yadin 1984). The woolen fragment investigated (number 1132/3), whose maximum measurements were approximately 2 × 4 mm, was unearthed in an area (locus 791) that was part of the refuse dump of the western palace and was situated at the northeast corner of that edifice (Netzer 1991). Based on the archaeological dating of the other artifacts found with this textile, it can be conclusively stated that this fabric belonged to the Herodian period of the first century BCE (E. Netzer, personal communication).

The fortress and palatial complex at Masada was built by King Herod, the Roman-appointed Jewish monarch of Judea, during the middle of his reign (37–4 BCE). History recounts that he built the palaces and other structures at Masada as a fortress in case a retreat by him and his family was necessary. King Herod's short-lived dynasty was to be the last monarchy of ancient Israel. The western palace was the first of the two that were built at Masada and it served as an important administrative center (E. Netzer, personal communication). Further, a "throne room" was discovered in that palace in which four rectangularly arranged niches were found in the floor in a corner of this chamber (Yadin 1984). These niches were undoubtedly used for the supporting poles of a royal canopy in a room that was large enough for people to have an audience with the king.

So, it was not to be an ordinary day. When the analyses on the small yarn were concluded, the chromatographic and spectrometric results indicated that the most probable molluskan source of this purple dye was the hypobranchial glandular fluid of *Murex trunculus* gastropods. Based on the history, archaeology, religion, and marine zoology associated with this molluskan dye, the significance of the discovery of murex purple on this royal fabric is three-fold: (1) This is the first time that a murex purple fabric from ancient Israel has been discovered, and it is among the oldest 'true purple' textiles discovered anywhere in the world; (2) The fabric found undoubtedly belonged to the western Herodian palace at Masada, and, based on the royal dye used and the physical structure of the weave, may have been part of the royal cloak or mantle of that king; (3) The color of this fabric was most likely that of the biblical *argaman* dye (fig. 15).

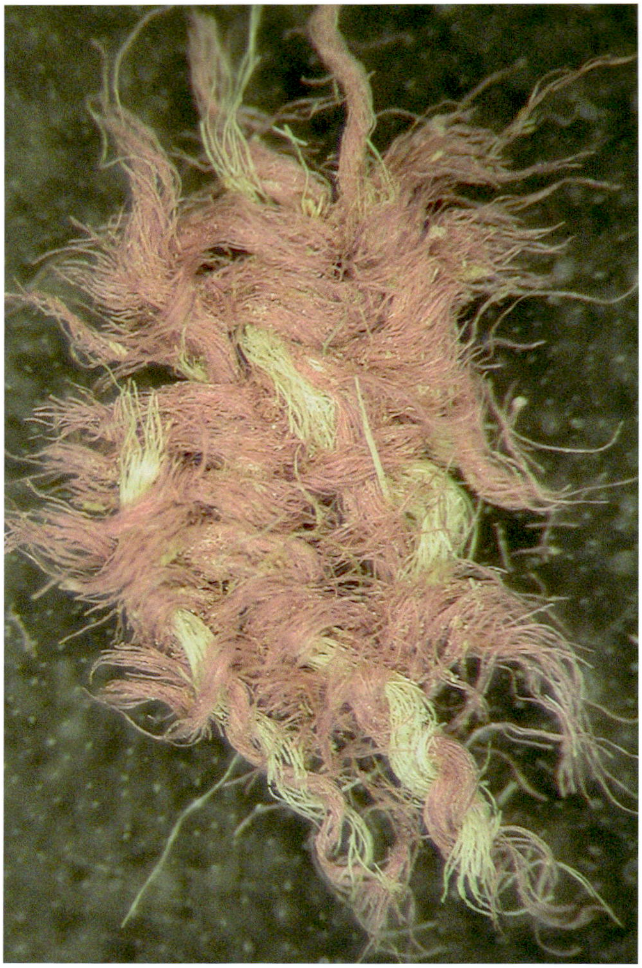

Figure 15. Microscope picture of a fragment of first-century BCE Herodian fabric. Each of the warp yarns in the fabric was produced by plying un undyed (now yellowed) yarn together with a purple yarn. The weft yarns are of purple alone. This construct indicates that the whole fabric was purple in color. The fabric is the only example of real molluskan Royal and Biblical Argaman dyeing found from ancient Israel.

EPILOGUE

Now that two of the three Biblical dyes have been deciphered, the red-purple molluskan *argaman* and the insect scarlet (orange-red) *shani*, much work still needs to be done regarding the nature and dyeing techniques associated with the third, and most holy, of the sacral dyes. The *tekhelet* dye was also produced from a *Murex* species, undoubtedly from a *Murex trunculus* snail, which already contains a bluer pigment than all the other molluskan pigments. Woolen *tekhelet* dyeings are probably violet or dark-blue in color. There is still much controversy related to this topic. However, the recent breakthrough research that we and John Edmonds of England and Inge Boesken Kanold of France independently conducted in decoding the riddle of how the ancients performed dyeing with the purple pigment with only natural means will hopefully resolve this last purple puzzle (Koren 2005b).

In trying to grasp the secrets of the ancients, one is simply bedazzled and awed by the advanced state of their empirical science in technology, chemistry, botany, entomology, marine zoology, biotechnology, and just as important, their artistry. Even several thousand of years ago, these scientific artisans were great individuals standing at the frontier of the civilized world, and producing great artistic products fashioned from skills honed over the centuries.

And so, my personal and professional scientific quest, cheered on by Clemens, is to help understand the chemical arts and technologies associated with the nature and use of color in antiquity . . . for the sake of humanity.

ACKNOWLEDGEMENTS

I would like to thank sincerely the Dr. Sidney M. Edelstein Foundation and Mrs. Mildred Edelstein (who passed away in 2005) for supporting this research. Since the departure of Sidney from this world, the Edelstein Foundation, and Mildred, Sidney's beloved wife, have steadfastly supported this research. In addition, I am most grateful to Professor Mary Virginia Orna of New York and to Professor Heini Zollinger (who also passed away in 2005), formerly of Zurich, for their expert advice during all these years, and to Professor David Samuel and Professor Amotz Weinberg for bringing me on to the Shenkar team. And, of course, I am very appreciative of

Mr. Clemens Nathan's efforts in championing these studies in science and art for the benefit of future generations.

REFERENCES

Abrahams D. H. and Edelstein S. M. 1963. "A study of the textiles from the color standpoint." In Yadin, Y. *The Finds from the Bar-Kokhba Period in the Cave of Letters (Judean Desert Studies)*: Israel Exploration Society, Jerusalem, 270–279.

———. 1964. "A new method for the analysis of ancient textiles." *American Dyestuff Reporter* 53, 19–25.

Bridgeman J. 1987. "Purple Dye in Late Antiquity and Byzantium." In Spanier E. (ed.) *The Royal Purple and the Biblical Blue: Argaman and Tekhelet. The Study of Chief Rabbi Dr. Isaac Herzog on the Dye Industries in Ancient Israel and Recent Scientific Contributions*. Keter, Jerusalem, 159–165.

Brunello F. 1973. Hickey B. (transl.) *The Art of Dyeing in the History of Mankind*: Neri Pozza Editore, Vicenza, 6–8.

Josephus Flavius. 1995. *Wars of the Jews*. In Whiston W. (transl.) *The Complete Works of Josephus:* Kregel Publications, Grand Rapids, Michigan, Book 7, Chs 8–9, 598–603.

Koren Z. C. 1993a. "Methods of dye analysis used at the Shenkar College Edelstein Center in Israel." *Dyes in History and Archaeology* 11, 25–33.

———. 1993b. "The colors and dyes on ancient textiles in Israel." In Sorek C. and Ayalon E. (eds) *Colors from Nature: Natural Colors in Ancient Times*, Eretz-Israel Museum, Tel-Aviv, 15*–31*, 47–65.

———. 1994a. "HPLC analysis of the natural scale insect, madder and indigoid dyes." *Journal of the Society of Dyers and Colourists* 110, 273–277.

———. 1994b. "Analysis of the Masada textile dyes." In Aviram J., Foerster G. and Netzer E. (eds) *Masada IV. The Yigael Yadin Excavations 1963–1965. Final Reports*: Israel Exploration Society, Jerusalem, 257–264.

———. 1995a. "An efficient HPLC analysis scheme for plant and animal red, blue and purple dyes." *Dyes in History and Archaeology* 13, 27–37.

———. 1995b. "Analysis of the Nahal Shahaq site textile fibers and dyes." *'Atiqot* 26, 49–53.

———. 1995c. "High-performance liquid chromatographic analysis of an ancient Tyrian purple dyeing vat from Israel." *Israel Journal of Chemistry* 35, 117–124.

———. 1999. "Microscopic and chromatographic analyses of decorative band colors on Nabatean 'En Rahel textiles – kermes and shaded bands." *'Atiqot* 38, 129–136.

———. 2005a. "Chromatographic Analyses of Selected Historic Dyeings from Ancient Israel." In R. Janaway and P. Wyeth (eds) *Scientific Analysis of Ancient and Historic Textiles: Informing Preservation, Display and Interpretation*: Archetype Publications, London, 194–201.

———. 2005b. "The first optimal all-Murex all-natural purple dyeing in the Eastern Mediterranean in a millenium and a half." *Dyes in History and Archaeology* 20, 136–149, Col. Pls. 15.1–15.5.

Koren Z. C., Sheffer A., and Granger-Taylor H. 1994. "Table v – Dye Analysis." In Aviram J., Foerster G., and Netzer E. (eds) *Masada IV. The Yigael Yadin Excavations 1963–1965. Final Reports*: Israel Exploration Society, Jerusalem, 251–255.

Netzer, E. 1991. *Masada III. The Yigael Yadin Excavations 1963–1965. Final Reports. The Buildings, Stratigraphy and Architecture*. Israel Exploration Society, Jerusalem, 369.

Sheffer A. and Granger-Taylor H. 1994. "Textiles from Masada: a preliminary selection." In Aviram J., Foerster G., and Netzer E. (eds) *Masada IV. The Yigael Yadin Excavations 1963–1965. Final Reports*: Israel Exploration Society, Jerusalem, 153–250.

Yadin, Y. 1963. *The Finds from the Bar-Kokhba Period in the Cave of Letters (Judean Desert Studies)*: Israel Exploration Society, Jerusalem.

———. 1980. *Masada: Herod's Fortress and the Zealots' Last Stand*: Random House, New York.

———. 1984. *Masada: Herod's Fortress and the Zealots' Last Stand*: Steimatzky, Tel-Aviv.

JULIUS LIPNER

Religion and Religious Thinking in the New Millennium

I AM delighted that this piece can be included in Clemens Nathan's felicitation volume. I have had the honour of knowing Clemens for several years; we are both trustees of the Centre for Jewish–Christian Relations at Cambridge, and I have had many opportunities to observe Clemens' breadth of vision and humanity, his gentle tact and good humour in this capacity. One of Clemens' qualities is his tendency to think ahead even in circumstances that seem to make it difficult to do so. It is no accident then that I have chosen the essay that bears this title for my contribution.

It would be as well to start with a kind of warning about our use of the word 'millennium'. A millennium is a thousand-year period and there would be very little we could say about the role of religion over such a long time. So let us begin with an act of humility and cut our reflections down to size. Useful comments can be made only with the next couple of generations in mind, not only because of realism concerning the scale of our inquiry, but also because of an inherent feature of a phenomenon like living religion. Living religion is not a compartmentalized reality; it is inextricably bound up with history, politics, and socio-economic changes. A brief glance around the events of our troubled world will bear this out. And this is all the more so with global faiths like Judaism, Christianity, Islam, Hinduism, Buddhism

This is an appreciably revised version of an essay first published in *Plurality, Power and Mission: Intercontextual Theological Explorations in the Role of Religion in the New Millennium,* ed. P. L. Wickeri, J. K. Wickeri, and D. M. A. Niles, London, The Council for World Mission, 2000.

and so on. In other words, we cannot lose sight of the fact that a crucial feature of religion as lived globally is its inherent *contingency*. And contingency implies unpredictability, even to the extent of the waning of religion in some cases. This is a salutary point to make in the context of millennial projections.

There is another where Christians in particular are concerned. Insofar as 'millennium' has religious connotations – after all, the term has currency with reference to calculations of time-spans starting from the birth of Christ – concern with millennia in one way or another has been primarily a Christian preoccupation. Though such a concern might impinge consequentially on non-Christians, most non-Christians do not find such thousand-year periods directly significant religiously. This is well exemplified in A. B. Yehoshua's novel *A Journey to the End of the Millennium*.[1] In this novel, millennial considerations are important only in so far as their Christian implications affect non-Christian (especially Jewish) lives. My point is that in our relationships with other cultures and faiths we must not act as if our own preoccupations are the order of the day. We require *methodological sensitivity* in these relationships if we wish to reach out to others, and methodological sensitivity is predicated on an act of decentring humility.

There is another consideration which puts millennial calculations in their proper place. This is the awareness that cultural trends, whether on a macro or micro scale, are not subject to millennial projections. Thus a political or religious movement is not going to change radically or disappear simply because numerically a multiple of a thousand has appeared in the calendar. Such movements have their own inner dynamic which is a resultant of various interacting social forces, and their life-span or structural transformations are governed by influences that are not simply numerical (yet how many analysts of human affairs succumb in one way or another to numerological presuppositions![2]).

Nevertheless, 'millennium' also has a secular connotation in an increasingly inter-connected world in which the fields of communications, politics, time-measurement, and commerce are dominated by the western calendar.

1 Published in 1997, and translated into English by Nicholas de Lange, New York, Doubleday, 1999.

2 One example would be the world-wide apprehension over the 'millennium bug' and its projected disastrous effects on computers, and the millions of pounds of useless expenditure this anxiety generated. When no widespread disaster occurred, the matter was quietly dropped by the media.

People seem to like to think in round figures, even large round figures. So there is some psychological value in thinking in terms of millennia. It is a time for taking stock and for considering emphases and forms of renewal. In this respect talk of 'the millennium' could be useful.

But such millennial projections today come into their own precisely because we live in what is called a globalized world. 'Globalization' can take on different connotations, but I would like to consider one set in particular. This comes from an article entitled 'Global Transformations: Politics, Economics, and Culture'.[3] The authors identify four characteristics of globalization: (i) 'it involves a *stretching* of social, political, and economic activities across political frontiers, regions and continents'; (ii) 'it suggests the *intensification*, or the growing magnitude, of interconnectedness and flows of trade, investment, finance, migration, culture, and so on'; (iii) in this context of worldwide interlinkage, it entails an increase in 'the *velocity* of the diffusion of ideas, goods, information, capital, and people'; and (iv) 'the growing *extent*, *intensity*, and *velocity* of global interactions can be associated with their deepening *impact*, such that the effects of even the most local developments may come to have enormous global consequences'. In other words, globalization implies a blurring of the boundaries between 'local' and 'national/international'.

The authors of the article mentioned do not expressly consider the role of religion in the globalization process, but it is obvious that religion, like other important features of human activity, is caught up in this process. I remarked earlier that living religion cannot be detached from the outworking of worldwide forces. As the new millennium develops, religion, that is, the particular religious traditions, will have to come to terms with the process of globalization in its various modalities. How can this be done? Clearly the different traditions, because of their different historical trajectories in the world, will have to tackle this problem in their specific ways. Note that the four characteristics listed above are descriptive, not evaluative. They do not purport to evaluate, either morally or otherwise, the phenomenon of globalization; they articulate what has become a matter of fact. But the various religious traditions cannot hope to escape first, discerning, and then negotiating, the moral dimensions of the stunning advances of information and communications technology that are developing exponentially in our world.

So we may ask: how will the religions cope with the potential *intrusiveness*

3 D. Held, A. McGrew, D. Goldblatt, and J. Perraton, in *Revision,* Fall, 1999.

in our lives of such technological advances as the Internet? Since the velocity of information-communication is so great and so graphic, will those who have control of such advances seek to manipulate the emotions, the judgements of religious people for their own ends? Will they employ surrogate models for religious services with financial gain in view? There are positive aspects to the new order: for example, using information technology to enhance solidarity among members of the various religions and genuine religious dialogue between faiths. I shall return to this last point in due course.

No doubt this feature of globalization – the development of the communication network – raises the question of editorial control and the responsible discernment of data received. This is particularly acute with respect to the existence of the worldwideweb. Who controls this net on a global scale? Is there any adequate editorial control, or is the volume of material on the web, both as to content and quantity, in effect out of control? So far, the latter seems to be the case, and this has repercussions not only for religion but also for the way the more vulnerable among us live our lives. And even if some manner of control can be asserted, according to what criteria should this take place? Globalization in the way mentioned is at the service of the fundamentalist as well as the liberal, the paedophile as well as responsible child-care agencies, the terrorist and anarchist as well as the peacemaker. Those who take a religious way of life seriously, whether institutionally or otherwise, will need to evolve procedures to come to terms responsibly with the mechanisms of information and communications technology as an ongoing phenomenon, as also with the techniques for regulating these constructively. At present, in the mainstream Christian Churches at least, it seems that this major issue is being tackled in a haphazard manner.

But the globalization of religion is taking place, willy nilly, in the context of what observers have called 'modernism' and 'postmodernism'. These are imprecise terms, but they convey meaning to the extent that in so-called modernist discourse cultural forces become an organizing agent that centralizes and excludes; people are marginalized and subordinated in various ways, e.g. through those modes of writing history that adopt a Eurocentric or androcentric perspective as an uncontested norm of value, whereas in 'postmodernist' discourse deconstruction and decentralization have acted as hermeneutic keys for understanding.

As a result of the dialectic between these discourses many religiously sensitive hierarchies and binary oppositions of the past – such as 'reason and revelation', 'faith and science', 'clerics and the laity' and so on – are being challenged in terms of new ideas such as 'hybridity', 'collage', and 'commonality'. A worldwide endorsement (in theory at least) of democratic and secular/humanist ideologies, the surge in migration and immigrant mobility across national frontiers, and increasing capitalization of resources and urbanization among other factors, have created multi-ethnic societies that have initiated new patterns of cross-cultural behaviour and thinking. In many cases, we are seeking shared values socially, politically and religiously without abandoning the specificity of difference. And an old hermeneutic of suspicion is giving way to a new hermeneutic of *cohesive pluralities* in terms of multiple but interconnected centres of meaning and activity. This is an advance on many features of the past.

Theology and religious reflection cannot but take these advances seriously, though the theologies of the world religions at any rate have generally been slow to respond to such changes. The reason for this is that such theologies have often been bound up with dominant power structures, such as colonialism, clericalism, and capitalism, for so long that even when some of these structures are dismantled the momentum of traditional exclusivist theologizing tends to continue. One example of this is the still poor record of inter-religious and cross-cultural dialogue in the mainstream Christian Churches. Too many Christian theologians still tend to discourse in naive supremacist terms.[4] But the multiethnic societies that have been created in so many parts of the world especially in the last century or so and the advances made in the hermeneutics of cross-cultural understanding over the same period demand new models of dialogic theologizing with respect to other faiths. Christian, and indeed other theologies, must act with boldness and purpose here or face the prospect of being spurned as increasingly obsolete.

A related phenomenon has been the rise of so-called new-age spiritualities. This development had started by about the middle of the nineteenth century as a result of the rationalist challenge to doctrinal faith in the west, greater sensitivity to intuitionist forms of philosophy, and increasing access to the 'mystic east'. The Abrahamic faiths in particular have still not learned to cope with the challenges of non-institutional and non-ritualistic forms of religious commitment. Interactive dialogue between the established faiths

4 For example, soteriologically by arguing for some form of explicit recognition of Jesus as Saviour of the world as a necessary condition of salvation, and epistemologically by claiming exclusive access to God on the basis of a particular revelation or its interpretation.

and the new religious trends is an urgent task facing traditional religion today.

The popularity of new-age modes of faith emphasizes a key feature of contemporary (westernized) middle-class culture the world over: the clamour for 'experience', for prioritizing sensation over intellection and 'praxis' over theory. This trend valorizes the body and bodily sensation over the traditional ideals of renouncer or ascetic forms of life. Consider the almost compulsive surge of interest in reality-TV (often a form of prurient, surrogate experiencing), drugs, exhibitionist sex and sexual discourse, adventure parks and sports, computer-generated role-play and so on. These forms of sensationalism are often associated with another phenomenon of consumerist society: the demand for 'choice' as a necessary condition of the freedom of democracy in every facet of our lives. But does proliferating choice have an inherent value? How does it affect the balance between our needs and wants, our family and social relationships, our ecological and environmental sensitivities, the behaviour of our financial markets, trading practices (especially with poorer countries), and the way we advertise products? The distinction between choice and licence and its moral consequences is rarely aired, let alone debated responsibly. Religious leaders and thinkers will have to take a much more assertive stand than hitherto in trying to challenge the consumerist lifestyles that threaten to engulf and destroy the values of human worth that religions have always proclaimed. This is no time for jargon, obscure terminology and introverted theologizing, for a loss of imaginative nerve. This is a time to take the battle to mammon, else well before the millennium is out our descendants' god will be the accumulation of wealth and 'choice' its mantra.

I am not advocating a drawbridge-mentality for the religionists. I am advocating robust dialogue and debate. Theologizing and religious commitment must become more and more interdisciplinarily sensitive. This harks back to my earlier point that religion cannot function in a vacuum, cannot be detached from the world. Religious faith must be like the yeast that leavens the whole batch (Luke 13.21). It cannot do this if it is intellectually uninvolved with the advances in the humanities, social sciences, and not least, the physical and biological sciences.

Modern astronomy and nuclear physics are changing our conception of the world in terms of stunning contrasts between macro and micro perspectives of reality. This is engendering new, and at times, apparently incompatible paradigms of space and time. But it is simultaneously forcing a reappraisal of the traditional (Newtonian) models of scientific truth which were part of the old antagonism between 'faith' and 'reason', and which the paradoxes of modern science are showing to be based on a simplistic grasp of the so-called scientific method of observation and experiment. Underlying this realization is an impulse in some of the leading scientists in this field towards oneness, that is, towards discovering a single explanatory principle for the apparent diversity of our universe.

All this is an opportunity for a new appraisal of the meaning and role of religious faith. Philosophers of religion must use this opportunity to play an important part in developing models of religious truth that are not covertly based on simplistic scientific and mathematical norms of truth. There may be one truth, but in the light of the principle of cohesive pluralities mentioned earlier there are analogical facets of this truth that have scientific, mathematical, moral, religious (and other) modalities. I believe that the thinkers of all faiths should be working towards the articulation of this cognitive goal.

But the advances of the biological sciences seem to be no less challenging. Indeed, their recent findings seem to have set the public imagination on fire. Today we have an early draft of 'The Book of Life' (a theological term originally), that is, a full decoding of the human genetic makeup. We have a new scientific discipline called 'Genomics'. For all its importance, 'The Book of Life' is no more than a massive uncovering of data. The real issue is what we do, in moral and religious context, with the seemingly endless possibilities of manipulating life in terms of the technological advances of medical research that this feat releases.

In fact, the metaphor of a 'book of life', the metaphor, that is, of conveying information, brings an important distinction to mind that we neglect at our peril. This is the distinction between *techne,* viz. the expertise to implement a discovery, and the readiness/ability to assess the human consequences of this implementation. The glamour of the first often overpowers the other. Indeed, it is not uncommon for scientists to claim that it is not their business to worry about the consequences of their scientific research, that their job is to make the discoveries in a totally amoral context. The moral of the following story, adapted from a version of the *Pancatantra,* an old collection of Indian fables, can help sharpen the issue.

Four Brahmins, traditional guardians of the knowledge-that-empowers in Hindu tradition, were journeying through a forest. Suddenly they came upon a pile of bones, and curious as ever, began to argue as to which animal the bones belonged to. Three of the Brahmins were experts in the lore of *mantra* – those power-packed formulae, which when correctly applied, invariably produce their (tangible) effect. The fourth Brahmin didn't have this esoteric knowledge; he was a practical man well grounded in the school of life. 'Don't meddle with those bones', he warned his companions. 'Leave well alone. Who knows what creature they belong too?' 'We can find out', said the others. 'We have the technology and we have the bones. All we have to do is recite the correct *mantra*s and we can re-create the owner. Our job is not to reason why, our job is to implement or die'. Alas, 'implement *and* die' would have been more to the point. For no sooner had they uttered their *mantra*s than a raging lion rose from the bones and devoured them. The fourth Brahmin, who had taken the precaution of climbing a tree in good time, escaped. Afterwards, when the lion had gone away, he came down and continued his journey shaking his head.

Techne, without wisdom and the prognosis of experience, has the capacity to devour not only its implementers but a great many others as well. *Techne* without the *logos*, the *scientia* or disciplined knowledge of moral and spiritual values, is blind. Theologians and moralists have an important role to play in creating *a climate of accountability* for scientific research and its backers. What is the true purpose of this research? What are likely to be its consequences in human terms? Will such research enhance the quality of human life? What role do commercial considerations, especially the interests of the funders of such research, play in controlling its benefits? Should you put a patent on information that can eradicate disease? No doubt questions are begged here: for example, what counts for 'enhancing the quality of human life'? But such questions cannot be tackled by science acting on its own. Since the great religious traditions have played such an important part historically in shaping the moral frameworks and spiritual values of our societies, their thinkers have a right to be heard in this discussion. What are these thinkers and the leaders of religious communities doing to educate and sensitize in this regard, to help set the moral agenda of the future? Not very much, you may conclude.

But religious thinking must also be ready to revise, even drastically, its attitudes and conceptual moulds through dialogue with scientific advances. New concepts and situations are being created by technology. Here is an example. Christians and Jews to a certain extent have traditionally related to God in terms of the idea of 'fatherhood'. This has been an important idea theologically, liturgically, and psychologically, especially for Christians. But in recent times, feminist insights have brought notions of 'motherhood' to the fore in the context of religion, and consequently of God's nurturing role as parent. But all three ideas – of 'fatherhood', 'motherhood', and 'parenting' – are undergoing substantial social change as a result of ongoing scientific research. We now have several functional notions of 'mother': the more traditional ones of natural mother, adoptive mother, spiritual mother, for example, but also newer ones such as surrogate mother and biological mother (i.e. someone who provides the ovum but does not become pregnant with the embryo). As processes for fertilization, bringing the foetus to term, and nurture after birth, change radically, the concept of parenting will change too. Our religious appreciation of this altered conception in terms of psychological resonance, symbolic power and theological articulation will have to come to terms with this change. We can extend this appreciation to sexual imagery, gender roles, the concept of personhood and so on.

Religion's dialogue with science is crucial for a pressing need in this new century: *a new theology of hope*. 'Love' – its use has become debased in so many ways ('making love' is often a euphemism for exploitative lust) – cannot exercise its influence of healing forgiveness and compassion unless it is in conversation with 'justice'. Like 'love', 'justice' is a word hard to pin down, but most of us have at least a working idea of what these words should mean as ennobling terms in the context of family, the market-place, employment, conflict-resolution. In a world where exploitation, avarice, oppression, violence and cynicism are rife, the everyday application of love and justice must give rise to a practical vision of hope. And a new power has risen, as a beacon of hope, in recent times: the *mass* mobilisation of ordinary citizens in *exocentric* causes, that is, in support of nations, people(s) other than their own. The huge demonstrations against the recent war in Iraq, the populist marches and concerts for the poor in Africa, the outpouring of aid for the victims of the tsunami in the Indian ocean in December 2004 and so on, are examples of a welcome and new phenomenon of globalization. Of course this is not enough. Corrupt governments, apathetic or compliant citizenry, unfair trading laws – are problems that must all be addressed as part of the larger picture. But the mass mobilization of which I speak is a crucial beginning for all those in power to sit up and take notice.

But, you may ask, is it not precisely the boon of modern science to be a harbinger of hope? Thus people who could not have children in the past, now have the hope, as the result of scientific developments, of producing children of their own; sufferers of various diseases untreatable in the past now have the hope of a cure; those who formerly faced a short life-expectancy can now hope to live longer, 'enhanced' lives. This hope is in the gift of science, is it not?

It is a hope that doesn't go far. For it is before and after the birth of the hoped-for child, the new cure, the life-enhancing treatment, that the real questions of meaning, purpose, value and right living arise, questions that science *qua* science cannot hope to answer. Scientific 'hope' is a pale shadow of the far richer dimensions of hope religions can offer and are seen as providing. This is 'deep' hope, that is, the hope of personal fulfilment. This is a crucial issue for our times.

It is here that the major religions, at least, come into their own. For deep hope is invariably linked to the use and abuse of power, and the major religions all teach (at their best) that we become fully human when we adopt what I may call *inverse strategies of the use of power*. This means that power is regarded as effective not when it results in the display of force but when it valorizes vulnerability in some way. These strategies are 'inverse' in so far as they contrast with the usual, i.e. worldly or raw uses of power where, to put it simplistically, might is right. Here power dominates, subjugates, pushes aside, humiliates, crushes. We are all familiar with these (ab)uses of power, not only on the battlefield, but also in the arena of gender relations, business competition, trading practices, aggressive advertising, family relationships, intellectual discourse. Inverse strategies of power, on the other hand, see and foster success when there is no attempt to dominate or manipulate. And to do this they valorize the vulnerability of trust, of weakness, the abjuring of violence and force. This impulse is at the heart of a number of the major religious traditions of the world.

Thus, a reading of the Hebrew Bible shows how God gradually weaned the ancient Israelites away from the blood-lust of conquest towards an appreciation of a covenant with him in which it is 'faithful love not sacrifice' that pleases him (Hosea 6.6). This was a covenant proclaimed faithfully by a long line of prophets, many of whom were ill-used or ignored. Yet God put himself (and continues to do so) in the vulnerable position of tirelessly seeking his people out in the faithful love of the covenant he had made. At the heart of the Christian tradition too is the proclamation of the Cross through which, by the death and resurrection of God's Chosen One, our broken world and lives are reconciled to our Father (and Mother) God. The Cross is not a symbol of assertive force; rather it is the sign of the strength of apparent weakness, of the power of vulnerability. There is the central teaching in the Buddhist faith, whether in the Theravada or Mahayana schools, that it is through wisdom and compassion alone towards every sentient being – not hurtful violence (*himsa*) – that one becomes a true follower of the Buddha, even to the point of sacrificing one's life. In Mahayana traditions it is emphasised that the *bodhisattva* (or Buddha-in-formation) yearns to defer achieving the ultimate goal of *nirvana* till every sentient being reaches that blessed state first. And it was not by egging on a people to violent revolt that Mahatma Gandhi, so emblematic of modern Hinduism, worked effectively to achieve self-rule (*svaraj*) in the Indian subcontinent, but by persevering in the path of truth-seeking and non-violence, even at the risk, on a number of occasions, of losing his life. Finally in Islam it is the spiritual, inner conflict with self in humble recognition of God's law that brings about the fruition on earth of the divine will for the welfare of all, not the lesser *jihad* of armed conquest (leave alone violent fundamentalism). The implementation of all these teachings decode into the inverse srategies of power mentioned earlier in everyday life. But they are hard to grasp, and even harder to follow. It will be the task of religion in the new millennium to more effectively propagate, exemplify, and seek to justify these strategies.

Let me conclude this essay, as we look to the future, by considering the role of university departments of theology and religion, and of the seminaries and theological colleges of the various faiths, in our modern societies. No doubt each of these kinds of institution of learning – university and seminary – adopts a different approach to the study of religion. The approach of the university is essentially academic/'secular', that is, it studies *what* the religious traditions say and practice – the contextual decoding of their scriptures, the consistency of their doctrinal statements and the potential coherence of the latter with other branches of knowledge, their historical development, and so on – without interjecting the commitment of personal belief as a necessary condition of such study (of course, such commitment may be contingently attendant on such study). The approach of the seminary/theological college on the other hand, while it may well deploy a high level of academic expertise, is driven by personal belief in a particular religious tradition. The 'shape' of the theological conclusion is taken for granted, so to speak, and its history and development, the means for its effective implementation, and arguments to generally support and defend it (and perhaps also to develop it in the light of comparative and interdisciplinary insights) are the object of its study. Nevertheless, in both cases, the objective is the reflective study of faith and religion, and this is a vital need for the societies in which we live. For it is traditional religion that has configured the frameworks of our core values and morals and of our understanding of the nature and destiny of the human person, that provides a critical dialogue partner for new departures from traditional models, that shapes the language of purposeful hope. If we undermine or close down the locations of such reflective study of faith and religion, we abandon a major resource for understanding, articulating and exploring what it is to be truly human. Then indeed our survival as a species on this planet faces a bleak prospect in this new age. Let us hope that all persons of good will have the vision to support in every way possible the responsible role of institutional centres of religious learning in our beleaguered societies today.

DAVID LOEWE

The Anglo-Jewish Association Past and Present

1. THE SOCIAL CONTEXT

From the Reform Bill of 1832 right through until, in 1928, Parliament finally allowed votes for all women, there was a steady stream of constitutional reform in Britain. In some cases, as in such matters as Sunday trading, alternatives to voting on Saturdays, and the granting of funds to denominational schools, specific provision was made for the Jewish community. One of the most significant acts was passed into law in 1867, when Parliament finally became free of control by the Crown, if not free from royal influence. But this was preceded, in 1858 and 1866, by two acts which, by freeing MPs of the obligation to swear a Christian oath, opened the way for Jews to enter Parliament.

Of course, many Jews were already prominent and successful members of British society. But the ability to enter Parliament was an important event for them, for two reasons. One was the immediate practical effect – Jews could now take a formal part in the government of the country in which they had lived for over two hundred years, and to the prosperity of which they had made a useful contribution. The second was that it marked the end of the second class status of the Jews in the country. It is unlikely that anyone believed that prejudice would disappear as if by magic, but it signified the last stage of formal acceptance of Jews in Britain.

At about this time the first practical thoughts about the serious intervention of the state into the community, for social purposes, were beginning to gain publicity. The effect of laissez-faire economics, combined with the industrial revolution, had been disastrous for some parts of the labour market, and the idea of modifying the purity of that doctrine was gaining ground. The philosopher Bradley was one of the most eminent to promote these ideas. Later on, of course, there were many other and more extreme thinkers. However, the general drift of their ideas – the need, that is to say, for the state to intervene in an organised manner to relieve the worst aspects of deprivation – was such as to find a response in the Jewish community. While the general approach tended towards changes in the regulations (or lack of them) governing employment, the Jewish tradition lay more in the direction of practical targeted assistance.

2. THE FOUNDATION OF THE ANGLO-JEWISH ASSOCIATION

These considerations provide some elements of the social context in which the Anglo-Jewish Association (AJA) was founded in 1871. But there were more immediate reasons for its foundation. In 1860 the French Jews had set up the Alliance Israélite Universelle in order to defend Jewish interests wherever it was necessary. Then, as in other times, the plague of anti-semitism was rife in the Middle East and indeed in eastern Europe. The occasion for its foundation was the notorious kidnapping of Edgardo Mortara, a Jewish boy from Bologna who was kidnapped in 1858 and brought up as a catholic. All efforts to get him released failed, and he eventually died a monk.

The AJA was founded for two reasons. One was the defeat of France in the Franco-Prussian war in 1870, and the other was the establishment of the Paris commune in the following year, during which the Alliance was unable to function. In these circumstances, it was felt prudent to ensure a British capacity.

The Alliance has, of course, developed into a far larger and more influential body than the AJA. The two organizations have always been on good terms; both sit on the Claims Conference, and on the Consultative Council of Jewish Organisations.

There was an additional reason for the AJA's foundation. Although the Board of Deputies had existed for many years as the representative body of Anglo-Jewry, it did not at that time, as a matter of policy, include the Reform congregations. Many influential and open-minded Jews were unhappy about the situation. On the one hand it would clearly have been wrong to set up an organization in opposition to the Board, which had and has a reasonable claim to be a representative body, but on the other hand an inclusive and influential body was needed.

The exclusion of Reform Jews from the Board of Deputies explains why one of the two founders of the AJA was Albert Löwy, the minister of the West London Synagogue, which was and is the leading Reform synagogue in the country. The other was Abraham Benisch, the editor of the Jewish Chronicle. The first president of the AJA was Jacob Waley, who was Professor of Political Economy at University College, London.

The original constitution, which, though it has been modified in detail, still retains its basic purpose, contains the following paragraphs defining the objectives of the AJA:

> To make every practical effort to remove any disabilities under which the Jews may labour, and to promote, wherever needful, the moral, social and intellectual advancement of our people . . .
>
> To give efficient aid to those who may suffer in consequence of being members of the Jewish community . . .
>
> To promote the publication of works calculated to advance these purposes.

Those objectives have been developed since then but their general thrust is unchanged. The humanitarian intentions of the founders in respect of Jews less fortunate than themselves have been evident throughout the existence of the AJA.

From the start the AJA was an independent body, and included members from all sections of Anglo-Jewry. This cross-community constituency was an outstanding feature of the AJA at the time of its foundation, and has been of critical importance to the Association ever since.

The social composition of the founders of the AJA reflected the upper crust of Anglo-Jewry, and it rapidly became one of the prestigious groups to which Jewish people who had made or were making their mark wanted to belong. The prestige which it gained was emphasized by its appointment as a Privileged Body of the Crown, giving it direct access to the monarch when it thought fit. It should perhaps be made clear that the AJA has taken no inappropriate advantage of this privilege. The Association soon included a large number of enthusiastic activists, and they recorded their work with the thoroughness typical of the Victorians. The Jewish archive at Southampton University became in due course the repository of their records, and is the source of much of the material in this paper.

3. THE WORK OF THE ASSOCIATION

The combination of basic philanthropic objectives with the thrust of social and political advancement produced a set of activities in which three strands can be detected.

3.1 The AJA and the Community

The first was the need to strengthen the cohesion of the Jewish community wherever that might appear necessary. Accordingly a large number of branches were set up, some of them in places which tell us quite a lot about the changes in social conditions and the problems of travelling in Britain. Local AJA branches appeared in Brixton, Edgware and North London. They also appeared in Edinburgh, Cardiff, Bristol, Sheffield and Birmingham, in Oxford and Cambridge, almost as a matter of course, one might think, but also in Canada, South Africa, Jamaica, Sierra Leone and Japan. It is unlikely that all these branches lasted very long – their demise is not always recorded in the AJA's archives – but it seems that they were intended to maintain the community and promote a wide-ranging and outward-looking Jewish culture.

3.2 Education

The second strand was educational, and here we begin to detect the philanthropic thrust of the AJA. The founders must have decided that their basic educational position in this country, both religious and secular, was satisfactory, because, although they founded some schools and took a benevolent interest in many others, these were all abroad and mainly, but not entirely, in the Middle East, which many of them knew.

Their interest and compassion seems to have been stimulated not simply by the need to secure the Jewish aspects of education but also a basic secular training for the children living under the regimes in that area. A report dealing with the children at Aden is instructive:

> There are government schools where about eight Jewish boys are sent; there is room for all who wish to be instructed, but unfortunately the Jewish parents prefer their boys to hawk about in the street, a disgrace to the community and an eyesore to Europeans landing at Aden.

The AJA supported a school at Aden, and there are some interesting figures dealing with the money involved. The costs of keeping a Jewish teacher and his (one assumes 'his' rather than 'her') family included annual sums of £40 for rent, £136 for housekeeping and £24 for two maids.

Apart from Aden, there is mention of a further fifteen schools which the AJA supported. They range geographically from Shanghai to Corfu. In both Baghdad and Basra they supported two schools, one for each sex. Some of the schools bear the names of benefactors who still figure in the AJA's current funds or supported the schools and who are well known in the community. They include the Shamash family, the Sassoon family, the Kadoorie family and the Rothschilds.

It would not have been possible to fund all these schools unaided. In its early days the annual subscription to the AJA was of the order of one or two guineas. There does not seem to have been a fixed amount, though there may have been a scale of charges. The accounts for the year 1879–80 show that the assets of the Association amounted to £3667 and the expenditure for the year, almost entirely balanced by income, was £3303. Of this sum, £1611 was passed to the schools which the AJA supported, and this support was continued until not long before the outbreak of the 1939 war. In almost every case the AJA's contribution, though far short of the total required, was sufficient to fund a significant activity.

3.3 The Evelina de Rothschild School

There was one exception to this generalisation. This was the Evelina de Rothschild School in Jerusalem.

This school evolved from small beginnings. In 1864 Sir Moses Montefiore and a French colleague, one M. Kahn, gave money to enable a class of fifteen girls to be given religious and secular education within the Old City. A little later on, Sir Moses persuaded the Rothschild family to take over the responsibility for this class.

The school was named in memory of the daughter of Baron Lionel de Rothschild, who was the head of the English branch of the family. She married her cousin Baron Ferdinand de Rothschild, but she died in 1867 after only a year of marriage. Her portrait can be seen in the Rothschilds' seat at Waddesdon, which is now open to the public.

A boys' school had been founded the year before the girls' school by the Alliance Israélite Universelle, and this school received some financial help from the AJA. This is on the record, but the AJA had initially no involvement with the Evelina de Rothschild School. It was not until 1894 that the AJA took responsibility for the teaching and administration of the school. It was now thirty years old, and it still reflected strongly the French influence from its foundation.

The AJA soon set up a ladies' committee to 'supervise' the school. The chair was, not surprisingly, Mrs Leopold de Rothschild, and the committee included Mrs Nathaniel Montefiore, the mother of Claude Montefiore, who was later to be a long-serving president of the AJA.

In the course of the next five years three separate reports on this girls' school were compiled by male visitors and passed to the AJA. The last of these, in 1898, was by Dr Israel Abrahams, and as a result – the report was not totally satisfactory – a trained English teacher, Miss Annie Landau, was sent out. Claude Montefiore had by then become president of the AJA.

From that moment the school took off. English and Hebrew were taught with equal prominence, the teaching of French was abolished, Arabic was introduced and, along with a proper emphasis on religious teaching and observance, a mild degree of what might be called muscular Judaism was also introduced. The school numbers rose to six hundred, and it was supported mainly by the AJA but also by the Rothschilds and by the payment of fees, effectively on a means-tested basis. The subvention from the AJA was initially £3 for each girl – in total not a negligible sum for the AJA in those days.

When the First World War broke out, Miss Landau was forced to leave the school – she was, after all, an English woman in enemy territory – and arrangements were made for funding to be continued during the hostilities. As soon as Palestine was freed she was back. She remained at the school until her death at the age of seventy in 1945.

When the Second World War ended, conditions had changed. The foundation of the State of Israel marked the beginning of a fundamental change in the school. Its preparatory section was transferred to the Municipality of Jerusalem, but not surprisingly the equal emphasis given to English alongside Hebrew was dropped. Some of the material shows that there was a significant degree of opposition to the teaching of English, though whether from natural chauvinism and a fear for the durability of modern Hebrew, or from resentment of the British government's post-war immigration policy, it is hard to say. Even so, the last headmaster valued the English teaching the girls receive as a valuable qualification and entry to many careers.

The secondary school remains as a free-standing organisation, but a somewhat anomalous one. The AJA no longer commands in real terms the financial resources with which it had supported the school in earlier days, and the school now depends on a mixture of tuition fees and grants, with some government assistance.

Nevertheless, the AJA maintains a beneficial interest in the school. The Association has been able to help in securing funds for some aspects of the school's work. Many honorary officers of the AJA have visited the school on a number of occasions, and are always made welcome. When the former prime minister, Yitzhak Rabin, was assassinated, interviews with some of the people of Jerusalem were shown on television in Britain. They included some of the girls from the Evelina de Rothschild, and they conducted themselves in a manner which reflected the greatest credit on the school. It is fair to say that the AJA's association with this school is one of the most important and creditable components of its history, and reflects the combination of religious faith and humanitarianism which the founders promoted.

3.4 The AJA as Employers

There is one more point to be made in connection with the AJA's educational activities. They displayed a practical but generous attitude to those who had served them. Though they consistently refused to make any contractual arrangement for paying pensions, they set up a scale to which they hoped their former employees' means would conform, and sometimes made ex gratia provision for those who had served them well and fallen on hard times. Indeed the AJA still possesses a fund for assisting teachers who have retired from the Evelina de Rothschild School, though since the school is now largely publicly funded, there is now little call on the fund.

3.5 The Humanitarian Work of the Association

The third strand in the activities of the AJA was humanitarian. The community in the UK supported a considerable number of charitable institutions – hospitals, and homes for incurables, for the deaf and dumb, for the blind, and for the homeless. There was also the Jewish Board of Guardians, now known as Jewish Care, which exercised itself in various types of charitable activities. The AJA contributed annual sums, which were significant in the context of the time, to up to ten such bodies, and these contributions continued until the Second World War.

However, the secure and emancipated position occupied by the Jews in this country was not available to their brethren in other parts of the world, and the AJA took an active interest in the well-being of Jewish communities elsewhere, in particular in eastern Europe and the Balkans, and in the Middle East. The early reports have sections dealing with Romania, Czechoslovakia, Bulgaria, Turkey and Iraq among other countries. The incidents covered in the following paragraphs took place between 1872 and 1890 – quite soon, that is to say, after the foundation of the AJA. An exact year can usefully be given in some cases, but very often the reports are vague and may well have been written considerably later than the events they describe.

The means by which the AJA attempted to achieve its ends was openly political, though in no sense party-political. There was presumably no other route open to it. The broader constituency of the AJA enabled its members to feel that they were entitled to a degree of influence comparable with that of the Board of Deputies, and there was initially some overlap and hence difficulty with the latter body, which is considerably older than the AJA. However, these difficulties were smoothed away over time, and in 1878 an agreement was reached to co-operate in foreign affairs, and from that agreement grew in due course the 'Conjoint Committee' which was set up in 1918. This proved to be a temporary arrangement, and was soon replaced by a more plainly named Joint Committee which remained active and useful until 1943, when it was terminated in circumstances which will be covered below.

The early records show a consistent pattern in two respects. One was the regular occurrence, year after year, of the same countries in the list of those in which the AJA thought it necessary to intervene. Morocco, Turkey, Serbia, Romania, Bulgaria, Russia and Egypt were regular offenders.

The AJA and the Board of Deputies, as already mentioned, co-operated in the area of foreign affairs, and a few of the initiatives they took are of interest. There is a record of a deputation sent by the committee to see Lord Salisbury – the exact date is not clear from the AJA record, but it was probably when he was foreign secretary – on the subject of persecution inflicted on Jews by or with the connivance of the authorities in Bulgaria. The record contains the text of the Jewish submission and Salisbury's reply. The latter concluded, 'You may think me curt if I do not go further into this subject ... I will only give you the assurance that as far as I know the feeling of those powers, with whom we are acting in concert, has not altered from those they entertained last year.' Apparently this reply was adjudged highly satisfactory by the deputation. One fears they may have been more easily pleased than a modern group would be by this stark response. Perhaps they were simply making the best of a bad job.

In Morocco, the AJA intervened to obtain compensation for a widow whose husband had been murdered by brigands. She was awarded 1500 francs, and the hill tribesmen who had committed the murder were brought to order and punished. Two Jews had in fact been murdered, but one suspects that the real impetus behind the punitive expedition was that they had also murdered no less than fifty Moslems. It is also of interest that the AJA's activities in Morocco at that time also covered the encouragement of smallpox vaccination among the Jews, whose conditions of life rendered them, it was thought, particularly liable to this dreadful disease.

This was in 1879 and 1880. There is, however, a record of an earlier intervention in Serbia, where a tolerant ruler had been replaced by a much less scrupulous figure who repealed the legislation which emancipated the Jews, and who connived in brutal practices against them. It is to the credit of the AJA that it persisted in its attempts to get this situation put right, and though it could not get the civil rights of the Serbian Jewish community restored, at least after some years the cessation of the brutalities was procured.

The other area of similarity lay in the process and the progress of these interventions. Information would reach the Jewish community in Britain that some form of anti-Semitism was being practised abroad. Sometimes it was necessary to send the AJA's own representative either to confirm the reports, or to conduct urgent legal transactions on the spot. Two names which occur in the reports as having conducted such missions are Neville Laski and A. S. Diamond, whom many will remember today. After getting confirmation, the Joint Foreign Affairs committee already described would approach the Foreign Office. After a protracted wait, during which exchanges between the Foreign Office and the diplomatic representatives in the country concerned took place, the Foreign Office would triumphantly produce a document which either declared that the discriminatory legislation would be repealed, or stated that the grievance concerned had been resolved.

In fact, these interventions were partly, but only partly, successful. In some cases the problem was discrimination, not so much against Jews as in favour of Moslems; Christians also suffered under rules which effectively precluded them from earning a decent living. Undertakings to change the law were sometimes more honoured in the breach than in the observance, and some governments resorted to legal subterfuges to get round the problem. On the other hand, in a number of individual cases, it was possible to get Jews released from arbitrary arrest, and to get their possessions restored to them.

Before dealing with the War and the post-War period, there is one pathetic incident to be recorded. There appear to be no records of any follow-up activity, nor is it possible to put a precise date on it, but it seems likely to have occurred just before Hitler came to power. The AJA received a document asking the Association 'to interpose its good offices with regard to the dangerous anti-Jewish agitation in Germany.'

Clearly the AJA contacted the German Jewish community in this connection, because the response from that community is on record. It said that they could thoroughly rely on the non-Jewish Germans. Pitiful and tragic as these exchanges seem now, it is hard to believe that any intervention possible in the contemporary political climate could have materially affected the course of history.

4. THE ASSOCIATION SINCE THE SECOND WORLD WAR

4.1 The Issue of Zionism

Two factors have influenced the fortunes of the AJA since the Second World War. One is the greatly accelerated pace of social change within the UK, and the other is the question of Israel. Both these factors have combined to reduce the power and influence of the AJA.

A form of Zionism was present in this country in the first half of the nineteenth century, not so much as a political force with the objective of a Jewish state, but rather as a movement to revive traditional Jewish culture and enable individuals to return to Palestine. That changed with the outbreak of the First World War. The story of the negotiations which led to the Balfour Declaration are of course well-known and on record.

Though there was and is only a limited amount of common ground between the extreme Jewish religious right and progressive Jews, it is true that both deplored, though for different reasons, the idea of a Jewish state. The extreme religious Jews thought that, wherever they happened to be, to live by the Torah was sufficient and that Judaism should have as little truck as possible with external authorities, though they conceded the necessity of obedience to the law of whatever land they inhabited. The Progressives regarded Judaism as a purely spiritual matter and accepted, as a matter of course, not only the civil laws of whatever state they happened to reside in but also, to a considerable extent, its general culture, and thus saw no need for a Jewish state.

This is no doubt an unfair and inadequate summary, but there is an element of truth in it. Certainly it is true that many Jews in this country, in the days before Israel existed, and perhaps today, had or have doubts about where they really belong. Some of them regarded with horror the possibility that once Israel was established, pressure, subtle or not so subtle, might be applied to them to move there.

Over the years, the political wing of Zionism pitched its camp, or more correctly one of its camps, within Anglo-Jewry, in the Board of Deputies, while the AJA remained the stronghold of the Jews who wanted a Jewish group within Palestine. It was partly this polarisation of attitudes which finally led in 1943 to the termination of the Joint Committee for Foreign Affairs in which the two bodies had previously participated. It was claimed at the time that Zionism was not the issue which caused the split, and it was possible to defend this contention, in that both sides supported the movement of Jews into what is now Israel. What separated them was the nature of the state to be established there.

There were two further points. The first was that the sentiment of large numbers of British Jews lay with the Board of Deputies. The second was that the social developments in the UK, both during and after the War, led to a reduction of the influence which bodies like the AJA, which was largely run by the rich, aristocratic and successful segment of Anglo-Jewry, could and should exert, and the Board of Deputies itself had almost from the beginning exerted pressure on the AJA to reduce its representation from the near parity at which the committee was set up. However, this was probably simple community politics.

4.2 The Association in the Post-War World

In 1947 the AJA submitted a memorandum to the British Government about Palestine. It is highly significant not only as an illustration of the AJA's attitude but also as a light on its view of both the Government's approach to Palestine and the situation which had developed in that country.

Firstly, it gave credit to the British Government for allowing the Jews to develop a physical infrastructure for their existence as, at least, an entity within the area.

Secondly, it advocated partition.

Thirdly, it recommended that both Arabs and Jews should assume responsibility for their own affairs.

Fourthly, and, one might think, critically, in view of the current situation, it reiterated 'that a settlement doing justice to Jewish rights and needs in Palestine could and should be carried out in conjunction with measures designed to further the progress and enhance the prosperity of the Arab states and generally to contribute to the peaceful development of the Middle East.'

However, later that year the AJA changed its tune, recommending an undivided Palestine in which all would enjoy equal opportunities and in which each group would be able to pursue unhindered its own way of life and preserve its own culture and traditions.

This is not the place for controversial matter about the Middle East today. But it is fair and probably uncontentious to say that the views of the AJA at that time at least evinced a high degree of idealism and would be recognised as decent, humane and civilised now. On the other hand, the AJA's approach to the problem was more in tune with the traditions of educated Englishmen than the passions of those who had suffered or were homeless and effectively stateless, or who saw themselves about to be dispossessed. Very large numbers of Jews were sympathetic to these latter sentiments.

Apart from the issue of Zionism, the records of the AJA during the War years are less interesting; this is natural enough, since its foreign activities were necessarily severely curtailed, though in 1940 the Association contributed nearly five thousand pounds to the Evelina de Rothschild School, and just over five thousand pounds in 1944. But there are important records of activity in the post-war years. In 1950 Zelman Cowen – now Sir Zelman Cowen, a former governor-general of Australia and a past president of the

AJA – intervened in the immigration problem with a published paper. He advocated temporary asylum for all genuine refugees and made the distinction between them and those whom we now call economic migrants, an interesting foretaste of later developments.

In 1947, the AJA produced a paper on Restitution and Compensation.

It dealt with some of the problems of property restitution in Europe, which, even with good will, proved very hard to resolve. Even today, these difficulties are still a problem.

The paper also recognised that not only was Germany insolvent, but furthermore that she had sustained so much damage to her productive capacity that it would be a very long time before reparations could be made. In fairness, it must be said that since then very large amounts have been paid in reparation in one form or another. The Conference for Material Claims against Germany – the Claims Conference, as it is now generally known – was set up in 1951 to deal with this problem. The AJA was a founding member and has a seat on the Board. The Claims Conference has attracted its share of controversy, but the AJA's contribution has always been oriented to the use of resources to bring aid and comfort to the needy, rather than to engage in political manoeuvres.

In any event, the overall record of the Claims Conference, in spite of individual complaints, does not admit of very much argument. With a small staff and a world-wide community it has dispensed vast sums where they were needed, and enabled many survivors of the Holocaust to pass the latter part of their lives in peace and comfort.

The AJA still operates in other areas internationally. One example is its membership of the Consultative Council of Jewish Organisations, and Clemens Nathan, a former president of the AJA, played a large part in the negotiations, which were eventually successful, to obtain compensation from Austria for the Jews from that country who suffered during the Second World War.

It also holds occasional functions, usually in order to give a platform to a speaker whose views are controversial or to deal with matters which concern the Anglo-Jewish community in the national context, for the AJA is always conscious both of its cross-community membership and of its national as well as its religious affiliation.

However, the AJA's core function today is the provision of assistance to those in higher education. In the UK, primary and secondary education is provided free by the state, though those in religious schools pay a supplement to cover religious education, for which it would plainly be improper to charge the taxpayer. However, university education is another matter. Not only are fees now going to become chargeable, but very many students attend universities remote from their homes and therefore incur subsistence expenses. It is clear, therefore, that this is the level at which the educational shoe pinches hardest, and, therefore, where the AJA directs its resources. Before the stock-market collapse following the atrocity in America on September 11, it probably gave more grants directly to individual students than any other UK organisation, and it also operates a similar service for at least one additional major charitable donor.

The AJA possesses great experience and knowledge in this area, and the record of those it has helped is excellent. It should be added that the subjects which the recipients of these awards are studying reflect an immense breadth of interests, ranging from theological subjects through history, engineering and medicine to advanced physics.

Today the AJA is functioning in the context of a shrinking Jewish community in Britain. It is building a new role against the background of intermarriage and a steady loss of faith. It was built by men of vision who understood the needs of their time. The general principles of tolerance, charity and compassion which they espoused are the essence of the tradition which they established in the AJA. That tradition must be a guide to the future of the AJA and its inspiration to meet the challenge of a changed and unpredictable world.

RAPHAEL LOEWE

Imitatio and Ethics in Judaism and Christianity

DICTIONARIES, especially concise ones, are dangerous tools in the hands of the half-trained. A contemporary English–Hebrew dictionary of Israeli Hebrew[1] tells us that the Hebrew for *ethics* is *torath ha-musar*, or *'ethiqa*; but *musar* means, in biblical Hebrew, *discipline*. In post-biblical Hebrew it does, indeed, shift in the direction of ethics when associatively tinged by other terms such as *derekh 'ereṣ*, but its adoption as a translation equivalent, *tout court*, is probably due to the prominence in the nineteenth century of the so-called *Musar*-movement[2] in eastern European Jewry, whose leaders sought to raise ethical standards both by the discipline of an exemplary *regimen* and by popularising mediaeval Jewish ethical writings. The only reason for drawing attention to this linguistic situation is in order to point out that as an established, hit-or-miss translation, it is liable to mislead modern Hebrew speakers and others unfamiliar with traditional Jewish sources into misconstruing the centre of gravity of Jewish ethical endeavour. For it would surely be a work of supererogation to demonstrate that, despite lack of a specialised vocabulary, the Hebrew Bible reflects an understanding of what ethical endeavour is about, and expresses it in terms of *derekh* (way), *leb* (heart or mind), and the verbal idiom *le-hithhallekh liphney 'elohim* (to

Based on a paper read to the Cambridge Theological Society on 25 February 1993.

1 M. Segal and M. B. Dagut, Jerusalem, 1977.

2 See the bibliographies to the articles in the *Encyclopedia Judaica* (henceforth *Enc. Jud.*) on *Musar-Movement* (H. H. Ben-Sasson), vol. 12, p. 534f., and *Salant, Joseph* (Y. Alfassi), vol. 14, p. 623.

walk before God), etc. Rabbinic Hebrew enlarges the relevant terminology by semantic extension of such terms as *minhag* (custom), *ma'alah*, (degree), that is, quality, and *middoth*, (measures), some of them perhaps being calques on Greek loan-words found also in Aramaic: κανών in Syriac can mean *rule of life*[3] a sense in which it was employed in Greek from Clement of Alexandria.[4] The point need not be laboured further, except to say that, similarly, while the invention of the adjective ἠθικός, *ethical*, is one of Aristotle's,[5] it would be absurd to contend that before him the Greeks had no notion of what ethics was about; one has only to remind oneself of such words as εἴκος and 'επιεικέια, ὕβρις, and of Sophocles' unforgettable appeal to the unwritten and unshakeable laws established by the gods.[6]

Greek ethical philosophy impinges on our topic but marginally. Despite the occasional assumption in non-philosophical contexts of divine endorsement, as by Sophocles as just quoted, or his assertion in the same play (*Ant.* 128) that Zeus particularly hates vainglorious boasting, for the philosophers ethics, like law, is man-made, and based upon social contract.[7] As such, Greek ethical writing is essentially irrelevant to Jewish and Christian ethics; but

3 R. Payne Smith, *Thesaurus Syriacus*, 2, (Oxford, 1901, 3660, *s.v.*, 1), cites J. P. N. Land, *Anecdota Syriaca*, 2, Leiden, 1868, 75.18.

4 G.W. H. Lampe, *Patristic Greek Lexicon*, p. 701, *s.v.*, D. 1.

5 *Eth. Nich.* 1103a, 5.

6 ἄγραπτα κἀσφαλῆ θεῶν νόμιμα, *Ant.* 454. The Greek notion of "unwritten laws" is well established. R. C. Jebb, Sophocles, *Oedipus Tyrannus*[3], on l. 865, quotes Plato, *Legg.* 793a, cf. Xenophon, *Mem.* 4, 4, 21, Aristotle, *Rhet.* 1 13 2. Contrast the Greek adage cited by R. Eliezer b. Pedath in the Palestinian Talmud, *Rosh Hashanah* 1.3 (57a), παρὰ βασιλέως ὁ νόμος ἄγραφος, "as proceeding from the king the law is unwritten" (i.e. not binding upon himself). See S. Lieberman, *Greek in Jewish Palestine*, 1942, pp. 37f. (It should be noted that while the context makes quite clear that ἄγραφος here means *not binding* (almost "capricious"), this meaning is not recorded by either Liddell-Scott-Jones or Lampe (see n. 4).

7 As Rabbi Louis Jacobs reminds me, Maimonides distinguishes between self-discipline leading to the ethical avoidance of such acts as murder and theft, "which are publicly acknowledged by all mankind as being reprehensible", and the self-discipline of compliance with the (specifically Jewish) precepts enunciated in the Torah (*Eight Chapters* introducing Mishnah, *'Aboth*, ch. 6). More significant for our present purpose is the differentiation, near the end of his Halakhic code (*Hilkhoth melakhim*, 8.11) between those non-Jews who accept the "seven commandments for Noah's descendants" (see below, n. 26) that are a formula for civilised behaviour as being divinely sanctioned, and who are therefore to be automatically considered "righteous gentiles", and those who abide by the code out of intellectual conviction (*hekhra' ha-da'ath*): the latter are to be reckoned [humanist] sages (reading *'ella'* in place of *we-lo'* as the penultimate word). (English translation, A. M. Hershman, *The Code of Maimonides Book Fourteen The Book of Judges*, Yale Judaica Series III, New Haven, 1949, p. 230).

mediaeval Judaism and Christianity could no more remain untouched by Plato and Aristotle than could Islam. My diagram (fig. 1), certainly oversimplified, endeavours to represent this influence, which consists almost entirely in providing a conceptual schematisation for the traditional springs of ethical endeavour in Judaism and Christianity respectively. To cite two examples on the Jewish side, both from eleventh century Spain: Ibn Gabirol's Neoplatonic system in effect subsumes ethics within a psychology that is largely conceived in traditional Jewish terms, notwithstanding the fact that he takes for granted the Aristotelian tripartite soul which had become a mediaeval commonplace,[8] and his near-contemporary, Bahya ibn Paquda, who is also to be reckoned a Jewish Neoplatonist, constructs his *Duties of the Heart* around the three principles that appear to anticipate Anglicanism, namely scripture, reason, and tradition, but he leavens his application of these to such ethical topics as the examination of conscience, or humility, by calling in aid the Aristotelian mean.[9]

The ethical system, whether of Christianity or Judaism, concerns us here to the extent only that it either has room for, or requires the notion of *mimēsis* (I shall generally prefer the Greek term to the Latin) as a generator of ethical energy; and I shall begin with a thumbnail sketch of the situation in Christianity, since although this is familiar ground its comparison with Judaism is essential to our purpose.

The familiarity of Jesus himself with the institutional framework and the values of pharisaic Judaism, with Torah in its plenary sense as their foundation, needs no demonstration. However, for the early Church, incarnation transcended Torah, lip-service to the validity of which was accommodated by reductionism: the Ten Commandments, Lev. 19.18 as regards the love of one's neighbour, and the *Shema*ʿ (Deut. 6.4f.; Matt. 19.18f.; 22.23f.). The authority

8 See J. Schlanger, *La philosophie de Salomon ibn Gabirol. Étude d'un néoplatonisme,* Étude sur le judaïsme médiéval, 3, Leiden, 1968. Cf. Ibn Gabirol's *Kether malkhuth*, sections 25, 31, ed. D. Jarden, *Shirey ha-qodesh*, 1, pp. 52f., 57. R. Loewe, *Ibn Gabirol*, 1989, pp. 137f., 143, also pp. 32f. I. Husik, *A History of Medieval Jewish Philosophy*, 1916 (1946), pp. 65f; C. Sirat, *A History of Jewish Philosophy in the Middle Ages*, Cambridge – Paris, 1985, pp. 71f., 75f., 77–79. W. J. van Bekkum, "The Motif of the Soul in Ibn Gabirol's Poem *shikhehi yegonekh*". E. G. L. Schrijver et al. (eds), *The Literary Analysis of Hebrew Texts*, Amsterdam, 1992, pp. 60–71.

9 On Bahya see the bibliography *s.v.* (G. Vajda), *Enc. Jud.* 4, 406f; M. Mansoor, *The Book of Direction to the Duties of the Heart ... of Bahya ... Ibn Paquda*, London, 1973, Introduction, pp. 12f. For the application of the doctrine of the mean, see e.g. the section on asceticism, Mansoor, pp. 411f.

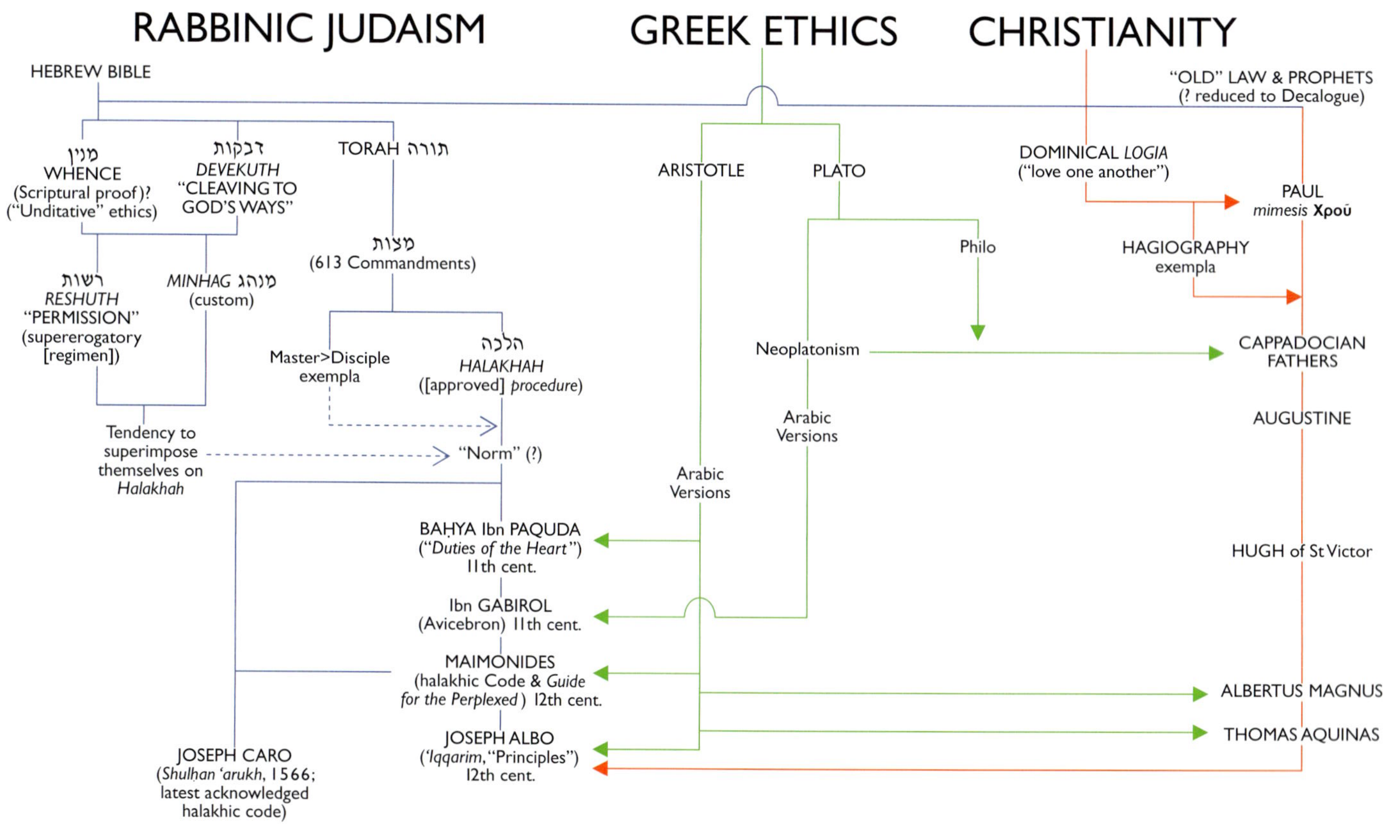
RABBINIC JUDAISM
GREEK ETHICS
CHRISTIANITY
HEBREW BIBLE
"OLD" LAW & PROPHETS
(? reduced to Decalogue)
מנין
WHENCE
(Scriptural proof)?
("Unditative" ethics)
דבקות
DEVEKUTH
"CLEAVING TO
GOD'S WAYS"
TORAH תורה
מצות
(613 Commandments)
רשות
RESHUTH
"PERMISSION"
(supererogatory
[regimen])
MINHAG מנהג
(custom)
Master>Disciple
exempla
הלכה
HALAKHAH
([approved] procedure)
Tendency to
superimpose
themselves on
Halakhah
"Norm" (?)
ARISTOTLE
PLATO
Philo
Neoplatonism
Arabic
Versions
Arabic
Versions
DOMINICAL LOGIA
("love one another")
PAUL
mimesis Χροῦ
HAGIOGRAPHY
exempla
CAPPADOCIAN
FATHERS
AUGUSTINE
HUGH of St Victor
ALBERTUS MAGNUS
THOMAS AQUINAS
BAHYA Ibn PAQUDA
("Duties of the Heart")
11th cent.
Ibn GABIROL
(Avicebron) 11th cent.
MAIMONIDES
(halakhic Code & Guide
for the Perplexed) 12th cent.
JOSEPH ALBO
('Iqqarim, "Principles")
12th cent.
JOSEPH CARO
(Shulḥan 'arukh, 1566;
latest acknowledged
halakhic code)

Figure 1

of Torah is, in effect, replaced by that of the dominical *logia* – in which, as it happens, Jesus was not averse to using the preceptive formula as emanating from himself in a manner that no rabbi would have presumed to do: "this is my commandment [ἐντολή, the regular septuagintal rendering of *miṣwah*], that ye love one another as I have loved you" (John 15.12). The seven so-called rabbinical commandments[10] concerning institutions for which no source in the written Torah, i.e. the Pentateuch, could be either identified or contrived allusively, are accompanied by the same benedictional formula as the biblical commandments, asserting that their authority inheres in God, "who has sanctified us by his commandments". Administrative ordinances introduced by the rabbis on their own authority are not called commandments but *takkanoth* (enactments) or *gezeroth* (decrees). The Johannine passage that I have adduced may be said to point the way forward to the Pauline centrality of *mimēsis*, *imitation* of God (Eph. 5.1, μιμηταὶ τοῦ θεοῦ ὡς τέκνα ἀγαπητά). The imitation of Christ, ἡ Χριστοῦ μίμησις, becomes a patristic commonplace[11] and indeed for all subsequent Christian thought and action; its centrality did not need, and indeed tacitly disposed of any prop provided by the commandment-formula familiar in Judaism.

It is important to pause here in order to expose the fallacy inherent in the assumption, or fiction, that in this process Torah is transcended – that is to say, yields place to something which, whilst organically not dissociable from it, nevertheless operates in an entirely different manner. W. D. Davies – and possibly others before him – speaks in this connection of transcendence,[12] if I recollect rightly; in my view it would have been better to speak of transfiguration. The teachings of Torah are embodied in *miṣwah*, "commandment": and obedience to a command, be it joyfully responsive or enforced, cannot be identified with the emulation of a model. The only situation that I can think of in which these two things coincide, without however constituting an identity, is in a school gymnasium, where a drill-instructor with a class of young children may prefer to call out a peremptory "Do this!" rather than "Arms bend!" Dr Hugh Montefiore has cited Lev. 19.2 as an example of *mimēsis* in the Old Testament: "Ye shall be holy, for I, the Lord your God, am holy". But that the Hebrew imperfect tense – *qedoshim tiheyu* – is here mandatory is made clear by the preamble: "Speak unto all the congregation of the children

10 For these see *Jewish Encyclopedia*, 4, p. 180, col. ii.
11 E.g. Basil, *de Spiritu Sancto*, 35, Migne, *Patrologia Graeco-latina*, 32, 128D.
12 *Paul and Rabbinic Judaism*, 1948, cf. pp. 111f.

of Israel and say, ye shall be holy". Curiously, despite the emphasis in parallel texts (11.44; 20.7), Maimonides does not list the cultivation of holiness as one of the 248 positive commandments, apparently considering the nuance of the imperfect tense here to be parenetic.[13]

Mimēsis, then, cannot as I see it be legitimately claimed to constitute the ideal and the ultimate implementation of Torah, even though Torah is misrepresented if it is simply equated with *law*. Imitation may be the sincerest form of flattery, but flattery is not the same thing as obedience. Nevertheless, it is understandable that, from a Christian point of view, *mimēsis* should replace responsive implementation of precept as an ethical dynamo. If the Deity subjected Itself to incarnation in order to share human experience to the full, it would follow that its incarnate reaction to such experience must, *ex hypothesi*, evince ethical perfection, and consequently constitute a paradigm for humanity. A theoretical paradigm, that is: from which it will be necessary to extrapolate virtually all specific indications, in view of the quite limited number of examples arising out of concrete situations in the life of Jesus as recorded in the gospels. It is significant that Thomas a Kempis' *Imitation of Christ* contains no references to events in the career of Jesus that constitute *exempla*; what we find there is encouragement to conform to Christ,[14] to emulate his acceptance of the role of victim[15] and the quotation from the fourth gospel "If any man love me, he will keep my word".[16] In point of fact, despite its title, rather than being a summons to *imitatio*, Thomas a Kempis' book is rather an education in the cultivation of submissiveness

13 A numbered catalogue of precepts, excerpted from Maimonides' *Sepher ha-miṣwoth* on the subject, is printed at the beginning of some editions of his great Halakhic code *Mishneh torah*. For a numbered list in English, see *Jewish Enc.*, 4, pp. 181f (preferable to that in *Enc. Jud.*, 5, 762f.). The traditional number of positive (248) and negative (365) commandments in the written Torah (i.e. Pentateuch) ascends at least to Rabbi Simlai (Babylonia, second half of third century), TB *Makkoth* 23b; the identification of the positive ones involves some subjective decisions on the part of jurists regarding distinction between the mandatory, the commendatory, and the permissive, and Maimonides' catalogue replaced earlier ones in popular acceptance. See below, n. 43.

It is apposite here to refer to Leon Roth's study of *mimēsis* in Judaism, *ha-hidamoth la-el we-ra'ayon ha-qedushah* (Ahad Ha'am Memorial Lecture, published in 1931 and in a collection of the memorial lectures, 1937; English translation by R. Loewe ('Imitatio Dei and the Idea of Holiness', in L. Roth, *Is there a Jewish Philosophy?* 1999, pp. 15–28).)

14 I 25; for convenience I have used the English translation by L. Sherley Price, London, 1952 (p. 64).

15 II I (pp. 67f.), III 13 (p. 110), 18 (p. 116), 56 (p. 174).

16 John 14, 23 (II, I, p. 67).

to the divine will; expressed in Christian idiom, it parallels the words of a noble prayer that is to be found in the Talmud[17] and thence taken up into the Jewish morning prayers, "Subdue Thou our self-assertive drive (*yeṣer*) to enslave itself to Thee" (*we-khoph 'eth yiṣrenu le-hishta'bed lakh*).[18]

When we look for the Jewish counterpart of Christian *mimēsis*, we shall distort the perspective if we fail to keep clearly in view the major categories within which the Torah finds expression. As already indicated, *law*, *nomos*, and *lex* are inadequate as one-word translation-summaries, and even *instruction* is not completely satisfactory. Since we are not editing a pocket dictionary we may abandon insistence upon a word-for-word rendering, and fall back on a brief definition. I myself would define Torah as the sphere in which revelational experience and the response thereto take place. And since response to revelation may be expected to express itself in the conviction that any practical directives as to action, or refraining from action, are binding (*Write! Paint! Preach! Prophesy! Refrain from blood-sports!*) inasmuch as they emanate from above, it is easy to see how *Torah* = *law* passes from being an over-succinct summary into a cliché. The complete system is set out in figure 2, which would be clearer if it could be three-dimensional, the whole being visualised as a domed cylinder. At the core stands Torah in its most limited, concrete sense, that is, the Pentateuch or "Torah in writing" – a term which is sometimes tacitly extended to embrace the other two sections of the Jewish biblical canon, namely the prophetic works and the Hagiographa. This inner column is encased within the so-called "oral Torah" which, because of the dynamic quality of its revelational source, is to be considered a continuously expanding element, the contents of which are comprised under the twin categories of *halakhah* and *'aggada*. Every Jewish institution, value, and concept falls under one, or (as we will explain in a moment) both of these headings. To change the picture, Torah is a golfing-umbrella, not an infinitely extensible bus-shelter; inasmuch as some things (for example, the blurring of the distinction between Creator and creation, idolatry, or the perversion of civilised morals) will not be admitted beneath it.

Jewish tradition identifies in the pentateuchal text 613 precepts, 248 of them positive and 365 negative;[19] and the processes – jurisprudential,

17 TB *Berakoth* 60b.

18 See e.g. S. Singer, *Authorised Daily Prayer Book*, ed. 1929, p. 7, and I. Abrahams, *Companion to the Authorised Daily Prayer Book* 2 (1922), p. xix.

19 See above, n. 13.

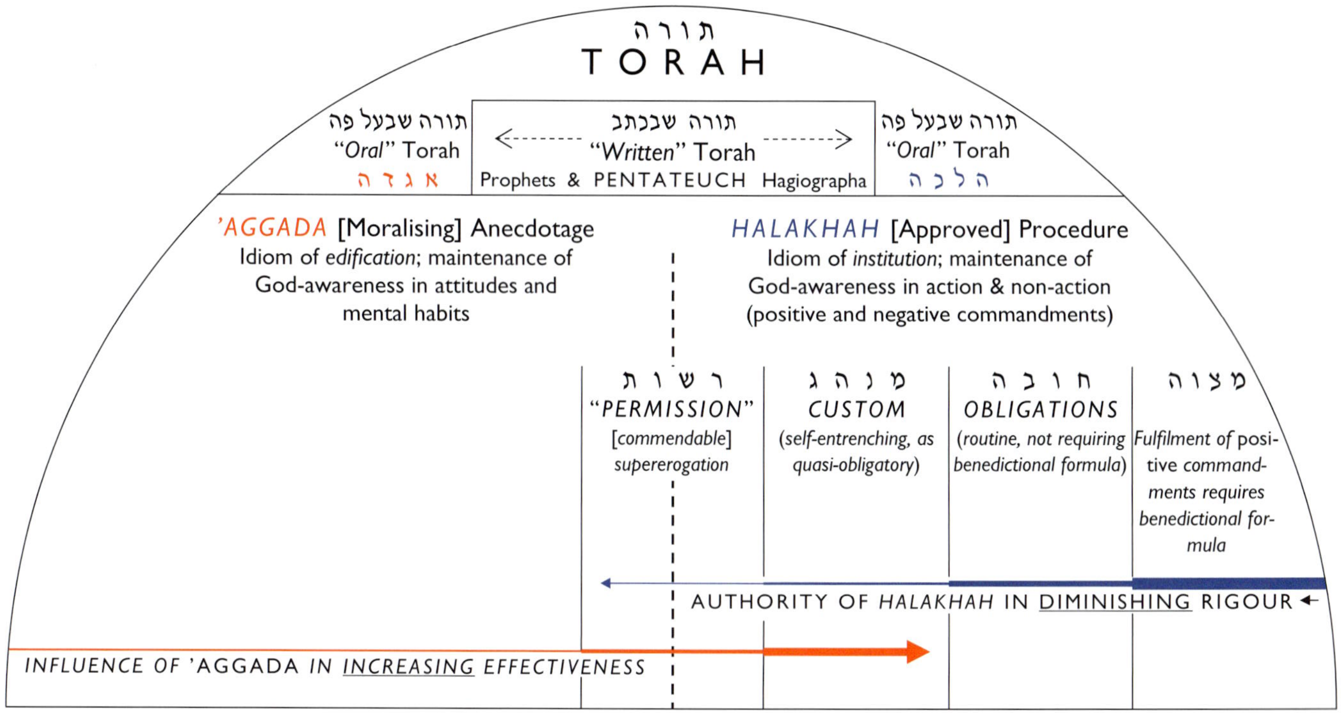
תורה
TORAH
תורה שבעל פה
"Oral" Torah
אגדה
תורה שבכתב
"Written" Torah
Prophets & PENTATEUCH Hagiographa
תורה שבעל פה
"Oral" Torah
הלכה
'AGGADA [Moralising] Anecdotage
Idiom of edification; maintenance of God-awareness in attitudes and mental habits
HALAKHAH [Approved] Procedure
Idiom of institution; maintenance of God-awareness in action & non-action (positive and negative commandments)
רשות
"PERMISSION"
[commendable] supererogation
מנהג
CUSTOM
(self-entrenching, as quasi-obligatory)
חובה
OBLIGATIONS
(routine, not requiring benedictional formula)
מצוה
Fulfilment of positive commandments requires benedictional formula
AUTHORITY OF HALAKHAH IN DIMINISHING RIGOUR
INFLUENCE OF 'AGGADA IN INCREASING EFFECTIVENESS

Figure 2

casuistic, and supervisory – subsumed under the title *halakhah* are in part concerned with the cumulative development of their detailed applicability, under rabbinical authority, and subject to sundry very clear terms of reference, in order to meet evolving social conditions, economic constraint, and so on. *Halakhah*, then, which – like the Greek μέθοδος, means no more than *procedure*, i.e. *approved procedure* – is concerned with maintaining God-awareness in all the practical aspects of life; not merely with cultic and ceremonial aspects, but all else, from private matters like personal hygiene and marital considerateness, through domestic concerns and education, to public administration at all levels – civil, commercial, forensic, religious – by imposing upon them a discipline of both action and enjoined non-action. Here are all the *dos*, *don'ts*, *mays*, *shoulds*, and the *ideally nots* of Judaism. Small wonder, then, that in simplistic Jewish popular thinking Torah often equals *halakhah* = rules = Judaism, anything without practical import being assumed to be peripheral, or even disposable.

In point of fact, without reference to *'aggada* the description of rabbinic religion is incomplete, but before we look at *'aggada* it is important to understand the internal anatomy of *halakhah*, as represented diagrammatically by the vertical columns at the bottom right of figure 2. The positive precepts of institutional Judaism, *miṣwoth*, such as the observance of the Sabbath, are incompletely implemented unless accompanied by a benedictional formula declaring that they are fulfilled in obedience to the divine command. Certain other actions, of a routine nature, require no such enunciation, even though they are obligatory (*ḥobah*, duty). In addition to these two divisions there are those of *reshuth*[20] (option[al supererogation]), and *minhag*, custom, these two comprising pietism and intense ethical sensitivity, such as generosity and regularity in the practice of charity that transcends statutory minimal scales. These four Halakhic sub-categories, *commandment*, *obligation*, *option*, and *usage*, together with their negative corollaries and counterparts, subsume and articulate Jewish ethical syntax; and it will not be feasible to consider the role of *mimēsis* in Judaism without reference to them.

'Aggada means *recounting*, that is, anecdotal rapportage; and it refers to the exuberant elaboration of the biblical story – not, be it noted, elaboration of the legal matter, which is the province of *halakhah* – with legendary material. Much of it is heuristic, being concerned to fill gaps in the bald narrative

20 For the categories *miṣwah, ḥobah, reshuth* see TB *Ḥullin* 105a, *infra*. Maimonides, *Hilkhoth berakhoth* 11, 2, uses these terms somewhat differently.

by resort to folklore material and fictional improvisation, without shying away from ribaldry where it can, without prurience, enhance the drama. But integral to the whole endeavour is the aim of moralizing those episodes which, on the face of things, raise serious questions as to the behaviour of the biblical heroes; of intensifying such spiritual and ethical sensitivity as leaps to the eye from the text; and of emphasizing the concern of the Godhead to involve Itself in the whole enterprise, by calling in aid anthropomorphism and anthropopathism, blithely untroubled by philosophical problematic or theological inhibition. The whole rich corpus can be best studied by those without access to the Hebrew sources in Ginzberg's monumental digest, *The Legends of the Jews*,[21] and it invites some comparison with the function of stained glass windows and the *biblia pauperum* in the mediaeval western Church. *'Aggada* may thus be shown to complement *halakhah*: whereas the purview of *halakhah* is God-awareness in practicalities, *'aggada* is concerned to infuse God-awareness into mental attitudes. Nor are the two to be considered watertight compartments – hence the interrupted line between the two of them in my diagram – since each can impinge upon the other. The concern of *halakhah* to establish continuity of institutional practice makes the *midrash* assert that even the early biblical heroes were pre-cognitively familiar with its *minutiae*, as was Abraham when he applied the legal fiction of the rabbis to permit cooking on a festival food for an immediately ensuing sabbath.[22] And the *'aggada* would predispose us to greater awareness of the virtue of charity, by encouraging us to emulate the example of David, who, it claims, never retired for the night without first ensuring that he had, on that particular day, performed some act of charity.[23] To the significance, for our purposes, of Aggadic material relating directly to the alleged activity of the Deity we shall return below.

In view of the foregoing, it will now be the more understandable that Hebrew has no specific term for *ethics*. Indeed, the whole concept of human rights is one that is, in my view, alien to rabbinic jurisprudence – a view shared by the late Haim Cohen, a judge of the Israeli Supreme Court, in his

---

21 Seven volumes, Philadelphia, 1913–38. The abridged version lacks the notes on the source material, and the index.

22 TB *Yoma* 28b, cf. *Genesis Rabbah, Wa-yera'*, 49, 2, ed. Wilna, f. 100b cols. i–ii, and parallels, for which see Ginzberg, *Legends*, 1, p. 292, 5, p. 259, n. 275.

23 *'Alpha Betha de-ben Sira,* ed. M. Steinschneider, 1858, f. 8a, cf. TB *Sanhendrin* 7b; Ginzberg, *Legends*, 6, pp. 260f., n. 78.

book on the subject.[24] What there is, is a categorical distinction between "commandments applicable between man and God" and "commandments applicable as between fellow-men":[25] all humankind are the reciprocal beneficiaries of the duties which each individual owes to God – this formula also potentially embracing the gentiles, who are subject to their own, streamlined code designated "the seven commandments given to Noah's descendants".[26]

The apparently comprehensive framework constructed by *halakhah* may be thought to set out to provide, so to say, a rule-book answer for any situation involving an ethical problem. In point of fact, of course, it cannot, and, recognising this, rabbinic jurisprudence uses a couple of formulas to demarcate gaps. Between them, they can cover much of the wide area which attaches itself to the most important term in the ethical vocabulary of biblical Hebrew – a term which, up to this point, I have left unmentioned. That term is *ḥesed*, commonly rendered mercy, or loving kindness, although *loyalty* perhaps comes nearer the mark. *Ḥesed* is that reciprocal solidarity which binds together, at the level of both individual and group, superior to inferior, advantaged to disadvantaged, man to God and God to man, and it may be considered to be the Hebraic equivalent of what Aristotle was referring to when he described man as a πολιτικόν ζῶον[27]. I would myself surmise that, insofar as what nowadays purports to describe itself as secular Judaism admits any specifically Jewish roots for its own ethical endeavours (the standards of

24 Haim Cohen, *Human Rights in Jewish Law*, New York, 1984, pp. 17f. The formula *miṣwah ʿal peloni* ("a commandment *in connection with N*") is significant; see quotations in E. Ben Yehuda, *Thesaurus,* 4, p. 3242, col. ii, e.g. "commandments [incumbent upon] a son *towards* his father".

25 See Maimonides, *Mishneh torah, Hilkhoth berakhoth* 11.2, end (commandments applicable between man and God), and Joseph Caro, *Keseph mishneh, in loc.* ("as distinct from those applicable between fellow-men"). I am grateful to Rabbi Louis Jacobs for directing me to this passage. In spite of the difficulty in locating references to the categorical distinction, its antiquity and importance seems clearly to be implied already in the Mishnah, by the corollary distinction drawn between transgressions (*ʿaberoth*) as solely between man and God, and as involving another human party [also] (*Yoma* 8, 9). The correlation effected between the Ten Commandments, disposed symmetrically 5 + 5 on the two tablets (e.g. "I am the Lord thy God" and "Thou shalt not murder"), seems to imply awareness of the same categorical distinction, even though the formula itself is not mentioned; see *Mekhilta, Bahodesh,* 8, ed. I. H. Weiss, f. 78a, English translation by J. Z. Lauterbach, Philadelphia, 1933, 2, pp. 262f.; Ginzberg, *Legends* (see n. 21), 3, p. 104, 6, pp. 43, n. 236, 49, n. 258.

26 See bibliography to the article *Noachide Laws* (S. Berman) in *Enc. Jud.,* 12, 1189f; R. Loewe, 'Universalism in the Halakhah, in R. Loewe (ed.), *Studies . . . in Memory of Leon Roth,* London, 1966, pp. 125f.

27 *Pol.* 1253a 3.

which I am in no way concerned to belittle), it is the notion of *ḥesed*, and the rarer term *ḥemlah* (clemency), that is pointed to as the sheet-anchor, since for the rabbinic mode of address to the subject secularism has little time.

Of the rabbinic formulas to which I refer the first is positive: certain things, the Halakhic sources recognise, are *debarim ha-mesurim la-leb*, left to the heart: for example, just what may constitute either material or verbal oppressiveness (*'ona'ah*) in connection with the biblical injunction (Exod. 22.22) not to vex a stranger, or, as rabbinically interpreted, a proselyte. A biblical pointer to the indispensability of the role of conscience in such connections is discovered in the recurrent phrase "and thou shalt be fearful of thy God" in some of the pertinent contexts (e.g. Lev. 25.17).[28]

The second formula, which is negative, is applied in order to reprobate what is reprehensible, even though it may be legally admissible; and it is reduced to the two introductory words of a sentence, rather as in English law the phrase *nisi prius* can become self-substantive. The formula is *mi she-para'*, and the full phrase runs, "He who punished [*mi she-para'*] the generation of the Flood and the generations dispersed from the tower of Babel will in due course exact punishment from those who do not keep their word" (Mishna *Baba Meṣi'ah* 4.1). It is applied to deprecate sharp practice in business, for example the use of comma-hunting to justify retraction from a commercial deal at the very latest stage.[29]

But despite this acknowledgement that individual conscience must play its part, there is frequently operative what we may call an Halakhic bridle-rein, that prevents either self-discipline or social responsibility from being ignored. A famous example is the beginning of the Mishnaic tractate *Pe'ah*, that deals with leaving the corner of the field for the poor to harvest (Lev. 23.22). Just how large or how small is a corner? The Mishnah[30] begins with the rehearsal of things regarding which Scripture itself ordains no fixed measure – the corner of the field, deeds of mutual charity (*gemiluth ḥasadim*), study of the Torah, etc. But whilst acknowledging that tariffs are not to be set on the upper range of the scale of generosity, the rabbis appreciated the social consequences of turning a blind eye to rampant parsimony. In theory, a single square yard, or even less, could constitute the corner of a

---

28 TB *Baba Meṣi'a* 58b.

29 Mishnah, *Baba Meṣi'a* 4, 2, TB 44af.

30 Mishnah, *Pe'ah* 1.1.

field; but in the immediately ensuing paragraph the Mishnah[31] declares that there is an Halakhically established minimum of one-sixtieth of the total harvest-bearing area. It may be apposite to observe that awareness of such jurisprudentially established parameters need not stifle ethical spontaneity; in view of the concept of *miṣwah* constituting privilege, the implementation of the consequential responsibilities should evoke feelings of gratitude and joy. Significant here is the popularity of an adage of the otherwise almost unknown tannaitic rabbi Hananiah b. Aqashyah to the effect that the plethora of precepts contained in the Torah is the mark of privilege divinely accorded to Israel, a proof-text being contrived from Isaiah 42.21.[32] The circumstance that eudemonistic considerations may well be present here would merely underscore the point.

The coordinates established, we may focus on the function of *mimēsis* in Judaism: and it should by now be clear that its writ, so to call it, is constitutionally limited to the upper left-hand area on figure 1 or, on figure 2, to the central area. That, however, does not preclude its influence being subtly pervasive. What is the mainspring of that influence? Simply to refer it to the uninhibited anthropomorphism of the Hebrew Bible would seem facile, in view of Jewish insistence, from the time of Deuteronomy (4.11–18) at the latest, on the incorporeality of God. More significant for our purpose is the rabbinic exegesis of two passages. In the first of them[33] Rabbi ʿAqiba turns anthropomorphism upside down by rigorous attention to the text of Genesis (1.27). "Favoured is man", he said, "in that he was created in the [divine] image; but it was an extra mark of favour that he was made aware of the fact."[34] It is not unreasonable to assume that what ʿAqiba meant was something

31 "*Pe'ah* should not be less than one-sixtieth part [of the harvest]. And although they have said that no measure is prescribed for *Pe'ah*, it should ever accord with the size of the field and the number of the poor and the yield [of the harvest]" (H. Danby's translation, p. 11).

32 Mishnah, *Makkoth* 3.16. For Hananiah b. ʿAqashyah see W. Bacher, *Die Agada der Tannaiten*, 2, 1890, p. 376, *Jew. Enc.*, *s.v.*, 6, 208. In Isa. 42.21, [*lemaʿan*] *ṣidqo*, "[for] his righteousness' [sake]" refers probably to the servant of the Lord (v. 19), but possibly to the Deity (v. 21). Hananiah's "proof" is achieved by revocalising as *ṣaddeqo* and treating the suffix as objective, "[in order to effect] righteousness [(and consequential merit) in] him" (*scil.* Israel). The quotation became the established preamble to recitation of *qaddish de-rabbanan,* i.e. the form of doxology with which collective study of rabbinic texts is concluded (*Enc. Jud.*, 10, 660) and hence very familiar. See Montefiore – Loewe (*infra*, n. 44), p. 219.

33 Mishnah, *ʾAboth*, 3.14.

34 Thus Maimonides understands the words *ḥibbah yetherah nodaʿath lo*; commentary to the Mishnah, *in loc.*, and similarly Obadiah Bartenora's commentary.

similar to Maimonides' own interpretation of the same text, namely that the image of God refers to man's faculty of intellectual cognisance.[35]

But the *locus classicus* is a piece of exegesis to be found in the *Sifrē* to Deuteronomy, which must consequently ascend to at least the period of 'Aqiba and Ishmael, that is, the early second century CE. The biblical text (Deut. 11.22f) reads: "For if ye shall diligently keep all these commandments which I command you, to do them, to love the Lord your God, to walk in all his ways, and to cleave unto Him, then will the Lord drive out all these nations from before you". And here is the *Sifrē*'s elaboration, in which I abbreviate the proof-texts in the interests of space:[36]

> "To walk in all his ways": The following are the ways of the Deity. He is a merciful and gracious God, of whom it is said that whosoever calls on his name shall be delivered[37]. [The *qal, yiqra'*, might be vocalized as *niph'al, yiqqare'*: "whoso is *called* by God's name".] But how is it conceivable that humankind could be called by God's Name? Just as God is called merciful, so be thou merciful; the Holy One, blessed is He, is called gracious, righteous, loyally appreciative [of remorse] (*ḥasid*), so do thou be gracious, righteous and loyal.[38] Proverbs [16.4] states that "the Lord hath made all things for Himself". [The problematic *lema'anehu* in that text is apparently here interpreted as a derivative of the root *'anah*, "answer", in the specific sense of testify:[39] in other words man, in emulating the divine qualities, bears witness to God.]

The text of Deuteronomy continues: "and to cleave unto Him". How, asks the *Sifrē*, could man conceivably ascend on high and cleave to God, who is stated[40] to be a consuming fire? "Nay," it rejoins, "cleave to scholars and their disciples" – perhaps meaning, learn from them the implications of the foregoing invitation to cultivate *mimēsis*; although I have to record that

35 *Guide for the Perplexed*, I, I, English translation by S. Pines, 1963, p.21, by M. Friedlander², 1910, p. 13.

36 *'Eqeb*, 49, ed. E. (L.) Finkelstein, Berlin, 1940, pp. 114f.

37 Joel 3.5 (English 2.32).

38 Ps. 145.8; 11.7; Jer. 3.12.

39 F. Brown, S. R. Driver, C. A. Briggs, *Hebrew . . . Lexicon of the Old Testament*, Oxford, 1906, p. 773, 3.a. See *Yalquṭ of Proverbs*, loc. cit.

40 Deut. 4.24, cf. Dan. 7.9.

the Talmudic parallel[41] understands it to mean the extension of patronage to scholars.

It would seem that, in non-technical language, this exegesis is anticipating Maimonides' assertion that the only attributes which can be predicated of God are attributes of action.[42] It is also pertinent to take note of the circumstance that Maimonides understands the call to walk in God's ways and to cleave to Him not as parenesis, but as precept, and lists them as numbers 6 and 8 of the positive commandments on the basis of parallel texts (Deut. 10.20; 28.9) in one of which the verb is clearly mandatory, and in the other is so construed by him.[43]

The call to emulate God's mercy and righteousness is hardly more specific than the exhortation to submissiveness in a Kempis' *Imitatio Christi*. But the Hebrew scriptures are so replete with accounts of God's dealings with man, details being either stated or exegetically inferable, that practical instances are to be found in plenty. Thus, God Himself has paradigmatically buried the dead, for it is said of Moses (Deut. 34.6) that "he buried him in the valley": modern grammarians may here recognize the impersonal third person singular, but the nearest named subject for the verb is God (v. 4). He likewise visits the sick, for his appearing to Abraham (Gen. 18.1) is recorded immediately after the account of Abraham's self-circumcision in his ninety-ninth year. And He dowers fatherless brides, for He brought Eve to Adam (2.23) – inconceivable that He omitted to provide her with bridal ornaments – and must Himself have read the seven benedictions of the marriage service over them, for does not the text declare (1.28) that He blessed them?[44] He likewise clothes the naked (Adam and Eve, Gen. 3.21), and comforts those in mourning (Isaac, after Abraham's death, 25.11[45]). Indeed, God's paradigmatic deeds even preceded the creation of the world, for, having consulted the Torah as to whether or not He should do so, He approved the Torah's argument that, were He not to bring creation into being, his would be but an empty sovereignty, thereby enabling us to learn that an autocracy without a cabinet is constitutionally unacceptable.[46] There are hosts of similarly inferred divine

41 TB *Kethubboth* 111b.

42 *Guide*, I 54, S. Pines (see above, n. 35), pp. 124f; Friedlander, pp. 75f.

43 See above, n. 13.

44 *Tanḥuma, Genesis, Wa-yera'*, 1; cf. C. G. Montefiore and H. Loewe, *Rabbinic Anthology*, London, 1936, p. 281.

45 TB *Soṭah* 14a.

46 *Pirqē de-R. Eliezer* 3; Ginzberg (see n. 21), 1, p. 3, 5, p. 3, n. 3.

exempla, most readily traceable from the index to Ginzberg's *Legends of the Jews*,[47] the sixteen columns of references to God in which are most helpfully articulated. It is worth observing that a number of these *exempla* are introduced by the formula *minayin* (whence?) that seeks scriptural evidence for a homiletic assertion.[48] I have elsewhere[49] drawn attention to the importance of this exegetical form, *whenceness*, or, as I have ventured to style it, *undity*. Since the appeal is to Scripture as yielding the authoritative source, it seems reasonable to claim that to a far greater extent than they are mimetic, rabbinic ethics are "unditative".

If the anthropomorphism of the Hebrew Bible lie on its surface, clear instances of anthropopathism have to be discovered by those concerned to authenticate it: even the most obvious example, Isaiah 63.9, "in all their affliction He was afflicted", *be-khol ṣaratham lo ṣar*, has been achieved by massoretic substitution of the third person prepositional *lo* for the negative, as against the septuagintal text and the Hebrew text 1QIs[a] from the Dead Sea caves, which yield a much superior sense. But the theological significance of patripassianism did not have to await the arrival of a Christian heresy. A striking instance occurs in the Mishnah;[50] after the detailing of the ghastly procedures of judicial execution, there is recorded the following rumination of Rabbi Me'ir:

> "When man is suffering agony," he said, "what does the divine Presence say? If one may venture the expression, it says, 'I am light – that is, diminished – in regard to my head, or my arm'. And if it be the case that the Deity suffers agony over the shedding of the blood of the wicked, how much more so over the blood of the righteous!"

Exhortation to *mimēsis* is surely implicit here. The notion is applied in an

---

47 Vol. 7, pp. 183f.

48 Eight examples, most of them relevant here, are listed by Aaron Hyman, *'Oṣar dibrē ḥakhamim u-pithgemeyhem*, Tel Aviv, 1934, p. 417.

49 "Midrashic Alchemy: Exegesis, Ethics, Aesthetics in Judaism" in H. J. Blumberg et al. (eds), *"Open Thou Mine Eyes" . . . Essays . . . Presented to William G. Braude . . .*, 1992, pp. 113f. A *Midrash minayin* was published by S. A. Wertheimer, first in his *'Oṣar midrashim kithbe yad*, i, and a revised text in *Battē medrashoth*, (ed. A. Werheimer), 2, Jerusalem, 5713/1953, pp. 75f, from Yemenite MSS; it was cited by Isaac Aboab (fourteenth century) in his *Menorath ha-ma'or*. The main focus of the collection (51 items) is liturgical, but the following concern ethics: series i, no. 26, p. 81, envy forbidden, citing Job 5.2; ii, no. 21, p. 87, payment not to be delayed (Deut. 24.15).

50 *Sanhendrin*, 6.5.

ethnic sense, in order to assert that God shares the collective sufferings of Israel, by means of Midrashic re-vocalisation. "For your sake have I sent [*shillaḥti*] to Babylon" (Isa. 43.14), which is a prophecy of redemption, was read by Rabbi Simeon b. Yohai as *shullaḥti*, "I was sent", for, he declared, God always shares his people's exile.[51] If the theology of the exegesis is – as one would anticipate from its author – obsessed with national identity rather than being focused on ethics, the *exempla* that point to God's being frustrated, or even victimized, which adduce the formula "it is good enough for a slave to share his owner's predicament" (*dayyo la-ʿebed li-heyoth ke-rabbo*, or *shaweh be-qono*) have a clear mimetic thrust. Thus, when Israel worshipped the golden calf, God bade Moses "get thee down, for thy people have corrupted themselves" (Exod. 32.7). Rabbi ʾAbin paraphrased as follows:

> God said to Moses, "Be not upset at my telling you to go down – I, too, have several times had cause to go down from heaven in order to observe the corruption of my creatures; at the Tower of Babel [Gen. 11.5, 7], and again at Sodom.[52] So, too, must you go down from Sinai: 'tis enough for a slave to find himself no less flouted than his owner." Moses deduced [from God's having cited the precedents of Babel and Sodom] that pardon for Israel was out of the question, and God, reading his mind, sought to assuage his distress. "Did I not tell you at the burning bush", God said, "that Israel were destined to do this, when I said[53] 'I have surely seen [*raʾoh raʾithi*] the *poor quality* [*ʿoni*, that is, affliction] of my people'? You say[54] 'I have seen this people, and behold it is stiff-necked.' Exercising but one degree of vision [*raʾithi*] you saw them arrive at Sinai and receive my Torah. But I, with second sight [*raʾoh raʾithi*], foresaw also that when I had come to Sinai

51 *Baraita* at TB *Megillah* 29a. *Ex.* 14, 30, *wa-yoshaʿ*, "and the Lord saved [Israel]" is re-interpreted as reflexive (*wa-yiwwashaʿ*) by Rabbi Me'ir (*Yalquṭ Shimʿoni* ii, 577, on Zech. 9.9, from an untraced source, reflected also in the liturgical *hoshaʿnah*-hymn *ke-hoshaʿta ʾelim be-lud ʿimmakh* (I. Davidson, *ʿOṣar ha-shirah we-ha-piyyuṭ*, 2, *kaph*, 110, p. 466), where likewise *Ex.* 6.6, "and I will bring you out" is treated as passive, "I will be brought out with you" (*ke-hoshaʾta . . . wa-yoshaʿ le-gohabh meṣuyyeneth wa-yiwwashaʿ . . . we-hoṣeʾthi ʾethekhem naqud we-huṣeʾthi ʾittekhem*). This poem, despite a possible acrostic signature *Samuel* at its end, is reckoned to be by Eleazar Qalir (Kal(l)ir, ? sixth century). See similar exegesis in *Exodus Rabbah*, 15, 12, ed. Wilna f. 27b, col. ii, on 2 Sam. 7.23; also 15, 16, f. 28b, col. ii. W. Heidenheim, *Sepher Qeroboth*, *Maḥzor*, Passover, vol. 16, Rodelheim, 1832, f. 100a, on the *silluq be-ʿeser makkoth pathrusim hiprakhta*.

52 Ibid. 18.21.

53 Exod. 3.8.

54 Ibid. 32.9.

> to give them the Torah and had subsequently returned to my τετράμουλον [i.e. *quadriga*, that is, the divine Chariot of Ezekiel 1], they would study the car, and, having unharnessed one of its four mystic beasts – for each has on its left the face of an ox[55] – would use it to provoke Me."

The moral is clear. Even after the classical example of Israel's collective apostasy, divine pardon was still possible; Moses – and like Moses, we also – are, by implication, called upon in emulation thereof to enunciate in our own conduct the message that the quality of mercy is not strained.

It will therefore be apparent that such uninhibited exegetical anthropomorphism affords a quarry for the derivation of ethical teachings; and it should be emphasised that it never seriously compromises Jewish conviction as to the absolute distinction between a creator-God and matter. The impetus within what would in due course become Christianity, emancipated from the Synagogue, towards postulating an incarnation, stems from Hebrew messianism; and it appears to me to owe nothing to Jewish openness to anthropomorphic myth. On the other hand, within the Jewish body politic during the middle ages, propensity towards literalism did briefly fuse with mysticism to produce the notion of a divine body; its text, which starts form the physical description of the lover in the Song of Songs[56] and is entitled *shi'ur qomah*[57] ("proportions"), describes the supposed divine physiognomy in dimensions so fantastic as to exclude comparison with incarnation. Leaving these proportions aside, we may cite as an example of its methodology the location of the seat of the divine attribute of grace in the ear, on the basis of the text[58] "and I will hear, for I am gracious". Maimonides, at the outset of the *Guide for the Perplexed*, exposes the fallacy of the whole idea, and was endorsed by Jewish consensus. But one can understand how it came about, at the time of the renaissance, that Christian scholars studying rabbinic Hebrew recognized – in the much less gross conceptual vocabulary of the Kabbalah

55 Ezek. 1.10.

56 5.10f.

57 See article and bibliography *s.v.*, (G. Scholem), *Enc. Jud.* 14, 1417f; Martin S. Cohen, *The Shi'ur Qomah: Liturgy and Theurgy in Pre-Kabbalistic Jewish Mysticism*, Lanham, 1983, and *The Shi'ur Qomah: Text and Recensions*, Tübingen, 1985; R. Loewe, "Apologetic Motifs in the Targum to the Song of Songs", A. Altmann (ed.), *Biblical Motifs Origins and Transformations*, Studies and Texts III, Cambridge (Mass.), 1966, pp. 184f., with a correlation of the detail with Theodoret's christological exegesis of the same passage.

58 Ex. 22.26.

– notions which they found it apposite to superimpose upon the Christian mystery of the incarnation.

Nevertheless, Theophile Gautier's jibe[59] is not without point – that God created man in his own image, and ever since man has been returning the compliment; for, as Xenophanes observed long before Gautier, were horses given to theologising, they would postulate an equine deity.[60] The popular Judaism of unsophisticated rabbinic religion, as distinct from what the philosophers and intellectuals made of the faith and institutions which were their heritage, found it difficult to think of the Deity otherwise than as the archetypal Jew, with inverted *mimēsis* as the occasional result. Despite that inversion, the nobility of God's own alleged prayer deserves a place within a study of *imitatio* as an ethical generator, inasmuch as its influence can resemble a hall of mirrors. According to Rab – a third century Babylonian rabbi, who was far from being unsophisticated – the prayer runs thus: "May it be my will that my mercy suppress my wrath, that my acts of mercy may overwhelm my [sterner] attributes, and that I may conduct Myself towards my children in accordance with the attribute of mercy."[61] One wonders, however, about God's phylacteries (*tephillin*). Phylacteries are worn by Jewish men, on the forehead and right arm, at morning prayer on working days, and they contain texts commencing with Israel's cardinal declaration of faith, the *Shema'* (Deut. 6.4), "Hear, O Israel, the Lord is our God, the Lord is One [*'eḥad*]". It being inconceivable the Deity Himself should not parallel an institution upon which Judaism lays so much stress, Rabbi Isaac felt prompted to ask, whence (*minayin*, "undity") the evidence that He does in fact wear *tephillin*? And he found it in Isaiah 62.8, "The Lord hath sworn *by his right hand, and by the arm of his strength*, etc.", since, he claimed, the *tephillin*, worn on the arm, are the source of Israel's strength (evidence is adduced for this from Deuteronomy 28.10). What, then, of the textual contents of these divine phylacteries, corresponding to the *Shema'* that proclaims Israel's monotheism? Rabbi Ḥiyya bar Abin had no doubt as to the answer. God's text is taken from 1 Chronicles 17.21, "and who are like Israel, a unique people

59 I have heard this attributed to Gautier, but do not know whether there is a written source for it.

60 Quoted by Clement of Alexandria, *Stromata* V 14, Migne, *Patrologia Graeco-latina,* 9, 168A; H. Diels and W. Kranz, *Fragmente der Vorsokratiker*⁶, Berlin, 1951, pp. 132f; G. S. Kirk and J. E. Raven, *The Presocratic Philosophers*, Cambridge, 1960, p. 169.

61 TB *Berakhoth* 7a. The occasion for this conceit is Isaiah 56.7, "my [house of] prayer". See Montefiore–Loewe (above, n. 41), p. 368.

[*goi 'eḥad*] on earth, whom God went to redeem for Himself as a people?"[62] It is true that the underlying thought here is the reciprocal relationship, deemed to have universal relevance, of God and his people:[63] but it is easy to see how jingoism could take the bit between its teeth.

It is appropriate to append to this study a brief note in regard to Kabbalism and Hasidism. The classical text in Deuteronomy 11.22f. upon which Jewish *mimēsis* bases itself centres round two phrases – to *walk* in God's ways, and to *cleave* to Him (*le-dobeqah bo*). In the later middle ages the abstract noun derived from this, *debequth*, became an integral item of Kabbalistic terminology,[64] indicating the acme of spiritual communion – not union[65] – with the Infinite (*'eyn soph*) to the attaining of which the intensity of the Jewish mystic's spiritual energy has to be directed; it being generally appreciated that although during this life passing moments of ecstasy might be achieved, consummation was something attainable in the hereafter only. To that endeavour, ethical conduct and the self-discipline that this imposes are indispensable, but at the same time merely incidental.[66] In the eighteenth and nineteenth centuries, Hasidism, operating through the notion of the

---

62 TB *Berakhoth* 6a.

63 For a mystical interpretation on these lines by the Hasidic Master Dov Baer of Mezhirech (died 1772) see M. Idel, *Kabbalah, New Perspectives,* New Haven–London, 1988, p. 48.

64 See G. Scholem, "*Devekut,* or Communion with God", originally published in the *Review of Religion,* 14, 1949–50, pp. 115–139, whence reprinted in his *The Messianic Idea in Judaism,* London, 1971, pp. 203–227,and again in G. D. Hundert (ed.), *Essential Papers on Hasidism, Origins to Present,* New York–London, 1991, pp. 275–298, to which I refer; more briefly, *s.v.*, (J. Dan), *Enc. Jud.*, 5, 1598f; M. Pachter, "The Concept of *Devekut* in the Homiletical Ethical Writings in Sixteenth-Century Safed", in I. Twersky (ed.), *Studies in Medieval Jewish History and Literature,* 2, Cambridge (Mass.), 1984, pp. 171–230 (I regret that I have not seen this paper); M. Idel (see above, n. 64), ch. 3 "Varieties of *Devekut* in Jewish Mysticism", pp. 35–38. I am grateful to my colleague Dr Ada Rapoport-Albert for guidance regarding recent literature on this subject.

65 Scholem, *Devekut* (see previous note) insisted on this distinction, pp. 275f., 277, 285f., 294f., 297f., cf. Idel (see previous note), pp. 42f., 44, 46f., 49, 56. But in his following chapter ("Unio mystica in Jewish mysticism", pp. 59–73) Idel challenges the dogmatic distinction between union and communion, adducing evidence from the writings of Abraham Abulafia (born 1240; see *Enc. Jud.*, *s.v.* (G. Scholem, 2, 185f.) and Idel, "Abraham Abulafia and *Unio Mystica*", in I. Twersky (ed.), *Studies, etc.* (see above, n. 65), and likewise from Hasidic sources. He points out that not only did such Kabbalistic views not, apparently, elicit protest, but that they were not fastened upon by the critics of Hasidism at a time when the movement was subject to severe attacks (*Kabbalah,* p. 70). Such silence is certainly significant.

66 See, however, Pachter (*supra,* n. 65).

charismatic spiritual leader (the *ṣaddiq*) and his devotees (*ḥasidim*), whose anticipated spiritual capacity was naturally expected to be of a lesser order, inherited the notion of *debequth* but modified it semantically, so that it came to refer not simply to the spiritual climax of communion, but also to the quest.[67] Henceforth it would mean spiritual self-training, through constant maintenance in the daily routine – and not just in one's prayer-life – of an intensified sensitivity to the divine; and here the level of ethical behaviour is once again to the fore. However, it is not to be expected of the ordinary member of an Hasidic circle that he will be able to command the requisite spiritual concentration to implement this; and despite Scholem's opinion[68] that to do so is precisely the challenge confronting all *ḥasidim*, it is now the view of academic students of the subject that such is the vocation of the *ṣaddiq* alone.[69] For his followers, *debequth* consists in the intensity of cultivation of, and personal subservience to, their charismatic leader – very much as the Talmudic comment on the Deuteronomic text cited above[70] understood cleaving to God to mean patronage of scholars and choosing them as sons-in-law. At both levels, the charismatic and the common, ethical endeavour is requisite, but is taken for granted. More important, for our present purpose, is the circumstance that the element of *mimēsis* operative at the common level does not involve immediate consciousness of an address to the *imitatio Dei*, but rather consciousness of emulation of the *ṣaddiq* in the spirit of the Talmudic tradition which assumes that the disciple will identify in his master a role-model:[71] and although the *ṣaddiq* himself will generally deprecate, and ought positively to discourage such emulation, his attempts to put a stop to it will generally be of no avail.

By way of conclusion, let us return to classical rabbinism, and its tech-

67 Idel, *Kabbalah* (see n. 64), pp. 49f., points to this same notion of *debequth* as the quest itself as present already in the *Me'irath 'eynayim* of Isaac of Acre (c. 1300), and suggests that the notion of a radical Hasidic re-interpretation is deceptive.

68 Scholem, *Devekut* (see n. 65), pp. 280f., 283, 285, 287f. *Enc. Jud.*, 5, 1598f.

69 Cf. A. Rapoport-Albert, "God and the Zaddik as the Two Focal Points of Hasidic Worship", *History of Religions* 18, 1979, pp. 296–325, whence reprinted in G. D. Hundert (see n. 65) pp. 299–329, in which see pp. 318f., 325, n. 37.

70 TB *Kethubboth* 111b. See above, n. 41.

71 The formula "it is [a matter of] Torah [about which] I have got to learn" (*torah hi' we-lilmod 'ani ṣarikh*) is proffered as a justification of a discipline's insisting on [endeavouring to] observe his master somewhat too intimately: TB *Berakhoth* 62a, cf. *Megillah* 28a. It is difficult to conceive of a rabbi, even if confronted by such environmental temptations as those prevalent in Corinth in Paul's time, ever appealing to his flock to avoid them by imitating himself, *qua* their spiritual leader (1 *Cor.* 4.16, μιμηταί μου γίνεσθε).

nique of exploiting a figuratively intended literalism in the exegesis of biblical anthropomorphism for the promotion of *mimēsis* as an ethical endeavour. Appended to the *Sifrē*'s[72] interpretation of Deuteronomy 11.22f. from which we began, there is a note to the effect that it was an apothegm of those who expounded Aggadic items that if one would fain get to recognize Him who had but to speak for the world to come into existence, one should study the *'aggada*; "for", they declared, "through so doing, one will both come to recognize Him, and cleave to his ways."

72 See above, n. 36.

BERTRAND RAMCHARAN

The United Nations and the Future of International Law

INTRODUCTION

Unless the United Nations can help uphold the international rule of law it will have no future. Sadly, in recent times, the very core of the international rule of law has come under severe strains that have rocked the world organization. The United Nations Secretary General established a panel on new threats and challenges, which reported to him at the beginning of December, 2004.[1] It has unfortunately paid only scant attention to the role of international law in under-girding international security. This is unfortunate.

The United Nations can only address new threats and challenges within the framework of the law. The strategic centrality of international law for the success of the United Nations idea has not been sufficiently recognized by those setting course for the future of the world organization and its role in contributing to international security. How can the United Nations recover and re-assert the centrality of the rule of law internationally? In this essay we shall explore the challenges of the United Nations in shaping the future roles and effectiveness of international law. We shall argue that the time is overdue for the UN to establish a high level commission on the effectiveness and future of international law. To begin with, we look briefly at the crises of contemporary international law.

The author exercised the functions of United Nations High Commissioner for Human Rights from May 2003 to July 2004.

1 'A More Secure World: Report of the High-level Panel on Threats, Challenges and Change'. United Nations, 2004.

1. THE CRISES OF INTERNATIONAL LAW

International law, at the present time, is experiencing the following acute crises:

(a) Open flouting of the United Nations Charter and the Security Council

The United Nations Charter requires its member states to settle their disputes peacefully, to uphold human rights and humanitarian law, and, save in self-defence against actual or imminent attack, not to resort to the use of force against one another. When Iraq invaded Kuwait the United Nations moved forcefully to restore international legality. When coalition forces went to Afghanistan to respond to threat of international terrorism from the Al Qaeda/Taliban coalition they did so within the framework of legality laid down by the United Nations Security Council. In contrast when coalition forces moved against Iraq the Security Council was bitterly divided and the Secretary General of the United Nations, an arbiter in international affairs, is on record as having declared that there was no authority in international law for such an operation.[2] This was a moment when the United Nations experienced one of its worst crises, and international law and legality were under severe stress.

Whether it be in the imposition of sanctions against recalcitrant Governments, or in relation to the management of particular crises, mandatory recommendations of the United Nations Security Council have been openly flouted by a number of states. International relations are marked by the power configurations among states, but it surely must be wrong for any state to flout a mandatory call by the United Nations Security Council. The international community is entitled to expect that all pressure will be brought to bear upon states in breach of United Nations Security Council mandatory decisions to comply with their legal obligations under the Charter. We have here a fundamental crisis in contemporary international law that requires urgent attention.

(b) Widespread violations of human rights and humanitarian law

In an address to the UN Commission on Human Rights on 18 March 2003, the president of the International Committee of the Red Cross, Jakob

2 The USA, the UK and other coalition countries contest this vehemently.

Kellenberger, noted that human rights law, refugee law and international law shared the common objective of protecting human life, safety and dignity. These bodies of law and their supervisory mechanisms formed an interlocking web of guarantees for individuals particularly in times of emergency – when they were most vulnerable. Sadly, breaches of all the three bodies of law were widespread in the contemporary world.

The United Nations High Commissioner for Human Rights, in his Human Rights Day message on 10 December 2003, lamented the gross violations of human rights attributable to poverty, conflicts, terrorism, state violence, inequality and bad governance. The United Nations High Commissioner for Refugees has, on numerous occasions, chided governments for not respecting the provisions of international refugee law. In all three instances – international humanitarian law, international human rights law and international refugee law – breaches of the law are rampant in the contemporary world. International law is thus in acute crisis.

(c) Global terrorism

The United Nations General Assembly and the United Nations Security Council have for many years now declared terrorism in all forms and manifestations, and for whatever reason, unlawful and unacceptable. Yet, alas, as the terrorist attacks in the United States of America on 9 September 2001 and subsequent terrorist attacks have shown, terrorists mount open challenges to international legality. The law is in acute crisis on this front, especially as there has so far been no agreed definition of terrorism in an international treaty.

(d) Partial resort to the International Court of Justice in the great political legal questions of our time

In an assessment we offered of the International Court of Justice at the millennium, we concurred with Professor Ian Brownlie's evaluation a quarter of a century earlier that states used the International Court of Justice only in a limited category of issues particularly related to land and maritime boundary disputes. The ICJ is occasionally called upon to render an advisory opinion, and, even then, the Court is sometimes subjected to heavy pressure when politically sensitive issues are involved. It surely must be right to assert that a deliberate search should be initiated for ways and means of strengthening the authority of the International Court of Justice.

(e) Atrophy in the codification and progressive development of international law.

One of the acute crises affecting contemporary international law concerns the almost total atrophy in the process of codifying and developing international law. The International Law Commission currently has under consideration the following topics: diplomatic protection; responsibility of international organizations; shared natural resources; international liability for injurious consequences arising out of acts not yet prohibited by international law; unilateral acts of states; reservations to treaties. At its fifty-sixth session in 2004 it decided to include on its long-term programme of work the following topics: obligation to extradite or prosecute; expulsion of aliens; and effects of armed conflicts on treaties.[3]

The codification and progressive development of international law is expressly provided for in the United Nations Charter. In the early days of the United Nations, the great Sir Hersch Lauterpacht did a survey of international law to stimulate the work of the International Law Commission. A second survey was prepared by the UN Secretariat in 1973; thirty years later no such document is emerging in the horizon. The ILC is locked in consideration each year of mainly technical issues – albeit important ones – of international law. In the early days of the United Nations, the Sixth (Legal) Committee used to prompt the ILC on topics requiring attention. Great initiatives such as the Maltese initiative to revise the law of the sea are now rarely seen. The major national societies of international law are producing very little that is intended to shape the future development of international law. It is as if paralysis has set in nearly sixty years after the establishment of the United Nations.[4] How is international law to prepare for and address the emerging risks? There is largely silence on this matter. But risks there are, as we shall see in the section that follows.

3 Report of the International Law Commission. Fifty-sixth session. General Assembly Official Records. Fifty-ninth session, Supplement No. 10 (A/59/10).

4 On the International Laws Commission generally, see J.S. Morton, *The International Law Commission of the United Nations*. Columbia: University of South Carolina Press, 2000.

2. EMERGING RISKS

A recent study by the Organisation for Economic Cooperation and Development on 'emerging systemic risks in the twenty-first century', which discusses changes likely to affect risks and their management in the coming years, identified four contexts: demography, the environment, technology and socio-economic structure.[5] On the demographic front world population is projected to increase to nine billion by 2050 in comparison with today's figure of six billion. In this scenario, migration is expected to intensify and, by 2050, South–North migration might become the norm. On the environmental front, the earth's climate is changing and will continue to do so. Water will be increasingly scarce. Over half of the 12,500 cubic kilometers of freshwater available for human use is already used, and ninety per cent will be used in 2030 if current trends continue. Worldwide polluted water is already estimated to affect the health of about 1.2 billion people and to contribute to the death of about fifteen million children under the age of five every year. Reduction in biodiversity could have dramatic consequences.

According to the study, three aspects of emerging technologies will influence risk: connectedness, the speed and pervasiveness of technological change, and the fundamental changes in the landscape they might induce. Some emerging technologies change living matter and represent an unprecedented potential to change the environment. They are even starting to challenge the definition of 'living' and could ultimately change the whole notion of 'human'. While the hope is that biotechnology, for instance, will improve living conditions and the quality of life, the long term consequences of interfering at such a basic level are impossible to evaluate, and irreversible damage could be done before the danger is understood or when it is too late to stop it.

As to socioeconomic structures, the study continues, governments' role in directly managing the economy has been shrinking over several decades, and especially in the past twenty years, through privatization, deregulation and regulatory reform. Poverty has persisted and in some cases increased in recent years. The living conditions of the poor rendered them more exposed to risks, but poverty and income gaps also had direct impacts on risk in that

5 *Emerging Systemic Risks in the Twenty-First Century*, ISBN 92-64-19947-0, OECD 2003.

they fuelled social tensions and weakened the social cohesion needed to assess and respond to potential dangers.

The question that arises when it comes to the future of international law is whether any international legal body is paying attention to these future risks and engaging in research and studies with a view to developing appropriate legal responses. One has the distinct impression that, at the present time, no legal body at the United Nations is giving serious attention to topics such as these. The Office of Legal Affairs of the United Nations must urgently commission a new survey of international law for consideration by the Sixth Committee, by the ICJ and by the ILC on the legal aspects of emerging risks.

3. THE STATE OF THE LAW

We have already argued in this essay that there is a crisis in the application of the law, and we have pointed out the need for an urgent survey of international law to help identify future legal challenges. In this section we offer a snapshot on the technical state of international law.

In comparison with the situation at the start of the twentieth century when a deliberate process was initiated of consolidating the basic rules of international law, the twenty-first century began with a detailed body of law to be found in treaties, restatements of international law and learned treatises. International conventions do exist on the law of treaties, the law of diplomatic relations, the law of the sea and other foundation issues.

Learned societies such as the International Law Association, the Institute of International Law, the American Society of International Law and the British Society of International Law have produced major legal compilations. The Max Planck Encyclopedia of International Law is a magisterial work on the technical content of the law. Learned commentaries have been produced on the Charter of the United Nations.

Regional bodies such as the Asian–African Legal Organization, the Inter-American Juridical Committee and the Council of Europe have contributed to the discovery and systematization of international law.

Between them, the Permanent Court of International Justice and the ICJ have rendered landmark decisions and advisory opinions.

Technically, the law is far better off at the start of the twenty-first century than at the start of the twentieth century. However, there are some notable problem areas still. More recently the ILC has been concerned about difficulties arising from the diversification and expansion of international law. Following its consideration of a feasibility study on 'risks ensuing from fragmentation of international law', the ILC established a study group on this topic. At its fifty-sixth session in 2004, the study group of the Commission discussed a paper by its chairman, Professor M. Martti Koskeniemi, and considered proposals aiming at drawing up interpretative guidelines on normative conflicts and regime-collisions; the suggestion that the Commission might seek to indicate what 'general international law' is and what a 'special regime' is. During its deliberations the study group noted that the difficulty presented by the relationship between the general and the special were relative, with differences arising depending on the circumstances of each case. The Commission has agreed to continue its deliberations of these issues.[6]

4. THE PROMOTION AND DISSEMINATION OF INTERNATIONAL LAW

If, as we have suggested in this essay, the international rule of law is so strategically important for the future of international security and the United Nations, it should be a matter of the greatest importance for the United Nations and sister organizations to act energetically to promote and disseminate international law. Sadly there is a major crisis here as well. The United Nations runs an annual international law seminar alongside the annual sessions of the ILC to which some two dozen participants are admitted. UNITAR has the occasional seminar on international law, but this is the extent of the United Nations' involvement in the promotion and dissemination of international law. The repertory of practice of United Nations organs has been hit by budgetary constraints and is way behind in its coverage. Something is clearly amiss here.

The Hague Academy of International Law continues to hold its annual summer courses. Some three-hundred students are admitted each year to the public international law segment. The International Law Association and the Institute of International Law hold biennial congresses for practitioners and professors.

For the public at large international law is like the milky way: it is known to exist; but what it is remains a mystery.

6 Report of the Commission, supra, Chapter X.

5. UPHOLDING INTERNATIONAL HUMAN RIGHTS AND HUMANITARIAN LAW

In his address to the Commission on Human Rights to which we referred earlier, the president of the International Committee of the Red Cross told the Commission:

> Improving respect for international humanitarian law remains a huge challenge. Without greater respect for existing rules the credibility and protective value of existing and also of any new rules is very limited.
>
> How can respect be improved? First, and quite simply, by spreading knowledge of the rules to authorities, to combatants, including of course, organized armed groups, and to civil society.
>
> Secondly, by the adoption of preventive steps in times of peace, such as the implementation of relevant treaties into national laws, military manuals and other instruments.
>
> Thirdly, in the heat of conflict, by the mobilization of all those who can contribute to the better respect of the law. The representations made on a daily basis by ICRC delegates in the field to those participating in hostilities are often a lifesaving contribution.

The 1951 Convention Relating to the Status of Refugees, which defines the rights of refugees including asylum and sets out legal obligations of states, is the cornerstone of international protection. In 2003, UNHCR launched 'Convention Plus', an important initiative that is aimed at strengthening the original Convention. The objective is to improve refugee protection worldwide and to facilitate the resolution of refugee problems through special multilateral agreements. The agreements will focus on three priority areas: (1) the strategic use of resettlement as a tool of protection, a durable solution and a tangible form of burden-sharing; (2) more effective targeting of development assistance whether in countries of asylum or upon return home; and (3) clarification of the responsibilities of states in the event of secondary movements of refugees and asylum-seekers from an initial country of refuge to another country. These measures are intended to secure for refugees a higher standard of protection as close to home as possible and also to increase the level of state involvement as an effective system of international burden sharing. Five states are currently facilitating the work of these multilateral agreements: Canada (on resettlement), Denmark and Japan (on development assistance), and South Africa and Switzerland (on secondary movements).

When it comes to improved implementation of international human rights law, five avenues are currently being pursued. United Nations Secretary General Kofi Annan has called for a plan of action to strengthen national protection systems; for enhanced treaty implementation; and for the better functioning of special procedures such as special rapporteurs dealing with human rights problems. During the 2004 session of the Commission on Human Rights, the United Nations High Commissioner for Human Rights called for an international convention on human rights education and for a program of cooperation with judges in different parts of the world.

CONCLUSION

This essay will have shown that while, technically, there is a solid body of international law to govern international relations, severe problems of compliance are being experienced, and there is no serious long range thinking about the future risks and challenges the law will be called upon to address. In our view these problems and challenges would warrant the empanelling of a United Nations commission on the effective application and future development of international law which should be asked to report within two years from the time of establishment so as to help stimulate the future growth and effectiveness of international law. We would end by repeating the caution with which we opened this essay: 'Unless the Untied Nations can help uphold the international rule of law it will have no future.'

AUBREY ROSE

Crime – An Assault on Human Rights

> ❧ Violence shall no more be heard in the land, desolation nor destruction within thy borders; but thou shalt call thy walls Salvation, and thy gates Praise (Isaiah lx)

THE prophets of old sought a Utopian world in which violence ceased, men learned war no more, beat their swords into ploughshares, and nation spoke unto nation in peace. It is a wonderful vision, but it never happened, at least not in this terrestrial sphere.

Millennia later, young America preached man's inalienable rights to 'life, liberty, and the pursuit of happiness'. Again, a glowing vision, born alongside the idea of human rights, whether natural, inherent, or God-given. But the problem remained. How could men, women and children enjoy rights when they were under constant attack by waves of crime, whether emanating from individuals, groups or governments?

The 1948 Universal Declaration of Human Rights, inspired by René Cassin, heralded a host of Conventions, Protocols, Declarations, too numerous to list. Again, like the prophets, like Jefferson and his friends, those documents sought a vision of human beings living together in justice, well-being, freedom and peace.

A wonderful world, and a shining light we should ever pursue, but it has never happened. Devoted people, like Clemens Nathan, to his enormous credit, have spent a lifetime pursuing this Holy Grail.

Yet here we are, almost sixty years after the original Declaration, witnessing a worldwide rampage against the basic human rights of people on every continent. One would have thought, after the unbelievable horror of the

Holocaust, that lessons would have been learned, but madness erupts constantly, from the irreligious blasphemy of suicide bombers, to the persecution of innocent souls in the Sudan, and the unspeakable attack on Russian schoolchildren in September 2004.

I have been close to crime much of my life. As a lawyer I have defended many criminals in the courts, handled some of the largest cases in British history, have observed a variety of crimes committed for a range of so-called reasons. My mind, however, goes back to the 1960s in an idyllic West Indian island. The people were God-fearing, went to church, showed mutual respect, were extremely literate (a higher rate than in England), and altogether enjoyed life, liberty, and the pursuit of happiness. The island had four criminal courts only. People left their front doors open, rarely locked their cars. Children could wander freely, never in fear of molestation.

It was the nearest I could conceive of Isaiah's vision. It was based on strongly held and practised moral beliefs. Humans had rights because they were all children of God and made in His image. Judeo-Christian teachings held sway.

Decades passed. That happy world became less happy. Doors were locked, guard dogs kept, the fight against drugs increased, the perennially violent pictures of television influenced the young in their minds and behaviour. Money, and its acquisition, became more and more important, even though there was no poverty on the island. It is still a happy place, and better than most. The rule of law applies, a law fairly administered, but there has been a change.

In a way it reminded me of my early years in East London, when again no one locked doors, when violence rarely stalked the streets, and children could wander far and wide with no one to make them afraid, unless it was the uniformed policeman, held in great respect. That world is no more. The Second World War, with its grim catalogue of horror piled on horror, seems to have released a disease of violence. Since 1945 there have been over fifty wars in our world, a world that is now, slowly, so slowly, beginning to understand the deadly threat of Islamic terrorists, who, with their medieval mind-set, shame all the peace-loving Muslims who seem unable to influence their more violent element.

Crime is a crime is a crime; a constant assault on human rights. I turned to the writers of books, experts, criminologists. No need to look at Stone, Archbold, the recognised textbooks, and practical guides. As crime expanded, so has the number of pages in those works. They are weighty volumes. So also have the Criminal Justice and allied Acts of Parliament. I could list dozens of them: the Police Act 1964, Criminal Justice Act 1967, Police and Criminal Evidence Act 1984, down to the Crime and Disorder Act 1998. More and more laws; in 1999 ... 2000 ... endless laws. Meanwhile there are more inmates of prisons than ever before.

What did the books tell me? Book number one had 267 pages, whilst the list of books and authorities quoted at the end numbered over five hundred! It included the report of a Royal Commission on Crime to which I had given evidence.

Book number one discusses the aims of prison (where population doubled in twenty years), reflects on the role of the police and concludes that 'no government has been successful either in prevention of crime or the rehabilitation of criminals'. What a forbidding conclusion, despite the home secretary's assertion in 2001 that 'rehabilitation is the highest possible priority for those who enter the criminal justice system.'

The writer made mention of the human rights of victims. The process of law has been lethargic in this field. A Green Paper in 1988 referred to 'compensation to victims and reparation to the community'. This was encouraging. The courts had power to order compensation, but this was not enough. A Quaker magistrate, Margery Fry, took up the cudgels for victims, but slow motion was the speed. By 1990 'A Statement of the Rights of Victims of Crime' emerged, and later a victim statement scheme, giving the victim some say.

So the authorities swayed backwards and forwards, between police, prison, rehabilitation, compensation, with a minister even saying 'prison is an expensive way of denying people liberty', a strange way of putting things. Another minister said simply, 'Prison works.'

Book number two was quite critical and incisive. The writer even suggested prisoners should pay the state for looking after them in prison. He launched into figures. In 1921, 103,000 recorded crimes; in 2001, over five million! In 1937, 209 robberies with violence; in 1966, over one million! What the writer is trying to say is that, even with population increase, pre-1939 poverty produced less proportionate crimes than post-1960 affluence. Hence, whilst poverty may be one cause of crime, it is far from the whole story.

The author provides figures for recidivism. Those who emerged from prison continued to carry on a life of crime. The figures are appalling. So, while prison protected society, it achieved little to encourage criminals to adjure crime. Even with almost full employment in Britain, and a liberal welfare state, crime has not disappeared. It has increased.

The book emphasises the vital importance of the presence of police on the street, indicating that in July 2001 street robberies in Lambeth, an inner London suburb, increased by fifty-six per cent when police eased up on drug prosecutions. He is quite biting about the threat to free speech by all kinds of emergency measures, concluding that 'Government has lost control of crime, does not understand the moral basis of crime and does not know what to do'.

He has touched on a crucial point. Crime is a constant threat to human rights. Human rights have a moral base: respect for the person and property of individuals. This is, I believe, the crux of the problem of crime. My West Indian island people believed in the moral teachings of the Bible and acted accordingly. Even in poverty, my experience in pre-1939 East London showed that crime was low. I recall Disraeli's comment, 'It is not in the increased feebleness of its institutions that I see the peril of England; it is in the decline of its character as a community'.

Book number three was even more critical of the whole system of criminal justice, seeing it as a 'ritualised game'. His comments on our prosecution, court, and prison procedures are devastating. He sees the collapse of the traditional family as a major cause of current crime. He does not see the courts as a quest for truth. In fact he heads one chapter 'The Collapse of Criminal Justice', questioning our adversarial system and laws of evidence that impede the search for truth.

He concludes, and I agree with him, that the whole procedure must become victim-orientated, and the best elements of the inquisitorial system, as on the Continent, should enter our procedure. The human rights of the victim should be elevated to a prominent place.

He sees the authorities lurching from scheme to scheme, with no understanding of how to tackle the underlying cause of either crime or the crisis in criminal justice.

The last book was the best of all. It is impossible to summarise its contents, but it delved deeper than the others. It tried to define crime, and noted the great number of male compared to female criminals, the nefarious influence of the media, and the importance of compensation for victims, quoting a

United Nations 1985 Charter for Victims, and pointing out that as long ago as 1963 New Zealand had a state comprehensive scheme for victims, long before our limited Criminal Injuries Compensation Scheme came into being.

What I found most gratifying, however, was a far wider look at the causes of crime. The writer considered genetic influences, pollution (lead in air and water), physical environment (emphasised by Giuliani recently in New York), biochemical effects, and, *mirabile dictu*, diet and nutrition, a subject of enormous importance in my view.

More and more trials, here and in the United States, are showing the vital effect of diet, nutrition, blood sugar level, allergies, vitamins B and C deficiency, and constitution of the central nervous system as causation, triggers, of criminal action. And it goes without saying that excessive alcohol and mind-influencing drugs play a significant role in so much violence.

Bearing all this in mind, the author turns, as no one else had, to different forms of treatment rather than punishment, the pathway to future rehabilitation. Indeed a whole chapter is devoted to the 'Ecology of Crime'. Even the effect of noise on criminal behaviour is considered. How refreshing to find such a deeper perception of crime and its causes in this *Text Book on Criminology* by Katherine S. Williams.

All the books I have referred to emerged from academics in universities. I turned therefore to day-to-day events. The newspapers are full of crime reports, so I took a short period in July–August 2004. This is what I found:

20 July: MOTHER TELLS HOW EX-LOVER RAISED HIS KNIFE HIGH THEN SLASHED THEIR SON'S THROAT

HOW CRIME HAS CONTINUED TO RISE: Graphs show rising crime 1999–2003 in violent disorder, mugging, rape, common assault, gun crime.

22 July: 'We have created a vicious breed of young monsters', says police chief, under a massive front-page headline: THE PRICE OF BEING TOO SOFT ON CRIME.

EXTRA POLICE BUT DETECTION RATE STILL FALLS. (One almost feels like calling in Holmes or Poirot.)

31 July: TEN VIOLENT PUPILS A DAY EXPELLED

3 August: MAN KNIFED TO DEATH AS 40 CLASH IN STREET

17 August: ARCHITECT STABBED IN STREET MUGGING DIES

A study of our newspapers over any short period would reveal similar headlines, similar accounts of crimes. It has become a daily event, just as the fear of crime spreads, leading to the expansion of self-help groups to deter criminals.

I could go on with these examples:

THE GIRL WHO MET DEATH AT HER FRONT DOOR

AN ARMY OF CHILD YOBS BRINGING MISERY TO EVERY CORNER OF BRITAIN IS GROWING AT A TERRIFYING RATE

The only positive report, surprisingly, was whether fish and fish oils were 'the latest weapon against crime'. Indeed, trials in a young offenders' prison, using fish oil minerals, reduced the rate of offending by thirty per cent. Optimistically, a headline claims, 'Fish is the only treatment of serious offenders shown to work.' Extraordinary!

These new perceptions as to cause and treatment are encouraging. They may open new and untried paths.

The battle against crime is one aspect of the battle for human rights. It must also involve a campaign for the recognition of human duties.

In the autumn of 2004 I was asked to address a seminar of lawyers. I chose for my title 'A New Approach to Crime and Punishment'. Since it summarises my approach to the subject, I now set out much of my talk, indicating radical new pathways to treating crime and compensating victims.

A New Approach to Crime and Punishment

INTRODUCTION

CRIME, like sin, has always been with us, but, whereas sin emerges from the moral sphere and is personal, crime is a breach of the law and an attack not only on the individual but also on the peace and harmony of society.

Yet the two cannot be divorced. There are crimes, breaches of the criminal law, which have no moral content, such as parking a car incorrectly, forgetting to obtain licences for certain sales. On the other hand most of our criminal law is based on our moral beliefs at any particular time.

Thus libel and adultery were once criminal offences. Adultery still is in some countries, as are bigamy and polygamy here. But on the whole the law as to serious crime is based on the sanctity of life and respect for property. Therefore murder, assault, burglary, theft are breaches of accepted moral tenets reflected in criminal law.

In Britain, we have reached almost crisis point in dealing with crime. A recent study showed the annual cost of crime control at £10 billion, an enormous figure, a sum that excludes private and commercial expenditure.

In the United States more is now spent on crime control than on education. The total amount spent there by all authorities in 1996 was over £100 billion!

A recent report here stated that 'the prison system is a failure', that three-quarters of all burglars released committed more crime within two years of release, and that the reconviction rate for male prisoners under the age of twenty-one was seventy-four per cent!

The UK has the highest imprisonment rate in Europe; currently over seventy thousand, it is likely in a few years to rise to a hundred thousand. Thus prison may work for some, who cannot safely be released into society, but on the whole none of the present methods are either preventing crime or rehabilitating criminals.

It would be wrong to blame the agencies involved – police, prison, probation, welfare, courts. They do their best within the confines of present procedures. What I set out later are proposals for a radical change of approach. If such a change commends itself, it might release funds for more constructive efforts elsewhere.

I turned to the writers on crime, mainly professorial and academic. I do not find clear answers. First, they ponder on exact definitions of 'crime' and 'disorder', and then a whole torrent of words appears: community safety, the meaning of 'community', New Managerialism, bureaucratisation, social exclusion, late modernity, new penology, distributive justice, ontological insecurity, essentialism, deterritorialisation, disembeddedness, and so on.

These writers are dealing with crucial subjects. If only they would write simply, they could have greater effect and gain more sympathy and understanding, as they have wide knowledge and relevant things to say.

In analysing recent legislation, one professor comments, 'The Crime and Disorder Act 1998 marked a repudiation of both 1960s "welfarism" and 1980s "progressive minimalism" on the grounds that both approaches represented soft options which failed to confront the moral dimension of youth crime and disregarded the "rights" of victims.'

While I am not too clear about the meaning of some of the expressions, it is encouraging to see mention both of 'moral dimension' and concern for victims. In the past we have seen such emphasis on the rights of the accused. The 'Norfolk farmer' case has highlighted this aspect. If there had been no burglar invading his property, there would have been no shots fired by the irate householder. How far can defence of life and property be 'commensurate' to the danger? We draw a different line here from that in America.

Also we are very much in the period of 'rights', especially with the Human Rights Act, but how far has anyone commented on the human rights of society itself? A crime can be seen as an assault, not only on the individual concerned, but as a breach of the human rights of society. This is the case of groups of football hooligans. They may attack property and individuals, but they are attacking and despoiling the rights of society to life and liberty.

I would like to analyse why people commit crimes. I will put forward a number of reasons. I will then briefly deal with the police and judicial process, an area in which I have had some practical experience. Lastly I set out some new procedures which I believe can have a positive effect in deterring crime, and assessing those who commit crimes with appropriate sanctions.

SECTION I.1
WHY PEOPLE COMMIT CRIMES

THERE is no single answer to this question. We could as well ask: why are there wars and conflicts throughout the world? The First World War, 1914–1918, was naively described as 'the war to end wars'. The United Nations, set up in 1945 after the Second World War, was to be the means to rid the world of the scourge of war. Since that date there have been over fifty wars, some lasting many years, including the continuing horror of Central Africa.

In some ways, the actions of individuals within society can be compared to the action of nation states within world society. Hard as it may seem, there are certain nations or groups who are naturally aggressive. There are other groups who regard war and violence as something to be proud of, as traditional, as satisfying something in the national psyche or ego.

I doubt whether Switzerland, in the last few centuries, has attacked any neighbour, whereas Germany, since the 1860s, has attacked neighbours north, south, east and west. As with nations, so with individuals. In the early part of the twentieth century, one could still find cannibalism in parts of south-east Asia: men eating men. In that very same century lived caring figures like Mother Theresa, Mahatma Gandhi and heroes and heroines of peace endeavour, life-saving endeavour.

Thus to talk of 'mankind' is facile. There are 'mankinds' at different levels of moral development. Even most of the major world religions, whilst espousing certain wonderful levels of moral teaching, have hideous histories of torture, murder and violence as perennial blots on their records.

So one comes back to crime within society. It does not begin because of some notion of 'original sin' or fall from grace, or predestined behaviour. Within certain boundaries, a human being has freedom of choice to commit crimes or to desist from crime. In some societies, criminals are in control of the government and crime becomes official policy. Witness the terrible examples of genocide in and since the Second World War, and recently in Sudan.

There is one non-physical aspect of crime which I will touch on later, which, if properly acknowledged and understood, could make a big impact on human behaviour. For the moment I would wish to itemise a variety of causes, familiar to those involved in this field. Let me enumerate them, with perhaps a comment on each.

SECTION I. 2
CURRENTLY ACCEPTED FACTORS CONTRIBUTING TO CRIME

1. GROWTH IN POPULATION

Britain is a small place. Its population has increased by fifty per cent in the last sixty years. Parts of south England have become one vast housing estate. There are proposals to ease planning laws. If so, houses will sprout where once there were green fields.

It is known that if you constrict a few thousand chickens in a broiler house – not in cages – you will lose ten to fifteen per cent due to 'cannibalism'. Too many people likewise in close proximity can create a similar problem. Although rural crime has increased, it remains predominantly urban.

2. IMMIGRATION

This has enlarged the population numbers. On the whole, immigrants – there are now over fifty minorities in Britain each with over ten thousand people – have contributed positively to the country, and Britain has a fine record in taking in refugees, people escaping from persecution. But, just as immigrants from certain countries can bring in health problems, so Britain can find itself with newcomers with different mentalities and standards of behaviour.

Thus we see gun- and drug-proliferation among some coming from the West Indies, prostitution and violence from East Europe, and anti-social violence among young Muslims and others. An analysis of criminal cases and prison population will immediately confirm these problems.

It would be an interesting exercise for the Home Office to analyse the prevalence of crime, and type of crime, among each minority and majority grouping in the country. One could then try to understand why there is little crime in some groups and more in others.

Britain is a small, compact country with no wide open spaces like Canada, or Australia or the United States. There is a limit to the number of people it can take in. There is already a right of entry to citizens of European Union countries, now increased in number.

Refugee status is linked to the well-founded 'fear of persecution' test of many decades ago. On the basis of this test there could be ten million or more who could qualify for refugee status in view of tyrannical regimes in

Africa and Asia and elsewhere. That test therefore is no longer the only one that is relevant.

As it is, the Home Office and Immigration Service cannot cope administratively with applicants for entry. It has recently allowed a host of illegal immigrants to remain, itself a discriminatory policy against those trying to remain here legally.

If civil peace, and the lessening of crime, is desired, there has to be a far stricter control which works in limiting entry to Britain with a right to remain. Such a change would be greeted with howls of 'racism' from people who are sincere about refugees, but who do not see the wider problems if the present policy continues. Violence, on a group basis, has already erupted in some northern cities. Should there be widespread unemployment, those disturbances will increase, crime will increase, and the burden on police, prison, and probation authorities will reach breaking point. This is confirmed by recent French initiatives to limit crime in inner cities, but shown in 2005 violence to be woefully inadequate.

Crime is often linked to social deprivation, and this could escalate if there is no policy of stricter control of those people given right of entry and settlement into this country.

The sensible policy of the Commission for Racial Equality (CRE) in working towards integration of present minorities will only be made more difficult if there is no breathing space in the movement of peoples.

3. THE ENVIRONMENT, INCLUDING FAMILY ENVIRONMENT

There are two aspects. One could almost parallel Claude Bernard's medical assessment of internal and external environment. I will categorise these:

(a) *The Home* A close, loving family is a great inducement to peaceful behaviour. There are emotional and psychological reasons for this statement. However, as family life has changed its nature in many homes there is less closeness and emotional support. Compare, for example, the rates of divorce in the 1930s and the 1990s. 'Broken homes' is the expression often used, but broken families create so often broken children developing into broken adults.

This is not a universal picture, as often second marriages, or 'partnerships' as we now have them, can have positive aspects. But there is no doubt the absence of the right relationship, with its internal unexpressed discipline, can, and does, lead to criminal and anti-social activity.

There is a second less attractive aspect of the home environment. You can have a cohesive family relationship whose joint objects are criminal. This is rather jocularly referred to in John Mortimer's superb Rumpole series, but, less jocularly, I can confirm this sad pattern from my own criminal court experience.

I recall the many occasions I appeared in court defending members of the same family, usually on vehicle theft charges. Just as a family can have a tradition of study, or sport, or education, so a family can have an accepted code of behaviour and language which sees no moral defect in removing other people's property.

Thus family can be a preventative and a cause of crime.

(b) *The Physical Environment* In 1981 there were inner-city riots in South London, followed by the Scarman Tribunal Enquiry, in which I participated. There were a number of stated causes: the 'stop and search' policy of the police; the lack of sporting and leisure facilities for young people; a feeling, right or wrong, of group oppression; antagonism of authorities; and even the effect of rumour.

As I wandered around the area, I was struck by the proximity of the mass of people living close to one another in old tenement-type housing, as well as the absence of trees, flowers, and the green lawns of surburbia.

What one sees, day in, day out, makes an unconscious imprint on the mind. There is a kind of urban architectural and environmental brutality that enlarges into the individual's conception of his environment. If you add to this a mass of graffiti and litter, you create a devalued world around you in which nothing matters, no one cares, and especially no one cares about you. Thus, again, it would be interesting to compare the statistics of crime in these types of inner cities with the statistics of crime in less concentrated types of housing in suburbs and small towns, where trees, gardens, lawns and flowers are visible daily.

I believe the recent experience of New York and its zero tolerance of graffiti, litter, and other visible impedimenta may provide a lesson, gradually being learned here.

4. NOISE AND THE TELEVISION

Many people have little idea of the subversive and corrosive effect of noise. We have a younger generation attuned to a level of decibels that, decades later, will cause them serious hearing problems. If one contrasts the 1930s with the present, we have an overwhelming increase in the assault on the ears, reflected in the brain.

We have today constant motor vehicle and aeroplane vibrationary noise. We have radio, television and the newer technologies, which are compelling both visually and aurally. In addition, we have repetitious, rhythmical sets of sounds in the musical world, electronically based, that are largely devoid of romance, melody and true feeling. The barrage of sounds are both stimulating and unsettling, and seem to be everywhere: in shops, vehicles, etc.

As for television, those of us who recall the 1940s and 1950s can only regret the passing of standards of clear pronunciation of English and the current prevalence of swear words and semi-coherent speech at every opportunity.

All this may seem minimal, some may think irrelevant, but it is really cumulative, alongside other factors.

5. DRUGS AND ALCOHOL

The consumption of alcohol has been a constant feature of this country for centuries. The inns and pubs have grown up around its sale. Read Dickens' *Pickwick Papers* and notice the never-ending imbibing of alcohol. The television soaps – East Enders and Coronation Street – so beloved by millions, revolve around public houses. For some reason, the consumption of beer and spirits here is regarded by young people as a sign of virility. It has become the major pastime of millions.

In no way is this basic urge or need going to be eradicated. The question is, how far can it be modified and channelled into safe patterns. Car crime – whether removal of vehicles, or injuring pedestrians or damaging other vehicles – is often based on excessive consumption of alcohol. How often do families grieve for a child, a parent, killed on the road by drivers who are drunk or under the influence of drugs?

The law has been strengthened. There are breathalyser tests, blood tests; perhaps some motor crime has been reduced as a result. Yet alcohol consumption remains a cause of crime.

Just as serious is the taking of prohibited drugs, from cannabis to heroin, ecstasy to amphetamines. There are no completely safe drugs. They are the cause of deaths and crimes. Inhibitions are loosened, as with alcohol; a sense of fantasy may take over; and society, as well as the consuming individual, is put at risk, often with fatal consequences.

Why do people take these destructive drugs? Has any deep analysis been done? Has the publicity against them achieved anything? How often are drugs linked to gun crime in this country where it is still easy to obtain guns, notwithstanding the tragedy of Dunblane and subsequent gun control legislation.

A teaching black sportsman, Garth Crooks, has warned that 'the glorification of drugs, guns and misogyny by the street culture surrounding "gangsta rap" is a deadly virus threatening black Britons'.

My comments here are brief only, but these elements – alcohol, drugs, and guns – are a lethal combination in the hands of already disturbed young people. And it is young people who commit more crimes, especially of violence, than older generations.

6. ALTERNATIVE OUTLETS FOR YOUNG PEOPLE

For some years I was the adviser to the Lottery Promotion Company, the body which was the effective motive force in creating the National Lottery. Its objects were to finance arts, environment and sports. Government then got at the Lottery and spread the objectives wider. At the same time Government has sat on £3 billion which could make an enormous impact in advancing the original objects.

There is ample evidence that a national expansion of sports facilities would give an outlet for the energies of youngsters. There is no reason for them to hang about street corners or deviate into petty, and later serious, crime.

The company and its director, Denis Vaughan, as well as prominent MPs, have urged time and again a massive programme of sports facilities to combat crime. It makes sound common sense – financial and otherwise – to give an impetus to such a programme, rather than to allow playing fields to be converted into blocks of flats.

This country invented so many sports: tennis, cricket, football, rugby. It was pre-eminent in them in the past, yet mediocre now. Every school, every club, should have the best facilities. They do not have them now. Australia, the energetic Victorians of the modern age, offers a potent example, as does the United States. Crime can be considerably reduced if every child, with the wish or ability, has an outlet for sporting achievement.

7. THE MORAL DILEMMA

This is linked to the failure of both education and religion. Once, both these elements would have provided a framework and a discipline for people to follow a non-criminal path. Both have, to a large extent, failed.

Religious leaders have been frightened to speak out boldly on basic moral issues, to condemn unequivocally the greed of the poor and the rich alike, the obscenity of suicide bombers and sex-abusers. How on earth can people accept guidance when there is no clear direction, when some church officials themselves have committed crimes against children? Thus, for many, religion as we have known it has become irrelevant. Sunday has ceased to be a day of rest and prayer. It has become just another day. Even Christmas has been devalued and turned into a materialistic orgy.

Some religious leaders from abroad have even advocated publicly criminal activity, yet have rarely been prosecuted, and this limited violence escalates into the terrible war of terrorism in which we are now plunged. And it is a real war, a third world-war, though different in character from previous world wars.

Education is no panacea. It is merely a tool that can be – has been – used by tyrannical Nazis and Communists, religious and terrorist bodies, in many parts of the world. Is it not strange that the wider education has spread in Britain, the more crime has increased?

Is the answer the failure to inculcate moral standards and human values into our schools? Is that why religion-based schools are in such demand by concerned parents, and why those schools achieve such laudable results? Do those schools instil a sense of respect, discipline, right behaviour, largely absent from so many state bodies?

Allied to comparative failure of education and religion is the all-pervasive campaign, subtle and well-financed, to encourage people to spend and buy into a world of intense materialism. Since when has any public commercial advertisement urged action that advances moral standards and behaviour?

This materialistic urge is reflected in the widespread looting from shops that takes place whenever there is any rioting. This happened here, as in the USA.

8. DIET AND NUTRITION

Before concluding this section, I would commend a study of the dietary and nutritional basis of crime.

When, in the late nineteenth century, Dr Semmelweis urged doctors to wash their hands before operating, he was laughed at. When Pasteur presented his theory of bacteria, he was abused and jeered.

It is time to turn our attention to a largely neglected but vitally important cause of crime.

A generation ago most people would have looked askance at any suggestion that diet and nutrition were relevant to criminal activity. Indeed twenty-five years ago I presented papers to the Scientific Advisory Committee of the Imperial Cancer Research Fund urging a study of dietary elements in the onset of cancer. The response was dismissive.

Today, Cancer Research Campaign advises that one-third of all cancers have a dietary and nutritional base. Perhaps authorities and researchers have also learned from the crises emerging in the food industry – salmonella, CJD/BSE, listeria, e-coli, etc.

It may well be that criminologists will adopt the same approach to my suggestion as their medical colleagues did in the past to cancer. Indeed, reading a volume on crime with contributions by ten professional experts I note not a single mention of any link between diet and crime. There is a great deal about welfare and socio-economic matters, enlivened by the kind of turgid phraseology I have mentioned, but nothing about food and drink and crime.

Yet it should be obvious, if one just looks at the effects of alcohol. Dr Mackarness had the same problem when he posed diet as a cause of certain mental conditions described in his epoch-making book *Not All in the Mind.* Dr McGarrison described the link in great detail in studies of the prevalence of illness in different parts of India.

But in all the probation and similar reports I have seen I cannot recall a single reference to this issue.

It might therefore be useful to look briefly at some of the evidence:

(a) Studies in USA jails showed a marked decrease in violence among prisoners when their diet was changed and minerals and nutrients added.

(b) Dr Robert Mayer, PhD, a consulting psychologist, noted the effect of chemicals on the mind, emotions, and behaviour. Our food is full of chemicals. A study acknowledged that 'there are 30 chemicals in the workplace that can cause apathy, 26 that cause delirium, 40, depressions, 25, hallucinations, 39, irritability, 29, nervousness or tension.' This is an American experience, but relevant to all industrial societies, including our own. Even schizophrenia is being linked, not to parental attitudes in early years, but to a food allergy affecting the brain. Likewise many young women would be horrified if they were aware of the contents of some toiletries. It is a massive problem, and a solution is bound to conflict with commercial enterprises.

(c) I record two quotations from an article by the well-known Dr Thomas Stuttiford in The Times.

'The research into the effect on young offenders' behaviour, after discharge from custody, of taking a Forceval, a multi-vitamin and mineral preparation, while inside, will add considerable weight to the argument that, far from being valueless, vitamin supplements can have a profound physical, and now it seems, psychological benefit.'

While our food was fresh, clean and unadulterated, we did not need vitamin and mineral supplements. Today they seem to be essential for health.

He adds:

'The Royal College of Psychiatrists' report, which showed a twenty-five per cent reduction in re-offending and a reduction of forty per cent in the number of serious violent crimes, cannot unfortunately isolate the beneficial effect of individual vitamins and minerals, but it shows the importance of minerals and trace elements in maintaining good physical and mental health.

(d) Mr Matthew Adams notes that to keep one hundred thousand people in prison – the 2009 projected figure – could necessitate a rise of two and a half per cent in income tax. He notes the failure of rehabilitation in that, on his figures, two-thirds of offenders will return to prison. He links this to the de-mineralisation and de-vitaminisation of our food. He refers to a study by Professor D. Bryce Smith entitled *Crime and Micro Nutrients*. That study reports that 'violent offences (in a young offenders institution) fell by almost forty per cent among those who took nutritional supplements.'

Professor Bryce Smith comments that the study 'may have identified one of the most important yet neglected factors in human affairs'. I believe that comment to be a restrained understatement.

(e) William Walsh, PhD, conducted chemistry and physics research in a national laboratory near Chicago. He compared the behaviour of forty-eight sets of brothers. He found a notable contrast between the well-behaved brothers and those imprisoned for crimes they committed. The findings were the same regardless of race. He concluded that the difference in behaviour could be directly linked to minerals. He found that 'one of the criminal patterns was a high copper-to-zinc ratio, low levels of sodium potassium and manganese; and high levels of lead and cadmium which are toxic.' He describes the adverse effect of this imbalance on behaviour.

A further study details another mineral imbalance directly linked to violence.

(f) It is encouraging that both the Home Office and elements in Parliament are beginning to take an interest in the crime-nutrition link. An article in the magazine *Here's Health* by Siobhan Mason outlines some of the current initiatives in this field. She refers to bodies already involved, e.g. Natural Justice, and concludes with the lively comment, 'strange to think the humble herring might one day sweep crime off our streets.'

(g) Few experts today would disagree that diet and nutrition are vitally linked to health. They have only to look at the effect of limes on scurvy in the eighteenth-century navy. If they look at the extraordinary link forged by Dr Max Gerson in the mid twentieth century between cancer treatment and diet they will see remarkable results from his efforts. The same applies to the excellent results being achieved today by Mr John Carter in advising treatment of cancer by a strict dietary approach linked to vitamin and mineral supplements.

Even IQ is susceptible to improvement from omega-3 fatty acids.

I have provided but a few examples of the present trend of expert opinion. The evidence is extremely important and a full-scale study should be set in motion to determine the dietary and nutritional basis leading to criminal activity.

9. THE SPIRITUAL ELEMENT

I come now to what will undoubtedly be the most controversial section in these notes. Gibbon, the historian, regarded history as a record of man's crimes and follies. On the other hand, we have achieved wonderful things in the realms of science, medicine, and understanding of human beings, the worlds within them and beyond them.

Religions have developed moral codes, as well as identifying a life beyond our material one. Whatever errors there are in religious dogma, the faiths all represent a reaching up of hands to a Being – whatever name is given, and whatever the nature of that Eternal Force or Spirit – who is beyond our understanding, just as flowers and plants reach up to the sun of which they have no comprehension.

There have been terrible perversions of the religious instinct. The Inquisition murdered thousands in the belief that they were thereby saving souls. Suicide bombers, totally indoctrinated, believe their actions will ensure for them a place in paradise. Time and again religion has been at the base of so much persecution, prejudice, crime and violence. Yet it also has thrown up rare moral teachers of the quality of Isaiah, Jesus, Buddha – teachers of the ways of justice and of peace.

Recently, the European Union Monitoring Centre dealing with racism sent two experts to seek my ideas on the subject. I told them my views and recounted my experiences, but I also told them two other things. The first was based on the physical. I indicated that racism emerged from our evolutionary group development and allegiance – almost a Darwinian interpretation. The group may be identified by what it has in common, as opposed to the different characteristics of the outside groups, whose very existence is regarded as a threat, resulting in conflict. This was a totally materialistic cause of racism, dealt with more fully in the writings of Elias Canetti.

The second thing I told them related to the purely spiritual, something modern, materialist philosophers and scientists would condemn as a non-existent chimera or delusion.

Yet one of the causes of crime is based on the low level of spirituality that exists world-wide. There has been physical evolution. Alongside it there has also been spiritual evolution. The latter has not kept pace with the former.

The facts, as disclosed so fully over the last 150 years, are clear, and, in my view, the evidence for survival after death of the individual is overwhelming, if people, scientists especially, will only take the trouble to study it. Just as energy and matter cannot be destroyed and may change in form, so there is a spiritual element in human beings that cannot be destroyed and that survives physical death.

What survives can be called spirit, soul, mind or consciousness; but survive it does, and proceeds to a level in the world next to our own dependent on the moral evolution, sense of service, and purity of motive of that person in this 'nursery school' here on earth.

Hence to be able to reach a suitable future level we have to rise above our instincts and prejudices, and live in accordance with the highest moral teachings we have, eschewing violence and crime and hatred.

Thus we have every reason not to commit crimes, but to spread goodwill – if not love – of neighbour as far as we can, and certainly not to harm our neighbour.

This is a truth, though how to convince the world, so enmeshed in a love of material, and currently technological, things, remains an enormous problem. It may be the most fundamental and vital challenge to those intent on crime. Few rational people today believe in separate realms of heaven and hell, harps and brimstone. Hence that sanction for good behaviour has gone, but nothing has taken its place. Somehow those who believe as I do have a duty to bring home to people these truths, and, in a way, these new sanctions.

I appreciate how sceptical many people will be of these words, but they should recall the examples of previous sceptics I have quoted who were subsequently proved wrong.

Is human nature destined to sink into self-destruction, or is there a motive force that will raise the spiritual level of humanity just one step above the present escalating violence and lead to a new and glowing era of positive human experience? Can mankind awake from its materialistic sleep, and begin to perceive a deeper reality?

With these words, perhaps unusual to some, I conclude the section as to the causes of crime, and turn to the judicial process, police, courts, probation, prison.

SECTION II
PRESENT PROCEDURES IN DEALING WITH CRIME

THIS section, shorter than the previous and later sections, deals with four 'p's: police, procedure in courts, probation and prison.

1. POLICE

The prevention and detection of crime is in the hands of the police. They have an unenviable task. There was a time when the authority of the police and respect for the individual police officer was enough to deter the commission of crime.

That is no longer the case. We see the assaults on police – even fatal assaults – with the use of firearms.

This has come about through a variety of reasons. The ubiquitous television has often shown police in a bad light. In the Miss Marple, Poirot and Sherlock Holmes series the police officers are shown as rather wooden, unimaginative, unperceptive, formal practitioners whose ability to solve crimes is limited.

On the other hand some television series indicate police as boorish, ignorant, even violent. Perhaps the Morse series is one that showed police officers as human, all too human.

Secondly, we have seen an assault on police morale by enquiries that label the whole force as institutionally racist, or internally corrupt, or externally inefficient. This is grist to the mill for the criminal element, whose defence in the courts is invariably to attack the integrity of police officers, something almost unthinkable in earlier decades.

There is sadly an element of truth in some of the accusations. When a police officer knows the accused has committed a crime, he or she sometimes elaborates, even invents, evidence so that justice should not be evaded. When this is done, and exposed, the whole force suffers.

Sometimes the technicalities of the legal process infuriate police, who may have worked tirelessly, often dangerously, to bring offenders to justice, only to see that effort negated by legal formalities in the courts.

So the police have a forbidding task, open to criticism from all sides, yet they continue to risk their lives daily, something their critics would never contemplate for themselves. One hears constant criticism, often from minority groups. But one rarely hears whole-hearted public praise, when, through determined police efforts, a drug gang are exposed and brought to justice, or a serial killer or rapist apprehended.

The police are in the front-line of society, but, as at present constituted, are unable to cope. Hence their support for properly approved, local self-help policing operations and patrols.

In the past, police training was different, especially in dealing with minorities. This was clear from the evidence given at the Scarman Enquiry, resulting in radical changes in training and the setting up of police consultative and other committees to link police with local communal cooperation.

For the fight against crime to succeed, there has to be general respect for the police, and self-respect by the police. I have set out in my book *Brief Encounters of a Legal Kind* examples of police failures and successes, but the crucial importance of the police force to the health of society must never by undermined.

2. THE JUDICIAL PROCESS

Home Office notepaper today bears a slogan, 'Building a safe, just and tolerant society'. A just society depends on confidence in the judiciary and the judicial process. We are fortunate in having an honest judiciary free from corruption.

Yet in recent years its powers have been restrained, first by the Human Rights Act and the jurisdiction of the European Court of Justice, and secondly by an Executive determined to combat terror by more draconian legislation.

The judges are concerned about the latter, naturally, but the judges do not have responsibility for security in what is now a new form of warfare. Thus that conflict with the Executive will remain.

Judicial procedure in criminal cases has not altered much over the years. Perhaps there is more pre-trial disclosure of evidence, more control by judges, but the defects remain.

Sometimes in many of the criminal cases in which I was involved – from the Old Bailey to the magistrates' courts, from the first kidnapping case in England to a rash of shoplifting exercises – I have felt immensely frustrated. I really would have liked to ensconce judge, jury, accused, witnesses and lawyers in a room, seated around a table, none of them allowed to leave until the truth emerged one way or another.

For, after all, in my eyes, that is what a trial is all about – to discover truth. The first jurymen centuries ago were chosen because they had personal knowledge of the accused and would have a good idea as to his guilt or otherwise. We have completely reversed that process, disqualifying any jury member who knows the accused.

Our judicial process has the danger of becoming something of a game. Much depends on the ability of the lawyers representing the parties, of the shaking of witnesses by rigid, sometimes fearful, questioning, by the mood created in the popular media, press and television.

We have a proliferation of lawyers. Over sixty per cent of all lawyers in the world practise in the USA. We have nothing like that, but their numbers seem to increase in direct proportion to the number of prisoners in our jails. I often wonder how valuable it would be if a fair number of criminal lawyers saw the other side of the problem by becoming special constables.

I am intrigued to note that Sir Thomas Moore, in his vision of the ideal society, Utopia, states, 'They have but few laws.' (They don't need them in an improved moral state). In his visionary state, 'they utterly exclude and banish all attorneys, proctors, and sergeants at the law; which craftily handle matters, and subtly dispute of the laws.'

In Utopian courts there is no need of lawyers. 'Every man should plead his own matter', and in that process 'the truth shall sooner come to light'.

For that is the crux of the matter: how best to arrive at the truth. My having made a number of suggestions as to improving the judicial process, the Home Office replied to me that 'the Government is certainly aware of the difficulties with the criminal justice system and the lack of public confidence in the criminal justice system.'

They then referred me to the White Paper *Justice for All* (2002), which 'sets out a coherent long-term strategy to modernise the criminal justice system end to end, from detection to the rehabilitation of offenders, with a clear focus on fighting and reducing crime.' This strategy includes 'ensuring a better deal for victims and witnesses, fairer more efficient trials, clearer, consistent and constructive sentencing,' etc.

These are striking and encouraging words, especially the better deal for victims, which I refer to in the last section of these notes. It will be instructive to monitor progress of this laudable, almost Utopian official strategy.

I would therefore limit my comments on the judicial process to just three points, as follows:

(a) *Human Rights* Whilst I would love to see an equal emphasis on human duties and responsibilities, on civics and the privilege and benefits of citizenship, I acknowledge that the current mood relates to human rights, and particularly the rights of the individual.

Where an individual commits a crime, or is accused of a crime, a very expensive process is set in motion, at considerable cost to society.

How is a person found guilty of a crime to repay not only the individual affected, or his or her family, but also the society he or she has wronged? There is a communal human right, that of the individuals who make up society, to live out their lives free from fear and violence, and, to quote American sources, to enjoy life, liberty, and the pursuit of happiness.

I believe that whenever the Human Rights Act is invoked on behalf of an individual, there should be a comparable consideration of the human rights of the individuals who make up the wider community.

(b) *Juries* Many countries do not have them. Assessors or special individuals sit with judges to hear cases. The United States still retains grand juries to determine whether there is a prima facie case. This procedure was fortunately abolished in the UK many decades ago.

Some countries have cases tried by judges and magistrates sitting alone. England, which evolved the Common Law, emanating pragmatically from the common sense and common experience of the people, evolved the jury system, also a product of the people.

This system has many advantages, which need no itemising here. Certainly there are defects, but the system provides checks and balances to the professional individual judge and the professional lawyers. It therefore should continue to play a role in serious criminal cases. The vast majority of crimes are dealt with by magistrates, also a system that emerged from the people and which should be retained.

Where juries deliver perverse judgments there is always an opportunity of reviewing such decisions, but the system is one process of arriving at the truth and is therefore valuable. Juries can be wrong, but often have an instinct for where the truth lies.

(c) *The past history of accused persons* Whilst there are current rules as to evidence, particularly hearsay evidence, which should be reviewed as to their limitation on arriving at truth and relevant facts, I raise now a matter of considerable controversy, but one I think crucial to the pursuit of truth in our criminal judicial system.

I recall a case in which I was involved, at that time the largest criminal case in English history, in which the most fundamental fact never emerged, despite weeks of evidence and speeches. The prosecution obviously did not think it relevant in achieving a conviction, whilst the defence were constrained, either by policy or the particular accused's instructions, from raising the matter.

It was a bizarre case, with the strangest of features, later incorporated in books and television programmes. It was only after conviction that the court heard of the mental history of the accused, which, given in evidence, would have been most relevant to everything that had transpired.

Similarly, there are those who hold the firm and honest conviction that the past history and record of an accused should never be mentioned, and that the jury should simply come to a decision on the facts of the particular case before them. I cannot, in the interests of both truth and justice, support such a view. It makes a game of the process, a blind-folding of those making the decision, an opportunity for 'deceit', as Thomas More described it.

I believe no crime can be properly understood, no truth arrived at, without a full story being presented to court or jury.

The recounting of a person's history and criminal record may or may not sway a jury in their final decision, but it would be part of the price, and the punishment, a wrong-doer would pay for past offences, as well as deterrent to future criminality. It would also enable a court to consider in a different light the question of sentencing and the best methods of preventing commission of further offences, as well as providing justice for victims, to which I refer later.

How absurd it is for a person to be convicted of rape, or child abuse, or violence, or even fraud, whilst a jury sit amazed as a litany of past offences are recounted of which they had been previously unaware.

My view is that the 'whole person' should be presented to a court or jury, and this should be linked to a definite rehabilitation process, as is now more and more the view in the treatment of illness.

I believe rehabilitation is extremely important and needs to be dealt with in a separate document, utilising the experience of other countries.

At its extreme, could one prosecute a Nazi Holocaust murderer on one single case without providing a background of systematic slaughter? The same applies to the various war crimes trials now slowly wending their way towards a solution.

In my book, mentioned above, I set out the cases of five examples of shoplifting in which I was involved as lawyer for the accused. None of them could be adequately dealt with by a court, no truth perceived, no action explained, without reference to the person's whole history. Simply to deal factually, with no surrounding information or past events leading up to the acts, would be unfair to the accused themselves and to those judging them.

If we regard our trials as the pursuit of truth, then the truth about the history and record of the accused should be disclosed to jury and court before any judgement is passed.

3. PROBATION

I will not expand here on the work of the Probation Service. Yeoman work is done by its officers, whilst its remit has expanded in recent years. I propose a radical change in this field which I detail later.

I notice that the home secretary proposes (January 2004) that fewer offenders be sent to prison, but that they be dealt with by a range of non-custodial orders and procedures. This may relieve the prisons for a time, but the burden on the Probation Service can only increase.

In any event, there is little, if any, evidence to show a reduction of offending by expanding that policy on its own. The home secretary, however, is trying to find a way out of the dilemma by creating a National Offender Management Service, merging the prison and probation services. This could prove beneficial, provided it is not bogged down in bureaucratic red tape. It could take on board some of my proposals for change contained later in this document, and is a move in the right direction.

4. PRISON

Prison works and prison does not work. Prison is one of the core elements in the fight against crime. It is one of the Home Office's responsibilities, administered through the Prison Service. It tries its best, initiates new schemes and experimental ideas in some of the 136 prisons, including 19 women's prisons, for which it is responsible.

It is not alone. There are other excellent bodies trying to cope with the problem. I name but a few: NACRO, who seek ways of rehabilitation; the Lattice Foundation, training young offenders for jobs; and the Howard League for Penal Reform. There is also a Restorative Justice scheme operating in Thames Valley, bringing offenders and victims face to face; the Smart Justice Campaign, suggesting alternatives to custody; the Prison Reform Trust; Hibiscus, helping Jamaican and other women prison inmates; and positive post-prison schemes in Wales under the Homeless Persons Order 2001.

I mention others who have an interest, wholly or partly, in prison affairs: the National Association of Probation Officers, Prison Officers Association, Youth Justice Board, Social Exclusion Unit, Commission for Racial Equality and a variety of human rights organisations.

There is no shortage of goodwill, and perhaps some of the current, limited initiatives will bear fruit.

Meanwhile, it continues to cost £37,500 to keep one prisoner in jail for a year. Nineteen jails have been opened in the past ten years. A few privately-run jails are an experiment, and the tax-payer continues to bear the cost, in excess of £10 billion annually. Yet it seems that three-quarters of young offenders and half of all offenders commit another crime within two years of release. One commentator states: 'Such failure would be unthinkable in any other public service. Imagine the public outcry if seventy-five per cent of young people went into hospital and come out worse.'

One home secretary is reported to have said of prison that it is an expensive way of making bad people worse.

The Woolf Report on Prisons (1991) referred to over-crowding. This problem remains a serious one. It is estimated that more than seventy per cent of prisoners have mental disorders, and half have a low reading ability. Many are unemployed and have a drug problem, while others suffer from homelessness or have emerged from care as a child. Some of those in custody frequently accuse prison officers of adopting racially antagonistic attitudes to coloured and Irish prisoners. In my period as a CRE commissioner, and as chairman of its legal committee, I came across some evidence for this.

There is also the social and personal tragedy of mothers who are imprisoned and separated from their young children. Some of these mothers have come from the West Indies or West Africa, used as 'mules' to bring drugs into the country. Often this leads to suicides whilst in prison.

We learn, in fact, that in 2001 sixty-seven prisoners committed suicide, increasing to ninety-four in 2002, many in the 30–39 age group, over eleven per cent of them women, though women represent but six per cent of the prison population. Few women are in prison for crimes involving assault. Recognised authorities state that men are twenty-four times more likely to kill or assault another person than women. An Irish human rights group has drawn attention to seven Irishmen who took their lives over a thirty-month period whilst in custody, some only on remand. It all presents a forbidding picture.

But efforts to improve the situation continue. Rescue, a black church body, tries to retrain young black offenders. Project Fullemploy works to assist inner-city unemployed into gainful occupations. The Prince's Trust does much in this field. But the problem remains, even increases. The conclusion is that punitive sentencing does not solve the problem. Much hope rests on better re-offending results being achieved by community sentencing and similar non-custodial policies.

In the 1990s I was one of a panel of speakers at Feltham Young Offenders Institution. A fellow-panellist was Sir David Ramsbotham, a retired army general and former inspector of prisons. I was greatly impressed by his sincerity, energy and concern. He was in the first year of his inspectorate post. After five years on the job Sir David produced a book which he entitled *Prisongate: The Shocking State of Britain's Prisons and the Need for Visionary Change.*

His account details the enormous frustration he felt at getting anybody to have a sense of urgency and do something about the problem. This reflected a conversation I had once had with Sir Stephen Tumin, a previous inspector.

Sir David admits that no one has found a better alternative to prison. In fact it appears that 'criminals on probation and community sentences have comparable – possible higher – rates of re-offending to those released from prison' (*Sunday Telegraph* 2004).

The view is that detention amounts to nothing but a series of incentives to return to crime. So the fundamental problem remains.

Sir David Ramsbotham's title includes the words 'need for visionary change'. I believe this to be true. I believe a number of individuals and organisations have the capacity for visionary change, and some schemes are in actual though limited operation. I would like to make my own particular suggestion in this direction which I put forward in the next section of these already lengthy notes.

SECTION III
A NEW APPROACH TO PUNISHMENT AND CRIMINAL JUSTICE

ALTHOUGH this section may repeat points already made, it reflects some aspects of a paper I presented to the Home Office minister which elicited the reply I have quoted. There are three headings to this part of my notes as follows: (1) Case adjourned for a report; (2) Change in treatment of person convicted of crime; (3) New form of financial assessment and compensation.

1. CASE ADJOURNED FOR A REPORT: A NEW APPROACH TO SENTENCING

I used to practise a great deal in the British criminal courts, handling cases from the largest to the smallest, from the 1950s to the 1990s.

Frequently cases were adjourned so that the judge or magistrate could read a report before deciding on sentence, often thereby trying to gauge what caused the criminal activity, and how best to relate the sentence to the crime and the criminal.

The reports I used to see contained the familiar catechism of family and occupational history, yet rarely, in my view, did they touch on what I consider to be most important elements. The decision of a court is crucial to the future life of the individual offender and his or her family. Reports should therefore be truly comprehensive. Modern research has shown much wider elements linked to crime than previously imagined, and these should be included by those who compile reports.

Today I would recommend that reports should include the following:

(a) History of criminal behaviour in the family and its sense of values. How often did I find son following father or brother in the same criminal acts.

(b) Nature of a person's daily work; not merely a job description, but precise details: the level and nature of noise, lighting, repetitious processes, problems and effect of travel to and from work, relationship with colleagues. Also most relevant are periods of no work, of unemployment, and how that might be linked to criminal activity.

(c) Precise daily diet: the balance of protein and carbohydrates, the quantity of food eaten and at what hours. For those who would scoff at this suggestion, I would recommend a reading of the studies I have previously mentioned discussing the link between diet and criminality and dietary experiments in U.S. jails, as well as the researches of Dr McCarrison, a gifted pre-1939 medical officer of health in India. Dietary changes have had remarkable results.

(d) Many people have little idea of the subversive and corrosive effect of noise (unlike those living close to airports). We have, as mentioned, a younger generation attuned to a level of decibels that, decades later, may well cause them serious hearing problems. I would recommend itemising the nature and quantity of noise to which an accused person is subjected daily. I would include radio, pop music, television and its adverts, telephone, computers, mobile phones, transport – all elements that assault the ear. It is well worth reading research done on the effect of noise on behaviour, as well as the positive effect of the absence of noise on the nervous system. I appreciate the difficulty in making this assessment, but would draw attention to the remarkable results of therapies in religious and other retreats.

(e) Years ago men in shipbuilding and other industries worked with asbestos. Many have since died from the effect. Few knew the dangers then. We learned the truth later, to our terrible cost. I believe the same applies to radiation today. Small amounts are emitted from equipment in the home: televisions, computers, microwaves. Larger amounts are emitted from masts, pylons, even nuclear waste, etc. No one knows the *cumulative* effect of all this. Indeed the recent Stewart Report gave no unconditional clean bill of health to the masts. A German scientific report recently itemised their very real danger to cattle and children. Only now, after years of confident denials, do scientists admit the possible link between magnetic fields from pylons and leukaemia in children living nearby.

I recall too that, at the Scarman Tribunal in 1981, the quality of air in Brixton was mooted as one of the contributory causes of the riots. Do we know the accumulated effect of radiation on the actions of people? Officialdom, experts included, are as dismissive as they were over causes of cancer.

(f) Consumption of alcohol: quantity and nature. Which lawyer has not had to deal with acts of violence, road accidents, family assaults, linked to an excess of alcohol? Our two main television soap operas revolve around pubs. It is a national characteristic, yet a dangerous one at times. A report should look at this in detail, and, of course, into the use of forbidden drugs. The Criminal Injuries Compensation Authority would benefit greatly from steps that limited the effect of alcohol and drugs. It pays out so much to victims of assault occasioned by these.

(g) How does the accused spend his/her spare time? What hobbies, pastimes, if any? This would throw much light on the values and mental processes which are at the base of criminal activity, often the influence of peer groups and the desire to conform or assert oneself. A major benefit from the National Lottery should have been a great expansion of sports and recreational outlets which in turn would limit the temptation to criminal activity. People have to have a purpose, an objective, rather than while away the time aimlessly.

(h) A detailed medical history is relevant, but, more than that, what precise medicaments are being taken. I recall a cough mixture that so affected a person's mentality that for that reason alone a court dismissed a shop-lifting charge.

How many pills, e.g. Ativan, Thalidomide, have been withdrawn because, only years later, did their effect on the metabolism, mental, emotional and physical condition become known. Any medical expert can provide a list of such medicaments and their effects, particularly on those with greater sensitivity than others to these effects. There is barely a pill prescribed today that does not indicate a whole range of side effects in its descriptive literature. Sensitivity tests to allergies or intolerances would not be out of place

(i) Most reports include a history of a person's relationships with friends, family, work colleagues, clubs. This process can often elucidate facts not otherwise available.

(j) I would include, as a final point, the visual aspects of a person's home and work, relationship to parks, flowers, trees, open spaces. All these, or their absence, are relevant. Inner-city crime can be influenced by visual effect and, in my very personal view, high impersonal buildings. The anonymous, run-down residential towers of the 1960s have been a hotbed of crime. I have dealt with many cases from these types of estates.

With all this, I can well visualise a probation or reporting officer throwing his or her hands up in the air in despair, commenting, 'Yes, all very well, but I have neither the time nor the resources, nor often the expertise to deal adequately with all these points.'

And he or she would be right.

Yet we, as a community – apart from the individual concerned and his or her family – may be saved an awful lot of future expense if a full and proper assessment of an individual is made in this way, which complementary or alternative health practitioners would call a holistic approach.

There is something to be said for regional assessment centres to be set up for this very purpose, with specially trained assessors, including probation officers, in charge of specialist staff. A really complete profile of a person, based on a detailed and standard set of questions, might be obtained that would result in a more perceptive judicial response or a sentence which could prove more efficacious and communally valuable than repeated and costly prison sentences.

Indeed the centres could be a halfway house between society and prison, with an opportunity to observe the accused under non-prison conditions. The effect may be to reduce the eventual numbers sent to prison, or else to confirm prison custody as the correct sentence.

I realise that it is not difficult to make these preliminary recommendations. However, to judges, magistrates, probation officers and legal advisers, I do say that it might be worth thinking about these suggestions and perhaps delving a little further than we do at present. You never know what you might find, and how a new and valuable procedure may gradually develop.

2. CHANGE IN TREATMENT OF THOSE CONVICTED OF CRIMES OF VIOLENCE AGAINST THE PERSON OR VIOLENCE AGAINST PROPERTY

(a) There is no way our present procedure will reduce the level of crime in society. Britain has well over seventy thousand convicted criminals in prison. America has almost two million. The cost to the state is enormous. The rate of repeated crime after release is very high. We retain rightly the abolition of capital punishment, but remedial, rehabilitation procedures have had very limited success.

(b) The history of dealing with crimes of violence to person or property has varied from time to time. Emphasis has changed, according to government or theory or politics, in the areas of prevention, imprisonment, rehabilitation, protection of society, forms of punishment.

None has been wholly successful. A new approach is needed.

(c) In respect of the crimes mentioned, a new attitude should be taken. At present a few people charged with these crimes may be treated as mentally ill and sent to Broadmoor or special institutions.

(d) That approach should be extended to those who commit the type of crimes I have mentioned. The convicted person should be treated, after the trial and any appeals, *as an ill person*, albeit a person who knew what he or she was doing when committing the crime and the nature of his or her act.

The stigma of illness would have a far greater effect than the stigma of imprisonment.

(e) The major difference this would entail is in the subsequent assessment of the person. That person would remain in custody in existing institutions while an assessment in depth is made.

(f) This would entail a personal assessment in a regional assessment centre which could include elements of the existing Probation Service and similar bodies and the points I have set out. The assessment of each person may well take up to three months. The person would remain in custody (or out of custody if that was deemed safe, but on specific conditions), and a final sentence would await the report of the personal assessment centre.

(g) The present procedure of a judge postponing sentence until after receiving a probation or medical report will be followed, but the nature of the report and the issues to be considered will be far wider than at present.

(h) A document will be necessary as a guide to the assessment service that will have to deal with each point. At present many matters relevant to the commission of crime are ignored.

The points will include:

(1) Details of previous offences and incidents, cautions, etc., whether convicted or not. Data laws will have to be looked at.
(2) Conviction of other family members with whom the person is living.
(3) The educational level and history of the person.
(4) Medical problems.
(5) Mental and psychological history, including treatment.
(6) Medicaments, drugs, alcohol, taken by the person.
(7) The quality of air in the district in which the person lives.
(8) Relationship with other individuals and groups.
(9) Religious and moral teachings received by the person, and his/her

beliefs. This element has now become increasingly important.

(10) A detailed assessment of diet over a period, highly relevant to behaviour.

(11) Consideration of past reports: medical, psychological, school, college.

(12) Pastimes, hobbies, sports.

(13) Assessment of noise volumes in the person's daily routine.

(14) The immediate physical, town or country environment.

(15) Assistance to the person to change patterns of behaviour by individuals, groups, charities.

(16) Marital or other relationships.

This list is long, but essential for a proper assessment. As an example of one item, research in American prisons has shown a vast reduction in acts of violence on a radical change of diet. In addition, the amount of lead and chemicals in the air can affect the behaviour of people, just as consumption of excess alcohol or mind-affecting drugs can affect behaviour.

The effect of noise is also well known, especially the metallic repetitive noise of some current forms of music.

(i) One element in the assessment is to establish which public figures, past or present, the convicted person admires, sees as a hero or heroine or role model. This would give an entrée into the moral standards and values of that person.

(j) The main objection to the procedure I recommend is likely to be the cost. Against this should be reckoned the cost of long-term imprisonment or custody. For some the latter is no alternative, but for many, an assessment combined with an *enforceable judgment debt*, (see later) and subsequent supervision, may vastly reduce the cost of mass, extended imprisonment.

Some have to be imprisoned, partly as punishment, partly to protect the human rights of peace-loving members of society. But prison in its present form rarely operates as a rehabilitation process, and punishment, even capital punishment, an effective deterrent.

(k) The emphasis should now shift to the assessment of crimes of violence against person and property as *an illness*.

In purely material terms this would change the way crime is viewed in society. In spiritual terms it would treat the person as an individual with an individual soul, accountable in the hereafter.

While it might be very difficult to get this approach understood or respected, one could explain that a person's behaviour and conduct in this life will affect his or her life after death.

This is a truism, but unlikely to weigh heavily, in the present moral and materialistic climate, with either the person, the judge, or the assessment service.

(l) Much of my career in law has given me experience of criminal courts, sentences, procedure. That process has not affected the level of crime and on occasion has resulted in the conviction and punishment of the innocent. The Home Office review mentioned in their letter may help eventually, but this should not affect the main proposals contained in these notes.

(m) Alongside my suggested changes, there should be wider research, involving universities, psychologists, etc., looking into:

(1) societies which have a low level of crime, and why;
(2) individuals and groups who do not commit crime, and why;
(3) reports of the effect on crime of television, noise, diet, air pollution, family pattern, and often of racial and religious elements and attitudes. For example, why is crime so high in certain minorities and not in others? Also, the effect of home and school on future patterns of behaviour, as well as link to facilities for sport.

It is my view that a new approach is crucial to the future treatment of crime. It could herald a major shift in public thinking. It will also, in due course, be cost effective.

3. COMPENSATION AND FINANCIAL ASSESSMENT

(a) Any conviction against a person for an act of violence against another person shall be deemed a breach of the attacked person's human right to live his or her life in peace.

(b) When a person has been so convicted the details shall be placed before the Criminal Injuries Compensation Authority or a local/regional branch.

(c) The CICA shall then assess the money payable by the convicted person, not on the basis of the present schedule, but on the basis of a new schedule which would include the following elements:

(1) The figures as contained in the present schedule for compensation.
(2) An element of what would have been awarded in a civil claim for damages, including pecuniary loss resulting from the crime.

(3) An element reflecting the cost to society in bringing the prosecution, including cost of police time, the prosecution and court process. This element would thereby emphasise what society has suffered by the criminal activity.

(d) Notice would then be sent to the convicted person who would have an opportunity to be heard as to the figure assessed.

(e) When the final figure has been stated that sum shall be entered as a *judgment debt* enforceable against all assets, present and future, of the convicted person. That registered sum can be reduced periodically, dependent on the lawful efforts made by the debtor to meet his or her obligation.

(f) Where the CICA makes a payment to the attacked party, CICA shall have the equal right to enforce the judgment debt against the offender(s) for that amount.

(g) This judgment debt will also include a figure reflecting part of the cost to the state of keeping the person in prison, which CICA alone could enforce.

(h) This procedure may seem hard at first, possibly impractical to some, but it is likely to have an increasing effect publicly on those who commit violence and those who have in mind to commit crimes. A financial sanction may have a greater impact than fear of prison. Alongside this proposal it is important to look at the training and employment opportunities for such offenders so that payment is practicable.

(i) The same procedure will apply to violating a person's human right to property, e.g. burglary, housebreaking, theft, and criminal damage. I would suggest this new form of compensatory scheme be brought in gradually, at first limited to certain serious crimes against the person, and then extended, in the light of practical experience, to lesser crimes against the person and property.

(j) This procedure would remove a court's assessment of compensation to an injured party, which is often based on a quick calculation, not on a continuing loss and the wider elements I have mentioned..

(k) The procedure would not apply to any other crime, but only where violence to the person or property is involved.

(l) The above applies to penalising financially the person causing the death, injury to another person, or damage or theft of property. It would not interfere with the sentence given by the court for the crime.

Thus there will be a continuing financial obligation, life-long if need be, against the criminal. It will have a much more salutary effect than a simple apology to the victim, or even bringing victim and offender face to face, however valuable though transitory those processes may be.

To sum up, there would be a new approach to crime and sentencing, an in-depth assessment of the criminal, a sentence that bears relationship to the nature of the crime, the victim and the offender, a move to see criminal behaviour as an illness, and a financial sanction to compensate both victim and society.

It might be worth a try.

RUTH ROTHENBERG

Volunteering in the Jewish Community

VOLUNTEERING in the Jewish community is such a widespread phenomenon that it is hard to know where to begin. Communities depend so fundamentally on this civic spirit that they could not function without it.

And the people are there. Some start in their teens, others while surrounded by their toddlers. But the majority probably come forward only when they feel established in their homes, families and careers. At whatever stage of life they begin, they can find some voluntary activity to suit them.

Jewish voluntary work is hardly a recent phenomenon. It goes back a long way, albeit under different terminology. At the heart of the synagogue service itself, following the Torah reading, is tucked a blessing for a series of people who contribute to our social and educational well-being, including 'those who provide lamps for lighting and wine for Kiddush and Havdalah, food for wayfarers and charity for the poor and all who faithfully occupy themselves with the needs of the community.' (Singer's *Prayer Book*, 1990 edition, p. 379.)

In modern-day terms, this highlights first the work of synagogue guilds (which used to be the ladies' guilds, but the term is no longer acceptable); then hospitality, the one voluntary sector which, due to the development of rapid transport and the modern hotel industry, has seen a real decline; then a welfare safety net; and finally a catch-all for voluntary work in the social, cultural and welfare spheres.

What that little paragraph also demonstrates are two features that hold just as true today: the expression of appreciation that constitutes the volunteer's true payment, and the sheer assumption that volunteers exist. It is a Jewish fact of life that, despite regular cries of woe at a lack of volunteers in some specific field or other, people do come forward to answer a need. As one executive director of a national fund-raising charity put it: 'There's a lot of it about.'

Not surprisingly, the nature of voluntary work has changed over the years and decades – in fact, over the centuries. Where the welfare state has moved in to provide for basic physical needs, the charitable field has developed into providing psychological support and giving individual attention. Simply visiting a housebound person is as important for that person's well-being as providing food and winter heating.

The Jewish tradition of visiting the sick – one of the oldest of all Jewish charitable missions, dealt with extensively in the Mishnah tractate *Peah* – has now been translated not only into 'befriending' or visiting someone in their own home or residential home, but into a huge operation bringing housebound people to day centres that allow them to socialise and follow interests old and new in company with others.

It is not just the work that has changed. So have the people, the volunteers. Whereas fifty years ago the typical volunteer was a middle-aged woman with time on her hands, often comfortably-off and with affluent colleagues of her husband to approach for fund-raising events, today's volunteer is just as likely to be a man who has taken early retirement after selling a business and is now driving old people to hospital appointments or serving meals in a day centre.

The change in women's lives and careers, bringing women out of full-time motherhood and home-making and into the working economy, has made an enormous difference to the composition of the volunteers' pool. But rather than dry up, the pool has simply adapted.

One of the biggest users of voluntary female labour is the League of Jewish Women, founded in 1943 during the Second World War. Out of its approximately 3500 members, some 160 – admittedly a tiny proportion – are men. But since they have been drawn into the organisation and had their work officially recognised, if only for insurance reasons, the 'lads' (League Association Division) are now part of the various teams active in the Jewish and general community.

Wizo UK, the women's fund-raising organisation supporting family projects in Israel, has also seen the admission of a few men, though they tend to do their own thing, such as organise an all-male backgammon evening. Wizo (Women's International Zionist Organisation) also made news when it appointed a man as its executive director in 1998, the first time that a man sat at the heart of such a powerful all-female organisation.

This was a paid post but significant as a response to the profound effect on the volunteer sector of the new generation of working women since the 1975 Sex Discrimination Act. However, men's support for their wives' voluntary work can generally be seen as the counterpart of the tribute paid to women as the unsung partners in their husbands' professional success.

The recognition by men of the importance of their wives' voluntary work, which applies across the whole voluntary sector, forms the backbone of all community work. It allows for teamwork, where a communal worker such as a rabbi is paid, while his wife, the rebbetzen, doing as much if not more, is unpaid. The value placed on charitable deeds has traditionally given scope to a woman's energies and abilities without threatening her husband's sense of authority as head of the family.

Such emphasis on gender roles may be unfashionable now, but working it out in the past has laid down long-lasting foundations. Women still fill roles in the traditional spheres, looking after the young and old, the sick and poor; men are found as trustees, handling an organisation's finances, or as heads of building committees or chairmen of cultural institutions.

The stereotypes are surprisingly durable, but the main thing is that the work gets done, as many an honorary officer has learnt to his cost. In today's pressurised world, the paid–unpaid work balance means that for many well-intentioned people it becomes a struggle to find the time to earn a living. The demands of the voluntary sphere can become all-devouring.

With an ageing community, the welfare emphasis has largely, though not entirely, shifted from the young, who used to be sent to large institutional orphanages, to the old, who now find themselves at home alone or placed in residential care homes. Jewish Care, Britain's largest Jewish charity, with an annual budget of over £4 million, has some 2500 volunteers on its books. Its volunteer services administrator, Sylvia Malnick, reckons that people devote on average one and a half man-hours per week to volunteering.

This can range from four days a week for someone who visits old people, to once a month or even once a year for the organiser of a social evening or summer fête or Chanukah party. 'People don't even realise they are volunteering,' Mrs Malnick points out. 'They go to visit their relative in a care home, find that the relative is unavailable because of, say, a chiropodist's or hairdresser's appointment, and finish up chatting to other residents while they are waiting.' They may not realise it but what they are doing is befriending.

Most of Jewish Care's volunteers work in the organisation's day centres, which house a wide and disparate range of services and activities. They lead groups in discussions, arts and crafts activities, reminiscence sessions and seated exercises. They run shops on the premises selling safety aids and practical clothing, and give advice in mini-CAB (Citizen Advice Bureau) sessions.

Others help out at mealtimes in residential care homes, setting tables and serving dishes, or do routine but essential administrative chores such as filing, or run a library book service for the housebound. More specialist activities include a cookery class for the younger disabled, a computer class for disabled and older people to keep them up-to-date with modern developments and maintain contact with relatives, and an audio service by voluntary readers who tape articles of Jewish and general interest for people with failing or failed eyesight.

Jewish Care, created in 1990 from the amalgamation of two long-established charities, is London-centred. But its aims and services are replicated around the country in communities such as Birmingham, Bournemouth, Brighton, Cardiff, Glasgow, Leeds, Liverpool, Manchester, Newcastle, and Southend. The scope of service provision varies according to local conditions, but the principle is the same. Professional care is provided by non-Jewish staff. Volunteering, which gives the Jewish touch, comes from Jews. It is the Jewish visitor, sharing culture and religion, who understands the request for a particular food or book or piece of music.

The League of Jewish Women, a national organisation, was once best known for its meals-on-wheels service. It still does that, but a lot else besides. A recent scheme in Watford is an excellent example of how a well managed voluntary organisation can contribute to a social service scheme and then keep it running by taking it over when the original funder – often a local authority – pulls out.

The Contact Centre was set up by Watford Social Services in 1989 as a means of allowing supervised contact between children and estranged parents, usually fathers, in a safe environment, following referral from a family law court. Aware that the League of Jewish Women was an active force in Hertfordshire – the League has a policy of helping in both Jewish and general causes – Watford Social Services asked the League to provide volunteers to be present with the children and their parents.

Other voluntary organisations were also involved, but the League provided the bulk of man- (or woman-) power. Watford Social Services provided a management framework and paid for a volunteer co-ordinator.

A few years later, realising that Watford's funding was to be withdrawn, the borough's social services department contacted Gingerbread, a non-Jewish one-parent group, to keep the highly useful contact centre running. Gingerbread received a lottery grant – among the aims of the National Lottery, launched in 1994, was precisely the direction of funds to good causes – and took over control of the centre in September 1998 with a year's funding to pay for a professional contact development worker.

The League volunteers remained, supervising appointments on Sundays, the most convenient day for fathers to meet their children. Aware of the precarious financial situation, they approached Northwood and Pinner Liberal Synagogue, which agreed to include the Watford Contact Centre in its New Year appeal. This kept the Gingerbread-appointed professional in place until the end of 2000, when Gingerbread wanted to move on to other initiatives.

Negotiations with the national organisation, the Women's Royal Voluntary Service, which had been involved in establishing the centre, fell through when the WRVS informed the League that, because of a policy decision to concentrate on the elderly and on accident and emergency projects, it could not take on responsibilities with this child-directed project.

At this point the League volunteers decided that, having stayed with the centre throughout, they were not going to let this valuable service disappear. One volunteer, herself a former professional social services worker in the area, acted as unpaid development worker while her colleague did the administrative work, including making the necessary police checks for workers and, crucially, obtaining charitable status for the centre in December 2002. Together with volunteers from other sources, the centre continues to thrive.

A similar process took place at Barnet Hospital, where speech therapists running a successful stroke group were directed to concentrate on speech therapy alone. Unwilling to see the disappearance of their beneficial project, in 1993 they asked a League of Jewish Women volunteer, involved in the hospital's work, if she could set up a stroke unit.

She found church premises nearby, applied to local trusts and foundations to get the project off the ground and arranged for help from seven volunteers, three of them League members. Now affiliated to the Stroke Association, the unit still gets hospital referrals but does not cost it anything. The twenty or so people who receive help with speech and writing difficulties pay a £2 session fee, and money is raised through traditional fund-raisers such as bring-and-buy sales.

'But our members don't take the credit for it,' says the League's head of development and communications, Jackie Baines. 'They just get on with their work quietly.'

The core of League activity lies in such basics as meals-on-wheels, hospital visiting and taking over non-medical chores at Christmas to allow non-Jewish staff time off to celebrate at home. In this they are not alone. Ajex, the Association of Jewish Ex-Servicemen and Women, which started in 1929, has also provided this valuable service over the last half-century when Jews were the only sizeable non-Christian minority in Britain.

The situation has changed enormously with the influx of Hindu and Muslim immigrants from the Indian subcontinent in the 1970s and 1980s, but Jewish help still continues over this holiday period. Major hospitals covered by the League around the country include Poole Hospital in Bournemouth and Christie's, the cancer specialist hospital in Manchester.

Another League responsibility is prison visiting. Today's main duties are running tea bars and crèches at Brixton in London and Strangeways in Manchester. The Manchester volunteers were on the tea bar rota just before the April 1990 prison riot at Strangeways. They admitted afterwards to noticing a strange atmosphere and feeling 'there was something wrong' when they went to their regular Thursday stint.

On the Sunday they saw on television 'the faces that had been causally exchanging chit-chat during visiting time', only this time on the prison roof. The following Thursday was back to routine for them, but now 'stepping over rubble and fire service hoses' as they set up the tea bar for policemen, firemen and prison staff. A year later, after the prison had closed for refurbishment and then reopened, the rota restarted, to the obvious enjoyment of the volunteers.

The League is particularly proud of two unique initiatives, Skin Camouflage and Headstart, which tackle the psychological distress of people suffering the burden of physical disfigurement. In Skin Camouflage, a project going back twenty years in three Manchester hospitals, patients are shown how to camouflage unsightly birthmarks, tattoos, scarring and sometimes self-mutilation. The volunteers who carry out this work are trained by the Red Cross – a clear example of cross-charity cooperation.

Headstart teaches women who have lost their hair through chemotherapy to tie headscarves elegantly and literally hold their heads up high. The success of this service, set up in Christie's Hospital to help women cancer patients, has led to its replication in London, where volunteers are trained by a recent arrival on the Jewish charity scene, Chai Cancer Care. This support organisation, founded in 1990 in response to the growing scourge of cancer, has itself spawned its own volunteer groups to man phones and help-lines and give non-medical advice.

Another League cross-charity interlinking is the 'twins and triplets group', which works in conjunction with Norwood, the old-established Jewish children's charity, to give mothers of multiple births a break by looking after these groups of children once a week. But as Jackie Baines observes, 'for the volunteers this is not work. They get to play with the children while the mothers can speak to a Norwood Child Care professional and have a chat in the next room.'

Volunteering and professional charity work go hand in hand. The original charity is set up and financed by volunteers, historically male, to answer a specific need – financial, educational or health-related – for those not in a position to help themselves.

When Jewish Care started life as the Jewish Board of Guardians in 1859, it incorporated the 1779-founded Jewish Bread, Meat and Coal Society. These responsibilities were organised and implemented with the active participation of various ladies' committees. The Sephardi Jewish community was particularly concerned with providing dowries, to ensure that young people got married. Wrapping festival parcels, particularly of Passover food, is still a hardy annual for any number of Jewish organisations today around the country, while schoolchildren enjoy making and delivering Purim gift packs and providing entertainment in residential homes.

The 'old families' have disappeared, and the welfare state has taken over many of the initiatives introduced by yesterday's volunteers. But new money and new volunteers have come forward to take their place, not least in the

Jewish community. Fund-raising committees organise the garden parties and bridge-playing evenings which pay for the residents of care homes to enjoy excursions or hair-dressing salons.

The professional is needed at the core, but whatever can be provided voluntarily means more resources can be spent on the service and recipient, and less on keeping the charity afloat. A lean charity policy, i.e. avoiding duplication of charities, is the most efficient way to harness a community's resources. External factors can combine charities which have different origins and outlooks. But their volunteer needs remain.

The Ravenswood Foundation for special-needs children is a case in point. It was set up in 1953 by a group of parents determined to create a sympathetic Jewish environment to nurture and educate their children, who suffered from learning disability. Ravenswood, the name of a country house where the children lived at an early stage in the charity's history, became the highly regarded state-of-the-art Ravenswood Village in Berkshire.

But the external climate was already in a state of flux. The welfare state, which had stepped in with funding, began to realise the unsustainable bill which lay ahead and withdrew its generosity – this applied even more to care of the elderly. The 1990 Care in the Community Act, which closed the old adult mental home institutions, affected attitudes towards children's institutions. At the same time and perhaps even more influentially, people's attitudes towards mental disability were changing, so that children suffering from mental or motor disability were no longer shut away as shameful.

Ravenswood found itself moving ever closer to a far older and larger Jewish organisation, the Norwood Orphanage. Norwood, so named from the South London suburb where it moved seventy years after its foundation as the Jews' Hospital and Asylum in London's East End in 1795, had already downsized considerably from the four hundred children housed there in the 1950s.

The orphanage, which, despite its image of orphans and abandoned babies, in fact largely took in the children of penniless widowed mothers, left its institutional premises in the 1970s. It still took in the children of unfortunate family circumstances but now housed them in scattered small residential units.

Changes in the welfare system, including allowing single mothers to stay with their children by means of benefit grants, meant that Norwood was left with hard-core cases, often involving behavioural problems. The two major Jewish children's charities found themselves working closely together, a co-operation enhanced by the fact that the heads of each were married to each other. Ravenswood merged with Norwood in 1996.

Today, Norwood is Europe's largest Jewish child and family services charity, with a highly professional staff. But this leaves plenty of room for volunteers, as the 'twins and triplets' project, mentioned earlier, so imaginatively demonstrates. Another important volunteer group in this specialised field is the children's club Unity, which allows special-needs children to mix with mainstream youngsters. The teenagers who give their free time to engage with these children – playing with them, reading to them, just talking and listening to them – are taking their first steps in the voluntary sector.

The Jewish Deaf Association is a further example of change and adaptation. Its establishment in the early 1950s was, as so often, due to parents' dissatisfaction with existing provision for their children's disability problems; they therefore took it upon themselves to improve facilities. Although a school for Jewish deaf children existed in London up to about 1980 – a residential school in Wandsworth closed in 1965 and moved first to Tottenham and then South Woodford – problems of isolation arose once the children grew up and left school.

With a minimal administrative core and maximum input from its members, the JDA conducts a successful operation but happily calls on volunteers as drivers to take members to their centre and as mealtime helpers. Once the volunteers are established as regulars, they behave like anyone else in a work situation, eager to communicate with those around them, and often finish up learning lip reading, sign language or both. The whole situation can take on a momentum of its own, as when a synagogue holds a service for the deaf. The entire congregation is then roped in to help in one way or another.

Another more recent example is the emergence of JAMI, the Jewish Association for the Mentally Ill, where again parents took the lead in pressing for a Jewish response to the tragedy of young adults struck down by mental illness. The campaign for recognition got going in 1989, in advance of the closure of mental institutions envisaged by the 1990 Care in the Community Act. Twelve years later, in 2001, JAMI appointed its first executive director to run its own day centre and small-scale residential home.

Once again the founding parents were the outstanding volunteers, raising funds and providing support against a backdrop of general indifference if not outright rejection. Indeed, one of the most important tasks performed by both volunteers and professionals today is raising awareness of problems which used to be swept under the carpet.

One of those hushed-up situations was domestic violence, nearly always practised against women, and made more difficult by the reluctance to admit that this could be found in the Jewish community. The issue has a long history of breaking through to the surface – there was apparently a Jewish refuge for battered women registered in Lodz in 1906 – but then being pushed down again.

However, by the 1970s the problem had become acute in Leeds, and in 1988 a group of Leeds Jewish women set up the first telephone help-line. One of the decisive factors in rousing these women to action was the disparity in sentences handed down in cases which came to court. Husbands who killed their wives could successfully plead provocation and be acquitted or receive remarkably light sentences. Wives who finally retaliated after years of abuse were given long prison sentences.

The Leeds group got in touch with people in London and other cities, and in 1992 Jewish Women's Aid was registered as a national charity. Together with a fund-raising campaign for a battered wives' refuge, which opened in 1997, it launched a national help-line in 1993 for victims of domestic violence, manned by volunteers.

Telephone volunteers are a manifestation of the way volunteering adapts to the changing environment and techniques. The old collection tins and house-to-house calls have dropped out of use, thanks to fears of mugging with the rise of drugs and street crime. As well as taking calls from people in distress, volunteers also make calls to appeal for money. The technique is popular with old-established charities like the Jewish National Fund and United Jewish Israel Appeal, where a friendly response can be assumed in the lists of previous donors.

Over the last fifteen or more years, a growing source of charity funding has been the charity shop, which has given unpaid employment to hundreds of volunteers. The development of charity shops is a neat illustration of the way the charity and volunteering sector fits into a bigger picture.

Up to the 1980s charity shops were largely confined to a few organisations, such as Oxfam or the Red Cross, selling donated second-hand goods in a secondary retail location. Sometimes while a high street shop stood empty in between lettings, a charity moved in for a week or two, fielding its volunteers as sales staff and sorters of donated items. They invariably reported brisk business.

But they really took off as the result of the retail revolution caused by the growth of supermarkets and out-of-town shopping centres. Trade on the high street was badly hit and unit after unit stood empty. Local newspapers recorded the changing face of the high street as empty units were taken over by building societies, estate agents and charity shops.

It was a trio of enterprising Jewish ladies of leisure, the almost archetypal volunteer, who saw the business-cum-charity opportunity. Under the aegis of the Jewish umbrella body, the Board of Deputies of British Jews – whose work is mostly done by volunteers – they set up a company in 1988 to launch and run Jewish charity shops.

The All Aboard shops, named after the Board of Deputies, now comprise a chain of some twenty shops in and around London and the country, staffed by 150 volunteers. A recent list of charity beneficiaries included Jewish Care, Kisharon (a 1976-founded school and training centre for children with learning difficulties from Orthodox families, supported partly by the enormous efforts of pupils in Orthodox Jewish schools), Ajex, Sage (an Orthodox residential care home opened in 1992), JAMI and Side by Side (a 1997-founded nursery in the Stamford Hill heart of Hassidic Jewry absorbing special needs and mainstream children). Stock is donated or sometimes acquired for a nominal amount and the shops have raised well over £2 million for their chosen charities.

The importance of volunteering in a national context has now been officially recognised. In his November 2004 pre-Budget speech, the chancellor of the Exchequer, Gordon Brown, designated 2005 as the Year of the Volunteer.

The recognition is long overdue. But charities themselves are aware of the debt they owe their volunteers. Many, particularly those concerned with the elderly (such as Nightingale House in South London, which goes back to 1840; Jewish Care; and the Association of Jewish Refugees, a 1943 wartime foundation whose members now need support in their old age), hold annual receptions to show their appreciation to the group, and highlight outstanding service by individuals.

The United Synagogue, responsible for over sixty congregations in Greater London, has an exceptionally wide range of operations, and volunteers are involved in practically all of them. In 1999 it started working on a programme, 'Volunteers Are US' (i.e. the United Synagogue), to celebrate its members' voluntary work. The organiser was a professional volunteer co-ordinator, newly employed thanks to a grant from the then five-year-old National Lottery. Like so many others, the co-ordinator, Sue Soloway, observed: 'People go quietly about doing all these things. They like a thank you but they don't make it a big deal.'

In May 2001 the Chief Rabbi's awards for volunteering were introduced, to great fanfare and excitement. Among some seventy nominations, individual awards went to an older man who was the mainstay of a small out-of-town community, a young man who despite Down's syndrome was the unpaid beadle of a new suburban community, and a mother who had started a synagogue kindergarten. Group awards went to the United Synagogue women's *chevra kadisha* (burial society), the youth leaders of one community and the volunteer team of another.

Subsequent years have seen awards for work in education, with young marrieds, in synagogue magazine production and, in 2003, a once-in-a-lifetime award for the chairman of the governors (Arnold Wagner) of JFS(the old Jews' Free School) for guiding the school's move from inner-London Camden to the leafy north-west suburb of Kenton.

By May 2004, nominations reached nearly 170, representing over two hundred individuals. They ranged from synagogue security teams to youth service organisers to the group of women running the over seventy-year-old Stepney Settlement. The overall individual award that year went to the founder of the North West London Singles Group. David Rose, a middle-aged man, whose discovery three years earlier of the lack of social opportunities to meet people after divorce – or separation or bereavement – led him to action, showed that no volunteer need lack imagination or determination. (Mr Rose subsequently remarried and the group expanded beyond North West London.)

What these awards have clearly shown in the few years of their existence is that volunteering cannot be pinned down to any single place or base. Once it has taken root, it just grows. No less than two hundred nominations were expected for 2005.

The bulk of charitable work, and its associated volunteering, falls naturally within the field of welfare, with youth and education as a significant extra. But Jews, as always, have a double load. For diaspora communities, and certainly for Anglo-Jewry, this work is duplicated to benefit both the local community and Israel.

Work for Israel, whether on behalf of universities, hospitals, arts or social welfare amenities, is essentially fund-raising. Volunteers may find all sorts of ways to drum up money and enthusiasm, from bazaars to concerts to fashion shows to bike rides and jungle treks. Their efforts are valuable and successful and involve giving time (a vital element in the definition of volunteering), but they are not, and cannot be, hands-on in the same way as for local charities.

For charity abroad the contribution is everything, though here again a big effort is made to involve donors through visits to the projects they fund. This applies largely but not exclusively to Israel. Currently, both World Jewish Relief and B'nai B'rith are concentrating their efforts on aid for the elderly and impoverished Jewish population of Eastern Europe, which survived the horrors of the Second World War and the miseries of Communism.

The two organisations have very different aims and constituencies, but together they use their fund-raising talents to relieve hardship for marooned and isolated Jews, mainly in the Ukraine, and to provide them with a renewed sense of community.

The volunteers of World Jewish Relief go back to its inception in 1933 as the Central British Fund for German Jewry. This organised the committees which responded to the urgent appeal to sponsor individuals seeking asylum from Nazi Germany and to provide homes for the unaccompanied minors who came on the Kindertransporte, the children's transports which arrived from December 1938 to the following August, just before the outbreak of the Second World War. With a tiny professional core, backed by the groundswell of public and communal concern, the operation became a huge volunteer undertaking.

B'nai B'rith, founded in New York in 1843 as a Jewish counterpart to philanthropic networks, has an international reach. Indeed it is one of the comparatively rare Jewish charities firmly in the political field. Its twenty-two or so British lodges, with up to 1300 members, run their charitable programmes independently but combine on three main projects, which include helping the Ukrainian survivors. The two other projects support Ethiopian Jewish children in Kiryat Gat, a southern Israeli township, and encourage home-grown leadership through B'nai B'rith's own youth organisation, BBYO.

Charitable movements in Britain steer clear of political involvement but cannot avoid it altogether. Persecution in one country puts pressure on another. This has been the case throughout Jewish history and has continued despite the establishment of Israel as the ultimate Jewish refuge. When Israel itself was under threat in its wars of 1948, 1967 and 1973, Jews from abroad flocked to serve as volunteers.

The 1948 War of Independence saw foreign volunteer fighters (including non-Jews) fresh from combat give their expertise to Israel's fledgling forces.

By 1967 and 1973, with Israel's defence forces well tried and tested, the volunteer response was civilian. Thousands of volunteers presented themselves to the Israel Embassy in London, offering to work in hospitals, on the land or anywhere which required continuity of labour. Just a few hundred were selected, usually with specialist skills.

The one major exception to the rule of minimal, if any, political involvement for Jewish volunteers was the Soviet Jewry campaign of the 1970s and 1980s. This long-running saga of protest against the combination of traditional Russian anti-Semitism with Communism's refusal to let disillusioned citizens leave its paradise, turned volunteers into political activists.

It was an unusual but exciting process. Unlike the humdrum chores of everyday volunteerism, such as getting the disabled to their hospital appointments and distributing their meals, this was a dramatic series of events, involving protests against show trials, heavy prison sentences, exile, loss of livelihood and a bar on earning a living.

In Britain, synagogue congregations banded together to give moral and financial support to the dissidents who were thrown out of their jobs and, often, their homes. Long-distance telephone calls were arranged in an era when international calls were unreliable and expensive. Tourism to Russia suddenly became popular as Jewish travellers smuggled in Jewish and Hebrew literature for dissidents, whom they then had to track down. People took in new clothing, especially jeans – a highly popular fashion item – and left it behind for the dissidents to sell. It was one of the few livelihoods left open to Jews.

Action at home took a new form. The Women's Campaign for Soviet Jewry was a truly glamorous organisation with well-groomed, well-spoken, confident women clearly articulating their cause on television. Demonstrations became a regular feature outside the Russian embassy in Kensington, but with a difference. At the end of the day, the women stacked their fold-up seats, swept and tidied the area where they had sat, and removed any cigarette butts before leaving for home! The Russian embassy doors never opened while they were there but the British bobbies loved them. They had never seen anything like it.

Interestingly, when the campaign ended, thanks to Communism's collapse in 1990, the women stayed active but reverted to more traditional forms of volunteering. With the exodus of Jews from the USSR, they wanted to help with their resettlement in Israel. Government agencies in Israel provided the infrastructure, but at the individual level it was easy to become a casualty of bureaucracy and misunderstanding. The human touch was needed.

One to One, fund-raising for disadvantaged families in Israel and especially the children of these families, was established by veterans of the Women's Soviet Jewry Campaign (also known as the 35s). Its annual treks have become established on the adventure-charity calendar, attracting some 150 marchers who raise sponsorship money through their foot-slogging. The charity's remit has widened to cover children's medical needs in conflict areas worldwide. But the focus is Israel, especially child victims of terror attacks since the start of the second Arab intafada in 2000. Where violent politics intrude, charity and its workers – paid or unpaid – are not far behind.

Volunteering, a former Jewish Care worker explained, is addictive. You can start as a museum shop assistant and end up lecturing a school class on archaeological finds; you can start as a member of an old-age home house committee and end up influencing government policy for the elderly; you can start by trying to help someone in trouble abroad and end up in the midst of an international crisis.

This survey makes no claim to have covered every aspect of volunteering and has steered away from statistics. Trying to evaluate the economic worth of voluntary service would be sheer guesswork, though perhaps this is the aim of the Year of the Volunteer. Nor has any attempt been made to provide a comprehensive list of organisations which attract volunteers.

What this survey has tried to show is how volunteering is tied to charity, and charity tied to an ever-changing social environment. Nothing is done in isolation; everything has a context. It is a question of knowing what that context is at any given time. It is an activity that is widespread, infectious and adaptable, a sort of beneficial virus or parasite. Without it, this voluntary essay would never have been written.

DANIEL SPERBER

Ethical Investment: A Jewish Perspective

THERE are those who say 'Money doesn't smell', or as the English proverb has it, 'Money is welcome though it come in a dirty clout'. What they mean by this is that the source of one's wealth, and the means by which one accrued it, is largely irrelevant. One does with one's possessions whatsoever one wishes, good deeds or otherwise, without regard to their source.

This certainly is not the view expressed in the Bible. In Deuteronomy 23:19 we read:

> Thou shalt not bring the hire of a whore, or the price of a dog, into the house of the Lord thy God for any vow: for even both these are an abomination unto the Lord thy God.

In other words, money gained by prostitution or other unsavory practices may not be brought to the Temple to fulfill the obligation of a vow. Or to formulate this in more modern terms: 'tainted money' has no place in the house of God, even if the intent is to use it for an honorable cause.

However, it is not only inappropriate for 'tainted money' to be presented to the house of God (cf. Malachi 1:7–8), but indeed, any God-fearing person should distance himself from such 'spoiled goods'. It is for this reason that usury is forbidden by biblical and Rabbinic law (Exod. 22:24, Lev.25:36, Deut. 23:30, etc.), as it is also in Islamic law, though legal fictions were later developed to accommodate these laws to modern society and its economic infrastructure. Indeed, the Hebrew word for usury is *neshech*, from the root *nashach* 'to bite', for usury bites into one's possessions as a beast bites into the flesh. And just as one may not extract usury, so too we read in Exodus 22:26–27:

> If thou at all take thy neighbour's raiment to pledge, thou shalt deliver it unto him by the time that the sun goes down. For it is his raiment for his skin: wherein shall he sleep? And it shall come to pass when he crieth unto me, that I will hear, for I am gracious.

And just as He is gracious, so too are we enjoined to be gracious (see Babylonian Talmud, *Shabbat* 133b; Jerusalem Talmud, *Pe'ah*, chapter 1 *ad init.*).

And to much the same end, the Sabbatical year annuls all debts, as we read in Deuteronomy 15:1–2:

> At the end of every seven years thou shalt make a release [of debts]. And this is the manner of the release: Every creditor that lendeth unto his neighbour shalt release it; he shalt not extract it of his neighbour, or of his brother, because it is called the Lord's release.

The Rabbis devoted a whole chapter of the Talmudic tractate *Shevi'it* 'Sabbatical year' to this issue.

For we have no absolute ownership over that which we possess (or think we possess). Our land, our property, our wealth is God's gift to us, and we are no more than guardians over it. He bids us give tithes and other forms of charity from our earnings (e.g. Lev. 19:9–10, ibid. 23:22, Num. 18:21–24, Deut 14:22–27, 28–29, 23:19–22), and preserve the sanctity – i.e. moral integrity – of our possessions. The sanctity of our possessions, and indeed the sanctity of the land we live on, is preserved by our judicious and ethical use thereof, and that which is 'tainted' carries with it a stigma that bids us distance ourselves from it. As the Rabbis have said (*Derech Eretz Zuta* 2:8): 'Distance yourself from that which leads to sin, and all that is like it'; or again (ibid. 1:12): 'Distance yourself from the unsightly and all that is like it.' We have a further obligation to do all within our power to discourage the continuation of such unseemly activities.

Wealth poses numerous problems and challenges. Meir Tamari, onetime chief economist to the office of the Bank of Israel, in his seminal work *With All Your Possessions: Jewish Ethics and Economic Life*, (New York/London, 1987, p. 25), writes:

> Ever since the dawn of history, material possessions and wealth have been seen as posing basic ethical and spiritual problems. All religions, therefore, have had to offer some perspective regarding the scope and legitimacy of economic activity. Judaism is no exception in this respect, though it differs radically from all other religions in the answers it provides to the relevant questions.
>
> Two distinct sets of problems within the general issue of material wealth would seem to require a religious perspective: the proper allocation of time between work and spiritual activity (such as prayer, religious study, or the fulfillment of religious obligations), and the challenges to ethics and morality. Inequalities in wealth have given rise to injustice, theft, and often bloodshed, and the accumulation of wealth often looks as though it is linked to human lust. All of these behaviours are inconsistent with the ethical and moral teachings of almost all religions. In Judaism's approach to these and allied issues, we will be able to discover the foundations for a specific ethical framework with respect to economic activity, on the part of both the individual and society.

And indeed, in his 340-page book he attempts to paint a portrait of the vision of Jewish ethical economics.[1]

And with an even broader viewpoint, at a global level, we may note that 'the capitalist free market, perhaps the great innovation of the modern economic system, a system that has triumphed over its socialist and totalitarian foes, permits the individual to exert a good deal of control over his own private world. But capitalism is ill-equipped to redress injustice and inequity; in fact inequity is front-loaded into the system.'[2]

As Rabbi Jonathan Sacks, chief rabbi of the United Kingdom, in his recent book, *The Dignity of Difference: How to Avoid the Clash of Civilizations* (New York, 2002, p. 11), has so eloquently stated:

> The liberal democracies of the West are ill-equipped to deal with such problems. That is not because they are heartless – they are not; they care

1 Other books have confronted this subject. See, for example, most recently: Aaron Levine, *Free Enterprise and Jewish Law: Aspects of Business Ethics,* New York 1980; Moses L. Para, *Business Ethics: A Jewish Perspective,* USA 1997.

2 David Sasha, 'Cultural Diversity without Moral Relativism: a Review Essay of *The Dignity of Difference: How to Avoid the Clash of Civilizations,* by Rabbi Jonathan Sacks', the *Edah Journal* 3:2, 2003, p. 4. The following citations for Rabbi Sacks' book are quoted in Sasha's article.

> – but because they have adopted mechanisms that marginalize moral conditions. Western politics have become more procedural and managerial. Not completely: Britain still has a National Health Service, and most Western countries have some form of welfare provision. But increasingly, governments are reluctant to enact a vision of the common good because – so libertarian thinkers argue – there is little substance we can give to the idea of the good we share. We differ too greatly. The best that can be done is to deliver the maximum possible freedom to individuals to make their own choices, and the means best suited to this is the unfettered market where we can buy whatever lifestyle suits us, this year, this month. Beyond the freedom to do what we like and can afford, contemporary politics and economics have little to say about the human condition.

And he continues (ibid. p.32):

> Not only has the dominance of the market had a corrosive effect on the social landscape [and, we may add, the physical ecological landscape too – D. S.], it has also eroded our moral vocabulary, arguably the most important resource in thinking about the futrure. In one of the most influential books of recent times, *After Virtue*, Alasdair MacIntyre argued that 'We possess indeed simulacra of morality, we continue to use many of the key expressions. But we have – very largely, if not entirely – lost our comprehension, both theoretical and practical, of morality.' The very concept of ethics (Bernard Williams called it 'that peculiar institution') has become incoherent. Increasingly, we have moved to talking about efficiency (how to get what you want) and therapy (how not to feel bad about what you want). What is common to both is that they have more to do with the mentality of marketing (the stimulation and satisfaction of desire) than that of morality (what ought we to desire).

And in what may seem to be an obvious statement, but I believe is a very significant formulation, he remarks (ibid. p. 42),

> Religion and politics are different enterprises. They arose in response to different needs: in the one case to bind people together in their commonality, in the other to mediate peaceably between their differences.

Economic considerations play a key role in the political process. However, the single greatest risk of the twenty-first century (to paraphrase a Sacksian statement) *is* that economics become religionized. Religion should guide economics and not the reverse. Hence, ethics and morality should form the foundations of economic policy, whether at governmental or at non-governmental levels.

I believe it should be our aim, and indeed the universal aim of all faith groups, actively to encourage the socially responsible deployment of our assets and engage in a concerted effort to combat the use of unethical and harmful means to accumulate wealth. For this is an integral part of our overall duty and responsibility in striving towards providing the possibility of a fullness of life for all people (*tikkun olam* in Hebrew). And to this end we must jointly harness all our resources.

ADY STEG

Droits de l'homme et valeurs juives

POUR l'Alliance, le combat en faveur des droits de l'homme est celui de tous les hommes de bonne volonté, quels qu'ils soient, quelle que soit leur origine, comme le veut d'ailleurs la Charte élaborée par les fondateurs de notre Institution : « En tant qu'hommes – proclamaient-ils – n'obéissant qu'à notre conscience, nous sommes, inspirés par le judaïsme, les alliés de tous ceux qui luttent contre tout ce qui menace d'écraser l'homme ».

Mais il semble qu'aujourd'hui nous apportons dans cette lutte une dimension supplémentaire du fait de notre double fidélité :

– fidélité à la mémoire cruelle de la *Shoah*.

– fidélité à la tradition juive.

Pour notre génération, on le conçoit, la *Shoah* est l'événement historique central qui colore dorénavant notre vision des hommes et du monde et qui pèse de tout son poids sur nos engagements.

Comme l'a rappelé ce matin le Professeur Ruzié, c'est précisément cette épreuve qui a été l'un des mobiles de René Cassin. A l'occasion du 10e anniversaire de la Déclaration Universelle, il déclarait : « Ce sont les innombrables atrocités qui ont précédé et accompagné la Deuxième Guerre mondiale qui ont déterminé les chefs des pays éprouvés à susciter une protestation de la conscience universelle contre les attentats commis contre la dignité de l'homme, pour en éviter le retour ».

Communication prononcée le 11 octobre 1987, à la Sorbonne, lors d'un colloque organisé par l'Alliance israélite universelle, intitulé : « Droits de l'homme : tradition et devenir », à l'occasion du centenaire de la naissance de René Cassin.

C'est évidemment de la barbarie nazie dont il est question ici, mais pas uniquement d'elle. S'agissant de la violation des droits de l'homme, les démocraties occidentales ont, elles aussi, leur part dans ce qui a « précédé et accompagné la Deuxième Guerre mondiale ». On peut même estimer que la sauvagerie nazie était tellement monstrueuse, inhumaine, bestiale, qu'elle pose plus le problème de l'homme, de l'*humanité* de l'homme, que celui des *droits* de l'homme.

Il n'en est pas de même par contre des autres Etats d'Europe et d'Amérique qui se sont tus, ont laissé faire ou, en refusant dans ces heures de feu et d'horreur le simple droit d'asile, ont contribué à ce que cela se fasse :

– la traque impitoyable par les Anglais des Juifs cherchant à entrer en Palestine,

– le refus de laisser accoster le *Struma* qui devait disparaître corps et biens,

– l'ignoble jeu de ping-pong avec les Juifs polonais de Zbonszyn, chassés par les Allemands et refusés par le gouvernement polonais,

– le tragique renvoi, par Cuba et les Etats-Unis, vers l'Europe et ses camps, des passagers du *Saint-Louis* qui avait cependant atteint les rivages de l'Amérique.

Voilà quelques-unes des mille trahisons des droits de l'homme en ce temps. Quand on l'a interrogé sur le pourcentage de réfugiés juifs qu'il était possible d'accueillir au Canada, un ministre de ce pays a répondu : « Zéro pour cent, et c'est encore trop ! ».

« On n'a rien compris au sort des Juifs, écrit Manès Sperber, si l'on ne s'est pas rendu à cette évidence... la totalité de la population juive de l'Allemagne, de l'Autriche, de la Tchécoslovaquie, aurait pu être sauvée car Hitler les laissait partir, mais les pays leur fermaient l'entrée : les Juifs ont péri parce qu'ils n'avaient pas où aller ».

Voilà, par des pays où la morale avait son mot à dire, une vraie violation des droits de l'homme.

Pour en avoir mesuré et éprouvé les tragiques conséquences, nous nous sentons autorisés à insister sur la rigueur dont, en la manière, doivent faire preuve les démocraties : *la lutte en faveur des droit de l'homme commence d'abord chez soi.*

Mais cette nécessaire rigueur ne doit pas aveugler au point de nous faire ignorer que *seule les démocraties mènent ce combat avec sincérité*, et que cette lutte serait tout à fait inopérante et risquerait même d'avoir des effets contraire si elle était menée avec naïveté : je veux dire menée *par les démocraties* avec naïveté et face aux Etats totalitaires. Il suffit de se souvenir de la *naïveté* et de la complaisance, pour ne pas dire de la complicité de l'Occident quand Hitler invoquait les prétendues violations par les Tchèques des droits des Allemands de Sudète…

• Ce serait faire preuve de naïveté par exemple, que d'accepter les mensonges politiques et la « langue de bois » des droits de l'homme dont usent les Etats totalitaires pour couvrir l'oppression qu'ils exercent sur leurs peuples.

• Ce serait faire preuve de naïveté que d'imaginer qu'il est indifférent de laisser les droits de l'homme être tournés en dérision : il y a quelques semaines, le Comité des droits de l'homme de l'ONU a accepté sans broncher le Rapport du délégué irakien présentant son pays comme le paradis des droits de l'homme, à quelques vétilles près, comme par exemple la peine de mort (sans appel) pour toute insulte envers le Président de la République ! Ou encore « pour propagation de principes sionistes ou maçonniques » ! Et que dire par exemple d'une conférence des droits de l'homme organisée… à Moscou… par le gouvernement soviétique !

• Ce serait faire preuve d'une dangereuse naïveté que de prendre au sérieux la dénonciation indignée et bruyante de nos imperfections par les Etats bourreaux ou geôliers de leurs peuples. Les droits de l'homme sont bafoués par ceux qui les violent chez eux mais ils le sont doublement par ceux qui – comme dans les Etats totalitaires, ou dans ceux inspirés par le fanatisme religieux – tout en les ignorant chez eux, en dénoncent la plus minime atteinte chez les autres. Et même si cette hypocrisie est une sorte d'hommage rendue à la vertu, elle doit être dénoncée, sans relâche.

Le second facteur qui influe sur notre approche des droits de l'homme, c'est notre enracinement dans la traditions juive : plus qu'Athènes et Rome, Jérusalem est notre référence. On pourrait aisément, en regard de chaque paragraphe de la Déclaration Universelle, inscrire une citation de la Torah ou du Talmud. Ce qui ressortirait de cette confrontation serait certes identité ou très grande proximité des principes énoncés, mais en même temps une profonde différence dans la formulation :

– non pas « droit à la vie », mais « *tu ne tueras pas* »,

– non pas « droit à la propriété », mais « *tu ne voleras pas* »,

– non pas « droit à la dignité », mais, « *n'humilie pas* », « *n'humilie pas la veuve et l'orphelin, n'humilie pas l'étranger, ni ne l'opprime* »,

– non pas « droit à une rémunération équitable », mais « *n'exploite point le journalier, qu'il soit un de tes frères ou l'étranger qui est dans ton pays* »,

– non pas « droit à un jugement équitable », mais « *juge ton semblable avec impartialité* » ou encore « *même loi, même statut pour l'indigène et l'étranger* ».

Cette formulation est, on le voit, singulière à un double titre :

– d'une part, par le TU : elle s'adresse à l'individu, à chaque homme, à la personne humaine, tout en soulignant par l'incessante mention de l'étranger, qu'elle s'applique à l'homme en tant que tel, uniquement parce qu'homme et non pas à un groupe, une tribu, une caste, une race ou un parti.

– d'autre part, par l'impératif TU DOIS, elle associe aux droits de l'homme les devoirs de l'homme, devoir de droiture et de justice, le devoir envers l'autre, le prochain qui a acquis des droits sur vous. Il est clair que cette formulation personnelle et impérative TU DOIS, suppose qu'il existe un JE, le « *JE suis l'Eternel ton Dieu qui t'ai fait sortir d'Egypte, de la maison d'esclavage.* »

Autrement dit, la lutte pour les droits de l'homme implique des devoirs et suppose une référence à des valeurs, à une éthique, et la Déclaration Universelle des droits de l'homme, a à nos yeux, d'abord et surtout, une portée morale.

Se référer aux droits de l'homme – surtout lorsqu'il s'agit de ce que Raymond Aron a appelé « les droits traditionnels », « ceux qui expriment l'universalisme, la formule démocratique, les libertés personnelles ou intellectuelles » c'est se référer à une sorte d'impératif catégorique qui s'impose « ni par les armes, no par la violence, mais par l'esprit. »

Dans une récente réflexion sur les droits de l'homme, Jean Daniel suggère que ceux-ci pourraient un jour constituer ce qu'il appelle « la religion des incroyants ». « En assument la réhabilitation déterminée et militante d'un humanisme qui respecte le devin, sans sacrifier à Dieu », ces incroyants pourraient « se forger une religion grâce aux valeurs qui on été celles de l'incroyance ».

N'est-ce pas ici encore une façon détournée de reconnaître aux droits de l'homme un caractère en quelque sorte sacré ?

A nos yeux, la Déclaration Universelle, précisément parce qu'elle se situe dans l'ordre de la transcendance, constitue, dans ce monde instable et menacé, un thème rassembleur, une directive pour toutes les consciences religieuses ou laïques.

C'est par cette Charte que René Cassin a voulu que les hommes tirent la leçon de ce qui venait de se dérouler. C'est par elle qu'il est entré dans l'Histoire.

Une antique sentence du Talmud proclame qu'« *on n'érige pas de monument à la gloire des Justes, c'est leur œuvre qui est la garante de leur mémoire* ». Alors, n'en doutons pas, elle est assurée à jamais, la mémoire de René Cassin, Juste parmi les Justes.

GIDEON TAYLOR

Holocaust-Era Reparations – Morality, History and Money

HOLOCAUST-ERA reparations is truly the place where morality meets money. The amount of money handled by the Conference on Jewish Material Claims Against Germany (Claims Conference) is, by any standard, large. As a result of negotiations by the Claims Conference since 1952, more than half a million victims of persecution by the Nazis have received close to $60 billion.[1]

Yet Holocaust-era compensation and restitution is about much more than money. It is also about justice, history, law, politics and social work. It is about those who are entitled and about those who need help. It is about responsibility and about fairness.

1 Major Direct Compensation Programs for Jewish Victims Of Nazi Persecution, http://www.claimscon.org. For a comprehensive history of the Claims Conference and of Holocaust compensation programs, see: Nana Sagi, *German Reparations: A History of the Negotiations*, 33 (Dafna Alon, Trans., Magnes Press, 1980); Ronald Zweig, *German Reparations and the Jewish World: A History of the Claims Conference* (second ed. 2001); Angelika Timm, *Jewish Claims Against East Germany* (Central European University Press, 1997); *History of the Claims Conference: A Chronology 1951–2001* (2001) [hereinafter *History of the Claims Conference*]; *In Re Holocaust Victims Assets Litigation (Swiss Banks) Special Master's Proposal*, Sept. 11, 2000, Annex E; Karen Heilig, "From the Luxembourg Agreement to Today: Representing a People," *Berkeley Journal of International Law*, vol. 20, no. 1, 2002; Menachem Z. Rosensaft and Joana D. Rosensaft, "A Measure of Justice: The Early History of German–Jewish Reparations", *Leo Baeck Institute Occasional Paper* no. 4, 2003. See also Saul Kagan, "The Claims Conference and the Communities," *Exchange*, 1965, the author of which is one of the giants in the history of Holocaust-era restitution and compensation. Clemens Nathan has served as a long time and active Board member of the Claims Conference.

As Israeli prime minister, David Ben-Gurion wrote in a 1952 letter to Nahum Goldmann, founder of the Claims Conference:

> For the first time in the history of relations between peoples a precedent has been established whereby a great Power undertakes, under moral pressure only, to pay reparations to victims of its former Government. For the first time in the history of the Jewish people, oppressed and plundered for hundreds of years in all countries of the Old World, the oppressor and plunderer has had to hand back some of the spoil and pay collective compensation for part of the material losses.[2]

Half a century later, Israeli prime minister Ariel Sharon used the fiftieth anniversary of the 1951 founding of the Claims Conference to note that it "has been at the forefront of the struggle for justice for Holocaust survivors in Israel and around the world."[3] On the same occasion, U.S. president George W. Bush wrote to acknowledge the significant role of the Claims Conference in the search for a measure of justice for survivors of the Holocaust. He commended the Claims Conference "on your efforts to use the memory of the past to create justice in the present."[4]

Our society has a tendency to measure many complicated concepts in primarily financial terms. At the Claims Conference, we deal with one of the greatest moral challenges to humanity in the last centuries – the Holocaust – and seek to translate the quest for justice into one of the most basic forms of human interchange – money.

The task of the Claims Conference is, by definition, impossible.

The struggle to reconcile the irreconcilable goes back to the origins of the Claims Conference. Following efforts by Jewish leaders and the State of Israel, Chancellor Konrad Adenauer of West Germany addressed the German Parliament on September 27, 1951:

> The federal government and the great majority of the German people are conscious of the immeasurable suffering that was brought to bear upon

2 Letter from David Ben-Gurion to Nahum Goldmann, Sept. 17, 1952, reproduced in *History of the Claims Conference*, p. 14.

3 Letter from Ariel Sharon to Rabbi Israel Miller and Gideon Taylor, March 19, 2001, reproduced in *History of the Claims Conference*, p. 4.

4 Letter from George W. Bush, March 28, 2001, reproduced in *History of the Claims Conference*, p. 5.

the Jews in Germany and in the occupied territories during the period of National Socialism . . . Unspeakable crimes were perpetrated in the name of the German people which impose upon them the obligation to make moral and material amends, both as regards the individual damage which Jews have suffered and as regards Jewish property for which there are no longer individual claimants.[5]

The newly formed Claims Conference, while welcoming the statement of the Chancellor and making clear that it supported the concept of claims for compensation and restitution, issued a public statement after its first meeting:

Crimes of the nature and magnitude perpetrated by Nazi Germany against Jews cannot be expiated by any measure of material reparations. No indemnity, however large, can make good the destruction of human life and cultural values or atone for the agony of the men, women and children, tortured or put to death by every inhuman device.[6]

Some opposed the idea of any Holocaust reparations. Rabbi Isaac Lewin of Agudath Yisrael took the position that the offer of the Chancellor to commence negotiations should be immediately rejected. At the initial meeting of the Claims Conference, he cited the Bible: "Ye shall not take ransom for the life of a murderer that is guilty of death" (Num. 35:31).[7]

In Israel, the opposition was even more vehement. Angry demonstrators gathered outside the Knesset, Israel's parliament, and hurled stones as legislators inside gathered to debate the issue. The police responded and hundreds were injured.[8] Menachem Begin, a future prime minister of Israel, spoke to the huge crowd against accepting reparations: "That blood which was poured out in German concentration camps gave us courage to rise and overthrow the British . . . How shall we face the world after trading that blood for marks?"[9]

---

5 Declaration of German Chancellor Konrad Adenauer, September 27, 1951, reproduced in *History of the Claims Conference,* p. 6.

6 Statement issued by the Conference on Jewish Material Claims Against Germany, following its initial meeting October 25–26, 1951, reproduced in *History of the Claims Conference,* p. 8.

7 Ronald Zweig, p. 30.

8 Nana Sagi, p. 81.

9 John Authers and Richard Wolffe, *The Victims Fortune: Inside the Epic Battle Over the Debts of the Holocaust*, HarperCollins Publishers, 2002, p. 378.

Still, the Luxembourg Agreements of 1952, consisting of an agreement between the German Federal Republic and the State of Israel, and a parallel agreement between the German Federal Republic and the Claims Conference, ultimately came to be accepted.

Looking back, these agreements were truly remarkable in concept. In addition to the large financial sums that were paid to Israel and that continue to be paid to Holocaust survivors, the agreements paved the way for Germany's postwar relationship with the State of Israel and with the Jewish people.[10]

I have lost count of the number of times in the course of my work at the Claims Conference that I have sat at negotiations, a meeting or a briefing and started with the words "It's not about the money," to then continue with an explanation as to why this or that particular group of survivors needed to be included in a particular program and then to follow with the response to the inevitable question: "Well, how much does it cost?"

Is the mantra "It's not about the money" really true?

It is a question the Claims Conference faces every day. How does one take issues of justice and morality and translate them into dollars and cents? Is Holocaust restitution demeaning the memory of the Holocaust? Are the moral issues getting lost?

But what is the alternative? To agree that too much time has elapsed since these events took place? To abandon these claims? To say that survivors who have fallen through the cracks unfortunately just missed their chance?

The German Foundation agreement, which arose in 2000 out of negotiations for compensation payments for former slave and forced laborers, is, together with its implementing legislation, one-hundred pages long.[11] The agreement is of tremendous financial and legal significance. The Claims Conference has distributed some $1 billion arising from it. Yet, perhaps the two most significant documents are not part of the formal materials. Their significance goes well beyond their legal status or their financial importance.

The first document emerged from a small meeting on November 16, 1999,

10 Nana Sagi, pp. 202–204.

11 For details of the German foundation Remembrance, Responsibility and the Future see http://usembassy.de/policy/holocaust/index.htm. See also: Stuart E. Eizenstat, *Imperfect Justice: Looted Assets, Slave Labor and the Unfinished Business of World War II*, Public Affairs, 2003, the author of which played a pivotal role in the restitution process since 1995; Authers and Wolffe; Michael J. Bazyler, *Holocaust Justice: The Battle for Restitution in America's Courts*, New York University Press, 2003.

in Berlin, while the main negotiating session continued in Bonn. Rabbi Israel Singer, then chairman of the Negotiating Committee of the Claims Conference, and I, had requested a meeting with the president of Germany.[12] In postwar Germany the office of the president is a position of tremendous moral authority, and Johannes Rau, whose father was a preacher, had maintained the tradition of using the presidency as a forum for addressing important issues of morality and justice.

As we sat in a corner of the elegant reception room in his official residence, Schloss Bellevue, President Rau listened sympathetically to our request. We explained our concern: that if an agreement were reached, it would be perceived publicly as just another financial settlement. We told him that any agreement that dealt only with money would be of limited significance for the Jewish world. We asked that the president accompany any agreement with a statement that addressed issues of morality and responsibility. Without further deliberation, he agreed. Soon after, we were on our way to Bonn to rejoin our colleagues and to resume the arguments over financial details and legal definitions.

Just one month later, the negotiations had concluded and we were back in Berlin. The day began with last-minute discussions about technical issues and was followed by a signing ceremony that culminated in our return to Schloss Bellevue. This time, the meeting with the president was very different. In front of a simple podium was a battery of television cameras and journalists from the world's media, as well as the participants in the lengthy negotiations. The room was silent and the mood solemn as the president entered.

In a statement that took just a few minutes to read, he spoke of the history of those terrible times. He said:

> At the time, many companies profited from the victims of forced labor. Some of them have already publicly accepted the responsibility they bear and have concerned themselves with providing material compensation. It is, however, only with the Foundation Initiative of German enterprises that this commitment has been given a broader basis . . .
>
> The German state is making a very significant contribution. In this way all contributors to the Foundation Initiative, both government and

12 Joan Gralla, "Jewish Groups to Meet Germany's Rau on Holocaust," Reuters, Nov. 15, 1999.

business, accept the shared responsibility and moral duty arising from the injustices of the past.

We all know that no amount of money can truly compensate the victims of crime. We all know that the suffering inflicted upon millions of women and men cannot be undone ...

This compensation comes too late for all of those who lost their lives back then, just as it is for all those who have died in the intervening years ...

I know that for many it is not really money that matters. What they want is for their suffering to be recognized as suffering and for the injustice done to them to be named injustice.

I pay tribute to all those who were subjected to slave and forced labor under German rule and, in the name of the German people, beg forgiveness.

We will not forget their suffering."[13]

There are Holocaust survivors who believe that the moral issues are more important than the money and those who believe that they are less important. Regardless, the historical record now includes President Rau's powerful statement, which for the first time acknowledges that German industry was not an innocent party during those terrible times, but an active participant in the death and destruction that was the Holocaust.

The second document, of equal importance, is not an elegant statement publicly addressing issues of responsibility and morality. It is instead a rather dry and technical letter issued during the negotiations by a mid-level official in the German Ministry of Finance.

The agreement envisaged "legal peace" for German companies in U.S. courts, but this was far less important for survivors than the issue of the effect of the German Foundation agreement on future negotiations with the German government.

Early in the negotiations regarding slave and forced labor, some on the German side took the position that if an agreement were reached this would mean *schlusstrich*, or "closure." After this, there would be no more claims for Holocaust compensation against the German government. We indicated that we could not accept such a position. Ultimately, the German position was withdrawn. This led to the letter, which noted that the Claims Conference

13 Statement by German president Johannes Rau, Dec. 17, 1999 (translation).

had open issues with Germany and confirmed that "the Foundation legislation will not impede such discussions in any way."[14]

Certainly, this letter was important for ongoing negotiation efforts with Germany on Holocaust compensation. Indeed, in December 2000, March 2002, February 2003 and May 2004 (well after the German Foundation agreement was signed), the Claims Conference successfully negotiated the inclusion of thousands of additional survivors into the Article 2 program, which pays quarterly pensions.[15] The Claims Conference continues to fight for all remaining open issues.

However, for the Claims Conference, the letter was of importance well beyond its financial significance. There can be "legal peace" in courts for German industry. But this simple letter effectively acknowledged that there can never be "closure" with the German government. The German government is the legal successor to the Third Reich. There have been various forms of "closure" or "legal peace" with Switzerland, with other European countries and with German industry, but never with the successor to the entity that was responsible for the Holocaust. As long as there is one Holocaust survivor alive, we do not believe that anyone can grant such closure.

One of the key elements of Holocaust-era compensation is that it is fundamentally symbolic. No amount of money can ever make up for what happened. During the negotiations in the 1950s the Germans used the term *Wiedergutmachung* (which, translated literally, means "making whole").[16] We do not. Nor is the word "compensation" a satisfactory one; we use it as shorthand to describe payments to individuals that are in some way related to their suffering in the Holocaust.

In the negotiations regarding former slave laborers, there were suggestions by some to have a scale of payments for the survivors according to how long they were in a concentration camp. Ultimately our approach was that, as any payment could be no more than symbolic, every person who had been

14 Letter from German Federal Ministry of Finance to Dr. Karl Brozik, Claims Conference Representative in Germany, July 3, 2000.

15 Conference on Jewish Material Claims Against Germany, Inc., Annual Report 2001 with 2002 Highlights, p. 26; Conference on Jewish Material Claims Against Germany, Inc., Annual Report 2002 with 2003 Highlights, p. 21. Conference on Jewish Material Claims Against Germany, Inc., Annual Report 2003 with 2004 Highlights, p.28.

16 Susanna Schrafstetter, "The Diplomacy of Wiedergutmachung: Memory, the Cold War and the Western European Victims of Nazism, 1956–1964," *Holocaust and Genocide Studies*, vol. 17, no. 3, Winter 2003.

in a concentration camp or ghetto should receive an equal amount.[17] As one survivor graphically put it: "To be in Auschwitz for one day was like a lifetime."

Holocaust-era compensation is about absolute justice and yet it is also about compromise. "Time is our greatest enemy"; "The enemy of the good is the perfect"; "The clock is ticking": The clichés are no less true for being clichés. As the German Foundation negotiations dragged on the discussions continued ... fight for more, or settle now.[18]

What do the survivors want? Our negotiating team, composed primarily of Holocaust survivors themselves, grappled daily with these issues. Yet at our offices hundreds of survivors called daily to ask: "When will I finally get a payment? Will it be during my lifetime?"

When the founders of the Claims Conference first came together in 1951, they discussed what the name of the organization should be. After much debate they inserted the word *material* into an already unwieldy name: the organization would be called the Conference on Jewish *Material* Claims Against Germany.[19] They wanted to emphasize that negotiations regarding material compensation would never replace the moral challenges posed by the Holocaust. And half a century later, that remains the position of the Claims Conference.

Over the past few years there has been a cacophony of opinions as to how much restitution money is really owed and how it should be spent.

Yet lost amidst the figures and the ever present discussion of funds is perhaps the real achievement of the struggle for Holocaust-era restitution – the restitution not of money but of history.

As survivors seek restitution, their stories are being revealed to the world.

---

17 The emphasis on moral responsibility rather than legal responsibility was part of the Claims Conference position in the negotiations: "The compensation to be paid to slave laborers is based upon the acceptance by entities who benefited from slave labor of their moral responsibility for their acts and represents an attempt, however inadequate, to provide financial recognition of this responsibility in a material form." Conference on Jewish Material Claims Against Germany Position Paper, June 15, 1999.

18 "We not only want to see a measure of justice achieved but we want those who suffered indescribable horrors to be alive to see that a new generation in a new century has not forgotten them." Testimony of Gideon Taylor, Hearing before the Committee on Banking and Financial Services, U.S. House of Representatives, Restitution of Holocaust Assets, Feb. 9, 2000, available at http://www.financial services.house.gov/banking/2900tay.htm.

19 Ronald Zweig, p. 31.

When modest payments were made in 2004 to 2500 victims of Nazi medical experiments, it was after painstakingly identifying 195 medical experiments in thirty-two different concentration camps.[20] Dozens of these experiments were identified solely through survivors' individual testimonies submitted with their applications to this program. Until now, no book, no document, no list recorded their suffering. In just a few years the existence of those horrific Nazi medical experiments would have slipped from the grasp of history.

In Bulgaria, long thought to have protected its Jews from the Holocaust, Claims Conference historians working on Holocaust compensation cases combed through newly available local historical records and uncovered the full extent and horrors of labor camps for Jews. Archival documents combined with personal stories, letters and photos from applicants enabled an almost forgotten story to be told and led finally to the recognition by the German government of the persecution of these elderly survivors.[21]

In 2004, when the payments were made under the German Foundation agreement, there were some 130,000 survivors of concentration camps, labor camps and ghettos alive. More than 29,000 of them had survived Auschwitz. Yet others were the sole living survivor of their camps or ghettos. They lived in sixty-two countries. As memories fade after sixty years we must not allow them or their stories to be forgotten.[22]

When all the restitution money is long spent, what will be left? We will have rescued not just dollars and cents but also a little bit of the history of the Jewish people.

The testimonies of so many individuals and the stories they tell are part of the fragments that will enable historians today and historians a hundred years from now to have a glimpse into the lives not just of the perpetrators but also of the victims.

When settlements with European banks and insurers were reached a few years ago, we perhaps naively believed that everything was over. Amounts

20 Conference on Jewish Material Claims Against Germany, Inc., Annual Report 2003 with 2004 Highlights, p. 13, Jewish Week, January 30, 2004.

21 Conference on Jewish Material Claims Against Germany, Inc., Annual Report 2003 with 2004 Highlights, p.19, Jewish Week, July 16, 2004.

22 In the program for Former Slave and Forced Laborers, the Claims Conference undertook a massive research effort ultimately involving 150 archives in twenty-nine different countries. Conference on Jewish Material Claims Against Germany, Inc., Annual Report 2003 with 2004 Highlights, pp.14–16.

were determined and hands shaken. Years after the end of the Holocaust most of the victims were gone and many of the records were lost. But there were still claims to be handled, files to be looked at and archives to be gone through. It turned out to be a slow and difficult process – made even more difficult by the resistance of many of those same banks and insurers to giving access to the records even though the amounts to be paid by them were capped. Perhaps, on the part of some, there was a hope that few bank accounts or insurance policies would be found and it would all go down in history as what a former Swiss president called "blackmail."

Virtually every nation's history is built on a foundation of national myths. Swiss children grew up with the myth that the reason that Switzerland escaped the fate of most of Europe was its high mountains, elegantly dressed border guards and its rigorous and honorable neutrality. The stirring music as the Von Trapp family raced to freedom over the hills in the *Sound of Music* gave that myth to the world. The campaign for Holocaust restitution eventually brought out the truth – that Switzerland was simply more useful to the Nazis as a banker and trading partner than it would have been as a vassal state, and that Swiss officials were eager to do the Nazis' bidding.

The arguments over access to the files and the records will, no doubt, continue long after the settlements are reached. It is less of a fight over money than it is a struggle over history.

Perhaps the reality is that Holocaust compensation and restitution is not about the money and it is about the money. It may on occasion cloud the important lessons of the Holocaust, yet it can also be a vehicle to educate a wider public. At the end of day, it has helped many hundreds of thousands of Holocaust survivors around the world to live out the remainder of their lives with a little more dignity than they might otherwise have had. And it represents more than just the restitution of money; it represents the restitution of history.

EDWARD TIMMS

Remembering Refugees Lost at Sea
The *Struma*, the *Wilhelm Gustloff* and the *Cap Anamur*

DURING my ten years as director of the Centre for German–Jewish Studies, founded at the University of Sussex in April 1994, my colleagues and I developed a wide-ranging programme of teaching and research. Our London-based Support Group included Clemens Nathan among its members, and it is a pleasure to contribute to a book published in his honour. One of our priorities has been to research the experiences and achievements of refugees who escaped from Nazi-occupied Europe during the 1930s. In addition to completing a number of projects and publications in this field, staff at the Centre are compiling a database of British Archival Collections Relating to German-Speaking Refugees. More controversially, in my own writings, I have explored the concept of 'German–Jewish symbiosis' – the close identification of educated Jews living in central Europe with German culture, especially in the period around 1900.[1] This implies that there are certain convergences, both historically and conceptually, between German and Jewish cultural traditions – not least by virtue of their paradigms of remembrance.

The fundamental question is how national and cultural memories are formed and transmitted. As a consequence of the Holocaust, mainstream historiography has tended to picture Jewish and German traditions of commemoration in antithetical terms, as if the two were immutably fixed in their respective roles as victims and perpetrators. This paper will offer an alternative perspective, approaching the subject from the periphery by re-

1 See Edward Timms, 'Between Holocaustism and Symbiotics: New Approaches to German–Jewish Studies' in *Jewish Quarterly* (Summer 1994).

calling the fate of two ships laden with refugees that were lost at sea during the Second World War.[2] The first is the *Struma*, which was carrying Jewish refugees from Romania when it sank in the Black Sea in February 1942. The second is the *Wilhelm Gustloff*, which was laden with German refugees fleeing before the advance of the Red Army when it was sunk in the Baltic in January 1945. When we speak of these ships being 'lost at sea', the phrase has a double meaning: they were first sunk (with great loss of life) and then virtually forgotten (through collective amnesia). These specific cases provide a basis for reassessing the processes of public memory, while raising questions about refugees lost at sea that are still relevant in our own day. Hence the concluding section on the controversies associated with another refugee ship, the *Cap Anamur*.

REMEMBERING AND FORGETTING

The Hebrew narratives of the Old Testament provide an appropriate starting point, specifically the book of Deuteronomy, where the paradox of 'remembering to forget' is paradigmatically formulated. A celebrated passage in Deuteronomy 25:17–19 describes how the children of Israel were ambushed by Amalek, leader of a desert tribe from southern Canaan:

> Remember what Amalek did unto thee by the way, when ye were come forth out of Egypt; How he met thee by the way, and smote the hindmost of thee, even all that were feeble behind thee, when thou wast faint and weary; and he feared not God. Therefore it shall be, when the LORD thy God hath given thee rest from all thine enemies round about, in the land which the LORD thy God giveth thee for an inheritance to possess it, that thou shalt blot out the remembrance of Amalek from under heaven; thou shalt not forget it.

It would be fascinating to explore the paradoxes inherent in the precept (as formulated in the King James version of the Bible): not to forget to 'blot out remembrance'. The Deuteronomist is recalling another passage, from Exodus 17:8–14, which describes how the children of Israel, exhausted refugees fleeing from Egypt, were ambushed by Amalek at Rephidim; and how Joshua put Amalek to the sword, while Moses provided moral support, holding up

2 For helpful suggestions during the writing of this paper, I am grateful to Arun Bayraktaroglu, Susan Drucker-Brown, Saime Göksu and Stephen Nicholls.

his hands in benediction while watching the battle from a nearby hilltop. After Amalek's army had been put to flight, 'the LORD said unto Moses, Write this for a memorial in a book, and rehearse it in the ears of Joshua: for I will utterly blot out the remembrance of Amalek from under heaven'.

Moses is to write a memorial in a book so as to ensure that Amalek is forgotten. Indeed, Exodus *is* that book, traditionally thought to have been written by Moses, and the words of Moses, from Exodus 17:16, transform Amalek into the eternal enemy: 'the LORD hath sworn that the Lord will have war with Amalek from generation to generation'. There could be no more effective way of ensuring that Amalek's attack on the Jewish refugees will be always remembered, and it now forms part of the standard liturgy recited in the synagogue.

The biblical narrative identifies the factors that render certain military exploits or national disasters unforgettable. Such events are especially memorable if they are associated with the following factors:

1. a notorious perpetrator: Amalek
2. a specific location: Rephidim
3. eye-witness testimony: Moses standing on top of the hill
4. a monument or inscription: writing a memorial in a book
5. a territorial narrative: 'the land which the LORD thy God giveth thee for an inheritance'
6. a moral message: Amalek feared not God

If we think ahead 'from generation to generation', as the scripture instructs us, we may take this paradigm and apply it to massacres perpetrated in other periods, most notably during the Second World War. Certain parallels will immediately be clear. The crimes of National Socialism are vividly remembered because we have a notorious perpetrator; we have eloquent eye-witness testimony; we have an abundance of books containing written memorials; and they record the locations of atrocities far worse than those committed by Amalek. Moreover, the events of the Holocaust are publicly commemorated because they can be fitted into narratives which enshrine those events in a patriotic historiography: the founding myths of the state of Israel; the ideology of gallant little Britain resisting tyranny and providing a haven for refugees; the self-image of the United States as the saviour, not simply of Europe, but of thousands of Jewish lives. Finally, there is a clear moral message: we must learn the lessons of the past if we are not to repeat them.

However, on our mental map of the places where hundreds of thousands of persecuted Jews, prisoners of war and slave labourers were systematically put to death, certain locations are missing – places which have indeed been 'blotted out from remembrance'. This applies in particular to the victims of disasters and atrocities that occurred at sea. A particularly clear illustration of this process of amnesia is provided by my primary example from the Second World War: the sinking in the Black Sea of a Romanian ship laden with Jewish refugees.

THE *STRUMA*

In February 1942, off the coast of Turkey in the region of Cap Igne Ada in the Black Sea, a ship named the *Struma*, which had sailed from Constanza in Romania carrying Jewish refugees bound for Palestine, sank as a result of a mysterious explosion. Virtually all the passengers and crew, including over seven hundred refugees, were drowned. You may think it was only natural that such an event was soon forgotten. It was, after all, of marginal significance compared to the massacres that were being carried out during that same period by the German army and the SS in Poland and the Soviet Union. In this same period thousands of tons of British and allied shipping were being sunk by German submarines during the battle of the Atlantic, while the United States was reeling under the impact of Pearl Harbor. But the case of the *Struma* was special, since it had become the focus of intense diplomatic activity. It had actually passed through the Bosphorus and reached Istanbul on 15 December 1941, and it remained anchored within sight of the city for seventy-one days, while repairs were carried out and diplomats argued about its future. The Turkish government, which was anxious to protect its neutrality, refused to allow the refugees to land unless the British issued them with visas for entry into Palestine. The British refused, panicked at the possibility of losing Arab sympathies at a time when the German and Italian armies were advancing on Egypt. Finally, on 23 February 1942 the Turkish government lost patience and had the *Struma* towed back up the Bosphorus and into international waters in the Black Sea. Within 24 hours the ship had sunk without trace, after an explosion had torn it apart.

The fact that the *Struma* was so soon forgotten was certainly not due to ignorance. The ship's predicament had received considerable press attention, its sinking was widely reported, and the tragedy was debated in the British parliament, with Churchill's government under pressure to justify its policies and the *Manchester Guardian* calling for a more humane approach to the refugee problem. To understand the processes of erasure, we need to recall not simply the historical circumstances, but also the conceptual categories derived from Deuteronomy:

(1) There was no known perpetrator: For many years it was uncertain why the *Struma* sank. Was it attacked by one of the Soviet warships patrolling the Black Sea, or was it torpedoed by a German submarine? Given the decrepit state of its equipment, it was also possible that it might have been destroyed by an accidental explosion in the engine room.

(2) There is no known physical location. Despite recent efforts by salvage expeditions, the wreck has not yet been found.[3] There is thus no 'place of remembrance' ('lieu de memoire'), in the sense of the term developed by Pierre Nora and Aleida Assmann.[4]

(3) This is compounded by the absence of survivor testimony, which has made this tragedy difficult to conceptualize. The *Struma* has become 'invisible' – in the literal sense that there is not even a fully authenticated photograph of the ship. The purported photo in the Haganah Archives in Tel Aviv (fig. 1) may possibly be that of another ship. The sinking of the *Struma* was the greatest of the catastrophes in the seas around Turkey, but there is a reason for the shortage of survivor testimony. Of the estimated 792 passengers and crew on board when it reentered the Black Sea, 791 died. Thus there was only one survivor, a young Romanian Jew named David Stoliar, whose memories of events have only sketchily been recorded. It is even doubtful whether a reliable photograph of the ship survives. This helps to explain why for sixty years the sinking of the *Struma* remained, in effect, an 'untold story'.[5]

(4) There is no public memorial to mark the locus of the tragedy. The event has been virtually forgotten in Turkey, the country whose government

3 For information about attempts to locate the wreck, see http://www.alpas.net/uli/struma/struma_engl.htm (viewed 18 July 2004).

4 See Pierre Nora, *Les Lieux de mémoire*, vol. 1: 'La République' (Paris, 1984). For the development of similar ideas in Germany, see Aleida Assmann, *Erinnerungsräume: Formen und Wandlungen des kulturellen Gedächtnisses* (Munich, 1999).

5 The silence was broken in 2003 by the publication of the first circumstantial account, *Death on the Black Sea: The Untold Story of the 'Struma' and World War II's Holocaust at Sea* by Douglas Frantz and Catherine Collins (New York: Harper Collins). An appendix by Samuel Aroni (pp. 295–335) reviews the debate about how many were drowned and concludes that the most likely figure is 791.

Figure 1. The only known photograph of the Struma, *from the Haganah Archives, Tel Aviv. (There is some dispute about its authenticity.)*
Source: Haganah Archives; photographer unknown

actually sent the refugees to their deaths in the Black Sea. This is all the more surprising because the *Struma* was not the only ship loaded with Jewish refugees to be sunk in Turkish waters. In December 1940 a ship named the *Salvador*, carrying over three hundred Jewish refugees from Romania, was allowed to pass through the Bosphorus into the Sea of Marmara, only to be sunk by a storm, with the loss of over two hundred passengers. And in August 1944 the *Mefkure*, carrying 350 refugees from Romania under the Turkish flag, was torpedoed in the Black Sea, this time with only five survivors. But in none of these cases has a plaque been erected on the Turkish coast to mark the point nearest to the disaster. Only in Romania and in Israel are modest memorials to be found. A monument in the Giurgiului Jewish cemetery in Bucharest records the names of those who died on the *Struma* (fig. 2), while a sculpture at Ashdod near Tel Aviv is dedicated to their memory. For decades, accounts of the period tended to pass over this tragic episode in silence, as if it were a historical curiosity of interest only to naval historians.[6]

(5) Moreover, there is no national narrative to enhance the significance

6 The standard history of *The Jews of the Ottoman Empire and the Turkish Republic* by Stanford J. Shaw contains a single, rather misleading sentence about the *Struma* (p. 257). For an account by a naval historian, see Jürgen Rohwer, *Die Versenkung der jüdischen Flüchtlingstransporter Struma und Mefkure im Schwarzen Meer* (Frankfurt, 1965).

of the event. All the refugees were Jews, but the sinking of the *Struma* is of marginal importance for the founding of the State of Israel. For Zionist public consciousness, what counts are the ships that *did* run the British blockade and successfully reached the shores of Palestine.

(6) Finally, the sinking of the *Struma* contains no readily accessible moral message. Given the historical circumstances, no national group could claim the moral high ground. Indeed, all the key political players were compromised:

- the German regime, which in collusion with the Romanians had forced the seven hundred Jews to flee;
- the British government, which was responsible for refusing entry visas for Palestine;
- the United States, which failed in its attempts to put diplomatic pressure on the British and Turks to adopt a more humanitarian policy;
- the Russian government, which turned out to be directly to blame, after it was revealed that the *Struma* was actually sunk by a Soviet submarine;
- the Turkish cabinet which, for reasons which have never been satisfactorily explained, ordered the hapless vessel to be towed back into the Black Sea.

Shortly after the sinking of the *Struma,* the Turkish prime minister Refik Saydam, in a statement reported in the pro-German daily *Cumhuriet*, declared that 'Turkey cannot provide a home for people who are unwanted by all other countries'.[7] For the Jewish community in Istanbul, which had done its best to succour the refugees on the *Struma*, the situation became increasingly uncomfortable, as the Turkish government introduced a Wealth Tax that imposed severe burdens on non-Muslim minorities. For the Zionist Jewish Agency, too, which had its immigration office in Istanbul, the *Struma* episode represented a set-back, since its political weakness was exposed. The most detailed account of this affair concludes that the sinking of the *Struma* was 'the culmination of a policy of callous indifference on the part of the British and Turkish governments, carried out without interference from other Allied nations and, before the catastrophe occurred, with little outcry even from Jewish organizations'.[8] Thus every group had reason to feel implicated

7 *Cumhuriyet*, 25 February 1942; quoted in *Haymatloz: Exil in der Türkei 1933–1945* (Berlin: Akademie der Künste, 2000), p. 41.

8 Franzt and Collins, *Death on the Black Sea*, p. 228.

Figure 2. Monument to the victims of the Struma *disaster at the Giurgiului Jewish cemetery in Bucharest.*

Source: Timms Collection; photo: Petru Weber

in the disaster, and none could recall those events with pride. However, there may be other reasons for the process of amnesia, connected with aspects of Jewish historiography that deserve further discussion, after recalling the circumstances under which a second refugee ship was lost at sea.

THE *WILHELM GUSTLOFF*

In January 1945 the *Wilhelm Gustloff*, the largest of the cruise ships constructed in Germany during the Third Reich (fig. 3), set sail from Danzig carrying approximately ten thousand passengers. The majority were German refugees from East Prussia, fleeing from the advancing Red Army. The *Wilhelm Gustloff* had earlier been used as a hospital ship, protected from attack by the Red Cross, but on this journey it was also carrying substantial numbers of German naval personnel, due to be redeployed in the final defence of the Reich. Since it was also equipped with anti-aircraft guns for self-defence, it was technically a warship, at risk from attack by submarines. On the night of 30 January 1945 it was indeed intercepted and torpedoed by a Russian submarine, sinking within minutes. It is estimated that nine thousand passengers drowned, including thousands of women and children. This was followed by the sinking in the Baltic of two further German ships crammed with refugees, the *Steuben*, sunk by the same Russian submarine on 9 February, and the *Goya*, torpedoed on 17 April 1945.[9]

Measured in terms of loss of life, the sinking of the *Wilhelm Gustloff* may have been the greatest naval disaster of all time (we may recall that when the *Titanic* was sunk by an iceberg, the number drowned was 1,490). Moreover, the sinking of the *Wilhelm Gustloff* was not simply an unprecedented maritime disaster. It formed part of an even more momentous series of events: the expulsion of approximately twelve million Germans from the eastern provinces. How could events of this magnitude have faded from public memory? In fact, the sinking of the *Wilhelm Gustloff* was never as thoroughly forgotten as the loss of the *Struma*. The ship's purser, who was among the few hundred passengers that were rescued, was a man named Heinz Schön. He devoted much of his later life to collecting data about the history of the *Wilhelm Gustloff*, from the glorious day when it was launched in Hamburg, under

9 For eyewitness accounts by survivors, see *Letzte Tage in Pommern: Tagebücher, Erinnerungen und Dokumente der Vertreibung*, ed. Klaus Granzkow (Munich, 1984), pp. 47–66.

Figure 3. The Wilhelm Gustloff *setting out on its maiden voyage from Hamburg in April 1938.*
Source: Gustloff-Archiv Heinz Schön; photographer unknown

the eyes of Adolf Hitler, to the tragic circumstances of its sinking. Schön published a series of books on the subject, providing the basis for a black-and-white film made in West Germany in the 1960 under the title *Nacht fiel über Gotenhafen* (Night Fell over Gdynia), directed by Frank Wisbar.

There was an obvious obstacle to the process of more general public recognition, both for the thousands of refugees who perished on the *Wilhelm Gustloff* and for the millions forced to flee from the eastern provinces by the advancing Red Army. They were Germans, and the Germans – according to the dominant international historiography – were perpetrators, not victims. The fate of the *Wilhelm Gustloff* did not fit the master narratives, either in the East or in the West. How could the communist leaders of the German Democratic Republic commemorate the fate of a ship sunk by their Soviet allies? And how could the government in Bonn, committed to paying compensation for the millions of Jews plundered and murdered by the German Reich, campaign for international sympathy for its own refugees from the East? During the 1950s, the fate of the eight million expellees who had to be absorbed by the Federal Republic was certainly widely discussed, and the Bonn government ensured that systematic attempts were made to record their experiences and compensate them for their losses. There was also a series of specialist publications about the ordeals of refugees from each of the Eastern territories. But as the refugees became socially integrated, the Expellee Associations (*Vertriebenenverbände*) that represented their interests were sidelined, and a gap began to open between the private memories of those grieving for their lost *Heimat* and the public discourse of politicians with their eyes on the future. The young radicals of the 1970s tended to see their parents as perpetrators rather than victims, and it was hardly surprising that memories of the expulsions began to fade, despite occasional attempts by the media to address a topic that was becoming taboo. After Chancellor Willy Brandt had signed the Peace Treaty with Poland in 1970, the groups that still campaigned for a restoration of the lost eastern territories were marginalized and their testimony discounted as revanchism.

The combined efforts of conservative politicians and revisionist historians ensured that the losses in the East were never entirely forgotten. But to assign those events, including the sinking of the *Wilhelm Gustloff*, the place they merited in mainstream historiography required the combined efforts of independent-minded authors, democratic journalists and innovative film-makers.[10]

The most significant landmark was the publication in 2002 of a work of historical fiction, *Im Krebsgang: Eine Novelle* by Günter Grass, translated into English by Krishna Winston under the title *Crabwalk*. The narrator of this story is an invented figure: a man whose pregnant mother was supposedly among those rescued from the *Wilhelm Gustloff* and who was born (we are told) the very day after she was rescued. But the central events reconstructed in the story are based on fact: the history of the ship; the controversial personality of the Nazi leader, Wilhelm Gustloff, after whom it was named; details of the Soviet submarine that sank the ship; the rescue of survivors and their efforts to ensure that their fate was not forgotten. The captivating quality of the book lies in Grass's subtly suggestive narrative. He tells the story 'crabwise': as a complex reconstruction that scuttles in unexpected directions, combining the traditional framework of the novella with a topical use of motifs from the Internet. It is, according to this story, the creation of an Internet site about the *Wilhelm Gustloff* that has suddenly reawakened

10 For a detailed account of this process of 'remembering what was never really forgotten', see Robert G. Moeller, 'Sinking Ships, the Lost *Heimat* and Broken Taboos: Günter Grass and the Politics of Memory in Contemporary Germany' in *Contemporary European History*, vol. 12, part 2 (May 2003), pp. 147–81.

interest in this controversial episode. The narrator, a journalist who claims to have been commissioned by Grass – the 'old man' – to investigate the relaunching of this affair into cyberspace, suspects that the Internet site is the work of a group of neo-Nazis.[11] It turns out, as the personal story twists towards its unexpected conclusion, that the truth is far closer home.

Im Krebsgang is both a subtle psychological study and politically one of the most significant of Grass's texts. For the publication of this story prompted the weekly news magazine, *Der Spiegel*, to run a series of articles not simply about the sinking of the ship, but also about the partially forgotten fate of millions of other German refugees from the eastern provinces.[12] Suddenly, these extraordinary events from those cataclysmic early months of 1945 were making headlines again under the disconcerting title *Die Deutschen als Opfer* (The Germans as Victims). In 2001 a five-part documentary about the expulsions, entitled *Die grosse Flucht* (The Great Flight), was made for television by the director Guido Knopp, who also screened a reconstruction of the sinking of the *Wilhelm Gustloff*.[13] Confronted by these compelling images, a new generation of viewers and readers found themselves asking in astonishment: If it was really that bad, how could so much suffering have been repressed from public consciousness for so long?

The primary reason, strongly emphasized by *Der Spiegel*, was that anyone who espoused the cause of the refugees, appealing for sympathy for the victims on the *Wilhelm Gustloff*, was liable to be denounced as a neo-Nazi. The democratic credentials of both Günther Grass and *Der Spiegel* protected them from this suspicion, but there is an obvious risk that this renewed concern for the sufferings of German refugees will be exploited by the Far Right. There are signs that a new wave of historical revisionism may portray the Germans as the real victims of the Second World War: bombed out

11 References to the *Wilhelm Gustloff* proliferate on right-wing German websites, and revisionist pages like http://www.wintersonnenwende.com/scriptorium/deutsch/seiten/0905sosw.html (viewed 19 July 2004) give prominence to books by Heinz Schön about the expulsions from the eastern provinces, including *Die 'Gustloff'-Katastrophe: Bericht eines Überlebenden über die grösste Schiffskatastrophe des Zweiten Weltkriegs* (Stuttgart: Motorbuch Verlag, 1995).

12 These articles were collected and reprinted in a 130-page publication entitled *Die Flucht der Deutschen: Die Spiegel-Serie über Vertreibung aus dem Osten* (*Spiegel* special no. 2, Hamburg, 2002).

13 See Guido Knopp, *Die grosse Flucht: Das Schicksal der Vertriebenen* (Munich: Econ Verlag, 2001); and *Der Untergang der 'Gustloff': Wie es wirklich war* (Munich: Econ Verlag, 2002).

of their homes by the devastating attacks of the British and American Air Forces, and then driven from their ancestral territories in East Prussia, Silesia, Pomerania, Bohemia and other regions by the Red Army and the Czech nationalists. These two subjects, the obliteration bombing of German cities and the expulsion of German populations, have provoked widespread debate in the media. In 2002 Jörg Friedrich, an author who has developed strong right-wing sympathies, published a critique of the aerial bombardment of German cities during the Second World War under the title *Der Brand: Deutschland im Bombenkrieg 1940–1945*, which made a great impact when it was serialized by the mass-circulation newspaper *Bild Zeitung* (but has yet to appear in English translation). In September 2003 the same newspaper ran a series on the sufferings of German refugees from the former eastern provinces based on the book *Die Vertreibung* (The Expulsion) by Peter Glotz. The title they gave to one episode, published on 25 September, was '*Der Todesmarsch*' – 'The Death March' (fig. 4). The implication is that Sudeten Germans forced to flee from their homes by the vengeful Czechs suffered just as badly as Jews forced to endure death marches by the Nazis. In short, we are given to understand that there were simultaneous and comparable experiences of German and Jewish suffering.

To expose the muddled thinking underlying these revisionist arguments, we may recall the sufferings of Jewish concentration-camp victims during the real 'death marches', organized by the Nazis during this same period in the hope of destroying the evidence of German crimes. In several cases the SS, the force primarily responsible for the Holocaust, attempted to dispose of survivors in the Baltic Sea. In a notorious episode of May 1945, thousands of concentration camp survivors were loaded at Lübeck on the *Cap Arcona*. Although the Red Cross attempted to negotiate their release, their fate was sealed by the fact that the ship was indistinguishable from German naval vessels in the same flotilla. During an attack by the Royal Air Force, the *Cap Arcona* was sunk and most of its passengers perished.[14]

An even more gruesome episode occurred in East Prussia, just at the time when German refugees were embarking on the *Wilhelm Gustloff*. In the region of Königsberg (Kaliningrad), the capital of the province, camps were established in August 1944 for Jewish slave labourers, including many

14 See Wilhelm Lange, *Cap Arcona: Das tragische Ende der KZ-Häftlings-Flotte am 3. May 1945: Dokumentation*, 3rd edn (Neustadt, 1996).

Figure 4. 'Death March': Headline from Bild Zeitung, *25 September 2003, introducing excerpts from* Die Vertriebung, *an account of the fate of German expellees from the Sudetenland by Peter Glotz.*

Source: Timms Collection; copyright: *Bild Zeitung*

women, who were employed on construction projects.[15] By January 1945, as the Red Army advanced towards the city, the camps held approximately 6500 prisoners, whose fate was in the hands of the SS. With the land route to Germany already cut off, the problem of disposing of Jewish prisoners became as acute as that of shipping out German refugees. After consulting the head office of the Gestapo in Königsberg, the SS commanders organized a Death March, heading for Palmnicken on the Baltic coast, the site of celebrated amber mines. The plan was that those who survived the arduous fifty-kilometre march would be interred in one of the mineshafts and left to suffocate or starve. However, this was opposed by the manager of the mines, a courageous First World War veteran named Hans Feyerabend. Although Feyerabend was quickly eliminated (whether he committed suicide or was murdered is unclear), the plan was changed and approximately three thousand surviving prisoners were marched down to the beach under the pretence they would be transported to safety by sea from Pillau to Hamburg. Once on the beach, they were forced out onto the ice and into the frozen water and machine-gunned. According to eyewitness reports, the sea turned red with the blood of the victims and no more than fifteen survived. This massacre occurred on the evening of Wednesday, 31 January 1945, less than twenty-four hours after the sinking of the *Wilhelm Gustloff*.

LANDCAPES OF MEMORY – SEASCAPES OF OBLIVION

There can be no question of placing Jewish and German victims on the same plane, when the former were civilians murdered in cold blood, while the latter perished during a naval engagement in a fiercely contested region of the Baltic Sea. However, an underlying parallel does emerge when we return to the theme of remembering and forgetting, using maritime disasters as a point of reference. When we focus on the politics of memory, we may observe striking conceptual affinities between German and Jewish traditions. One of the most persuasive approaches to social memory is that adopted by the historian Simon Schama in his influential book, *Landscape and Memory*. This substantial and richly illustrated volume, which provides an intrigu-

15 The details recapitulated in this paragraph are based on the following article, which cites a wide range of German and Russian sources: Andreas Kossert, '*Endlösung* on the "Amber Shore": The Massacre in January 1945 on the Baltic Seashore – A Repressed Chapter of East Prussian History' in *Leo Baeck Institute Yearbook*, vol. 49 (2004), pp. 3–21.

ing counterpoint to the work of Pierre Nora, shows how specific landscapes become symbolic repositories for collective experience. But if any author were to plan a comparable book on 'Seascapes and Memory', it is likely to be far less substantial, since the seas – despite the valiant efforts of naval historians – are associated with oblivion. It may be relevant to recall that in Greek mythology *lethe* (forgetfulness) is symbolized by flowing waters, while incidents that we wish to ignore are dismissed as a 'drop in the ocean'. Ships, like the *Struma* and the *Wilhelm Gustloff*, which sink into a watery grave, tend to vanish from memory leaving few traces behind them. The burial of the dead in sacred ground constitutes one of the most fundamental rites of commemoration, but this process is frustrated when it proves impossible to recover bodies from the sea bed, and it is notoriously difficult to mark maritime graves. The implications for conventional modes of historiography are far-reaching. One of the reasons why the slave trade, sometimes known as the 'black Holocaust', has been erased from maps of history is that the most terrible suffering occurred at sea, during trans-Atlantic voyages of which there are few reliable records. It is only recently that radical historians have succeeded in compiling a more compelling picture.

While places may be remembered, even after their communities have disappeared, ships lost at sea tend to sink into oblivion. Of course, if we attempted to elevate this into a general principle, we would encounter the objection: What of the sinking of the *Titanic*? The *Titanic* constitutes the obvious exception, but for reasons which can be explained in terms of our original paradigm:

- it forms part of a grand narrative: the tragic hubris of technological progress;
- it expresses the fundamental conflict of modernity: nature versus the machine;
- it symbolizes the falsity of the class structure of England and the US around 1910;
- it is seen as a portent of the disaster that was to engulf Western civilization in the First World War.

Above all, the fate of the *Titanic*, like that of the *Lusitania*, sunk off the coast of Ireland by a German submarine in May 1915, is remembered because it can be fitted into the historiography of two nations with strong maritime traditions: the Americans with their founding myths of the Pilgrim Fathers and the Boston Tea Party; and the British with their celebration of Drake and Nelson, the defeat of the Armada and the Battle of Trafalgar. For maritime nations such spectacles have a compelling power, especially when exploited by skilful propaganda. In 1940, after Dunkirk, the humiliating retreat of the British army was transformed into a myth of national salvation through the symbolism of the 'little boats' bringing the troops back home.

What of nations that lack such maritime narratives? Peoples, like the Jews, whose sense of identity is linked to the land? Traditionally, the Jews were not simply the 'people of the book'. The Old Testament promises something more specific: land. The narratives of persecution and warfare, defeat and exile, from Genesis to the Book of Joshua, are governed by the twin themes of sacred law and promised land. To the present day, in theocratic Zionism, biblical sources are cited to justify claims to occupied territories. In the biblical narratives there are repeated references to God's gift of 'the land which he sware unto our fathers' (Deut. 6:23). But there is scarcely a glimpse of the sea. Lakes and rivers may be mentioned in passing, but water, generally speaking, is perceived as a problem. The great flood is pictured as a punishment, and it is only when 'the waters were dried up from off the earth' (Gen. 8:13) that Noah is able to make his burnt offerings. The counterpoint to this, towards the end of the Old Testament, is the attempt by Jonah to evade his duties by finding a ship and putting out to sea. This predictably incurs God's wrath. The reluctance to accept the sea as a constraining reality is epitomised by the most frequently recalled of all Jewish narratives: the escape out of Egypt. When the children of Israel reach the Red Sea, what happens? Do they consider constructing rafts or some other means of passage? Nothing could be further from their minds. Moses stretches out his hand over the sea, the waters are divided and they cross the sea on dry land (Exod. 14:21–22). The miracle is repeated when Joshua has to cross the river Jordan before the battle of Jericho. The waters cease to flow and all the Israelites pass over 'on dry ground' (Josh. 3:17).

The Exodus story is not only celebrated annually at Passover by every observant Jewish household. It forms part of a narrative of salvation, with feet safely on dry land, which persists to the present day. There is indeed an Israeli Maritime Museum, but ships do not feature prominently in Jewish national festivals. The potential is certainly there. In the history of Zionism there were indeed 'pilgrim fathers': those who landed on the shores of Palestine in order to escape religious and racial persecution. Those dramatic events certainly deserve to be remembered, not least in Britain, the country that caused considerable suffering by preventing Jewish refugees from landing at Haifa during the Palestine Mandate. We only need to recall the *Atlantic*, another refugee ship from Romania, whose passengers were prevented from landing at Haifa in 1941 and interned on the island of Mauritius.[16] A further notorious example is the *Patria*, blown up by radical Zionists within sight of harbour, after the British refused permission for its passengers to land. And of course the *Exodus*, whose passengers were brutally forced to return from Palestine to Germany by the British government after 1945. Those events certainly made headlines at the time (the *Exodus* affair became the subject of a best-selling novel by Leon Uris and a powerful film directed by Otto Preminger). But those events are by no means central to modern Zionist ideology, which privileges the land and its inhabitants, the Sabras: tough, native-born Israelis with their roots in the soil.

In short, for nations which conceptualize their heritage exclusively in terms of the land, disasters suffered by boatloads of refugees are likely to remain on the margins. When we turn again to Germany, we find – rather to our surprise – that German national memory, like that of the Jews, is curiously 'land-locked'. Costal communities may treasure their local memories of heroic exploits at sea. But the dominant concepts of German ideology have traditionally related to control of territory (*Land*), physical space (*Raum*), the soil (*Scholle*), forests (*Wald*), and rivers (especially the Rhine). Simon Schama, quite rightly, devotes one the longest chapters in *Landscape and Memory* to the Germanic forest, the central motif in a recurrent narrative that can be traced back to the account of the Germanic tribes by Tacitus. Schama shows how Latin texts of the first century AD, describing the defeat of the Roman armies by tribal warriors led by Arminius at the battle of the Teutoburger Wald, evolved into a compelling national myth. He also cites more modern variants in which influential German ideologists defend the land and the foresters against the city and the cosmopolitans. A striking example is the trilogy by Wilhelm Heinrich Riehl, published between 1851 and 1855 under the title 'Natural History of the German People'. The second volume, 'Land and People' (*Land und Leute*), defines closeness to the land, especially to the untamed forest, as the primary source of national identity.[17]

16 See Karl Lenk, *The Mauritius Affair: The Boat People of 1940–41*, edited and translated from the original German by R. S. Lenk (Brighton, 1993).

17 Simon Schama, *Landscape and Memory*, pp. 112–14.

This theme can surely be extended and linked with the '*Blut und Boden*' ideology of National Socialism eighty years later and the concept of a *Volk ohne Raum* (People without Living Space).

Volk ohne Raum was the title of a novel published in 1925 by Hans Grimm, a German author with imperialist ambitions. Conventional interpretations of the novel recall Grimm's formative experiences in Africa, where he envied the vast territories of the British Empire; and we know that its political impact was intensified when he became one of the most honoured authors in Nazi Germany. While Grimm was grieving over the loss of Germany's colonies in Africa after 1918, his slogan '*Volk ohne Raum*' became associated with Hitler's notorious '*Drang nach Osten*' – the conquest and settlement of territories in Eastern Europe, featured so prominently in the programmatic final chapters of *Mein Kampf*. Grimm was an antisemite who propagated the superiority of the Nordic race, stridently insisting that the Germans needed more national space. But when we consider where his concept '*Volk ohne Raum*' originated, and what was the source of its popular appeal, it is difficult to avoid the conclusion that it is partly biblical in origin.

German nationalists were not simply inspired by Tacitus, Wagner and Nordic myths. They also immersed themselves in the Hebrew and Greek bible – in Luther's translation. Their imaginations, too, were shaped by the narratives of Moses in the Torah, especially the escape from Egypt, the victory of Joshua over Amalek, the Battle of Jericho and the vision of the promised land. Through Luther's bible, a best-seller for four hundred years, the Old Testament narratives shaped German national consciousness, even though Luther was also notorious as the author of a fanatically anti-Jewish tract.

Thus Luther and his heirs gave the Germans two contradictory messages: to immerse themselves devotionally in the ancient Jewish narratives and to stigmatize politically the activities of modern Jews. German nationalists of the nineteenth century denigrated the Jews as eternal nomads, a hostile people dispersed through the Christian world with 'no piece of earth for their own habitation'.[18] Meanwhile, the nationalists took over from Judaism the idea of being a 'chosen people' destined to conquer a promised land. The biblical script was transposed into secular terms by Hegel's philosophy, which proclaimed that history had a divinely inspired purpose, casting Germany in the role of the world-historical nation, destined by the World Spirit to

18 Adolf Wahrmund, *Das Gesetz des Nomadentums und die heutige Judenherrschaft* (Karlsruhe, 1887), p. 58.

play the dominant role. However, this political agenda never entirely lost its theological basis, thanks to the identification of the Lutheran Church with the Prussian State. As head of both Church and State, Kaiser Wilhelm II was convinced that the Lord of Hosts would lead the German Reich to victory in the First World War, and this idea was endorsed by mainstream Protestant theologians. After the collapse of November 1918, such appeals to biblical authority lost their plausibility, although echoes of this sacralization can still be heard in Hitler's conception of the control of territory as the nation's 'most sacred right'.[19]

While territorial ambitions became especially potent for German ideologists of the late nineteenth and early twentieth centuries, the sea featured only marginally in their imaginations. This is surprising, for in reality the Reich had an extensive coastline. Water became significant for German political writers only when it formed a line of demarcation on land – a frontier marked by a river. From the 1840s onwards, the 'Watch on the Rhine' provided the rallying call for German nationalists. Rivers were equally significant in the text of the national anthem, '*Deutschland über alles*', a poem that becomes all the more compelling when sung to the tune by Joseph Haydn. In this poem the boundaries of Germany are identified not by coastlines, but by rivers: '*Von dem Maas bis an den Memel, von der Etsch bis an den Belt*'. This verse has been dropped from the version of the anthem sung in Germany today, since all four rivers are actually in other countries: Denmark, Italy, Holland and Lithuania.

There was one interlude in this dream of continental domination: the founding of the German navy, which was initially associated with nineteenth-century liberalism, later providing the basis for colonial aspirations. Wilhelm II, modelling himself on his English cousins, dreamed of a vast empire overseas, and loved being photographed on his yacht. But this imperial dream was displaced during the First World War by the idea that Germany's manifest destiny, both militarily and economically, lay in Central Europe – *Mitteleuropa*, the title of Friedrich Naumann's influential tract of 1915.

This geopolitical vision was further developed during the Weimar Republic by *völkisch* nationalists, who claimed swathes of Eastern Europe as Germany's 'cultural soil' (*Kulturboden*). The Nazis, who revived the primitive Germanic myths, showed little interest in reclaiming the imperial colonies, confiscated

19 Adolf Hitler, *Mein Kampf*, tr. Ralph Manheim (London, 1987), p. 607.

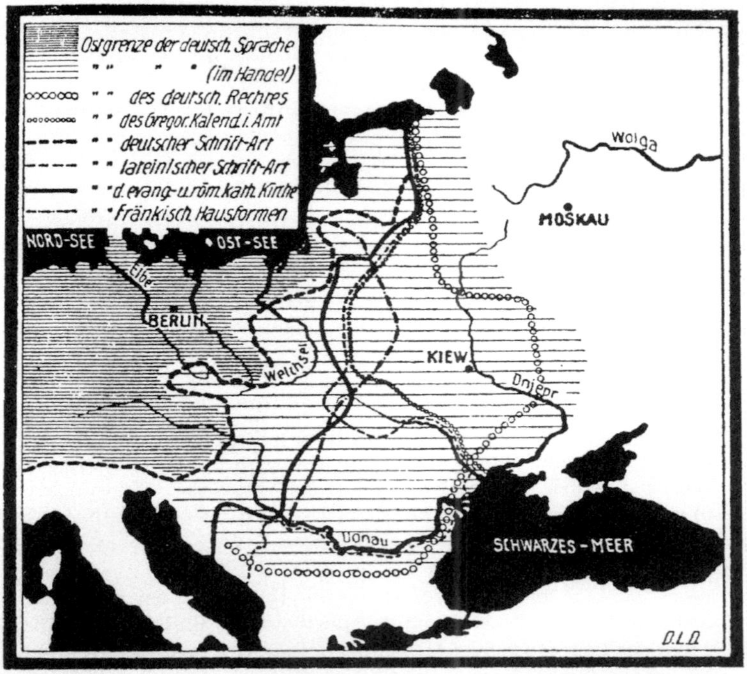

Figure 5. German cultural influences and territorial aspirations in Eastern Europe. (Karl Haushofer, Grenzen in ihrer geographischen und politischen Bedeutung, *Heidelberg and Berlin, 1939).*

Source: Haushofer, *Grenzen in ihrer geographischen und politischen Bedeutung*; photo: Stuart Robinson

from Germany under the Treaty of Versailles. Their ideology was again constructed in terms of the vast landmasses in Central and Eastern Europe, which Hitler claimed as German *Lebensraum*. These aspirations were supported by a plethora of nationalistic publications designed to prove that the influence of the German language, culture and commerce extended across swathes of eastern Europe, well beyond Königsberg, Kiev, Bucharest and Odessa (fig. 5). The aim was to create what their leading jurist, Carl Schmitt, the subject of a pioneering study by my successor at Sussex, Dr Raphael Gross, called a morality based on a 'grand territorial order commensurate with the *Volk*'.[20]

20 For the debates about German *Kulturboden*, see Guntram Henrik Herb, *Under the Map of Germany: Nationalism and Propaganda 1918-1945* (London, 1997). For Schmitt's conception of *volkhafte Großraumordnung*, see Raphael Gross, *Carl Schmitt und die Juden* (Frankfurt, 2000), p. 294.

Their inspirational concepts were *Heimat*, *Boden*, *Rasse* and *Lebensraum*, while Auschwitz and Stalingrad became the defining parameters of German geopolitics. Rivers continued to feature prominently in political discourse, as Hitler's armies tried to push the frontiers of the Reich ever further East. Reaching the Memel was not enough. As the German forces advanced on Stalingrad, they sang a song from an operetta by Franz Lehar about the Solitary Sentry defending the Fatherland on the banks of the Volga.[21] Even in the post-war period, after the enforced migrations from the East, political debate was still dominated by a fluvial frontier, the Oder–Neisse line – an issue which German nationalists to this day regard as unresolved.

By a strange historical irony, the state of Israel is embroiled in an even more bitter controversy about territories demarcated by a river, the West Bank of the Jordan with its potent biblical associations, occupied during the Six Day War of 1967. While the founding of the State of Israel was associated with the idea of the Jews as the principal victims of Nazi atrocities, the use of military force in the occupied territories has altered the picture, prompting pro-Palestinian groups to see the Israelis as aggressors. The situation is complicated by the fact that religious fundamentalists on both sides claim scriptural authority for their claims to 'holy lands', especially to the city of Jerusalem. More recently, a post-Zionist historiography has emerged that questions the biblical conception of a 'promised land'. The traditional theocratic claims are under pressure, not only from the Intifada, but also from debates about political 'legitimacy'. Concealed behind the conflict and bloodshed, a small band of liberal thinkers is trying to develop alternative models of Israeli identity that are more 'cosmopolitan' and 'multi-cultural'. Thus Jonathan Boyarin, in *Storm from Paradise*, his study of the 'Politics of Jewish Memory', criticizes the 'ideology of the land' that sustains modern Israeli identity.[22] Such critics argue that in place of the biblical promises, the focus should be on the practical politics of dividing the land between the two peoples that lay claim to it.

21 See the memoirs of German veterans, cited in Antony Beevor, *Stalingrad* (London, 1999), p. 307.

22 Jonathan Boyarin, *Storm from Paradise: The Politics of Jewish Memory* (Minneapolis, 1992), p. 126.

EPILOGUE: THE *CAP ANAMUR*

Disputes about control of territory constitute a recurrent source of political conflict, and the policing of borders remains a priority for all nation states, especially those that feel threatened by terrorism. However, maritime frontiers tend to be less securely defended, and this has made them attractive both to political refugees and to economic migrants. This is the reason why the fate of refugees lost at sea continues to be a subject of controversy. Since 1945 there have been innumerable cases of so-called 'boat people' – refugees prepared to brave the hazards of the high seas in order to escape political persecution or economic misery. This concept made headlines during the late 1970s after the communist take-over in Vietnam, when large numbers of Vietnamese attempted to escape across the South China Sea. Their plight aroused widespread sympathy as it became clear that hundreds of people crammed into decrepit boats were at the mercy of storms and pirates. The number who drowned when their ships were wrecked or capsized remains unknown, but an impression of their sufferings can be gained from the testimony of survivors who have made a new life in the western world.[23] By contrast, the sufferings of economic migrants who put their lives at risk by embarking in small boats tend to be treated with far less sympathy. Their plight may fleetingly make the headlines in newspaper or television reports, but their prospects as asylum seekers are problematic, not least because the law relating to territorial waters often leaves their status undefined.

The continuing spectacle of refugees exposed to the hazards of the high seas has prompted a humanitarian rescue effort that is all the more remarkable for originating in Germany. The government of the Federal German Republic has a creditable record for the treatment of refugees. Given its geographical position and extended land frontiers, it is understandable, especially since the ending of the Cold War, that official policies have focused on immigration from Eastern Europe. But in 1979, during the crisis associated with the Vietnamese boat people, a group of public-spirited German citizens led by Christel and Rupert Neudeck set up a committee to create a 'Ship for Vietnam'. They succeeded in chartering the freighter *Cap Anamur*, named after a cape on the coast of Turkey, which was despatched to the South China Sea. The project attracted widespread public support, and the

23 See Mary Terrell Cargill and others, *Voices of Vietnamese Boat People: Nineteen Narratives of Escape and Survival* (Jefferson NC, 2001).

journeys of the *Cap Anamur* and her sister ships achieved remarkable results. According to the website of the Cap Anamur Committee, they succeeded in rescuing over ten thousand people and providing medical treatment for a further thirty-five thousand. Further missions were undertaken around the globe with a special emphasis on Asia and Africa, and during the Balkan wars of the 1990s the charity's medical teams, still operating under the name Cap Anamur, provided a large-scale support programme for new waves of political refugees.[24]

The charity still operates a ship named the *Cap Anamur*, and a recent episode shows that under new leadership it has not forgotten its original mission of responding to the plight of refugees at sea. It is now the Mediterranean that has become the scene of a potential humanitarian disaster. To circumvent policies designed to protect the territories of the European Union from illegal immigration, many people from the Balkans, the Middle East and northern Africa entrust their lives to small boats in an attempt to reach Greece or Italy, France or Spain, seen as lands of economic opportunity.

In June 2004 a group of thirty-seven African migrants was approaching the shores of Sicily in a damaged and waterlogged dingy when they were spotted by the crew of the *Cap Anamur*, which was operating in the area. Acting in accordance with the laws of the sea, the ship's captain, Stefan Schmidt, in consultation with the director of Cap Anamur, Elias Bierdel, took the Africans on board in order to save them from drowning. The ship then found itself at the centre of an international controversy, as the Italian government refused the migrants permission to land, attempting to pass the buck to Malta (to which the ship had travelled after rescuing the Africans) or to Germany (which was where the Africans said they wanted political asylum).

For several weeks the *Cap Anamur* was left floating a few miles off the Italian coast with no country willing to allow her passengers to land, despite pressure brought to bear on the Italian government by the United Nations High Commissioner for Refugees. With the Africans becoming increasingly desperate, even threatening to commit suicide by throwing themselves overboard, the Italian authorities finally relented. In mid-July the Africans were allowed to land, and were taken to a reception centre, but at the same time

24 http://www.cap-anamur.org/eng (viewed 17 July 2004).

three Europeans from the *Cap Anamur*, including Elias Bierdel, were arrested and accused of promoting illegal immigration.

This provoked angry reactions in Germany, where the Cap Anamur organization is widely admired. After being released on bail, Bierdel summed up his position in an interview: 'According to official numbers, more than five thousand people have lost their lives in the Mediterranean. It has become a kind of floating cemetery. The situation is truly contemptible. As a humanitarian organization we have a boat and we try to save human lives.'[25] Clearly, the *Cap Anamur* has been successful not only in saving small groups of people from drowning, but also in highlighting a far larger problem. Concerted international action is needed to relieve the causes of economic migration and alleviate the risk that refugees exposed to the hazards of the open seas will continue to sink into oblivion.

25 Quoted by Peter Popham in 'Judge frees crew of ship that saved migrants', published in the *Independent*, London, 17 July 2004, p. 26.

ALEXANDER VERKHOVSKY

Radical Orthodox Anti-Globalism 1999–2002

Electronic Tax Codes – a Topical Theme for Fundamentalists

RUSSIAN Orthodox fundamentalism (hereafter simply 'fundamentalism') – a perception of the world based on extremely mythologized notions about the pre-revolutionary Orthodox monarchy – is very widespread in the Church. Moreover, fundamentalism in the Russian Orthodox Church (ROC) has been on the rise since the early 1990s, and there are no grounds for believing that this rise will stop in the near future.

Orthodox fundamentalists are basically opposed to liberals and Westerners, perceived by them as almost the same. The concept of 'the worldwide Kike-Masonic conspiracy' with its spear-point aimed precisely against Russia is to some extent characteristic of practically all Russian Orthodox fundamentalists. And when the theme of 'globalization' became popular in the West and then in Russia too, these assumptions naturally gave birth to a specific Orthodox anti-globalism.

This anti-globalism was first evidenced by statements against the commodity bar code, in which our fundamentalists – prompted by like-minded Greek ones – discovered the number 666.[1] Hegumen (presently Achimandrite) Tikhon (Shevkunov), father superior of the Sretensky Monastery in Moscow, became the main herald of this new trouble from the West, which is regarded as nothing less than the advance of the Antichrist,[2] as early as 1998. Given that Sretensky Monastery is one of the Church's largest publishing houses,

1 It is not appropriate to go into details of the bar code here. Suffice it to say that the presence of three sixes in it is a kind of optical illusion.

2 See, for example, Hegumen Tikhon (Shevkunov), *Amerikantsy ob Antikhriste: s nim*

the propaganda has proved to be rather successful. In the Church's press and parishes believers began to passionately discuss whether it was admissible for the Orthodox believers to buy bar-coded goods.

Then they began to discover 'the Seal of the Antichrist' in all kinds of codes, first of all on all kinds of magnetic cards (credit cards and so on). And the taxpayer's individual number (*individualniy nomer nalogoplatelshchika* – INN), which according to the Ministry of Taxes' plans should be given to each resident of the country, was considered the most obvious case. Besides, in the consciousness of the majority of fundamentalists, INN for some reason merged with the bar code and the belief spread that 'the Number of the Beast' was somewhere inside INN as well.

A powerful campaign was unleashed against INN in the autumn of 1999. Hundreds of parishioners, monks and even fathers superior of monasteries were signing petitions with the demand not to introduce INN. The motivation in all cases was apocalyptic, so the heat of passions at once became very high. Certainly, the actions in favor of the canonization of the last emperor Nicholas II and family, and against 'the heresy of ecumenism' continued too. But the anti-INN campaign was aimed directly against the policy of the state authorities, that fact giving it an additional impetus in the radical environment and creating an additional problem for the leaders of the Church.

The Synod tried to stop the new campaign by making a compromise proposal. The Synod's decision of 7 March 2000 ruled[3] that INN was not 'the Seal of the Antichrist', but repeated the assertion that the bar code contained the number 666. Without arguing against the introduction of INN in essence, the Synod actually asked the authorities to condescend to the most superstitious believers and introduce – no less! – a system of bar codes different from the rest of the world.

'I.N.N. JIHAD'

It was no surprise that the Synod's decision did not stop the campaign, but it was surprising that the campaign was actually suspended for a few months.

---

nam bolshe vezyot (Americans about Antichrist: we are more lucky with him); *Pravoslavnoye knizhnoye obozreniye* (Orthodox Book Survey), not numbered, June, 1998.

3 *Uvazhat chuvstva veruyushchikh. Khranit khristianskoye trezvomysliye* (To respect the believers' feelings. To preserve sober Christian thinking), statement of the Holy Synod of the Russian Orthodox Church, 7 March 2000. Accessible at: http://www.russian-orthodox-church.org.ru/nr00 3083.htm

And beginning in the autumn of the year 2000, after the Bishop's Council fulfilled the fundamentalists' main demand to canonize Nicholas II and his family, the campaign was resumed on a much larger scale. One observer has aptly called the movement 'INN Jihad'.[4]

At this point references to the authority of some elders, primarily that of Archimandrite Kirill (Pavlov), confessor of Troitse-Sergiyeva Lavra – the main monastery (and the main ecclesiastical academy) of the country – became the strike-force. Fathers superior of monasteries were taking more active stands, some (differently oriented) politicians traditionally lobbying for the interests of the ROC, and, of course, radical nationalists joined the campaign. Official consultations on the theme entitled 'Globalization and personal codes as an issue of the worldview choice of a contemporary human being' were held in the State Duma on 23 January 2001.

A summary of opinions voiced since the autumn of 2000 produces a rather homogeneous picture. It was alleged that, first, the number 666 is 'implanted' in the bar code, including the one used in taxation-related document circulation. Secondly, the act of giving a person a unique number to stay with him or her for their whole life substitutes his or her Orthodox Christian name. Thirdly, a uniform computer registration leads to total control over the people; the introduction of INN is just another step on the path toward such control. And, fourthly, the computer systems are all compatible with the global standards, making it possible to include the registry of Russian citizens into the world registration system controlled by the mystical global forces of evil – by the West, 'the new world order', 'the world Jewry leaders' or directly by the Antichrist.[5] One has to admit that bar codes were not mentioned then as often as before, and attention was focused on the idea that globalization inevitably leads to the kingdom of the Antichrist, while the mission of Russia and the Russian Orthodox Church is to defend national and religious identity in the face of such a dangerous trend. Therefore it

4 That definition was produced two years later by Sergey Grigoryev, editor-in-chief of the 'Russian Line' webserver, one of the active fundamentalists not supporting the campaign. See: S.Grigoryev, *Chego khotyat protivniki INN?* (What do the opponents of INN want?); *Russkaya Liniya* (Russian Line), 2 December 2000 (http://www.rusk.ru/News/00/12/new02_12a.htm).

5 Though it has happened very seldom, argument number 5, the most realistic one, was used: creation of a unified taxpayer database makes the taxpayers vulnerable not only to the state, but to the bandits as well, as all such databases very soon find their way to the black market.

was less important whether INN was literally 'the Seal of the Antichrist' and whether the sixes were in the bar code. The important thing was not to take a step back in the global confrontation.[6]

In addition, there were sometimes calls 'to escape into the wilderness' – cases of refusal to give the Eucharist to those parishioners who 'accepted INN' etc. – and thus some grounds for accusations of a split emerged. Some went as far as making barely disguised calls to overthrow the authorities.[7]

Such radical moods of the fighters against INN caused a delimitation within the ranks of the Orthodox anti-globalists. Comparatively moderate opponents to globalization believed that INN was not the boundary at which it was necessary to make a mortal combat stand. More precisely, they believed it was both possible and necessary to bargain with the state on that issue, but it was not worth bringing relations with the authorities into sharp conflict and subjecting themselves to the risk of real persecutions for the sake of INN.

Elder archimandrite Ioann (Krestyankin), a person of the greatest authority among conservatives, produced the most convincing arguments in favor of a moderate position. In his specially video-recorded late January appeal (that fact being extremely unusual in itself), he reminded believers: '... And what can be said about control and total spying, with which they frighten simple-minded people so much? When and in what state was there no secret office? All was ... and all is ... and will be ... but nothing prevents a believer

6 See, for example, the open appeal of the Orthodox priesthood, church clergy, and laymen of Vladimir-Suzdal Eparchy (Diocese) of the Russian Orthodox Church to the President of the Russian Federation V. V. Putin, Minister of Taxes and Charges G. I. Bukayev, and the Constitutional Court of the Russian Federation, 20 December 2000. Published on the website of the Movement For the Right to Live Without INN (http://infolab.spb.ru/anti-inn/text002.htm); *Yarko vyrazhenniy demonicheskiy kharakter* ... (A Clearly Evident Demonic Nature ...); The Appeal of the brothers of Svyato-Vvedensky Monastery of Optina Pustyn to the Orthodox Christians; *Rus Pravoslavnaya* (Orthodox Russia), no. 1, 2001; *Globalizatziya i lichniye kody kak problema mirovozzrencheskogo vybora sovremennogo cheloveka* (Globalization and personal codes as an issue of world outlook choice of a contemporary human); 'Russian Line' News, 27 January 2001 (http://www.rusk.ru/News/01/l/new27_01al.htm); V.Petrovm, *INN i plany 'knyazey tmy'* (INN and the Plans of the 'Princes of Darkness'); 'Russian Bulletin' server (http://www.rv.ru/super/2001/2/diablos.htm).

7 Celibate Schema Priest Nikolai [Uskov]. *Pravoslavnych zagonyayut v ugol* (The Orthodox believers are being driven into the corner); *Rus Pravoslavnaya* (Orthodox Rus), no. 12, 2000.

from seeking salvation.' In the same appeal Elder Ioann sharply spoke against the INN fighters' split-provoking manner of speech.[8]

Many Orthodox fundamentalist leaders, including Archimandrite Tikhon (Shevkunov), once the initiator of the entire campaign, the implacable opposition activist Konstantin Dushenov, editor-in-chief of the *Rus Pravoslavnaya* (Orthodox Russia) newspaper, Sergey Grigoryev, editor-in-chief of *Russkaya Liniya* (Russian Line), and others turned out to be in solidarity with him too. But they used to add also the argument that a refusal to be obedient to the state was obviously non-patriotic, as it implied that Putin's regime was a God-fighting one. And that went (and goes) counter to the hopes they pinned on Putin as 'their' president. Yet their arguments were accompanied by emphases that in general the opposition to liberal and anti-Christ globalization must be continued. As far as one can judge, Archimandrite Kirill (Pavlov) took a similar position.[9]

Few have stayed in the ranks of the staunch fighters. It is necessary to mention a Saint Petersburg priest, Alexey Masyuk, and the editor-in-chief of the *Svyataya Rus* (Holy Russia) newspaper, Konstantin Gordeyev, as well as Father Rafail (Berestov), an Athos Mountain elder. With such obvious non-equilibrium of forces the outcome of the struggle was predetermined.

A broadened session of the Theological Commission held on 19–20 February 2001 in Troitse-Sergiyeva Laura adopted a final document[10] which definitely denied any apocalyptic meaning of bar codes and INN and condemned the split-bound spirit of the fighters against INN, while as concerns the threat of globalization it said only that 'processes of globalization . . . may be used by a malicious will to enslave people and human communities'.

Besides, the minister of Taxes and Charges, Gennady Bukayev, personally promised as early as 31 January 2002 that his employees would not force people to adopt their INNs: the number is mandatory only for businessmen

8 Archimandrite Ioann (Krestyankin) on INN; *Pravoslavie.Ru.*, 1 February 2001 (http://www.pravoslavie.ru/jumal/society/ioannkrestyankin.htm).

9 See, for example, Archimandrite Tikhon (Shevkunov), speech in a *Radonezh* broadcast on 29 January 2001; *Pravoslavie.Ru* (http://www.pravoslavie.ru/jurnal/society/arhim tihon_radonezh.htm); Archimandrite Amvrosy (Yurasov), *Antikhrista boimsya, a Boga – net?* (We are afraid of Antichrist, but do we fear God?); Sergey Grigoryev, *Chego khotyat protivniki INN?* (What do INN opponents want?); Konstantin Dushenov, *Tzarsky put* (Tzar's way); *Rus Pravoslavnaya* (Orthodox Rus), no. 1, 2001.

10 Its text is accessible at: http://www.russian-orthodox-church.org.ru/nrl02206.htm

(and, of course, organizations). For INN opponents who get their incomes otherwise than from business, tax registration is possible without INNs.

RESPECTABLE ORTHODOX ANTI-GLOBALISM

The radicals were defeated and since then have displayed almost no activity for some time.[11] But the more moderate Orthodox anti-globalists are still active to make up for that.

In addition to the above-mentioned individuals, these include very many of the elders and fathers superior of monasteries. One can see that even by reading the officially published statements made at the Theological Commission session,[12] though not all judgements contrary to the opinion of the Patriarchate were published.[13] Archimandrite Kirill (Pavlov), who was absent at the session, did not sign the final document either.[14]

The Saint Petersburg Ecclesiastical Academy headed by Bishop Konstantin (Goryanov), on 3–4 May 2001, together with two secular institutes, held a conference titled 'Spiritual and social problems of globalization'. The conference adopted a final document[15] which was carefully drafted and has already become a theoretical basis for further development of the movement. It is therefore worth giving a rather extensive citation from it:

> (1) The ideology of globalization is in opposition to the Christian world outlook and incompatible with it; it takes root and is propagandized in secular society and the Church through the efforts of the world elite, and it expresses its interests. Globalization becomes an embodiment of the utopian idea of mondialism about the creation of a unitary, supranational and rigidly controlled community on Earth . . .
>
> (3) The historical calling of Russia as a country preserving the Orthodox

11 Even the information campaign has been waged relatively weakly. It is possible to learn about it at *Stoyanie v istine* (Perseverance in truth) (http://www.voskres.ru/truth) and *Svyataya Rus* (Holy Rus) (http://kongord.narod.ru) sites.

12 *Vestnik Russkoy Linii* ('Russian Line' Herald), no. 6, 2001 (http://www.rusk.ru/News/01/2/new24_02a.htm).

13 Interview by Konstantin Gordeyev fot the *Blagovest* (Church Bells Ringing) newspaper of Samara, *Stoyaniye za pravdu* (Perseverance for truth). (http://www.voskres.ru/truth/econtrol/inn/gord3.shtml).

14 Archimandrite Kirill Has Not Signed the ROC Final Statement on INN, NG-Religii, 28 February 2001.

15 The document has been published on the site of the Movement For the Right to Live without INN at: http://infolab.spb.ru/anti-inn/info09.htm

faith, culture and traditions is not recognized and is rejected by mondialists. Yet the values mentioned are important for the whole world.

(4) Changes in the traditional system of values; destruction of national culture, Christian morals and senses; primitivization of the people's thinking and universal work to make them accustomed to 'voluntary-compulsory' acceptance of digital identifiers (personal codes) replacing a human name in all state-public relationships are presently the main manifestations of the globalization process in the Russian Federation ... As confessor of Svyato-Troitskaya Sergiyeva Laura Archimandrite Kirill (Pavlov) noted with justice and precision, 'By accepting INN a person is incorporated into the system of evil ...

It is possible to find some differences in this document as compared to the final document of the February plenary session of the Theological Commission, but on the whole we see just more definitely and resolutely reformulated provisions of 'The Bases of the Social Concept':

In the field of culture and information, the globalisation has been conditioned by the development of technologies facilitating the movement of people and objects and the acquisition and distribution of information ... This process, however, has been accompanied by attempts to establish the dominion of the rich elite over the rest of the people, and of some cultures and worldveiws over others, which is especially intolerable in the religious field. As a result, there is a tendency to present as the only one possible a universal culture devoid of any spirituality, and based on the freedom of the fallen man unrestricted in anything, as the absolute value and measure-stick of the truth. The globalisation developing in this way is compared by many in Christendom to the construction of the Tower of Babylon.

... The spiritual and cultural expansion fraught with total unification should be opposed through the joint efforts of the Church, state structures, civil society and international organisations, for the sake of asserting in the world a truly equitable and mutually enriching cultural and informational exchange, combined with efforts to protect the identity of nations and other human communities.

... Efforts should be made to achieve such a world order which would be based on the principles of justice and the equality of people before God and exclude any suppression of their will by the centres of political, economic and informational influence.

It is not surprising that no reprimands, at least public ones, have come from the Synod.

PATRIARCHATE, STATE AND FUNDAMENTALISTS AROUND THE I.N.N. – THE PRESENT POSITION

INN opponents' influence on the state is in general very small, of course. They are supported by a handful of State Duma deputies: Alexander Chuyev, Anatoly Greshnevikov, Alexander Shulga. But it was in many respects due to their efforts that on 15 February 2001 the Duma rejected a draft law 'On the Basic Documents of the Russian Federation Certifying the Identity of a Citizen of the Russian Federation', because it suggested such innovations as a citizen's personal code and magnetic record of passport data. The draft was not saved even by the fact that it was submitted by a wide and authoritative group of deputies ranging from liberals to communists. A new draft submitted to the Duma in April does not contain anything 'mondialist'.

But that is the only success. Without wide and organized support, the anti-globalists cannot deter the government, with its initiatives aimed at further modernization of the economy, which implies improvement of accounting systems as well. For example, on 29 January 2002 the government approved a whole program of information modernization called 'Electronic Russia'.

The aforementioned deputies were also very active in the practical negotiations held by the Moscow Patriarchate with the Ministry of Taxes and Charges. The fact is that, despite Minister Bukayev's assurances, cases of pressure on the taxpayer demanding they acquire their INNs are still numerous enough. It is hardly caused by a purposeful policy of the Ministry, but rather by the momentum of the bureaucratic machine trying, naturally, to simplify its work as much as possible. The Patriarchate, in its turn, trying to pacify the conflict, acts against those breaches. And, as there are no principled contradictions between the Patriarchate and the Ministry, it is quite possible to discuss the breaches together. There is also the problem of INN being assigned without a citizen's knowledge: if that citizen is an INN opponent, he or she cannot get rid of the number.

During those consultations. the Ministry and the Patriarchate managed to prevent a serious crisis caused by an instruction of the Ministry and the *Sberbank* (Savings Bank) of Russia, dated 10 September 2001, prescribing that from 10 January 2002 it would be mandatory to indicate the INN when paying taxes, fines and other citizens' payments to the state. That measure would have concerned the overwhelming majority of the citizens, including INN opponents. The instruction was revoked on 24 December after negotiations with the Patriarchate's representatives.

There are also attempts to solve the problem in principle by means of amendments to the Tax Code. There is Alexander Chuyev's project to shift a person's name to his file at the tax inspection office, but officials are totally uncomfortable with it, as the files have already had their numbers, which still do not create a single system of accounting. By now Chuyev and some other deputies have joined Anatoly Greshnevikov's project obliging the taxmen to assign INNs only if they have a citizen's written consent. And the Ministry proposes an option more convenient for it – to make those not wising to use INNs come themselves and conclude a special agreement with the Ministry. But so far all these projects are far from the Duma's consideration.

Meanwhile, since the summer of 2001, radical opponents of INNs have again stepped up their activity. And this time their actions were aimed against the Patriarchate rather then against the authorities, and specifically against the moderate fundamentalists who shy away from the 'INN Jihad'. The Synod members' statements in support of the USA after September 11 added fuel to the fire.

On 17 July 2001, meetings in Moscow and Saint Petersburg adopted appeals to the Patriarchate urging 'a prompt convocation of the full-fledged Local Council' since Church leaders themselves were not resisting globalization. Since then the appeals have been actively disseminated among the Orthodox public. And at a meeting held on 4 October in Moscow by the Movement For the Right to Live Without INN,[16] the agenda contained, amongst other items, the following:

> (12) The ROC leaders as promoters of a globalization ideology inconsistent with a Christian world outlook (as exemplified by the lobbying of the ROC leaders for the digital identification, and 'theological' reasoning for the so-called retaliation strikes).
>
> (13) The role of the Church-sponsored media holdings (*Radonezh*,

16 A similar meeting in Saint Petersburg took place on October 30.

> *Russkiy Dom* and other) in the manipulation of public opinion and in the information support to realization of the globalist scenario in Russia.[17]

After the appearance of the above-mentioned instruction on taxes and the INNs the radicals held on 5 December 2001 a totally unprecedented action by arranging a meeting near the building of the Patriarchate in Moscow. Three activists, including the leader of the Union of 'Christian Revival', Vladimir Osipov, were given an audience by the Patriarch's closest associates, Metropolitan Sergius (Fomin) and Archbishop Arsenius (Yepifanov), and handed an appeal to the Patriarch (who, by the way, himself, as they said, renounced using his INN). And on 15 December the radicals picketed the entrance to the Temple of Christ the Savior, where on that day the Moscow Eparchy (Diocese) Meeting was being held. When they were not admitted inside, they made crusade walks around the temple.

These attacks forced Patriarch Alexis, usually temperate in his statements, to publicly declare on 14 December: 'INN rejection on religious grounds is a problem created on an empty space . . . There is an impression that these people persevere not just due to their ignorance, but possibly because they have been bought by somebody to bring confusion into others' conscience.'[18]

But it is impossible to simply ignore the radicals, as they are supported, albeit indirectly, by more than just rank-and-file priests or some elders. On 17 October 2001 three archbishops of the Urals, namely, metropolitan of Chelyabinsk Job, archbishop of Yekaterinburg Vikentiy and archbishop of Tobolsk Dimitriy, made a joint statement wherein they indicated that the continuation of the practice of assigning the INNs against the will of Orthodox citizens might lead to a new turmoil.[19] However, as Metropolite Sergius (Fomin) said, later they 'practically renounced their position'.[20] But it

17 Orthodox anti-globalists believe the ROC to be Antichrist's associate, NTV.Ru., July 25 2001 (http://txt.ntv.ru/religy/25Jul2001/antichrist_print.html); Public Movement *Za zhyzn bez INN* (For Life without INN), Information message no. 11; Site of *Stoyaniye za istinu* (Standing for truth), http://www.voskres.ru/truth/econtrol/INN/inn11.shtml.

18 Patriarch Alexis condemned the actions of some believers against the taxpayer's individual numbers, *Radonezh*, 14 December 2001 (http://www.radrad.ru/new/news/news_text.asp?newsID=2661).

19 *Pravoslavnaya gazeta* (Orthodox Newspaper), Yekaterinburg, 17 October 2001. Quoted from: http://www.voskres.ru/truth/econtrol/startsy/vikenty.shtml.

20 Minutes of the session of the Theological Commission of 24 December 2001. Quoted from: http://www.voskres.ru/truth/econtrol/INN/kom241201.shtml.

is well known that the ROC bishops do not make sharp statements by chance. Archbishop Vikentiy said:

> Believers . . . do not accept the INNs because of their unwillingness to join the system that is to oppress our Fatherland. In the end it might lead to the power of Antichrist, as predicted in the Revelation of St. John . . . as yet it is early to talk about the seal of Antichrist, but the people do not want to take even first steps into that system.[21]

It is indicative that on 24 December 2001 the Theological Commission again had to hold a meeting on the INN theme with officials' participation on the one hand and INN moderate and radical opponents on the other.[22] And that theme had to be discussed again at the Synod session of 26–27 December. The theme continues to be very hot.

Yet no new decisions were made then either. In one year the Patriarchate's position had not changed: the Church is prepared to endlessly hold talks with the authorities on a relaxation of the problem and amendments to the law, it 'urgently suggests for the numeration not to be related to a person, but to be assigned to a personal account or some other document wherein a taxpayer's incomes are fixed',[23] but it is emphatically against any conflicts.

A new round of the Patriarchate-radicals' confrontation has not changed the balance of forces, but rather aggravated the confrontation. If events continue to develop in this way, one cannot rule out a future secession of some groups of radicals from the Patriarchate. This will not happen, though, as long as the radicals have not depleted their capacity to expand their influence and have not lost hopes for victory. Against the background of a general tendency towards the consolidation of fundamentalist trends within the Church, such hopes still remain.

---

21 Archbishop Vikentius' interview to *Pravoslavnaya gazeta* no. 33, 2001, quoted from: Konstantin Dushenov, *Zhyveye vsekh zhyvykh* (More alive then all the living), *Rus Pravoslavnaya* (Rus the Orthodox), 2002, nos. 1–2.

22 See Minutes of the session of the Theological Commission of 24 December 2001.

23 Message from OVTZS, 27 December 2001 (http://www.russian-orthodox-church.org.ru/nr112271.htm).

JEAN-JACQUES WAHL

De La Clemence
Réflexions sur quelques textes de la tradition juive

La tradition juive accorde – comme d'autres cultures d'ailleurs – une importance évidente au nom porté par l'individu. L'étymologie des patronymes des grands personnages bibliques se veut source de sens, à commencer par le premier d'entre eux Adam, extrait du sol « *adama* » (Gen. 2,7), ou Moïse qui sera celui qui est tiré des eaux (Exode 2,10). Les chapitres 29 et 30 de la Genèse détaillent la naissance des enfants de Jacob en explicitant le choix des prénoms de ceux qui seront à l'origine des 12 tribus d'Israël. Ainsi « *Acher* » (en hébreu « bonheur ») doit-il son nom à la proclamation de sa mère Léa « Pour mon bonheur ! car les filles me proclameront heureuse ! » (Gen. 30,13). Plus significatif encore sont les modifications de noms qui annoncent un changement dans la personnalité de celui qui tel Abram se transforme en Abraham. « Et on ne t'appellera plus du nom d'Abram ; ton nom sera Abraham, car je te fais père d'une multitude de nations » (Gen. 17,5) ou encore Jacob qui devient Israël après avoir lutté avec l'ange (Gen. 35,10).

Dans ce contexte, porter le nom de Clemens Nathan est peut être aussi prémonitoire. Nathan, neuf personnages bibliques sont désignés par ce nom, le plus célèbre d'entre eux étant le prophète qui officie au temps des rois David et Salomon (cf livres de Samuel II et Chroniques I). Le terme Nathan signifie « donner » tandis que Clemens apparu dans différents idiomes européens trouve son origine dans le latin « *Clemens* » où il désigne, dans le vocabulaire ecclésiastique, la vertu dite « d'indulgence », elle-même reprise d'un attribut divin désigné en hébreu par « *ra'hamim* » qui est au centre d'une volumineuse littérature exégétique dont nous nous proposons d'aborder ici quelques aspects.

D'une manière générale, l'une des difficultés essentielles à laquelle se trouvent confrontés les théologiens est celle de la définition et de la représentation de Dieu. Comment décrire l'ineffable, comment expliquer l'inexplicable, évoquer celui qui refuse de « dévoiler sa face » ? Mais peut-on empêcher l'être humain qui aurait été créé à l'image de son créateur : « Faisons l'homme à notre image, selon notre ressemblance » (Gen. 1,26) de chercher à se représenter la divinité ? Pour s'en convaincre, il suffit de se référer à l'iconographie occidentale où ne manque pas la représentation d'un vieillard serein ou majestueux censé être le portrait du Tout-Puissant. Les philosophes juifs médiévaux tentent bien d' insister sur son caractère incorporel, mais considèrent qu'il est possible d'approcher Son essence à travers Ses attributs. La clémence est non seulement l'un d'entre eux, mais elle en est l'un des plus fondamentaux.

Dans la littérature biblique, le passage central pour soutenir cette approche est celui de la théophanie de l'Exode (chapitre 34) où Yahvé se présente à Moïse comme un « Dieu, clément (*ra'houm*) et compatissant »..., mais aussi « qui ne laisse rien impuni ». Cette dialectique entre miséricorde et justice, au centre de l'alliance entre Dieu et son peuple, se trouve confirmée chez le prophète Osée où l'Eternel s'adresse à Israël comparé à une épouse pour lui signifier « Je te fiancerai à moi pour toujours, je te fiancerai à moi dans la justice et le jugement, dans la piété et la clémence » (Osée 2,21). Cette opposition apparente entre justice et clémence repose sur un postulat d'évidence. Le créateur demande à ses créatures d'observer la justice, les lois et préceptes qu'il leur a transmis au moment de l'alliance du Mont Sinaï, mais l'être humain dans sa faiblesse se révèlera dès l'origine incapable de ne pas fauter. En toute justice s'impose donc le châtiment et ce qui devrait en être la conséquence : l'exécution du pécheur, autrement dit la disparition de l'humanité et c'est principalement là qu'intervient la vertu de la clémence divine.

Le Zohar, corpus fondateur de la tradition ésotérique juive, exprime bien cette problématique : « Viens et vois. Quand le Saint béni soit-Il créa le monde, il le fit par l'attribut du jugement et c'est par le jugement qu'il subsiste et toutes les œuvres du monde subsistent par le jugement, sauf que le Saint béni soit-Il, pour que le monde perdure et ne soit pas anéanti, étendit sur lui la miséricorde. Cette miséricorde empêche le jugement de détruire le monde ; et c'est selon la miséricorde que le monde est dirigé, il subsiste grâce à elle. »

Mais revenons à la question de l'image de Dieu. Nos sages ont proposé une concession entre la figuration anthropomorphique de Dieu et l'impossibilité de lui donner une représentation humaine en développant une comparaison de l'Eternel tantôt avec le roi, tantôt avec le père. Un double titre qui a le mérite de Le personnaliser mais sans pousser l'anthropomorphisme à ses extrémités prohibées.

En effet, lorsqu'il prononce la formule « Notre père, notre roi » qui se retrouve en particulier dans la liturgie du Nouvel An et du Grand Pardon, le fidèle sait bien qu'il ne s'adresse pas à un roi ou à un père de chair et de sang, mais à un être qui en a les qualités, en l'occurrence le pouvoir de rendre la justice, mais aussi la volonté de protéger celui qui est son sujet ou son rejeton, étant entendu que la royauté tend du côté du droit, tandis que la paternité incline du côté de la clémence. Ce n'est sans doute pas un hasard si un autre passage du Zohar (section *Vayechi*) précise que « le Saint béni soit-Il ne prodigue sa clémence sur le monde qu' après en avoir fait référence aux patriarches » (en hébreu aux « Pères »). Ce sont leurs mérites et en particulier ceux d'Abraham, dont nous l'avons vu, le nom signifie « Père » des nations qui plaident en faveur de leurs descendants.

L'accumulation de leurs hauts faits, de leurs vertus, des qualités dont ils ont su faire preuve est à verser au crédit des générations qui les ont suivis.

Cette relation de paternité magnifiquement illustrée par le verset des Psaumes (103,13) « Comme un père est clément vis- à -vis de ses enfants, tel est l'Eternel envers ceux qui le craignent ».

Mais n'oublions pas le caractère normatif du judaïsme. Ces spéculations n'ont d'intérêt que lorsqu'elles induisent pour l'homme une conduite à suivre « à l'image de Dieu ». Le Midrach Sifri nous rappelle : « de même que l'omniprésent est appelé clément miséricordieux, tu seras toi aussi clément et miséricordieux » (section *Equev*) et il ajoute (section *Tzav*) : « à chaque fois que tu feras preuve de clémence envers les créatures, le ciel t'offrira sa clémence » ou pour reprendre une formule encore plus lapidaire du Talmud : « Ressemble Lui : Il est clément et miséricordieux, toi aussi tu le seras » (Chabbath 133b).

Encore faut-il expliciter en quoi cette clémence se concrétise ? Qu'est ce qui la rend spécifique par rapport à d'autres qualités requises dans notre rapport à autrui.

Là encore, c'est le modèle divin qui va nous permettre de mieux comprendre ce qui nous est demandé.

Ce doit être avant tout un acte gratuit sans attente de reconnaissance qui fait abstraction du mérite ou plutôt de l'absence de mérite de celui qui en est le bénéficiaire.

Dans son ouvrage de morale « Le Devoir des Cœurs », Bahya Ibn Pakuda (xie siècle) note : « la clémence s'applique aux pauvres, aux démunis, aux malades et aux laissés pour compte » (3ème porte, chapitre 10), ceux dont on peut le moins attendre réciprocité.

Quant à Nahmanide, cabaliste et commentateur biblique du xiiie siècle, il développe ce thème autour d'un précepte assez étonnant du Deutéronome (22,6–7) : « Lorsque se présente devant toi un nid d'oiseau . . . et que la mère est couchée sur les petits ou sur les œufs, tu ne prendras pas la mère sur les jeunes, tu dois lâcher la mère et tu prendras les jeunes ».

Pour Nahmanide, l'un des buts de ce commandement est de nous apprendre ce qu'est la miséricorde. Selon son raisonnement qu'importe à Dieu les modalités par lesquelles sont tués les oisillons ou tant d'autres lois qui nous ont été imposées. Il veut y voir des règles qui ont pour seul objectif de renforcer les qualités morales de l'homme.

En l'occurrence s'abstenir d'un acte cruel ou qui peut apparaître comme tel envers l'oiseau, c'est nous éduquer à la clémence envers nos semblables.

Une limite toutefois, la mansuétude ne s'étendra pas à celui qui volontairement fait preuve de cruauté, le délateur, le traître, ou celui qui par provocation persiste dans l'abjection malgré les mises en garde dont il fait l'objet. En effet, accorder la clémence à ces pécheurs, ce serait ouvrir la porte à la propagation du mal.

Le caractère unique de la clémence comparée à d'autres valeurs qui lui sont proches tels la charité, la bonté, l'amour c'est sa gratuité totale. Elle n'est et ne doit être motivée ni par l'attente d'une reconnaissance, ni même par la satisfaction narcissique de faire le bien, mais par la seule volonté de permettre au monde de subsister en limitant les forces de la violence et de la cruauté.

Ceux qui comme Clemens Nathan ont choisi de se dévouer à la défense des opprimés, des sans-droits s'inscrivent, sans aucun doute, dans cette tradition illustrée par le message des Prophètes d'Israël.

GEORGE R. WILKES

Reforming the UN Commission on Human Rights

INTRODUCTION

The Annan years have witnessed a succession of attacks on the appearance of ostensibly 'political' abuses within the UN human rights institutions. Reform is an enticing concept, and the present chapter is a cautionary response to one of the most common aspects of the otherwise contradictory recipes offered for change – the contention that less politics will necessarily mean more human rights protection.

The politics associated with the operation of the United Nations human rights mechanisms can, of course, be dirty and dangerous. The margin which human rights abusers currently have for evading international scrutiny has provoked calls for a series of institutional reviews from across the UN and human rights communities. In the latest reform programme announced in December 2004, the UN secretary-general's 'High Level Panel on Threats, Challenges and Changes' called for reform of the Commission on Human Rights (CHR).[1] The Panel's main proposal was the extension of the 53-member Commission to include all member states of the UN, with the aim of curbing the influence of states which currently use their position to block effective action within the CHR. The reaction of professional human rights advocates was immediate and negative. Human Rights Watch suggested the change would do little to restrain the influence of human rights abusers within the CHR and urged restrictions that would prevent states with

1 'A More Secure World: Our Shared Responsibility', A/59/565, 2 December 2004.

poor domestic human rights records from playing active roles within the Commission's principal committees.[2]

Whereas the High-Level Panel described its proposal as a response to the need to make the CHR more 'credible', Human Rights Watch called instead for reform to 'restore the legitimacy' of the Commission. The choice of words betrays a fundamental gulf which frequently separates member state and non-governmental approaches to the role of the UN in advancing human rights. Among the former, the CHR is commonly presented as a device for increasing dialogue between states over international human rights, a dialogue which is often viewed as subordinate to the UN's mandate to maintain peace and security. Among those professional non-governmental bodies specialising in human rights protection, the Commission on Human Rights is rather seen as the focal point for the United Nations to advance and maintain human rights standards through public commitments made binding in international law. The achievements and continuing importance of these NGOs are a basic feature of any calculation about the future of human rights at the UN, and if the present essay gives more attention to the CHR and reserves more critique for some of the problems associated with NGO politics, it is only to redress an imbalance in the literature on the subject. The discussion which follows emphasises the need to explore the territory between the intergovernmentalist and idealist poles through reflection on the extent to which pragmatic 'political' calculations have been a necessary element of the development within the UN of the will to make advances to the consensus on universal respect for human rights.

THE COMMISSION ON HUMAN RIGHTS IN INTERNATIONAL POLITICS

In 2003, Libya was elected Chair of the annual session of the Commission on Human Rights. The subject of many allegations with regard to its respect for the human rights of its own citizens, Libya had also yet to acknowledge and make amends for its role in terrorist acts such as the bombing of PanAm flight 103 over Scotland in 1988, or the shooting of PC Yvonne Fletcher in 1984. The reaction of many human rights advocates was derisory: this was a prime example of the Commission being used as a 'club of human rights abusers', its operations hamstrung by a coalition of the worst state abusers

2 'UN: Good diagnosis, but poor prescription', HRW press release, 2 December 2004.

from across the world deliberately infiltrating and obstructing key sub-committees of the CHR. Much of the public meetings in the CHR session chaired by Libya were dominated by discussion of the situation in the Palestinian territories, while a series of proposed resolutions criticising states alleged to have engaged in far more dramatic abuses were watered down or dropped altogether.[3] The high level review of UN activities had been underway long before this, but the dramatic nature of the positions laid out in December 2004 corresponded to the immediate sense that the UN's most malignant human rights abusers had been able to take over CHR proceedings.

Still more consistent critics of the UN human rights system argued at the time that the trend was a reflection of organisational problems established early in the history of the Commission on Human Rights. In 2003, Libya was elected to chair the Commission as the preferred candidate of the African Union, and the election ultimately went through unopposed, in spite of much initial discomfort within the Western and democratic states, because the formal voting procedure is managed by regional blocs which take turns in nominating their candidates for the Commission. Within the politics of the African bloc, Libya is a well-accepted partner, indeed a key player – a generous financial supporter of radical groups across the globe which was alleged to have paid money for its nomination to the CHR. Long a leading member of the Arab League and Non-Aligned Movement, Libya's candidacy was embraced by a wide range of African states, viewing it within the context of a gradual shift towards greater international engagement on Libya's part which would encourage security and stability in the region. If some of Libya's erstwhile supporters were evidently willing to see the CHR's agenda sacrificed in the process, there were others, with South Africa, which judged the country's renewed commitment within the human rights field to be an essential element in its international rehabilitation. During the CHR session of 2003, Libya gave no sign that it would open its domestic record to great international scrutiny. In September 2003, however, after the Libyan authorities accepted responsibility for the Lockerbie bombing, the UN lifted its air and arms embargo on Libya. In December, Libya announced the dismantling of its programmes of weapons of mass destruction, and in February 2004 Libya granted Amnesty International access to the country, for the first time in 15 years, and ratified the Protocol to the African Charter on

3 'UN Rights Body in Serious Decline', HRW press release, 25 April 2003.

Human and Peoples' Rights establishing the African Court on Human and Peoples' Rights. This is not an irreversible process, but Amnesty and other professional human rights bodies have taken it as a credible basis for further dialogue and improvement.

It was always foreseen that states would play politics with human rights at the United Nations. The Cold War chasm between the Communist and non-Communist blocs quickly confirmed this, encouraging a deliberate balance between the pursuit of international agreements over civil and political rights and those focused instead on social rights. As newly-independent African and Asian states joined the UN in the 1960s, the Commission on Human Rights turned its attention to combatting contemporary forms of slavery, an issue which enabled cold war warriors to demonstrate their engagement with the interests of the peoples of the new member states. The Commission on Human Rights has fostered better human rights protection through 'open' diplomacy without any diminution of its political character. The dangers associated with the political nature of the CHR, however, are not easily dismissed.

In the 1960s and 1970s, the CHR sought to elicit commitments to halt gross violations of human rights from the dictatorships blossoming across the developing world, providing an instrument through Resolution 1503 (1970) by which states could exercise political pressure and persuasion on recalcitrant states, behind closed doors. The so-called 1503 procedure gives states an opportunity to keep their most glaring human rights violations out of the other UN sessions which meet in public, as long as they satisfy members of the committee responsible that they are investigating and responding to the accusations made against them. The secrecy maintained around the committee's sessions once enabled the Argentinian junta to keep its disappearances from making headlines at the Commission, encouraging Argentinian diplomats to target human rights defenders who threatened to disturb the status quo at the UN in Geneva.[4] In more recent years, the effectiveness of the (now revised) 1503 Procedure has nevertheless been loyally affirmed by the UN staff charged with overseeing communications to states and their responses. The real pressure on states whose violations are repeatedly serious enough to bring them to the attention of the 1503 Procedure occurs where it is feared that other states, and particularly potential trading partners, may

4 Ian Guest, *Behind the Disappearances: Argentina's Dirty War Against Human Rights and the UN*, Philadelphia: University of Pennsylvania Press, 1990.

react to the accusations with economic, diplomatic or other sanctions. It is a procedure which epitomises the intergovernmentalist understanding of the nature of the CHR as a body essentially founded upon a dialogue between the political perspectives of states primarily focused on realist conceptions of their interests.

The recommendations of the High-Level Panel treat the Commission on Human Rights in exactly this light, suggesting institutional revisions to extend the intergovernmentalist dimension of the reform programme of the Commission initiated by Kofi Annan on taking office as UN secretary-general in 1997. Successive reforms have restricted the mandate of the Sub-Commission on Prevention of Discrimination and Protection of Minorities (renamed the Sub-Commission on the Promotion and Protection of Human Rights in 1999), restrictions which the NGO community in Geneva viewed as an attempt to remove the CHR's activities further from the public gaze, but which a wide range of states, from the USA to South Africa, supported as reducing wasteful duplication and eliminating a source of polemic likely to disturb the interstate dialogue. While the length of CHR sessions was cut from six to four weeks, the CHR established new means for inter-sessional communication that extend this intergovernmental dialogue throughout the year. The moves reduce the impact of NGO participation, and strengthen further the role of the political groups to which CHR member states belong – a reflection of the strong hand played by these groups in the reform process itself. The most obvious winners from the changes are the diplomats in Geneva, charged with managing issues over the whole year, as against the high-level delegations flown in for the annual spring session of the Commission. This has consequences for the character and content of the intergovernmental discussions associated with the CHR. Thus, the political dialogue between the CHR's informal groups is largely conducted behind closed doors, and often turns around high politics and arguments over the sources and use of funding. Western groups, the main financial supporters of the UN's human rights programmes, are pitted against less developed states, such as those in the Non-Aligned Movement, concerned to underscore the means by which the First World attempts to advance its political interests through interference in the internal affairs of weaker states. In recent years, attempts have been made to forge the dialogue anew as one between a democratic and an undemocratic group, though at present tensions across regional blocs have contributed to the failure to create a functioning Democratic Group.

A range of issues divide the democratic states; crucially, the US takes a more forceful view of the need to pressure non-democratic states on their human rights records, while the EU has on the whole urged a more pacific dialogue with states in breach of international human rights norms. Faced with the unconditional and conditional approaches of the US and Europeans, their critics from the developing nations, grouped in a 'Like-Minded Group', have pressed for a culturally sensitive dialogue based on respect for states' rights and interests, appropriate, as they saw it, to the goals of peace and security between all of the United Nations.

The collapse of attempts to create a Democratic Group underscores the extent to which the CHR is swayed by differences over regional preferences and governmental styles. In an arena in which idealism has a particular premium, the developing states have increasingly drawn on discourse about distinctive Asian, African and Islamic approaches in order to lend weight to restrictive approaches to the definition of human rights at Geneva. Debate over the appropriate response to demands for a recognition of different cultural values has played a significant role behind the scenes during Commission sessions since the 1990s, particularly in response to the increasing self-assertion of the Organisation of Islamic States. While most of the Western states and NGOs in Geneva have stood firm against erosion of the universality and indivisibility of all human rights, states from the developing world have only viewed this as further evidence that the UN's human rights instruments are tools of the powerful if narrow political interests of the First World.

In debate at this normative (or 'idealist') level, all sides view politics as illicit. States from all regions reject interference where it can be cast as 'political' rather than strictly apolitical. It is in this context that the Russian president Vladimir Putin can hope to limit UN criticism over Russian actions in Chechnya, because the UN High Commissioner for Human Rights, Louise Arbour, is potentially an instrument for 'political criticism'.[5] The fact that every state engaged in conflict is faced with critique at the Commission has made rebuttal of political self-interest one of the most evident features of state and state-supported NGO interventions at the CHR. The politics of delegitimation lends further credence to the arguments of human rights advocates who cast the bulk of CHR politics as an obstacle to legal commitment

5 'Putin Firm On Russia Human Rights', BBC News (Online), 10 Feb. 2005.

and public identification with the process of identifying and developing a global human rights system.[6]

The resulting, more purist approaches to human rights protection, stripped of their appeal to a legal discourse which many states have not internalised, rest on the faith that states can be cajoled into better behaviour by a combination of public shame and a sense of the need for a moral dimension to inter-state trust-building. We shall examine further below the implications of human rights activities at the UN which rely on unsullied, direct assertions of international morality, adherence to which depends upon no less and no more than an act of collective will. This conception of the scope for asserting principles regardless of political context is less often a full account of the making of human rights law than may be suggested by legal texts or sensational journalism.

A more realist dimension to CHR politics need not detract from the assertion of a single, undivided global political will. Only in the more severe constructions of international human rights politics are state interests solely equated with narrow and illicit visions of the application of human rights intended to delay or obstruct progress to greater protection for victims of abuses. Two examples follow, each underlining how very different political approaches at the CHR may openly reflect state interests without detracting from the objective of asserting universal human rights norms. Since the fall of the Pinochet dictatorship, the government of Chile has spearheaded the negotiations of international principles on reparations for victims of human rights abuses – as an extension of its own internal reflection on the interests of Chileans in preventing abusive regimes from torturing citizens with impunity. By contrast, coalitions manifesting external disapproval of a particular regime often provoke a counter-coalition within the CHR, but even this more heavy-handed style of diplomacy occasionally gains acceptance as politically necessary, as it did at the time of the junta in Argentina. In the 1970s, CHR protocol prevented the naming of individual states in its resolutions, and the Commission, unable to reprimand Argentina openly for the reported kidnap and torture of thousands of its citizens, passed the resolution that would lead to the first UN Convention against Torture of 1975 – a declaration commonly referred to at the time as 'the Argentinian resolution'. Gradually, the UN member states have been drawn into a process of engagement with

6 *International Human Rights Monitoring Mechanisms: Essays in Honour of Jakob Th. Möller*, The Hague: Martinus Nijhoff Publishers, 2001, 913–926.

the phenomena of torture, and very gradually they have acknowledged the place of torture victims in the prevention of torture in the future. The NGO community played a central role in shaping the CHR's agenda, and Amnesty International also contributed its expertise to the drafting process for the Convention itself. However, if this highly political process can be improved, it will not be achieved simply through a rhetoric of reform which has no regard for the role that pragmatic inter-state politics has played in the CHR's history. At its heart, the CHR has always been construed as a tool for gradually drawing state human rights abusers into a wider community based on a minimal respect for common values, and if this does not remain an effective objective for the CHR it may jeopardise the interest of democratic states in the body. An institution to which only the willing make concessions risks making fools of those of good will, not of those who cynically ignore it.

HUMAN RIGHTS INSTITUTIONS

The aspiration to promote respect for human rights through institutions and laws raises the same problems for the Office of the High Commissioner for Human Rights (OHCHR) that governments have faced since Jean-Jacques Rousseau contended against the increasingly centralised bureaucracies of eighteenth century nation states and Rousseau's nineteenth-century liberal critics began to explore the limited popular impact of the high-flown ideas of the political elite. A range of thinkers – from Mill to Tolstoy and Weber – presented bureaucracy as one of the chief political problems of the nineteenth and twentieth centuries; indeed, only the Bahai community offers a defence of international bureaucracy and world government without apology, inspired by a faith in the divine direction and humane sensibilities of a world federation which few outside the movement appear to share. It is difficult to conceive of a bureaucracy which is humanising, which upholds the value of the human in the context of the defence against governments of a set of rights, but it is to exactly this kind of humanising agenda which the OHCHR aspires.

The peculiar flaws of officialdom within the UN's predecessor, the League of Nations, were given wry treatment of their own in Albert Cohen's semi-autobiographical *Belle du Seigneur*. Today, a host of international institutions have sought to counter the potential threat of public alienation through a discourse promoting greater democracy and transparency, spending a considerable portion of their budgets translating the legalistic discourse of the initiated elite into material thought likely to appeal to a wider audience. The Universal Declaration of Human Rights is available in over three hundred languages; the Office of the High Commissioner supports so many human rights education programmes around the globe that it is sometimes difficult to know which category of human rights abuse is being mainstreamed or given priority treatment as the theme of the moment. The need for some public re-evaluation of approach is pressed by a range of critics, according to whom the UN is in danger of spreading itself too thinly, and of projecting a vainly triumphalist image at odds with the grim realities across the globe, barely affected by UN activities. The professor of human-rights practice at Harvard, Michael Ignatieff, suggests that human rights have now become hopelessly diluted by their extension beyond campaigning against 'core' abuses like torture, classically the focus of the civil and political rights track.[7] Cut-backs and contentious re-statements of human rights ethics may not be an answer to the conflicts which accompany the growth of the UN's human rights system, but more publicity is equally patently not sufficient to respond to the force of these and similar critiques.

If further attention to reforming the UN's human rights institutions is to go beyond the trite and partial, it will draw on an awareness of the productive roles played by similar institutions in political processes elsewhere. In other words, would-be reformers will explore the senses in which this aspect of 'politics' can be a positive element in protecting humanity, as well as a source of possible threat. The officials who run the core 'charter bodies' which oversee the totality of the UN's human rights institutions are readily made aware by their interlocutors of their somewhat constrained legal status and contested situation vis-à-vis the representatives of member states.[8] While 'politics' appears as a problem in Ignatieff's stimulating critique, neither the 'political' nor the 'institutional' dimensions of human rights campaigning are conceived in positive terms, and this reflects a general poverty in political thought about

7 Michael Ignatieff, *Human Rights as Politics and Idolatry*, Princeton NJ: Princeton University Press, 2001, esp. 3–100.

8 Among the most insightful writers in this regard is former Deputy High Commissioner for Human Rights Bertrand Ramcharan, see, e.g., *The Concept and Present Status of the International Protection of Human Rights: Forty years after the universal declaration*, Dordrecht/London: Martinus Nijhoff, 1989. See also Fons Coomans, ed., *Human Rights from Exclusion to Inclusion: Principles and practice: an anthology from the work of Theo van Boven*, The Hague/London: Kluwer Law International, 2000.

international human rights mechanisms. This means the debate about the UN proceeds without careful attention to the role of officials as initiators of compromise, as public faces and exponents of the human rights procedures, or as experts providing practical translation for the broad and often conflicting visions behind the resolutions of the Commission on Human Rights and General Assembly. The relegation of the Sub-Commission on Human Rights to 'think tank' has not been accompanied by a forceful public clarification of the role of its 'expertise' in human rights, but has rather been construed as a statement of its limited, 'non-political' character – eighteen of the best legal minds required to give preliminary opinions and an independent basis for the drafting process, which the legal officers in Geneva's embassies then take over. If this expertise counts for more than an admission that the states left to their own devices would find the process of decision-making still more difficult, it has not been formally acknowledged. The Sub-Commissioners – and a few of the leading experts working within the Office of the High Commissioner or appointed as Special Rapporteurs by the CHR – are often lionised within the community of NGO representatives at Geneva, but their manifest contributions to the development of the UN's human rights procedures have been overshadowed in recent debate over reform largely thanks to the attention drawn by diplomats appointed to the Sub-Commission or to other independent expert roles whose concept of human rights politics is often defined by a narrow and partial agenda, in some cases manifestly determined by their governmental allegiance, and who in a number of cases have been pilloried as incompetent or uninterested.

If the role of officials and experts in forging progress in human rights at the UN is undervalued, this may change if the member states continue to become less reluctant to allow that UN officials might present a personal face with which a global public might identify. A major shift was initiated by the trend after the turn of the 1990s in favour of public dialogues over thematic problems and strategies for protecting rights, with increasing emphasis placed on the scope for recognising the distinctive identities of different groups of potential victims without losing the universal force of the human rights discourse as a whole, and without discarding the dignity and decorum historically associated with government and legal process. On the other hand, the institutions covering human rights at the United Nations in Geneva appear to have precious little by way of the media analysis by which prominent Western bodies track their impact on public debate as well as the challenges before them in terms of popular misperception and bias. This in spite of the probability that – like a score of NGOs in this field – they could have tailor-made information provided *pro bono*. The anonymity of officials in Geneva and the lack of provision for relationships between these officials and the public are disincentives for a global public to monitor the activities – and possible misdemeanours – of representatives of the UN's human rights mechanisms. If 'dialogues' are to have a meaning, they must be between two independent partners, aware of their role and in a position to be forthright about their respective contributions.

PRESSURE FOR CHANGE

It is often left to those who identify themselves as the representatives of the human rights community to provide the personal or human dimension to proceedings at the UN which would otherwise lose sight of the individual, of the full human implications of a compromise at the expense of a group of potential victims, or of delay while victims continue to suffer or die.

To the architects of the High Level Panel on Threats, Challenges and Changes, the NGO community is at best invisible, in spite of – cynics would perhaps unfairly say because of – the manifest success of NGO coalitions in creating consensus behind some of the most successful treaties in UN history. In 1983, for instance, an NGO coalition drew together in favour of a Convention on the Rights of the Child and the document was quickly passed through the UN system, opened for signing in 1989 and ratified by a larger number of member states (192 to date) than had hitherto joined any other treaty mechanism. Since the end of the Cold War, the number of NGOs accredited at the UN's umbrella Economic and Social Council has boomed from hundreds to thousands. In the autumn of 1998, the Chair of the Commission on Human Rights warned NGO representatives against further assertion of their interests, noting that NGO interventions at the Commission were frequently irresponsible, a criticism which characterises the attitudes of state representatives in the face of unelected critics presenting the views of groups which are generally representative of only narrow sections of the global population. The challenge this sets the NGO community is to give an effective account of its role in the wider political process surrounding the UN's human rights activities without sacrificing its essential nature, as a guardian of the principles underpinning universal human rights.

The rhetoric of all sections of the NGO presence at the human rights committees rests legitimately enough on the assertion that the public is an essential element in the process of building a global consensus, or community, in favour of human rights. A key to this now well-entrenched orthodoxy is the observation that human rights cannot be parcelled off and treated selectively: if human rights are not universal, indivisible and tackled comprehensively, then they are not being respected as human rights. In so far as there is an NGO or human rights 'community' in Geneva, it is divided on exactly what constitutes responsible activity at the UN. For many of the professional bodies which aim to divide human rights thematically into issues and legal responses, the wild and sometimes unashamedly partisan interventions of NGOs which support the rights of particular national, religious or ethnic causes are the Achilles heel of the NGO cause. As important as these professional bodies are in pressing human rights causes on the UN, professionalisation also contains dangers for the notions of universality and indivisibility, not least in the difficulties with which particularism is confronted. In so far as a degree of unity is important in imposing public pressure on the Commission and its related institutions, the division between a Western or Northern modernist camp and a group of like-minded and largely Southern section of global civil society is a threat to the notion of asserting human rights through popular will. This paradox goes to the heart of the role which NGOs have arrogated to themselves, in large part, and, where they have secured results, deservedly, to public acclaim.

This divide amongst human rights activists is clear enough to suggest a further realm of human rights politics within the NGO community. A response in realist terms runs deeply counter to the ethos of many of the bodies established to protect human rights, committed to what may be an unavoidable and sometimes a largely rhetorical attempt to circumvent politics through idealism, through law and through gestures of commitment. Some human rights advocates attempt to bridge the North–South (or 'East–West') gap through engaging with the relationship between human rights and the diversity of cultures and social groups engaged in rights work at the UN. Israeli academics Shlomo Avineri and Avner de-Shalit have suggested there is theoretical precedent for forging a compromise in respect to the common cultural opposition between Western individualist and non-Western communitarian approaches, since communitarian approaches to rights do exist within Western political thought.[9] It is hard to imagine such an intellectual solution alone will heal the divisions within the human rights community. Where NGOs are in a position to adopt more pragmatic responses in pursuit of common objectives, by contrast, they may help to move the NGOcommunity further to the centre of the UN dialogue on improving measures to safeguard human rights. The Association for the Prevention of Torture is blazing a path in this respect, providing professional advisory services for governments seeking to root out torture within their police and penal systems. As this dimension to professional human-rights work becomes more common, the NGOs' activities dilute the force of diplomatic demarches which dismiss NGOs as disengaged from the wider discussion of the place of human rights in international relations. As participants in an acknowledged political process, where politics is not a cover for cynicism or a threat to higher values but a vehicle for progress, they are in a better position to share with state representatives their understanding of the political obstacles to the most contentious and most difficult objectives of the human rights community – a community encompassing state representatives, and increasingly whether they are willing or not.

9 Shlomo Avineri and Avner de-Shalit, eds, *Communitarianism and Individualism*, Oxford: Oxford University Press, 1992.

CONTRIBUTORS

DAVID ABRAHAMSON, MBE, qualified in medicine at Trinity College, Dublin and trained in psychiatry at the Maudsley Hospital in London. His principle aim as an NHS consultant from 1971 to 2002 was to combine practice and research to promote a satisfactory transition from mental hospital services, followed by community care that reflected patients' choices, needs and potential. Consequent developments, including a multidisciplinary rehabilitation team and a network of supported housing, provided a partnership with patients that he came to value highly in one of the most socially deprived districts in Europe. He is now exploring historical aspects of institutional and community care.

ANNE BAYEFSKY is a senior fellow with the Hudson Institute, and a professor at Touro College in New York. She is on leave from her post as full professor at the Department of Political Science at York University in Toronto. From 1996 to 1999, she was the director of York's Centre for Refugee Studies, and from 1981 to 1996 was a professor of constitutional and international law at the University of Ottawa. She holds a BA, MA and LLB from the University of Toronto, and an M.Litt. from Oxford University. She is a barrister and solicitor of the Ontario Bar. She has launched a website, www.EYEontheUN.org, dedicated to the UN's record on identifying and condemning human rights, and another, www.bayefsky.com, dedicated to enhancing the implementation of the human rights legal standards of the United Nations.

Bayefsky has been awarded the Bora Laskin National Fellowship in Human Rights Research (1992), and a MacArthur Foundation grant in Peace and International Cooperation (1995–96). She is a member of the International Law Association Committee on Human Rights Law and Practice, and editor-in-chief of the series Refugees and Human Rights published by Brill. Bayefsky is a frequent contributor to the editorial pages of numerous newspapers, periodicals and online journals. She is author or editor of several books, including: *Human Rights and Refugees: Internally Displaced Persons and Migrant Workers* (Martinus Nijhoff, 2006); *How to Complain to the UN Human Rights Treaty System* (Kluwer Law International and Transnational Publishers, 2002); *The UN Human Rights Treaty System: Universality at the Crossroads* (Kluwer, 2001); *The UN Human Rights Treaty System in the Twenty-First Century* (Kluwer, 2000); *Human Rights and Forced Displacement* (Martinus Nijhoff, 2000); and *Self-Determination in International Law: Quebec and Lessons Learned* (Kluwer, 2000).

LOUIS BLOCH, avocat honoraire, né à Strasbourg (France) où il vit avec sa femme Tirtsa née Serfaty de Marrakech (Maroc). Père de trois enfants. Représente le CCJO au Conseil de l'Europe et au Parlement européen à Strasbourg. Membre du jury au Concours européen des Droits de l'Homme "René Cassin". Collabore au quotidien "La Voix du Luxembourg" ainsi qu'à des revues juives :"L'Arche" (Paris), "Unir" (Strasbourg), Almanach du KKL. A publié des ouvrages de poésie. Décoration: Officier des Palmes académiques.

SIDNEY BRICHTO is a leading Liberal rabbi who directed the Liberal Jewish movement from 1964 to 1989. He has been very active in communal life, particularly in his support for Israel through the Israel Diaspora Trust. He has written *Funny, you don't look Jewish: A Guide to Jews and Jewish Life*, and edited with Richard Harries *Two Cheers for Secularism*, both published by Pilkington Press; he is also the author of *Ritual Slaughter: Growing up Jewish in America*, and has already completed a translation of fourteen books of the Hebrew Bible as well as most of the Christian Bible, published by Sinclair-Stephenson as part of the People's Bible series. His translation with explanatory notes of the entire New Testament will appear next year.

JAN HERMAN BRINKS (Dr) is a specialist in modern and contemporary German and Dutch history. He was awarded research fellowships at the Zentrum für Zeithistorische Forschung in Potsdam, the Center for German and European Studies at Berkeley, the American Institute for Contemporary German Studies of the Johns Hopkins University, the German Historical Institute in Washington, D.C., Bath University, Birkbeck College and the Centre for German–Jewish Studies at Sussex University. His publications include *Children of a New Fatherland: Germany's Post-War Right-Wing Politics* (2000) and *Paradigms of Political Change: Luther, Frederick II, and Bismarck; The GDR on its Way to German Unity* (2001).

MARTIN FORWARD is the executive director of Aurora University's Wackerlin Center for Faith and Action, and the Helena Wackerlin Professor of Religious Studies. Previously, he was academic dean of Wesley House, Cambridge, and a member of Cambridge University's faculty of divinity. He helped to found the Centre for Jewish–Christian Relations in Cambridge, of which he remains a trustee. He is an ordained British Methodist minister, and was also ordained deacon in the Church of South India in Hyderabad, where he was a fraternal worker with the Henry Martyn Institute of Islamic Studies.

KENDRA GAINES (Dr) has been teaching English and related subjects since 1969. She received a Master's degree in philosophy of religion and literature from Claremont Graduate University (Claremont, California), and a Master's degree and a doctorate in English literature from Northwestern University in Chicago, Illinois. As an undergraduate, Dr Gaines studied at the then newly opened Warwick University, UK. Since 1986, Dr Gaines has taught writing and literature at the University of Arizona in Tucson.

LUCIEN GUBBAY was born in Buenos Aires and grew up in Manchester's Sephardi community. He is a past president of the Spanish and Portuguese Jews' Congregation of London, and is currently chairman of the Montefiore Endowment at Ramsgate. Lucien Gubbay was educated at the Manchester Grammar School and at Balliol College, Oxford, after which he served in the Royal Air Force. A consulting structural engineer by profession, he also lectures and writes on religious history and related topics. His books include *Origins*, *Ages of Man*, *The Jewish Book of Why and What*, *Quest for the Messiah*, *The Sephardim – Their Glorious Tradition*, *Sunlight and Shadow – The Jewish Experience of Islam*, and *Two Worlds*.

GENERAL THE LORD GUTHRIE OF CRAIGIEBANK, GCB, LVO, OBE, was born on 17 November 1938. Educated at Harrow School, he attended the Royal Military Academy Sandhurst in 1957 and was commissioned into the Welsh Guards in 1959. He served with his regiment as a young officer in the United Kingdom, Libya, Germany and Aden. In 1966 he joined the SAS, serving in the Middle East, Malaysia and East Africa. In 1970 he returned to the Welsh Guards and for two years commanded an armoured infantry company in Germany. After a year as a student at the Staff College, he served in the Ministry of Defence as the Assistant to the Head of the Army, the Chief of the General Staff. From 1975 to 1977 he was the Brigade Major of the Household Division, and from 1977 to 1980 he commanded the Welsh Guards in Berlin and Northern Ireland. He was appointed as a Colonel to the branch overseeing operations worldwide, and during his time there became briefly the Commander British Forces New Hebrides (Vanuatu), recapturing the island of Espirito Santo, which had been taken over by insurgents. In 1981 he was appointed Commander of the 4th Armoured Brigade in Munster, West Germany, following which he was Chief of Staff, Headquarters 1st British Corps in Bielefeld. He became the General Officer Commanding the 2nd Infantry Division and North East District in 1985. In 1986 he became Colonel Commandant of the Intelligence Corps. After a further tour in the Ministry of Defence he became, in succession, the Commander of the 1st British Corps, the Northern Army Group, and the British Army of the Rhine before becoming the Chief of the General Staff and finally the Chief of the Defence Staff (1997–2001). He is Colonel of the Life Guards, Gold Stick to the Queen and Colonel Commandant of the SAS. He is a director of N M Rothschild & Sons Ltd; a council member of the International Institute of Strategic Studies; a visiting professor and honorary fellow of King's College London University; chairman of the trustees of the Liddell Hart Centre for Military Archives; a member of the Steering Committee of the Center for Strategic and International Studies, Washington, D.C. He is president of the Army Benevolent Fund, Action Research, and the Federation of London Youth Clubs, and a governor of the Charterhouse, Clerkenwell. He is married with two grown up sons.

ARTHUR HARVERD is a chartered accountant and chartered arbitrator. He is a past chairman of the Chartered Institute of Arbitrators and is presently chairman of the board of the London Court of International Arbitration. He is engaged in compensation schemes for victims of persecution in World War II. Arthur has been a close friend of Clemens ever since they were in the same primary school class in Amersham, nearly sixty-five years ago. Their paths continue to converge in their professional lives. They are both governors and honorary fellows of the Shenkar School of Engineering and Design, Ramat Gan.

HIS ROYAL HIGHNESS PRINCE EL HASSAN BIN TALAL OF JORDAN has been at the centre of Middle East politics and diplomacy for many decades, in the course of which he has won exceptional respect for drawing attention to humanitarian and interfaith issues and the human dimension of conflicts. His Royal Highness has initiated, founded and is actively involved in a number of Jordanian and international institutes and committees. Amongst his many positions, the Prince is president and patron of the Arab Thought Forum, moderator of the World Conference of Religion and Peace, and one of the founders of the recently formed Parliament of Cultures. Prince Hassan is the author of seven books, which have been translated into several languages.

K. HANNAH HOLTSCHNEIDER, MPhil (Dublin), PhD (Birmingham), is Lecturer in modern Judaism at the University of Edinburgh. She was Research Associate in the Faculty of Divinity, Cambridge, UK, and Junior Research Fellow at the Centre for the Study of Jewish–Christian Relations, Cambridge, UK. Since 2002 she has been a member of the Pastora Goldner Symposium on the Holocaust, an international group of Holocaust scholars. Her first book is *German Protestants Remember the Holocaust: Theology and the Construction of Collective Memory* (Münster: Lit. Verlag, 2001).

EDWARD KESSLER (Dr) is founder and executive director of the Cambridge Centre for the Study of Jewish–Christian Relations and bye-fellow of St Edmund's College. He received his doctorate from Cambridge University and now teaches and writes on Jewish–Christian relations. His publications include *Bound by the Bible: Jews, Christians and the Sacrifice of Isaac* (Cambridge University Press, 2004), and he is also specialist editor of *A Dictionary of Jewish–Christian Relations* (Cambridge University Press, 2005). Kessler is a leading thinker in contemporary Judaism and Jewish–Christian relations. He writes for the printed media and broadcasts regularly on radio.

ZVI C. KOREN (Professor) (formerly Kornblum) has been the director of the Edelstein Center for the Analysis of Ancient Artifacts at the Shenkar College of Engineering and Design in Ramat-Gan, Israel, since the Center's inception in 1994. He was also head of the Department of Chemical Engineering at Shenkar from 1999 to 2004. Prior to making *aliyah* to Israel in 1990, he served as professor and chairman of the Department of Chemistry in the School of Engineering at the Cooper Union for the Advancement of Science and Art in New York. His main research area is the analytical chemistry of ancient colorants.

JULIUS LIPNER is professor of Hinduism and the Comparative Study of Religion at the University of Cambridge, and chairman of the Faculty Board of Divinity. Of Indo-Czech extraction, Professor Lipner was born and brought up in India, and has been teaching at Cambridge since 1975. He has lectured and published widely, and is the author of numerous papers and several books, including *Hindus: Their religious beliefs and practices* (Routledge, 1994, pbk 1998), and *Brahmabandhab Upadhyay: The life and thought of a revolutionary* (OUP, 1999); his English translation of Bankim Chatterji's famous Bengali novel, *Anandamath*, together with an extensive introduction and critical notes, under the title 'The Sacred Brotherhood', will be published by OUP in August 2005.

Professor Lipner is married to Anindita, and they have two children, Tanya and Julius, and a granddaughter, Amalia. Professor Lipner is a trustee of the Centre for Jewish–Christian Relations.

DAVID LOEWE was educated at St Paul's School and Oxford, and served his national service in Malaya. He worked in the computer industry, first with J. Lyons and Co., at the time a pioneer in the commercial use of computers, and later with International Computers Ltd. He was involved in many major government projects, including the DVLA project at Swansea, the Vat project at Southend, and in elements of the Inland Revenue project. He joined the Anglo-Jewish Association in 1981, and served a six-year term as its president in the 1990s. He is married, with three children and eight grandchildren.

RAPHAEL LOEWE held the Goldsmid Professorship of Hebrew at University College London. His scholarly work has focused mainly on the positive reaction of Judaism to its environment in late antiquity and the middle ages, and, particularly during recent years, on parallels between the sacred poetry of mediaeval Jewish Spain and the metaphysical poets of sixteenth- and seventeenth-century England. His published translations include Fitzgerald's Omar Khayyam in the Hebrew style contemporary with Omar, and, most recently, Isaac ibn Sahula's thirteenth-century rhymed Hebrew fables (*Meshal haqadmoni*) rendered into English couplets with a commentary elucidating the satirical description of events in the reign of Alfonso X of Castile.

BERTRAND RAMCHARAN was Deputy High Commissioner for Human Rights and Assistant Secretary-General of the United Nations when Mr. Sergio Vieira de Mello, then high commissioner, was killed on 19 August 2003 during the attack on the United Nations headquarters in Baghdad. Dr Ramcharan then assumed the post of acting High Commissioner for Human Rights which he held until July 2004 when a new high commissioner was appointed by the United Nations secretary-general. During his three decades with the United Nations, Dr Ramcharan served in the Centre for Human Rights as special assistant to the director, as the secretary-general's chief speechwriter, as director of the Office of the Special Representative for the Secretary-General in UNPROFOR (the largest-ever United Nations peacekeeping operation), as director of the International Conference on the Former Yugoslavia, as political adviser to the peace negotiators in the Yugoslav conflict, and as a director in the United Nations Political Department, focusing on conflicts in Africa. A barrister of Lincoln's Inn, with a doctorate in international law from the London School of Economics and Political Science earned in 1973, Dr Ramcharan was a commissioner of the International Commission of Jurists from 1991 to 1998 and has been a member of the Permanent Court of Arbitration since 1996. He was Adjunct Professor of International Human Rights Law at Columbia University and has written or edited some twenty books and numerous articles. He holds the Diploma in International Law of the Hague Academy of International Law, where he has also been Director of Studies.

AUBREY ROSE was born in London in 1926. He is married and has three children. By profession a solicitor, he was awarded the OBE in 1986 and the CBE in 1997, D.Univ (2000). He became the senior vice-president of the Board of Deputies of British Jews (1990–96), and is founder of the Commonwealth Human Rights Initiative and of the Indian–Jewish Association, UK. He served as deputy chairman of the British Caribbean Association and of the Commission for Racial Equality (1991–5), and acted as Adviser to Overseas Governements. He chaired the Jewish Working Group on the Environment. Aubrey Rose is editor of *Judaism and Ecology* and author of *Journey into Immortality* (a life of his 21-year-old son), *Brief Encounters of a Legal Kind* (his life in the law), and *The Rainbow Never Ends* (an autobiography).

RUTH ROTHENBERG trained as a journalist in the provinces, having found student journalism more interesting than Greats (Classics) at Oxford. She has worked mainly in the Jewish press, on the now defunct *Jewish Observer and Middle East Review* and the *Jewish Chronicle*, where she edits the obituaries page. She has covered every reporting aspect except sport and fashion and has specialised, in recent years, in welfare and education. She has also brought up four children, with a 'career break' before returning to fulltime work. In semi-retirement she volunteers by cooking lunch at a Jewish day-centre one day a week. Complaints only arise when the meat is not tender enough.

EDMUND LEOPOLD DE ROTHSCHILD was born in 1916. He is married and has four children. He was awarded the CBE (1997), VMH, and TD. He is former chairman of NM Rothschild and Sons Ltd. Major RA (TA). Served in France, North Africa and Italy 1939–46 (wounded). Deputy Chairman: British Newfoundland Corporation Ltd 1963–9; Churchill Falls (Labrador) Corporation Ltd 1966–9; Member, Asia Committee, BNEC 1970–71, Chairman 1971. Vice President, Queens Nursing Institute; Former President, Research into Aging; President, Association of Jewish Ex-Servicemen and Women; Vice-President, Council of Christians and Jews. Former Governor, Technical University of Nova Scotia; Honorary LLD, Memorial University of Newfoundland, 1961; Honorary DSc Salford, 1983; Order of the Sacred Treasure, First Class (Japan), 1973. Publications: *Window on the World*, 1949; *A Gilt-Edged Life: Memoir*, 1998.

DANIEL SPERBER (Rabbi Professor) is a member of the Faculty of Jewish Studies, Bar-Ilan University, president of the Jesselson Institute of Advanced Torah Studies, Bar-Ilan University, and a member of the Committee on National Religious Education, Ministry of Education, State of Israel. He is winner of the 1992 Israel Prize. Professor Sperber's areas of expertise include classical philology; the history of Jewish customs; Jewish art history; Jewish education; and Talmudic studies. His recent publications include: *The City in Roman Palestine* (New York, Oxford University Press, 2001); 'Nautica in Talmudic Palestine' (*Mediterranean History Review*, vol. 15, 2001); *Why Jews Do What They Do* (New Jersey, 1999); *Minhagei Yisrael* (Jerusalem, 1998); 'On the Bathhouse' in R. Katzoff (ed.) *Classical Studies in Honor of David Sohlberg* (Ramat Gan, Bar-Ilan University Press, 1996).

ADY STEG (Professor) was born in Czechoslovakia in 1925. He is married to Gilberte Nissim, a gynaecologist; they have two sons. Professor Steg is a surgeon and was head of the urology department in Cochin

Hospital. Since 1984 he has been the chairman of the Alliance israélite universelle and is a member of the Economic and Social Council and the National Academy of Medicine. His publications include numerous scientific papers in the field of urology. He has been awarded the following decorations: Grand officier de la Légion d'Honneur; Grand Croix dans l'Ordre national du Mérite; and Commandeur de l'Ordre du Ouissan Alaouite from Morocco. He has also been awarded honorary doctorates from the Hebrew University of Jerusalem and the University of Athens.

ALAN STEPHENS was born in Swansea, South Wales. He read law at University College London and was called to the Bar at the Middle Temple. He was on the board of editors of the *Netherlands Yearbook of International Law* (1975–84), and is currently on the board of editors of the *Journal of Religion and Human Rights*. He has given papers at the Henry Dunant Institute, George Washington University, the Australian Institute of Jewish Affairs, NATO and many others. He has been a panellist at the annual meeting of the American Society of International Law, and was interviewed on legal topics by radio and television companies in the UK, USA and Australia. From 1984 until his retirement in 2002, he was publisher, and later publishing director of Kluwer Law International / Martinus Nijhoff Publishers. In recent years he has initiated research projects with, inter alia, the International Bar Association, the Raoul Wallenberg Institute and the Hague Institute for the Internationalisation of Law. He is director of research of the Clemens Nathan Research Centre.

GIDEON TAYLOR has been executive vice president of the Conference of Jewish Material Claims Against Germany (Claims Conference) since 1999. He has overseen numerous negotiations for compensation and restitution of Jewish victims of Nazism, as well as the distribution of funds from several programs. Under Mr Taylor's leadership, the Claims Conference helped negotiate the creation of the $4.5 billion German foundation Remembrance, Responsibility and the Future, set up to compensate victims of Nazism. Using funds from the Foundation, the Claims Conference processed 265,000 applications from former

Jewish slave laborers in eight languages and distributed $1.1 billion to 143,000 Holocaust survivors within a three-year period. Mr Taylor has also overseen the creation of Claims Conference programs to compensate victims of Nazi medical experiments and former refugees to Switzerland. In addition, the Claims Conference continues to negotiate for the expansion of other pension and one-time payment programs, recover unclaimed Jewish property in the former East Germany, and distribute more than $100 million in institutional grants annually. Mr Taylor came to the Claims Conference from the American Jewish Joint Distribution Committee (JDC), where he served as assistant executive vice president. Mr Taylor was involved in the planning of Operation Solomon, the airlift of fifteen thousand Ethiopian Jews to Israel in 1991, and spent much time in Ethiopia. He also took part in JDC's rescue activities in Yemen and Syria. Originally from Dublin, Ireland, Mr Taylor is a law graduate of Trinity College in Dublin and received his master's degree from Oxford University. He lives in New York with his wife and two daughters.

EDWARD TIMMS is Research Professor in History at the Centre for German–Jewish Studies, University of Sussex, and a life fellow of Gonville and Caius College, Cambridge. He is best known for his book *Karl Kraus – Apocalyptic Satirist*, published by Yale University Press in two volumes as *Culture and Catastrophe in Habsburg Vienna* (1986) and *The Post-War Crisis and the Rise of the Swastika* (2005). He was awarded the Austrian State Prize for History of the Social Sciences in 2002 and made an officer of the Order of the British Empire for services to scholarship in 2005.

ALEXANDER VERKHOVSKY was born in Moscow in 1962. In April of 1989 he became co-founder and editor-in-chief of the *samizdat* newspaper *Panorama*, which has since been transformed into the Panorama Information and Research Center. Since 1994 his main interest is focused on the interrelation of religion and politics and on political extremism, nationalism and xenophobia in Russia. At the end of 2002 he became co-founder and director of the SOVA Center for Information and Analysis (http://sova-center.ru), which conducts monitoring and research in these areas. He is author of several books and many articles, published in Russia and abroad.

JEAN-JACQUES WAHL was born in Metz (France) in 1947. He married Elisabeth Bulz and has two children. He has a BA in the history of art, an MA in Modern Literature, and studied Bible at the Hebrew University. He was director of the Jewish Community Center, first in Strasburg, then in Geneva, and became director of the European Association of Jewish Community Centers. From 1982 to 1985 he was a Jerusalem Fellow. Since 1985, he has been working in the Alliance israélite universelle, first as director of the education department, then as the general director. He has published several articles in various French publications, and is a *chevalier de la Légion d'Honneur*.

RAPHAEL WALDEN was born in London and educated at Balliol College, Oxford and at the London School of Economics. He is an English solicitor and member of the Israeli bar. In 1974 he joined the Israeli Foreign Ministry, where he held the posts of director of the Treaty Division, director of the International Law Division, counsellor at the Israel embassy in Copenhagen, deputy chief of the mission to the UN in Geneva, and finally ambassador to Eritrea. He participated in the drafting of the Israel–Egypt peace treaty and subsequent implementation agreements, and was deputy agent for Israel in the Israel–Egypt Boundary Arbitration. He participated in many UN conferences, including sessions of the Security Council and the General Assembly, the Conference on the Law of the Sea, the Human Rights Commission and the Sub-Commission on the Promotion and Protection of Human Rights. Mr Walden retired from the Ministry of Foreign Affairs in the year 2000, and since retirement has been acting as adviser to the Consultative Council of Jewish Organisations and director of the Clemens Nathan Research Centre. He has edited a collection of essays published by Martinus Nijhoff entitled *Racism and Human Rights*.

GEORGE WILKES (Dr) is a fellow of St Edmund's College (Cambridge University) and Director of Studies for Social and Political Sciences. He has been engaged in human rights research and advocacy with the

Consultative Council of Jewish Organisations and other organisations since 1998. A research associate at the Von Hügel Institute for the Study of Ethics, he directs the 'Ethics and Politics of War' programme, and, through the CCJO, helped to renew the study of the relationship between humanitarian and human rights law by the Sub-Commission on Human Rights. His doctorate, 'British Attitudes to the European Economic Community, 1956–1963', is now being revised for publication.